Hello I am Erik

Erik Spiekermann:
Typographer
Designer
Entrepreneur

By Johannes Erler

gestalten

Erik Spiekermann on the type in this book

»That's ›Real‹. It's based on a special medium ›Akzidenz Grotesk‹ weight that was only used for very large poster type. Lighter than the ›medium‹ in hot metal, phototypesetting, and digital.

I have a lot of history with ›Akzidenz Grotesk‹ or ›AG‹. For me, it's the mother of all sans serifs. The real, non-fake version, as it were, the royal sans serif face (which is why it's called ›Real‹, apart from the fact that my typefaces have four-letter names).

The type foundry Berthold grew up with ›AG‹, and I grew up with Berthold. I learnt to know and appreciate ›AG‹ during evening courses with Günter Gerhard Lange. I still think it remains one of the best typefaces ever, which is why I've even had it cast in hot metal – in regular and medium in 8, 12, and 24 point.

I drew ›Real‹ digitally for this book, and passed the data on to Ralph du Carrois to clean up and complete. We changed what we wanted to have differently (e.g. an Anglo-American g, a serif on the l, old style figures with an Anglo-American 8, serifs on uppercase I for the text version, wider f and t, round points, etc.). So there's a bit of Spiekermann in the ›AG‹.

Buyers of this book can get ›Real‹ as a free download. Details in the colophon.«

Seven short pieces on Erik Spiekermann

By Johannes Erler

1. Greeting:
Why this book has its title

›Hello, I am Erik‹ is the opening part of a fairly typical Spiekermann sentence: »Hello, I'm Erik! Let's call each other ›du‹; I only say ›sie‹ to people I don't like.« (In German ›Sie‹ is the polite form of address, while the familiar ›du‹ is reserved for friends and colleagues). This sentence may sound naive, but in reality it is something of a policy statement containing much of what Spiekermann is about: openness, curiosity, and the need to engage people and draw them into his own special Spiekermann world, which is hard to drag oneself away from. That's how this book got its name.

2. The story so far:
How this book came to be

This is the first photo of myself with Erik Spiekermann. It was taken during a fabulous Meta-Design works outing to London in summer 1992. Fresh from graduation, I was working as an intern at Meta in Berlin.

Afterwards: I would have liked to have stayed at Meta but didn't get a job there / I returned to my home town Hamburg, and founded Factor Design with Olaf Stein, with whom I had worked at Meta / An advertising campaign for FontShop was one of our first jobs / I developed the symbol fonts ›FF Dingbats‹ for FontShop / Meta-Design became the largest and most famous German design company / Erik founded TYPO Berlin with Neville Brody / In the years that followed I spoke at TYPO four or five times / Erik left MetaDesign and founded ›United Designers Network, and later Edenspiekermann / I would meet Erik over the years at congresses and on design juries / Michael Bierut wrote a book on Tibor Kalman that I thought was so good I decided to write a similar one on Erik Spiekermann / Erik wasn't averse to the idea.

Now we are up to 2009. Another five years would pass before the book was ready.

During this time: I met the publisher Robert Klanten and we decided to do the book together / Erik received the German Federal Design Award for his life's work, to which I wrote

a laudatory speech / I left Factor Design and founded ErlerSkibbeTönsmann / The ›schriftgestalten‹ exhibition about Erik Spiekermann opened at the Bauhaus Archive in Berlin / I gave the opening speech / Erik received awards for his life's work from TDC New York and ADC Germany / Erik had his entire archives sorted, so that we could start working on the book properly / I became art director at the German weekly news magazine ›Stern‹ / the book ›Hello, I am Erik‹ was finally ready in summer 2014.

Twenty-two years ago I met Erik Spiekermann for the first time. At exactly the time when I started to work as a graphic designer. Our paths have crossed many times since. So this is not just a book about a great designer, but also about a person who has become familiar to me over the years.

3. The crunch question:
The chatterbox

Berlin in winter, after a long meeting at work. Erik's apartment. I save the last notes on my laptop. For the time being we have stopped talking. Erik puts the kettle on again. I think about how the book could begin. That's when I think of this question: »Erik, why did you become a designer in the first place?«

Normally he would deliver a razor-sharp response, but this time he hesitates. Erik takes the teapot to the table and sits down, mulls it over a bit before answering quietly, with the hint of a question mark at the end of the sentence, »Probably because I'm such a chatterbox?«

»A what?«, I ask him.

»Well,« says Erik, »Even as a child I used to talk all the time. I'd talk about anything I found interesting, which was just about everything. I'm very inquisitive. At home I would talk about my discoveries. I wanted to convey as precisely as possible what I thought was important. That's how I discovered speaking. Shortly afterwards I learnt to write.«

»From speech to information to type!«

»There was a printing press in our neighborhood. I used to go there and get scrap paper to draw on. To this day I can still hear the clatter of the jobbing press. When I was 12 my father gave me my first case of type.«

»That's how you got into typography.«

»Speech, type, typography. It was how I was able to describe things. At school I set the student magazine using my own lead type. After school I wanted to be a journalist, so I still wanted to report about things.«

»But you became a designer instead.«

»At first I carried on with lead type, and bought some more fonts. I got better at it, more precise. I found I could apply this experience to photo-typesetting, and write instructions for typesetters. That's how I earned my first money.«

»From a hobby to a job to a profession!«

»At some point I figured out how to get information across using typography. That's when I started to care not only about the information itself, but the way it looked too.«

»Form took on meaning.«

»Exactly. And from there it's only a small step to design. Communication design means designing communication. One develops information systems in order to inform, not to please. Which doesn't mean that it shouldn't look good anyway. Corporate design is the visual expression of identity. That's how it all connects. That's also the reason why I nearly always develop a corporate design from individual typefaces. Communication becomes type becomes design.«

»You are always concerned with communication.«

»I have always been, and still am, concerned with designing communication as precisely as possible. I aim to be clear, because I find there's so much to discover and understand. Throughout my life that's what I've wanted.«

We drank the tea.

4. Chaos and order:
Spiekermann in two sentences

»I'm totally chaotic! I'm so untogether, my left leg doesn't even know what my right leg is doing.«

»I need order. I need systems. I don't really do anything without a design grid. All my typefaces and designs are based on grids and systems!«

5. Type follows function:
On Erik Spiekermann's significance to communication design

The subject I studied is called »communication design«. I noticed back then that this term is difficult to explain. One can try saying »Communication design is designing communication,« but for most people that is too abstract. So one can try it differently: »In principle, a communication designer is a graphic designer. One can use it to work in advertising, or design books and posters, or newspapers and magazines. Or one can create corporate design« (The last one also usually requires an explanation). Such de-scriptions help people understand – whereas the term ›communication designer‹ remains impenetrable.

It is surely no coincidence that these four descriptions of what a ›communication designer‹ normally does – advertising, book and poster design, editorial design, corporate design – apply to the four most important graphic designers to have worked in Germany: Herbert Bayer, Jan Tschichold, Willy Fleckhaus, and Otl Aicher. Each of them worked in one of those four areas. Typography is the element that connects them.

Bauhaus teacher Herbert Bayer's name was synonymous in the 1920s and 1930s with the design and use of »New Typography«. His radically abstracted and eye-catching ›Universal‹ and ›Bauhaus‹ typefaces from 1925 marked a turning point in type design. These and other typefaces were the graphic vehicle for the Bauhaus credo »Design for everyone!«, a call to arms against all that was conservative, expensive, ornamental. Bauhaus thought ahead. Herbert

Bayer was one of these prophets of a modern world where design serves a purpose and makes life easier for everyone. This made him appealing to anyone who also wanted to appear modern. Thus, it was only logical to go into advertising, which Bayer did when he left Bauhaus in 1928. Bayer's outstanding design, above all his typography, was itself like the promise of a successful future. The simple but extremely effective equation is: modern design + modern type = modern product.

Jan Tschichold was also a fervent advocate of New Typography. In his typographic manifesto of 1925 he writes: »New Typography is functional. The purpose of any typography is communication (whose means it represents). This communication must appear in the shortest, simplest, most direct form.«

Tschichold's thorough journalistic know-how made New Typography popular in Germany, before the national socialists fundamentally abused it and Tschichold emigrated to Switzerland. His consequent renunciation of Bauhaus and return to classical design ideals (his main typeface ›Sabon‹ is a successful attempt to improve the old-style serif face ›Garamond‹) is only contradictory in appearance: Tschichold was always focused on basic structures and rules to keep typography and the way it is designed as meaningful and memorable as possible. Tschichold was an uncompromising perfectionist searching for timelessness. In book art he found the perfect environment to systemize his typographic developments and subsequently publish them in essays or textbooks. His findings on typographic systems and systematic design are still relevant today.

Willy Fleckhaus did not like to stick to the rules – that is how, between 1950 and 1970, he produced the most beautiful, surprising, and striking double-page spreads ever seen in German editorial design. Fleckhaus, who audaciously styled himself »Germany's first art director«, was looking for thrills and confrontation. His design thrived on dramatic contrasts: big against little, light against dark, loud against quiet. He delved into the enormous history of type to throw up daring combinations that appealed to him. His typographic specifications were feared by editorial staff, since he would often put form ahead of content; writers would have to fill his layout sketches with text perfectly, down to a character. He would rile the best photographers in the world by cutting up or altering their pictures. Willy Fleckhaus had balls. He was a transgressor, conqueror, plunderer, and egotist who was never afraid to be unpleasant – because when you cross the line you find the New, and Fleckhaus wanted to get there first.

Otl Aicher thought about everyone, and less about himself. In the tradition of Bauhaus, he felt design was a democratic instrument whose creative power was relevant to society as a whole. He used the term design in a more fundamental way than anyone else, in the sense that it was a product of communal life. The design program for the 1972 Olympic Games, to this day a milestone of international corporate design, was in this sense nothing less than the symbol of a revived and open German society that wanted to step away from the shadows of its past. Red was missing from the color palette rainbow used for the Olympic image, since it represented this dark past. It was this power of symbolism, popular and intellectual in equal measure, combined with eloquent arguments and derivations (Aicher often wrote entire books about his work) that made Aicher so easy to understand and corporate design so well known in Germany. Aicher always carefully drew the big picture, thereby making sure everyone could follow him. He managed to pry design out of its specialist box into the public consciousness. Aicher was convinced of his mission in the best sense of the word; he set himself a task and stuck to it consistently.

Erik Spiekermann studied them all carefully. The desire for modernity of Herbert Bayer, the systems and rules of Jan Tschichold, the iconoclasm of Willy Fleckhaus, and the sense of mission of Otl Aicher. One can clearly sense all of them in him and his work, and yet he has found a unique approach of his own. For Spiekermann everything is about language, communication, and information. Whereas the big four always had a concrete product in mind (an advertisement, book, magazine, symbol), Spiekermann first imagines what it is like to talk about or explain something. The character of such communication becomes the starting point for type (very often his own typefaces), that in turn forms the basis for a design system and eventually a product.

A good example of this method is his never-realized work for Deutsche Post, begun in 1984. The job description was: design us a new image! At the time that meant: redesign our logo, use it on our business cards and forms, and explain the design in a manual. But Spiekermann had other ideas. He thought Deutsche Post already had a good logo that hardly needed changing, but that their real job of transporting letters and parcels as efficiently and understandably as possible was being limited. Spiekermann recognized this as being due to poor communication between the postal service and its customers, an example being the huge amount of forms that were hard to read and fill out, and that made customers want to rip their own hair out. So how could a service provider that comes across as a badly organized institution make itself more popular with customers? Certainly not with a new logo!

So Spiekermann started redesigning the way they made forms before he hit another hurdle. The Deutsche Post house typeface was ›Helvetica‹, and it has (we all know Spiekermann's opinion) a bunch of weak points: numbers and small type sizes are hard to read, it is wasteful in its width, and has (that is its essence!) a cool, non-specific character. For Spiekermann ›Helvetica‹ was the antithesis in type of how he imagined the postal service. Postal forms ought to be easy to use even when really small, and they ought to look friendly.

The basic thinking behind the new image was that a postal form that was quick and easy to fill out was itself the perfect calling card for Deutsche Post.

Thus, he created the first drafts for the ›PT55‹ typeface, which was to serve as the basic model for the new image. A completely new, space-saving typeface readable in small point sizes that would – as Spiekermann was quick to grasp – be easy to manufacture in all necessary weights using the emerging digital type technologies, and could soon be used in digital typesetting. A thoroughly modern idea at a time when even most insiders in Germany had barely heard of Ikarus and Apple.

Legend has it that in 1985 Spiekermann borrowed one of the first available Apple Macintosh computers, took it to Bonn to the Deutsche Post head office and proudly told them that this box was the future. All postal forms and type would soon be inside the box, and it would make working on their image so much easier, and cheaper too. Spiekermann was euphoric, since he could sense that this technology would help realize his vision of communication and type-driven corporate design. All the more painful it must have been for him when his plan hit a brick wall. They simply did not understand him. The job never came off, and a furious Spiekermann said that the best solution would be to hurl a bomb at post office central.

However, the typeface was released in the end. Spiekermann called it ›Meta‹, like his company and his approach to design: Meta-design. Design that follows a basic and primary idea, whose driving force is language, communication, and information. ›Meta‹ became a worldwide success and is now a part of living type history in the typographic collection of the Museum of Modern Art (MoMA) in New York.

The Deutsche Post example is representative of all the major works by Erik Spiekermann. To name but three from the long list: the corporate design for the Berlin public transport company BVG in 1991 was created from the information system at bus stops and train stations (the typeface they used was ›FF Transit‹); the corporate design for Düsseldorf airport in 1996 is his own signage system, which had all eyes on it after a catastrophic fire damaged the airport (›FF Info‹ typeface); the corporate design for Deutsche Bahn in 2009 is founded on the knowledge that easily readable maps and schedules interest customers more than how many twists the Bahn logo has (›DB Type‹ typeface). Spiekermann is never primarily interested in representation or status in his work (nor, as a consequence, in logos themselves), but rather in communication, information, and the attempt to bridge the gap between businesses or institutes and customers in as simple and practical a way as possible.

Spiekermann works according to the premise that speech is the most direct way of showing character. The famous phrase by Paul Watzlawik that »One cannot not communicate«, which Spiekermann himself often uses, translates for him as: »You are what you say and how you say it.« Type is always the first reproduction

of speech and as a consequence is always the focal point of every communicative design. In its individualized form it is the basis of highly precise communication design.

This brings us back to the beginning of the text. Communication design is designing communication. Nobody has interpreted this term so thoroughly nor given so much life to it than Erik Spiekermann. In so doing, he has added a fundamental aspect to the history of design.

6. A plea for more controversy in design: The spat

In March 1994 the German news magazine ›Spiegel‹ published an article about the expletive-laden war of words between Kurt Weidemann, designer of the new Deutsche Bahn logo, and Erik Spiekermann. It is one of the few documents about graphic design that ever made it into a major German magazine:

Too many breast curves
Designers row about the new rail logo

No engine driver or sleeping car attendant had ever been aware that, by wearing the rail logo on their cap, they were making a »highly feminine impression«.

The design professor from Stuttgart, Kurt Weidemann, 71, saw it right away. He counted a total of 28 curves in the logo from 1952 – »breast curves«, »hip curves«, and »pregnancy curves«; the four »round corners« looked terrible to him; they symbolized a »deep psychological lack of decision making«.

Since the beginning of the year when Deutsche Bahn AG came into being, the state company has a new logo. It cost around 25 million marks to introduce the emblem; instead of the feminine curves – »too limp«, according to Weidemann – the Stuttgart designer had created »straight-forwardness, movement, streamlining«.

»This, in a sense, erect symbol,« jeered Erik Spiekermann, 46, a typographer from Berlin, in the design magazine Form, »is bereft of emotion, like men, who famously don't use their gut for instinct, but another body part lower down.«

Seldom have two designers rowed as nastily as these two stars of German typography. Weidemann struck back in the next issue of Form, because colleagues had prompted him not to spare »Spiekermann and his revolver mouth«. It is also rare for a new logo to stir up the sort of controversy Deutsche Bahn's has. Weidemann praised his own creation as »simple, strong, and to the point.« Spiekermann, on the other hand, found the logo to be »Haunted by the past, so respectable and backward-looking.« Two internationally known type designers bickering like fishwives. Spiekermann designed typefaces for Deutsche Bundespost and AEG, among others; Weidemann helped forge the image of companies such as Daimler-Benz or Zeiss. Creating a new type image for the railways is an ego boost for any graphic designer. According to Spiekermann, the professor from Stuttgart got the job because he was a friend of the Deutsche Bahn boss Heinz Dürr. Weidemann is an advisor to the Daimler-Benz board, which Dürr used to be on. Weidemann insisted that his »200,000 or so« fee for designing the rail logo was in no way disproportionate. In exchange, Spiekermann accused the professor of delivering »a heap of shit«. Weidemann countered that his colleague ought to take a good look at his own designs first: »Spiekermann himself made a really shitty typeface for the BfG:Bank.«

»Kurt had it in for me ever since the article appeared,« Spiekermann says today. »I didn't stay mad at him though. Now I think the DB logo is OK, really. At the time I thought his chauvinistic attitude was appalling.« In 2014, 20 years later, the squabblers are reunited in the current Deutsche Bahn corporate design. The logo of the since-deceased Weidemann continues to adorn caps and train nose cones, while Spiekermann designed a large font family in 2009, which Deutsche Bahn uses for its many means of communication.

7. Onomastics: A name that carries weight

A little onomastics – name research – is allowed for light relief when someone has a well-known and distinctive name like Erik Spiekermann, especially someone who is involved with language.

Andrej Kupetz (Rat für Formgebung) begins his contribution on page 199 with the words »Erik Spiekermann simply knows everything.« That fits the meaning of the name Spiekermann, which the Heimatbund für niederdeutsche Kultur e.V in Oldenburg, Lower Saxony informed us of. According to them a »spieker« (in low German »speiker«) is a speicher, a storage room or repository. It follows that a spieker-man is someone who works at or has a large storage facility, like Kupetz said.

Spiekermann's first name Erik is nordic in origin. The original word is »Eirikr«, which means »sole ruler«, no less. Combined, this gives us: »Storage man, the sole ruler«. Or interpreted somewhat more freely: Erik Spiekermann knows a lot, can do a lot, is allowed to do a lot and does a lot. That fits perfectly!

Seven Ages of Spiekermann:
User manual for this book

When one looks at Erik Spiekermann's life's work, one is not
only struck by the sheer abundance of quality work, but also
by how intertwined his many activities are. Words, type, and
design are connected to entrepreneurship, networks, and
technical knowledge. Over the course of nearly 50 years in the
profession, he has created an impressive graphic cosmos
that has had a massive influence on graphic design in Germany and abroad, and which is impossible to capture in its en-
tirety, even in this book.

     The works section of this book, which begins on page
28, divides Spiekermann's work into seven clusters: The ›typographer‹ shows the most important typeface designs (a complete index of all his typefaces is on page 292). The ›designer‹
documents his major work as a graphic designer. The ›entrepreneur‹ describes Spiekermann as the founder of numerous
companies. The ›networker‹ looks at his many professional
activities. The ›author‹ looks at his work as an author and col-
umnist. The ›technician‹ deals with Spiekermann's interest in
print and type technology, both vintage and new. The ›person‹
shows how Spiekermann's enthusiasm for design reaches far
into his private life.

     The clusters are indicated in the vertical text on each
page margin. They have been integrated chronologically in
order to show how one thing led to another. The works section
begins with his first company in 1967. The year numbers are
also presented vertically. They each indicate the start and the
end of a project.

     Erik Spiekermann puts his huge output down to his abil-
ity to keep on finding partners and colleagues to support him
in his work, and with whom he normally remains on good terms
as a colleague and friend. This book is also dedicated to
those colleagues. Credit is given to the many people involved
in collaborative works. Starting on page 308 is a list of these
colleagues and the contact details I was able to research.

Content

3   Introduction

28   Works

288   Seven questions

292   List of typefaces

308   Colleagues

314   Index

Texts

Contributors

3 ›Real‹ / On the type in this book
By Erik Spiekermann

4 Seven short pieces on Erik Spiekermann
By Johannes Erler

7 User manual for this book
By Johannes Erler

10 »I never had a plan« / Childhood and youth
By Isabelle Erler

24 »There is a thin line between ridiculous and banal«
Interview by Urs Willmann

154 The making of ›FF Meta Serif‹
By Yves Peters

160 A4 versus 8½ by 11 / MetaWest
By Erik Spiekermann

202 Leaving MetaDesign
By Johannes Erler

206 »I am officially unemployed«
Interview by Petra Schmidt

220 How does United Designers Network work?
By Erik Spiekermann

266 »Who is that guy?« / Edenspiekermann
By Julia Sysmäläinen

270 German Design Award
Laudatio by John L. Walters

275 Explain the world to me / Exhibition Bauhaus Archive
By Melanie Mühl

278 About cycling
Interview by Philipp Poll

37 Christoph Busse
47 Wally Olins
51 Joan Spiekermann
123 Jürgen Siebert
127 Neville Brody
135 Alexander Branczyk
145 Bruno Schmidt
153 Mirko Borsche
159 Bill Hill
167 Susanna Dulkinys
173 Jürgen Korzer
179 Robin Richmond
187 Stefan Sagmeister
199 Andrej Kupetz
217 Christian Schwartz
227 Michael Bierut
259 Erik van Blokland
267 Göran Lagerström
318 Christoph Niemann

Erik aged three at the Schützenfest fair in Stadthagen. Like all men he bears a wooden rifle and a top hat to commemorate the defense of the city by the people's militia against the Napoleonic army.

»I never had a plan – at least, not one that was longer than two hours.«
Erik Spiekermann's childhood and youth, and the years before MetaDesign

By Isabelle Erler

In the black-and-white photo Erik is three years old. He stands on sandy ground; in the background are some cobblestones and part of a tree trunk to the right. He wears lederhosen, a traditional jacket, sandals, and knee-length socks that have slipped down a little. On his head, sunk deep into his neck, is a top hat far too big for him. Erik's round face peers out from underneath it. His big eyes gaze with fascination through strong-looking metal-framed glasses at something in the distance. He carries a pointy piece of wood on his left shoulder. Erik clutches it with both hands, but it looks as though he has forgotten about it; what he sees is too fascinating. His mouth is agape, as though he were on the verge of excitedly saying something about what he has discovered.

Excessive and always very good.
Stadthagen, 1947 to 1956

Left: Erik aged 10 months
Right: Erik in 1951 with mother Barbara,
sister Angelika, and father Erich

On May 30, 1947 Erik Spiekermann was born
in Stadthagen, a small town in Lower Saxony near Hanover with a population of around
15,000 at the time. He was the first child
of Barbara Scheins, born in 1920, and Erich
Franz August Spiekermann, one year her
junior. Both parents were from lower-middle
class backgrounds. His father Erich was
from Dortmund. In 1939, at the age of seventeen, he volunteered for the navy. When he
was released from war captivity in summer 1945 he went to
Stadthagen, where his father had been evacuated during the
war. Although a trained mechanic, he had to drive coal from
Barsinghausen to the train station in Stadthagen under British occupation. To do so, he obtained a truck driver's license,
which would serve him for his later job as a long-distance
truck driver. Erik describes his father as sporty, charming,
and with good professional connections – connections
that he knew how to use, and that would subsequently also
get Erik a job here and there.

Left: Erik with his mother, 1948
Right: Holding his father's hand, 1949

His mother Barbara was from Aachen, where
she grew up with an uncle after being or-
phaned. She went to Stadthagen because
her best friend Ellen lived there (Ellen would
later move with her husband, a British soldier,
to Leigh in the North of England, where Erik
would go on the first of countless trips to
England). Barbara was an administration
secretary for the postal service. Erik describes her as hard-working and smart, if not
well-read at the time. Erik had three younger siblings: Wolfgang was born in 1948, but died at the age of one. Angelika
was born in 1950, and Michael in 1952.

The Spiekermanns lived modestly. His father was now
employed as a truck driver, while his mother worked as a
cleaning lady. His parents' marriage – only registered a few
days after their daughter's birth – was not a happy one. His
father had numerous affairs, which put a strain on his family.

A situation, as Erik's sister Angelika explains, that left their mother embittered and made the eldest son into a substitute head of family, due to their father's frequent periods of absence. In 1961 the family was living in Bonn and Erik was fourteen years old. Barbara Spiekermann sent her eldest son to Hamburg by train, wrapped in a trench coat with a small suitcase. After an eight-hour journey he met his father's lover at Hamburg's main train station in order to plead with her to return his father to his family. As soon as he had delivered his message, he went straight back to Bonn – an experience that etched itself deep inside Erik's memory.

The Spiekermanns allowed their children a lot of freedom in their interests. Even as a boy, Erik was very creative. At one point, according to his sister, he made mobiles which he hung all over their apartment. At other times he would draw and color coats of arms or illustrate poems. Erik followed his ideas, and busied himself with his interests. Everything he did, says his sister, he did »in excess, and very well«.

At the age of seven Erik visited, as he often did, the printing press nearby, which attracted him as North attracts a compass needle. He stood next to the printer, who checked on the proofing press that the forme was set perfectly. It smelled of steel, machine oil, and thick printing ink. Everything was dirty, especially the printer himself. Erik watched how he placed a virgin-white sheet of paper on the press, rolled it over the printing forme, and lifted the printed sheet with dirty printer's fingers and blackened fingernails. Not a spot of dirt. Clean text on a white background. A miracle that smelled of black ink. A miracle that instilled a sense of vocation in the young boy.

Left: Erik's first day at school in spring 1953. As on all school photos, he was made to take off the glasses he had worn since the age of two.
Right: In 1953 with mother Barbara and sister Angelika at Hanover zoo

There was always so much to do
Bonn, 1957 to 1964

Shortly before Erik went to high school in spring 1956, the family moved from Stadthagen to the capital, Bonn. Erich Spiekermann had found a new job as a chauffeur for the FDP, a political party. Later he became a dispatcher. As luck would

have it, the family lived near a printing press again, the University press.

At twelve, Erik received his first printing machine from that printer as a gift, a little old platen. His father gave him the instructions to go with it: Fritz Genzmer's book ›Vom Umgang mit der Schwarzen Kunst‹. Since Erik only had a few lead type letters, often he could not print a sheet in one go. In order to make the irregularities that cannot be avoided in a second run stand out less, he usually used red ink. Some people later speculated that this red had something to do with Bauhaus typography. However, in the late 1950s Erik did not know anything about that yet.

At high school in Bonn Erik wrote for the school magazine. Since he already knew something about printing, he was also responsible for the design, typesetting, and printing. Before he even knew what a compositor was, he found himself standing next to one at the printing press, observing how the magazine pages were constructed according to his ideas.

Left: Painting on the balcony of the apartment in Bonn, around 1958
Right: The same place a year later. Twelve-year-old Erik was a real bookworm; his favorite author was Karl May.

Obviously, Erik did not know what boredom was, even as a child. »I was thrilled to arrive home every day after school,« he says today. »There was always so much to do: my platen, reading, playing music. I really looked forward to it.« He would send carefully designed envelopes every week to his secret – she already had a beau – sweetheart Ulrike, who lived in nearby Bornheim. He would paint the envelopes, print the address using his platen, and design the stamps himself. These envelopes probably also contained letters, but the packaging was the most important thing for Erik. What motivated him was knowing he had the ability to design the envelopes. »I wasn't an artist; I was a practical designer. One needs a reason to design something.«

Even though he already had a great passion for print, Erik's artistic talents covered a broad spectrum. From the age of nine he was a member of the Bündische Jugend, a youth movement similar to the boy scouts, but which promoted an anti-fascist, independent way of thinking. This fellowship was important to him, and helped foster a political stance and team spirit that developed his ability to make decisions for himself. It also stirred a love of music in him, since collective

Erik aged 15 on a family outing,
full of beans and in a suit, as was usual
at the time

music-making was a fundamental part of the movement's outlook. Erik started to play guitar. Every weekend and during vacations in particular, they would head off without money but with a tent, kettle, and guitar on long journeys to the Spessart region, and even to Yugoslavia, the North Cape of Norway, and Lapland. Everywhere there were jamborees and singing competitions with other groups. A few years later, between 1964 and 1967, Erik was responsible for looking after English-speaking musicians at the folk festival Burg Waldeck, co-organized by the Bündische Jugend. He would drive them, without a driving license, in an old VW beetle convertible from the station to their lodgings and to the venues. The role that music played in the Bündische Jugend, and the legend-ary festivals in Burg Waldeck influenced Erik's taste in music. A musician he knew from the festival got him a job during the summer vacation at the Troubadour café in London. So Erik went to London for the first time, spending the summer clearing tables at the famous coffee house in Earls Court by day, and pouring free coffees in the evening in the basement below. Every night his musical heroes such as Martin Carthy and Bert Jansch would play, an experience that sealed Erik's deep connection with folk music. Perhaps he might have become a professional musician himself, had he not seriously injured his hand during a trip to Norway in 1962.

It feels just great to live freely!
Berlin, 1964 to 1967

In 1964 Erich Spiekermann urged his eldest son to move to West Berlin, to avoid conscription – until the reunification of Germany, men over 18 residing in Berlin were exempt from military service. His father was, Erik says, »fed up with war, which had robbed him of the best years of his life,« and want-ed to make sure Erik did not have to wear an army uniform.

By now his parents had separated, and Erich Spieker-mann worked from 1962 for the FDP-affiliated Friedrich-Naumann-Stiftung in Berlin as the local representative. Two years later the 16-year-old Erik went there too, going to the Erich Hoepner Gymnasium high school in Charlottenburg. His art teacher in Bonn had recommended it to him, since

it suited Erik's artistic streak. However, the high school student did not move in with his father and his girlfriend in their Schöneberg apartment. Instead, he lived in a communal apartment in Charlottenburg. Taking care of himself was not a problem for Erik, ever since his time in the Bündische Jugend. Quite the opposite: living alone and free in Berlin »felt just great«.

One year later Barbara Spiekermann and Erik's siblings joined him in Berlin, with the vague hope of rescuing her marriage. Erik moved in with them. The marriage was beyond rescue, and his parents divorced in the mid-1960s. Barbara began a new life, both privately and professionally.

Erik's friend Gert Wiescher with Erik on the left, and Erik with Gert on the right, 1986. They met in summer 1964 in Berlin and are still friends today.

Erik met Gert Wiescher on the Ku'damm in summer 1964, a young graphic design student who had learnt to be a sidewalk artist in Barcelona and Paris. Wiescher in turn taught Erik, and throughout the summer they drew chalk pictures together on the sidewalk outside the Hotel Kempinski. In exchange, Erik infected his teacher with an enthusiasm for typography: Wiescher is now a type designer in Munich. Erik used his father's connections to land a job at the Buck printing press in Wedding. Still a student, he worked there two or three afternoons a week as a combination of apprentice and assistant. There was no time for sidewalk art anymore; when summer was over the sidewalks were uncomfortable anyway. Gert Wiescher left Berlin, but would remain friends with Erik.

In 1966 Erik went to work at the Mercator printing press belonging to the ›Tagesspiegel‹ newspaper. As an assistant with printing experience and a talent for drawing and layouts he spent two years after school setting all kinds of advertisements while earning decent pocket money and developing a profound dislike of the ›Tagesspiegel‹ jobbing typefaces ›Candida‹ and ›Bodoni‹.

Erik on stage at the Ça ira club in 1966, sporting his tie and waistcoat combo

I don't remember money being involved
Berlin, 1967 to 1973

Music continued to be an important aspect of his life. In the music club he co-founded, Ça ira, where he regularly performed garbed in his strange-looking English-inspired style of three-piece suit, he met Joan Sargent, coincidently from Leigh, the first place he had been to in England. She was an au pair for an English journalist couple, and the girlfriend of a friend of Erik's. Erik and Joan soon became a couple, and moved into their first shared apartment shortly after Erik's university-entrance diploma. Two Englishmen lived downstairs who were setting up the German distribution for the British company Personality Posters that sold posters of pop stars and movie stars. Erik helped them from time to time, for instance with getting their posters through customs.

     Around this time Erik started to study history of art and English studies, and »liberated« a Boston platen that was standing around unused in the basement of a youth center. He used it to print calling cards, invitations, and private advertisements of all descriptions. Erik began to collect old letterpress machines – the same machines he grew up with, and that the printers were getting rid of due to the rapid rise of offset printing. One day some friends delivered a huge proofing press in a converted hearse right to his front door, saying »We've got a machine for you!«

     At that time type cases were literally being thrown out of windows in Kreuzberg, an area full of printing presses. Erik gathered whatever he could use from the streets and took it to his printing press in a rented factory floor in the same building where his brother-in-law, musician Udo Arndt, had his band rehearsal space. Word quickly spread about Erik's passion for collecting. »There's this idiot who collects stuff like that. Before we dump it, let's give him a call. He'll even collect it himself.« A dream come true for Erik, who soon owned a bunch of machines, type cases, and accessories of all kinds.

     Erik used these machines to do small jobs as a printer and graphic designer for artists, and musicians in particular. They either knew Erik as a musician, or they knew his brother-in-law. Sometimes they needed a poster in a hurry; some-

times they needed a record cover. ›You can do that sort of thing,‹ they'd say, so I'd come up with something. In those days there was no such thing as a preliminary design phase or anything like that.« Erik did everything without payment. »I don't remember money ever being involved,« he says today.

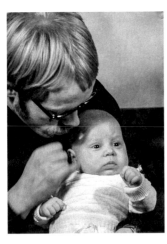

In 1968 Joan, who had married Erik five months earlier, gave birth to their son Dylan. One of their English neighbors had said »He looks like a Dylan« when he visited Joan at the hospital, and the name stuck. Joan was convinced throughout her pregnancy that she was carrying a girl, and had not even thought of a boy's name. And so Joan and Erik named their little son... Dylan. A year later their English neighbors suddenly disappeared without a trace. Joan and Erik were persuaded by the head of Personality Posters to take over the poster distribution. They rented an old butcher's shop from which they delivered British posters to West German shops, cross-ing East Germany to get there in their Mini Traveller. At the same time Erik designed and printed all kinds of little things on his printing machines, now housed in the cellar underneath the shop.

Left: Erik and son Dylan, December 1968
Right: The pair seven years later in London

Two years later Erik was selling posters for Objects & Posters. The young family moved into a large rented house in Arno-Holz-Straße, where Erik installed the Erik Spiekermann Hand Press on the first floor, with his little graphic design studio on the second floor. Their lodger was Gert Wiescher, who had himself started designing posters, sometimes together with Erik. At the beginning of 1973 Erik passed the poster distribution to his friend Hucki Schuppenhauer and Erik's brother Michael, and found steady employment for the first and only time in his life: as the director of pre-press at the Format printing press, for three whole months.

Left: The house at 7 Arno-Holz-Straße where Erik, Joan, and Dylan lived from 1970 to 1973. The Erik Spiekermann Hand Press was also housed here.
Right: Erik in the basement printing press, 1971

Erik was still enrolled as a student, but as a young father he had little time to study. Nevertheless, he gave workshop talks to English studies students, and – naturally – printed the flyers for it.

In 1973 the big house in Arno-Holz-Straße that Joan and Erik loved so much was sold. Since they were in no position to buy it, they decided to move to London. Erik's printing machines stayed in Berlin for the time being.

»Today,« says Erik, »I wonder how we managed to get by financially. Joan and I always did lots of different jobs. We never had a steady income, but neither did we have any debts.«

I was left with no alternative
London and Berlin, 1973 to 1981

In London a music journalist friend got him a position at the London College of Printing. There Erik imparted his practical knowledge of layout to journalists. He confidently managed to cover up the many gaps in his theoretical knowledge, reading up on it in his spare time.

In 1976 Erik returned alone to Berlin. He met Florian Fischer, a graphic designer who had heard of Erik's printing press. They started a design studio together, Fischer & Spiekermann, run from an apartment in Schöneberg. The office was in the front, with its own darkroom; Erik lived in the middle, and his sister Angelika lived in the back for a while.

A year later Erik decided to move back to London. This time he wanted to take all his machines with him, in order to run his own printing press and do ambitious work for artists. In the summer he packed it all into a big truck bound for London. He put the machines in a rented space underneath some railway arches and took the family off to Italy for four weeks. When he returned, nothing was left. Everything had burnt down, destroyed by a fire that broke out from the car repair shop next door. All that remained was a massive lump of lead. »And then I was left with no alternative.«

Erik began working as a typographer for the typesetters Filmcomposition, whom he had known since 1974, introducing typesetting onto positive film, which was still largely unknown outside Germany. Filmcomposition had Berthold phototypesetting machines, and thanks to Erik's good relationship with the world-famous Berlin type production company, the London typesetters could work with all the latest typefaces. Starting in 1978, Erik worked as a freelance con-

sultant for the Wolff Olins agency, where he met Dieter Heil. Together they were responsible for the German clients: Audi, VW, Faber-Castell, and the Bank für Gemeinwirtschaft. At the same time Erik started to design typefaces for Berthold, taught at the London College of Printing once again, and worked, as he puts it, as a »typo-freak« on big and little jobs, in addition to co-founding the Type Directors Club, today called the Typographic Circle, of which he is an honorary member for life.

On June 8, 1979 Erik, Dieter Heil, and Florian Fischer founded MetaDesign – the start of something which had really begun much earlier.

In 1979 Spiekermann founded MetaDesign with Dieter Heil and Florian Fischer. The road sign in the background with the two lines that change direction was the symbol of his collaboration with Florian Fischer before MetaDesign. On page 40 Fischer and Spiekermann carry this sign to their new office in Salzburger Straße.

»There is a thin line between ridiculous and banal.«

Urs Willmann is a science journalist who knows nothing about typography – the ideal requirements for a talk with Erik Spiekermann.

How do you explain the importance of selecting a font to a pig farmer? Everything we read, we perceive rationally and emotionally. When we look at a sentence, we react emotionally to its form before we even rationalize its content. That makes it part of the message. Type is full of expression, sound, and tone, since it is the form speech takes.

As a reader, however, I want nothing but pure, unadulterated information. As a typographer I visualize content, which makes me its translator. Let us compare it to music: a composer writes melodies, and a musician then arranges them and makes them ready to perform. According to Watzlawick, one cannot not communicate. Therefore there is no such thing as neutral type design. Everything has a voice.

One doesn't usually notice this voice. That's precisely when it works best. When you consciously notice it, it can distract you. You can develop an attitude towards it, but there's no defense against what you feel in your gut. It influences us subliminally, like background music in shopping malls. It gets under our skin.

But if I become aware of this acoustic treacle, I can actively try to ignore it. That may work on an intellectual level, but not emotionally. I might say that the weather doesn't interest me. However, it still influences my mood. It's the same with typography; all cultural expressions influence us. Take buildings, for example: the way they look, how they work. Even if we're ignorant about architecture, buildings still influence us a lot. The same goes for typography – it influences all of us.

Your main tool is type. What letter do you like least? For pragmatic reasons it's a drag that the lowercase r has a shape that can barely be changed. When an r is before an n, it always looks a bit like an m. It is also impractical that that m and n are so confusable; they have the same origin. Confusing n with u is also easy to do: they look the same when one of them is upside down. Or p and b and q and d. The brain gets used to distinguishing letters after a while. But really it's impractical that p and d and q and b are the same characters, just mir-rored or rotated.

Have you ever tried to change that? No, you can't do that. The skill in type design lies precisely in working within this 90 to 95 percent established framework. An a is an a. Once again, it's like music: you work with clearly defined notes, but an oboe A sounds different to a violin A.

So your work is bound by a convention that you mustn't harm? Sure. If I were to ignore the a, or change it so it doesn't look like an a anymore, then I'd be making art, not communication.

What is the most beautiful letter? A small a! It has a vertical limit and two possible types of construction. There is the a with the simple bowl against the vertical line, and there is the a with the double bowl. With this a, one crosses the surface three times: at the top, in the middle, and at the bottom. That means there are two counters – one closed and one open. It's very complicated; there's a lot happening. On the other hand, n is merely a stroke and another stroke and a connection and an open space. The e is also tricky.

Does e make life hard for you? On the contrary! The a and e may be complicated to design, but they give me the opportunity to play around with them. The same goes for s: like a and e, one crosses the surface three times. c, on the other hand, is nothing but a counter. This counter is separated in e, giving it two counters. What we really decode when we read is the contrast between black and white, between outside and inside. I find these to be clear points of reference; I can understand the letters better. One can compare it to people: I can't recognize you with the sun behind you; all I see is a masculine shape.

You would recognize me as soon as I walk. But only then. Walking effectively corresponds to the rhythm of the letter in a word. Just like I don't recognize you by silhouette alone, but by your movement and physiognomy – it's the same with words. Just like individual letters do, words have inner and outer spaces. If I look at the outer space of a word, the outlines, I can barely recognize anything. And I recognize more in a line with both uppercase and lowercase than one with uppercase letters alone, which is like a sterile high rise building with few contours. When there are upper and lowercase, I see the tower, the tree, the stream. That's why I prefer signage using upper and lowercase. However, engineers prefer to use uppercase letters, since they are easier to define, and bigger. Some people think capitals have more letter bulk, and that one can express oneself more clearly using them, but that's rubbish.

And that's why the small, unmistakable a is your favorite letter? Along with g. I like g just as much, because it's complicated too. Our alphabet is pretty refined, in spite of its weak points. The i, for example, is far too narrow.

How do you deal with it? I like to put a serif on it, to give it some white space – i has no white space. Neither does l; it consists merely of a stroke without inner space. But inner space makes it recognizable. That's why I often put a little arch at the bottom right, to give it some inner space of its own. And a head serif on the left of the i, so that it can breathe. Plus my t's and f's are wider than usual. The t has a little stick. This creates white space, which stops words from looking like picket fences.

That all sounds pretty cerebral. At this point our pig farmer will be thinking, »What is Spiekermann's problem?« Why? Pig farmers talk in the same way to one another. I'm sure they have their own distinctions: how many ribs, how many bristles? But I suppose you're right – when 70 grown men stand around together at typography conferences talking about i's and a's, I do sometimes wonder whether we've all lost our marbles. There are wars and disasters out there, while we're talking about rhythm in type. But everyone does that. All experts have a nerdy side to them. As long as you don't forget that there is more to life, then it's OK. If we were all average, nobody would have invented the wheel.

Why does type have to be not merely readable, but beautiful too? It doesn't – but consciously striving to make things beautiful is one of the things that seprates us from animals. How much history do we have as homo sapiens?

Max Frisch once wrote that Man appeared during the Holocene. And later he started to communicate. Not only when he was in pain or hungry – he started to reveal himself through signs and paintings: I was here in this cave, I killed four bulls. Later there was religion: the attempt to look for meaning in Nature. As social beings we have the urge to share our thoughts and to leave something behind. Culture also means that there is an aesthetic value beyond mere function. This value helps things work: if music sounds crap, nobody wants to hear it.

In the end, type has to be functional. But beauty itself is a function. Beauty is not free of function. Put simply, we need beauty. Ugliness doesn't sell. Soon after the fall of the Berlin Wall, in 1991, I designed the signage for the Berlin transport authorities. Naturally, a signage system like that has to work in the first place. Customers have to know where the exit is, and where to buy tickets. But I wanted to make it pretty too. Berlin is so gray! We used color for orientation, but also because it's decorative.

How do you work when there are a lot of parameters to take into consideration, like in this example from Berlin? I start with the worst case. In this case something like: an old man in a bad mood, in an unpleasant situation, in a rush, in dim lighting... most people don't ride the subway for fun; everyone wants to get somewhere. The subway is only an interruption. In that respect, nobody reads a train schedule for fun. I have to bear in mind the person who has to find something out without really wanting to. I want to give that person a tiny bit of joy, so that afterwards he's both smarter and happier.

Surely the creative act begins with dry analysis though? That's the way I learnt it. I'm very German and protestant like that. But after 40 years in the business I can no longer separate what comes from gut instinct, and what is down to experience. However, an analytical approach is always a good idea. The first thing is to gather material, write a briefing, and find out what the client says – and what they really need.

That sounds as though those are very different things. What the client wants from you is often not what they need. What they say often has a lot to do with the bal-ance of power, and constraints. We have to filter out and translate these aspects at the beginning, before we can start on intuitive design.

What skills does a good designer have? They are able to recognize patterns and mimic them. They need to be analytically and aesthetically-minded. They need to juggle facts and emotions. One can't be purely cerebral about this sort of work – that would be like an author having a computer generate his sentences. Any calculator could produce sequences of words. Subject, object, predicate, and even case can be mathematically derived. These are complete sentences viewed analytically, but they have no feel for language.

I imagine you're constantly upset at bad type when you're out and about. Age has mellowed me somewhat. It used to be different.

You'd see type or design and think »Oh dear«? I guess I was like a top chef disgusted at every hotdog stand, and who has a fit when he sees processed food at the supermarket. That was me a lot of the time! It was clear to me that with a little extra effort they could have got it right.

I would like to hear an example. I notice it most with paperbacks, even nowadays. A publisher who puts a book out every week should only need to develop one typographic concept for the inside of the books. But most of them don't bother to make the little effort required. Most paperbacks look dreadful. They all tamper with the cover: the sales people want this, the agents want that. But the inside is usually awful. And there's no excuse for that.

Why do they skimp on typographers? Because a lot of publishers think it costs too much money, when all they'd have to do is pay someone like me for two days, and they'd have some nice typography for all their books.

Maybe the publishers just think that type isn't so important for them. Of course it's important! One can't prove it, that's all. Even if a book sells more thanks to good typography, the head of marketing will still come around and say it's due to advertising, and the cover designer will say it's because of the cover, while the author will, of course, believe purely in the power of his brilliant text.

I have heard that much of your ire is reserved for the ›Arial‹ typeface. Are there any other typographic sins that you would call »environmental pollution«? It's not simply a matter of an aesthetic problem. What bothers me is the attitude behind it. There are enough experts to decide how to make a text more readable, and what adds aesthetic and functional value. ›Arial‹, or for that matter ›Helvetica‹, is a nightmare on an iPhone, for instance. Far too uniform, no contrast: it reads far too badly. Just try to make a password that includes 1's and l's and i's. You can't tell them apart! It's just a bunch of dumb lines; everything is way too tight!

Why don't these experts do something about it? Most of them are just too lazy to look around and try some thing out. They make the same soup every day, but they present it as a conscious, almost heroic decision. »I don't need any other spices,« they say, »I don't need salt or pepper; I'm happy pouring hot water onto some instant soup powder.« It comes down to laziness in the end though. Being too lazy to look at a typeface and take a risk. Instead, they'd rather have the same soup every day. In designer speak they call it »conscious rejection of the status quo«. New magazines come on the market set in ›Times New Roman‹, and the choice of typeface is somehow presented as being worthy in its unpretentiousness, as though it were a rejection of the commercial world of modern typefaces that nobody needs anyway. But really it's all about the instant soup powder thing.

That sounds like a snob talking. No way. Of course, some people moan about »these Spiekermen«. A massive hassle, and nobody will notice the difference anyway. I find that attitude cynical. That attitude is based on nothing but laziness.

Could it be a generational problem? Probably. In the seventies I used to get a lot of abuse from the generation above me. They thought I was a cheeky upstart who broke the rules. But I didn't know the rules; I was naive.

Does that make a difference? When one breaks the rules without knowing them, it's often naive or infantile. A toddler is allowed to pee in their pants, as long as they're not old enough to understand that they shouldn't do it.

The Rolling Stones are still allowed to pee in their pants. A breach of taboo like that is something else altogether. When one knows one isn't allowed to do something but does it on purpose anyway, that's an expression of culture, of civilization. However, if I break rules without knowing them, even though they are not hard to know, then I'm being childish. Music has no function, thank god. It's fine in art free of function. Childish can be a good thing in that case, because it's fun. But unlike art, it just isn't possible in an applied discipline such as graphic design, where you're commissioned to work for someone. I can mess up my own texts as I see fit, but not someone else's, not in a working relationship.

I draw the conclusion that you are definitively not an artist. But I work with artistic means, intuition, visual translation. Always on behalf of a client. Which doesn't mean I'm a slave. When I work for someone, I'm 100 percent loyal. You pay the penny, I sing the song. I have to decide beforehand whether they're an idiot or not. Of course, I have returned work that wasn't quite right in form or content, but that doesn't mean it's alright to get mad at the customer, or badmouth them later.

Didn't you once want to blow up the Bundespost, the German Federal Mail, with a petrol bomb? Yes, it's true – but I didn't have the contract then.

What made them think of asking you? They didn't ask me personally. It was a bid between a couple of design studios. The idea was to design a new image for the postal service. The invitation to bid in itself was idiotic. The bidding task was to design a given note paper and business card. They even specified where each line had to be! A banal activity that any village printer could do! But designing an image for a national service provider is a huge task that goes so far as to influence German culture.

You got the chance to do something of that magnitude later for Deutsche Bahn, something that people see wherever they go. The railway is another gigantic business whose image has influenced the entire republic. There's a lot of responsibility involved! That's why I had found the mail invitation to bid so petty. We still won it. Somehow they liked our note paper, as banal as it was. Before I knew it I was sitting at the postal ministry in Bonn, presenting my proposal. The Bundespost still used all kinds of different typefaces: in theory they used ›Helvetica‹ as a house typeface, but I counted more than 20 different typefaces when I analyzed it. Presumably the printers employed at the time by the Bundespost often didn't have the right fonts, and used whatever they happened to have to print. So over the course of time, the Bundespost appearance had become increasingly fragmented. It had lost its unified voice, its unified tone.

You wanted to tidy up. Yes, particularly since one could already digitize fonts and put them on different typesetting systems. I had already done it for a bank, so I knew it was possible. But the Bundespost people didn't understand me. I had borrowed a little Mac in Frankfurt, so I went to Bonn and set the thing on the table in front of them. They just stared at me as though I was from the moon. He's telling us there's type inside that thing? These guys had imagined trucks full of metal type! They furrowed their brows and looked me up and down. They probably thought »He's an artist! Just let him talk, he's harmless enough.«

Whatever happened to cooperation? We spent years working on the new image for the Bundespost. Some forms we redesigned were even set and printed in an early version of the postal typeface called ›PT55‹ at the time). But then the client, lacking foresight, got cold feet about the typeface, and the rest of the work was done using ›Helvetica‹. Later the Bundespost was divided into Telekom, Deutsche Post, and Postbank. None of those companies has any courage when it comes to typography.

So was your work all in vain? Not quite. I was lucky: I developed the ›Meta‹ typeface out of the postal typeface, and that turned out to be one of the bestsellers of the modern era.

It even made it into MoMA. ›Meta‹ in the early nineties was a new kind of thing. There hadn't been anything like it.

Perhaps we still needed new typefaces back then. Now there are countless typefaces. Do we still need new ones? Well, do we need new books, or new music? We don't really need them, but we get them.

But books and music are also expressions of culture. You've just taught me that typography is different. Then I have to put it into perspective. Naturally, typography is different from music or literature which are free of function, by definition. However, new digital technology makes it possible for everyone to simply make their own typefaces. So of course that's what's happening.

You must think that's just terrible! Not at all! The market will decide whether the world needs these typefaces. Many creative people would like to make their own typeface, just like many people dream of writing a novel. Thanks to computers they can do that too. Of course there's going to be a lot of junk, and most stuff is just imitation – but so what?

You make that sound very forgiving. I think it's perfectly alright. How many people have played Beatles songs? Millions! Just go on Youtube, you'll find umpteen thousand videos of spotty youths playing ›Yesterday‹ in their party basements, with mixed success. It's the same thing with typography in this day and age.

Cheese has been around for 10,000 years. Nevertheless it's always being reinvented. The same goes for wine. Who needs millions of kinds of wine? People have the need to keep being creative. I think that's wonderful! That's how culture emerges – from the need to communicate.

But does each company really need its own typeface? In competition they do. Of course Telekom wants to look different from O2. Type plays an important role as the tone of speech. If I'm a boring designer I'll use ›Helvetica‹. It goes with everything. That didn't really matter for a long time for companies that don't really have competitors. However, by now even those companies have grasped that it is even important for internal communication, to make it more identifiable. The company's own employees ought to notice: this note is from us; it has its own handwriting, it belongs to me. But one has to be careful when renewing things. I reached a certain limit with my typeface for Deutsche Bahn. It's expressive, almost too expressive. One can't go much further before it starts to get ridiculous. On the other hand, one mustn't be too cautious as a designer, otherwise the new typeface will be indistinguishable. There's a fine line between ridiculous and banal.

Isn't there a great danger of losing ones identity with a change of image? I often say to my clients they should behave as they are, and also stay that way on the outside. Nobody can do something that's not them. Just recently I had a Chinese car manufacturer. He wanted to be like Audi. He even wanted a German designer, so that his cars would look German. That can't work – everyone can tell. It's similar for me as a contractor: if I jump through hoops to get a contract, or if I prostitute myself, then things are bad. Before you know it, you're on your back, suffering. Then you have no pleasure, and without pleasure there can be no good outcome.

The logo for Großplakate GmbH was made in five minutes using Letraset letters. The address is hand-set in ›Akzidenz Grotesk‹ 8 point. This business card was printed in the basement on the Boston platen press.

In 1964, as a 17-year-old schoolboy, Erik Spiekermann went to Berlin to escape national army service, and got by painting sidewalks and busking on the street. After graduation he studied art history at Freie Universität. He lived in Friedenau with his future wife Joan. One floor below lived two Englishmen who imported posters of Hollywood stars from Britain and the US to Germany. Walls adorned with prints such as Personality Posters were still pretty unknown in Germany.

When the Englishmen suddenly left, Spiekermann took over their poster business. Since the company registration insisted on a German name for the company, Spiekermann called it Großplakate GmbH. He rented a shop with his stock upstairs and his hand press downstairs. Then he drove around in his Mini, selling the posters to book shops. Erik Spiekermann recalls: »We moved with all our stuff to Arno-Holz-Straße in 1971, but in 1973 the owner gave us notice to move out, so we moved to London in summer 1973.« That spelled the end for their poster business.

Grossplakate GmbH.
1000 Berlin 15
Pfalzburger Str. 72 a
☎ (0311) 883 59 98
Verlag & Vertrieb von
Posters & Plakaten

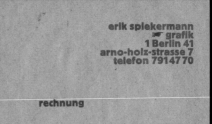

rechnung

After his son Dylan was born in 1968, Erik Spiekermann, in addition to selling posters, started printing note paper, business cards, and stationery for a travel agency, a book shop, and Friedrich-Naumann-Stiftung, among others.

His additional income as a self-employed graphic designer allowed him to finance his art history studies at the Freie Universität for a time. He printed things on an old Boston platen press that he had »found« in a basement and »socialized«. Over time, he gathered several more platen presses, a lot of type and a proofing press.

Stationery designed and produced for clients and his own office

The Spiekermann Hand Press in Arno-Holz-Straße. Behind him is an Adana platen press, and the proofing press is in the foreground.

New Year card from Joan and
Erik Spiekermann, 1973
Overleaf: Sticker for mini-press
conference in Mainz, 1971

Hier erha

PRODUKT

→ MINI-P

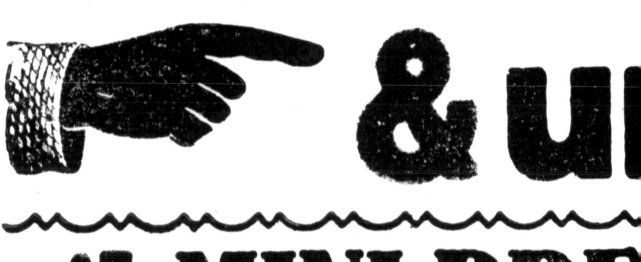 & u

!! MINI-PRE

ten Sie ☞

ONEN VON ◐◑

RESSEN ◀

d & ☞

S-REPORT !!

In 1971 Erik Spiekermann started managing the Berlin branch of Objects&Posters who made posters in Munich; he had made a name for himself selling posters for Personality Posters from Britain. While he was selling O&P posters, he also produced a few of his own, for example the Jimi Hendrix poster he made with Gert Wiescher.

»Our posters had all sorts of political motives at the time, plus there were a couple of op art patterns,« Spiekermann recalls.

In early 1973 he passed the business on to his friend Hucki Schuppenhauer and his brother Michael Spiekermann, who kept it going up until the end of the 1980s.

Final artwork on paper, repro proof made in his own darkroom. The printing presses hated Spiekermann's love of bled color elements, since it meant having to print a sheet of A4 oversize paper and then cutting it to size.

Rechnungsdatum:

Rechnungs-Nr.

Grützmacher was a typesetter in Berlin, where
Erik Spiekermann could always find work:
»I did all sorts of jobs there, and learnt how
to do many things: film make-up, repros, phototypesetting.«

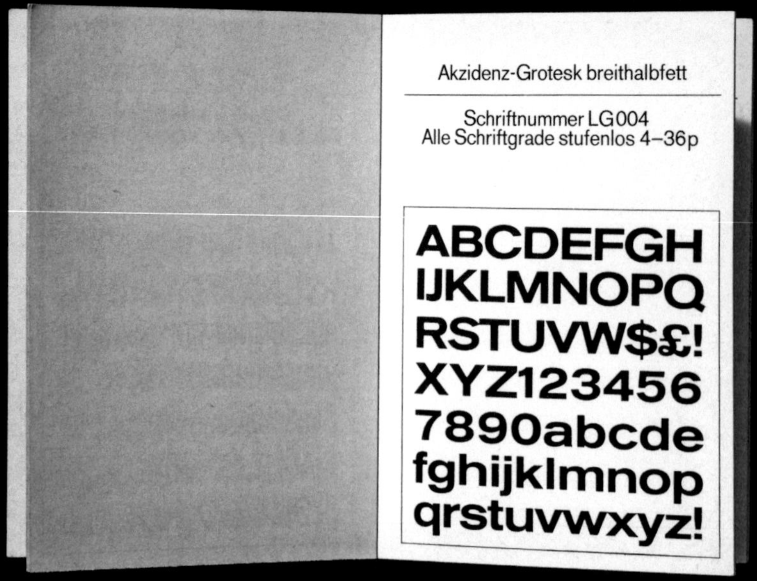

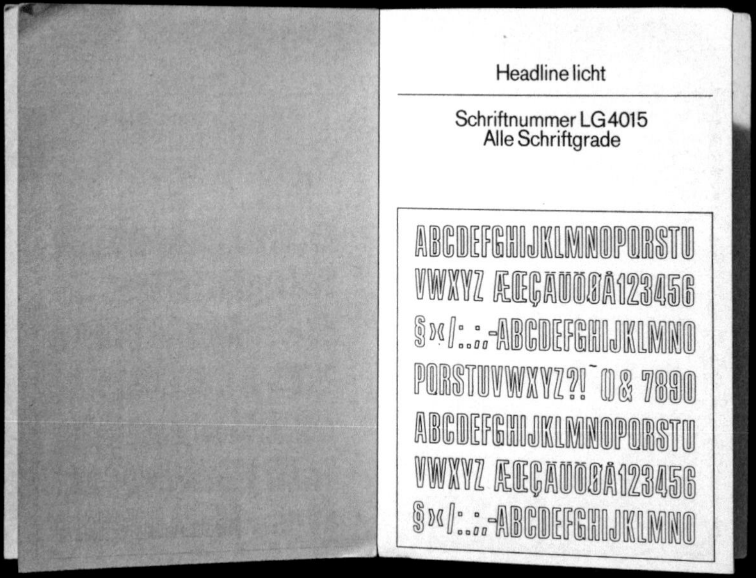

Akzidenz-Grotesk breithalbfett

Schriftnummer LG004
Alle Schriftgrade stufenlos 4–36p

ABCDEFGH
IJKLMNOPQ
RSTUVW$£!
XYZ123456
7890abcde
fghijklmnop
qrstuvwxyz!

Headline licht

Schriftnummer LG4015
Alle Schriftgrade

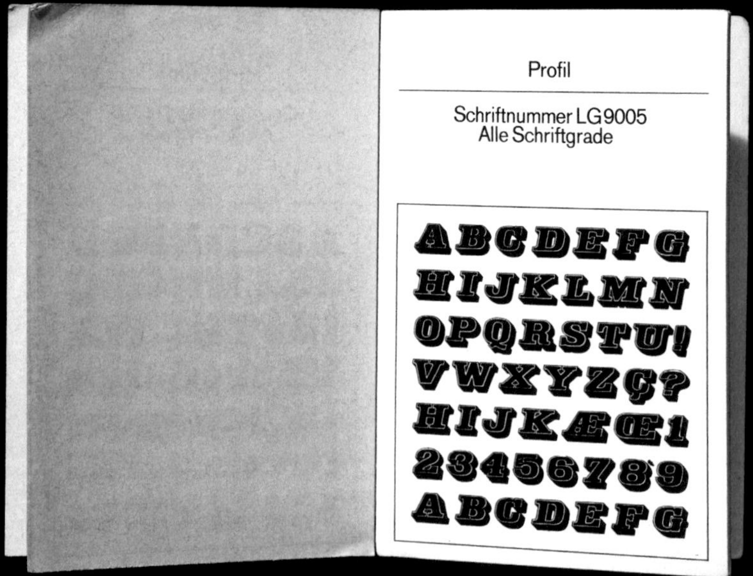

Profil

Schriftnummer LG9005
Alle Schriftgrade

Type specimens for Berthold typefaces
by Christian Grützmacher in Berlin.
Original size: 5 × 7.2 cm. In the late 1970s
there were only a few dozen typefaces,
so they all fit in a small book like this.

os mundi: 43 minuten.

In his youth Erik Spiekermann had dreamt of becoming a musician. He would act out this dream by designing record covers: ›43 Minuten‹ by the Berlin rock band os mundi in 1972; the eponymous debut LP by ZeitGeist in 1981; ›Gnadenlos!‹ by Hans Hartz in 1983, and ›Gib Mir Zeit!‹ by ZeitGeist in the same year, plus many other records over the years. All of them are characterized by unobtrusive design, an almost monochrome color scheme, and – somewhat untypical for a typographer – an emphasis on images and symbols rather than type.

The os mundi logo and the cover for this LP are by Spiekermann, who also designed posters for the band.

Christoph on Erik

Erik and I went to school together in Berlin in the 1960s. He had an artistic streak; I studied classical languages and played drums in a band with the really idiotic name The Safebreakers. The group's guitarist was Udo Arndt, who is still married to Erik's sister Gela. Erik already spoke excellent English and helped me with my first attempts at writing lyrics. Since he was very musical and familiar with the London music scene, his contributions were really creative (›The Green Cleaning Machine‹, or ›Dustman‹). More than anything, I was particularly interested in his hot picking technique on the acoustic guitar. I think he taught me my first basic guitar chords, although I never did manage to master fingerpicking. At home he had a record collection with everything a folkie could desire. He introduced me to the music of Steeleye Span, Fairport Convention, The Chieftains and and and... Erik could play a bunch of those songs on the guitar. We never asked him whether he wanted to join our band, even though we always hung out together. Perhaps he dreamt about it. If he did, he never dared ask. I always saw him as a lonesome solo artist.

It was three bands later when he finally had the chance to record his guitar picking in the studio. The band was called os mundi. It had developed out of the old school band and its successor, Orange Surprise. A fusion band, made up of musicians of various shades. Rock, beat, free jazz, classical; two drummers, and up to ten people on stage. Here too, Erik was always around, but as our designer. He designed the os mundi logo (inspired by Escher's triangle), which was later used on the album cover for ›43 Minutes‹, concert posters, flyers – anything to do with the graphic concept. He never got up on stage with us. But in the end we did invite him along to the studio to use his special guitar technique on the song It's All There‹. ›It's all There‹ was not a hit, but then neither were any of the other songs.

Christoph Busse
(born 1947 in Berlin)
studied directing at the
German Film and
Television Academy
Berlin. Busse works for
numerous well-known
international artists
and German television
as a composer,
producer, screenwriter,
and director.

Oakwood Court near Holland Park in
London. Spiekermann lived here with his
family from 1973 to 1981.

After Erik Spiekermann, his wife Joan, and son
Dylan had spent a few years in Berlin, they
moved back to his wife's home country. The
move was triggered by the sale of the much-
loved house they rented in Arno-Holz-Straße.
Once in London, a music journalist friend
got Spiekermann a job as lecturer at the London College of Printing.

»At the time I didn't know all that much
about design – only a little more than my students,« says Spiekermann. »I would take on
any work I could get. I renovated the musician

Terry Gould's house, laying tiles and so on.
I knew him from the Waldeck festivals, but he
made his living running a tea shop in Hamp-
stead, for which I designed some packaging.
I also wrote scripts for radio programs,
and interviewed people in London for WDR
radio. The programs were called ›Curiosity is
good‹ and ›Critical Diary‹.«

In 1976 he returned to Berlin on his own for
a year before spending another four years in
London.

Spiekermann with his son Dylan
(born 1968) in London, around 1976

Spiekermann and Fischer carrying
a detour sign as a symbol of their new
shared direction, 1976

Title and two double pages from the book
›1000 important tips‹, reprinted with
comments by Fischer & Spiekermann, 1977

Erik Spiekermann met Florian Fischer in Berlin; Fischer was looking for a business partner and had previously worked for four years as a communicator on the Quickborner Team. Together they founded Fischer & Spiekermann. The front part of their apartment in Salzburger Straße contained the office with a darkroom; Spiekermann lived in the middle part, and his sister Angelika lived at the back for a time. Most of their work was designing print and small advertisements; however, they also made their own publications. The pair continued to work together on projects after Spiekermann returned to London in 1977. They started to make plans to found a larger Anglo-German cooperative agency. These plans became concrete when Wolff Olins, for whom Spiekermann did freelance work, offered them a contract for a thorough corporate redesign of the Bank für Gemeinwirtschaft. After years of doing typographically oriented graphic design, the idea of »design for design« became the priority: the basic concept of MetaDesign.

With: Florian Fischer

Spiekermann met Peter Karow, who developed the Ikarus system, in 1976 at the ATypI (Association Typographique Internationale). Ikarus is a system that defines letters as coordinates with starting, join, tangent, and curve points. It made it possible to digitize fonts in good quality that had hitherto only existed as hot metal or phototypesetting fonts. »I must have been the only graphic designer who was interested in this technology, so I got commissions from lots of type manufacturers such as ITC, Adobe, Monotype, Linotype, and Berthold in particular. I designed type samples and advertisements, and I was an adviser on the cutting edge between technology and design,« says Spiekermann. In 1988 he digitized his own ›Fidia‹ (typeface design for the Italian pharmaceutical company Fidia) using Ikarus-M, a program that Petr van Blokland wrote for Macintosh.

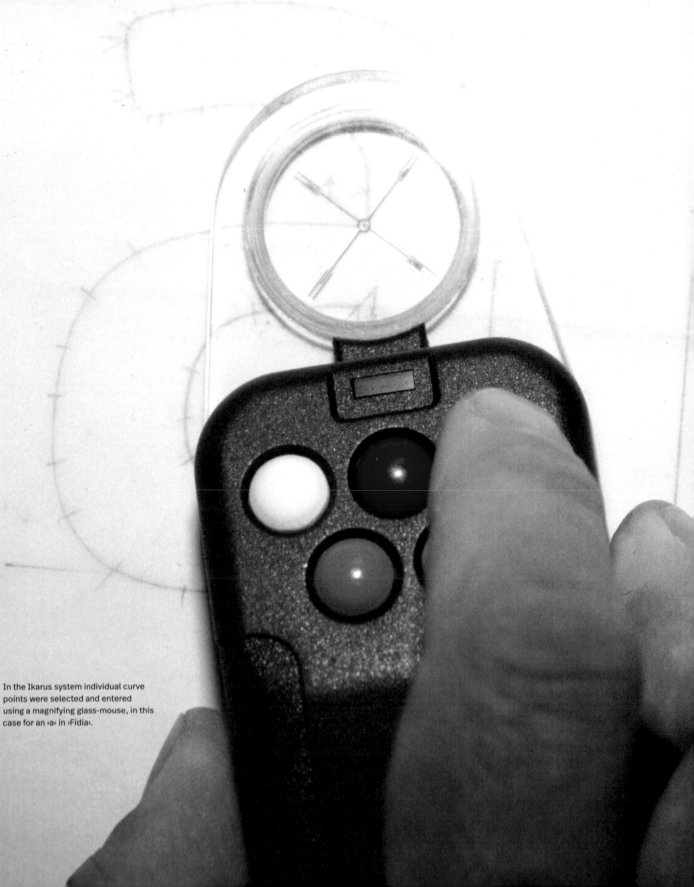

In the Ikarus system individual curve points were selected and entered using a magnifying glass-mouse, in this case for an ›a‹ in ›Fidia‹.

The Typographic Circle
presents
Erik Spiekermann

Thursday 18 November 2004

London College of Communication
London SE1
(Elephant & Castle ⊖)

Doors open 6.15pm
Talk starts 7pm prompt

Members £10
Non-members £15
Students £7.50

Contact:
angie@daltonmaag.com
(020 7924 0633)

www.typocircle.co.uk

Design: Jade Design. Material: Gmund Alexan Cult Chevreau 100gsm from GF Smith. Print: Benwell Sebard.

Poster by James Alexander for a
presentation by Spiekermann at the
Typographic Circle in London, 2004

Spiekermann founded the London Type Directors Club with Ed Cleary, the boss at Filmcomposition, where Spiekermann worked as a
typographer. Today it is called the Typographic
Circle, of which Spiekermann is an honorary
member for life. The model was the original
club founded in New York in 1946 by, among
others, Hermann Zapf, Bradbury Thompson,
Will Burtin, Aaron Burns, and Louis Dorfsman.

Spiekermann remembers: »Our motivation
was to make typography better known. Along
with myself and Ed, who emigrated to Toronto
in the late 1980s and founded FontShop
Canada in 1990, there were five other typo people from design agencies, among them Colin
Craig and Steve Legate.«

With: Ed Cleary

After a year in Berlin without his family, Erik Spiekermann decided to return to London. His plan was to run his own printing press and do work for artists. However, the machines, which were delivered to London by truck, were destroyed in a fire while the family was on vacation in Italy.

44

Nothing remained of Spiekermann's printing press after the fire in a railway arch in London. Welding work on the car in the foreground caused the blaze.

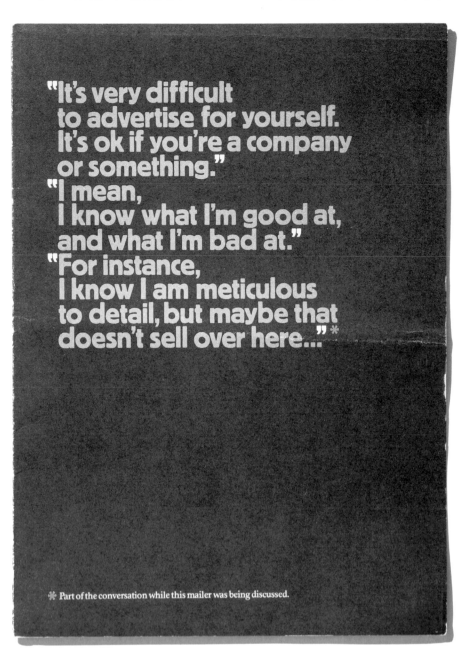

"It's very difficult
to advertise for yourself.
It's ok if you're a company
or something."
"I mean,
I know what I'm good at,
and what I'm bad at."
"For instance,
I know I am meticulous
to detail, but maybe that
doesn't sell over here..." *

＊ Part of the conversation while this mailer was being discussed.

In 1977, after his plans to open a printing press of his own were ruined, Erik Spiekermann sent a letter of introduction to various design studios, offering himself as a »fussy German«. Wally Olins, co-founder of Wolff Olins, soon responded by offering Spiekermann work as an adviser on German projects such as VW, Audi, and Bank für Gemeinwirtschaft. Through his experience at different typesetters, he quickly earned a reputation on the design scene as someone who knew all about modern typesetting methods, and who could do precise layouts. Thus, he got his first jobs from the type manufacturers Letraset and H. Berthold AG, as well as Wolff Olins and other design agencies such as Henri-on Design and Pentagram.

With: Ed Cleary

Self-advertisement to London agencies, text by Ed Cleary. Designed in the style of »copy-prep« for composing on Berthold spec sheets, such as Spiekermann had introduced at Filmcomposition, 1978.

Wally on Erik

One day, I guess it was back in the '80s, in the Wolff Olins office in London I heard in the middle of the usual hubbub a very sharp voice speaking colloquial, pungent, and witty English in a very strong German accent. The voice turned out to belong to Erik Spiekermann and, as I subsequently discovered, he was, characteristically, telling someone that his work was »absolute bloody shit«.

That, as far as I remember, is the first time I came across Erik Spiekermann. His total command of idiomatic English, combined with an extremely strong German accent and a powerful and direct, not to say abrasive, form of communication is funny, unique, and unforgettable.

I don't know how he arrived at Wolff Olins; I can't remember how long he was with the company. But he certainly made an impact.

I see Erik as clever, witty, fearless, difficult, amusing, and somebody who is well worth knowing.

The only other occasion I can remember Erik in full flood was when an eminent British designer had finished making a speech which was, I have to say, leaden, boring, self-aggrandizing, and lengthy. Erik got up and said, »That was a complete pile of garbage. Why waste our time talking that pompous rubbish?« He was saying what everyone else in the large audience had thought but no one dared to say.

That's my Erik.

Wally Olins (1940 – 2014), at his company Wolff Olins, was one of Erik Spiekermann's first employers and supporters in London. An internationally famous expert in branding and corporate identity, author, and professor, his last position was chairman of the Saffron design agency. He died during the making of this book.

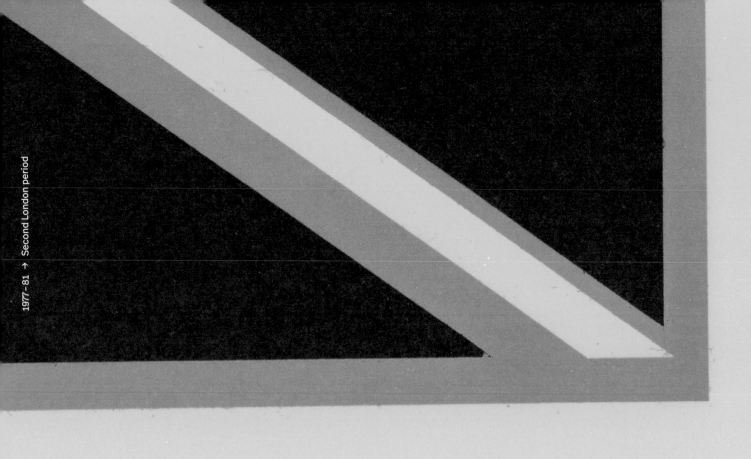

Person

Card sent to London agencies, 1977.
A rather unattractive combination
of the British Union Jack and the German colors.

Person

The Spiekermann family Joan, Erik, and
Dylan in their London apartment with
their collection of enamel signs, 1980

Joan on Erik

The second time I met Erik was at a pre-Xmas party of a mutual friend in Berlin where I was with my then boyfriend. It was 1966, everyone was dressed in student/Carnaby Street/early hippie garb and Erik was there in a suit, complete with waistcoat and tie. He definitely stood out.

We chatted a bit, then he asked if I was going home to England for Xmas. I said yes, he asked what date and how was I going. I told him; he said he was going on that very flight, so we could travel together! Unbeknown to me he went and booked it next day. That was typical Erik, charming, persuasive, spontaneous, and romantic – I think that every girlfriend since experienced something similar…

I soon found out about his love of type through that trip to England. We went to the Troubadour in London where he had worked as a busboy for a few weeks and which greatly influenced his love of enamel advertising signs and folk music. The Troubadour, a coffee house started in the 1950s and still there today, had an array of colourful enamel signs decorating the walls and a folk club in the basement where notable musicians such as Bob Dylan played. That was the beginning of his love affair with visual type ephemera, particularly English sign writing compared to German ones.

Years later when we lived in London we started to collect enamel advertising signs we found or bought on our travels, and had about 80 of them on the walls of our flat.

Not long after the trip to London we began to plan a longer trip: we would buy an old car and travel through Europe for a few months. We saved as much as we could from the bit of money we were earning doing odd-jobs, bought an old citroen 2CV called ›Weekend‹ which we could just about sleep in if we couldn't pitch the tent, and started to take driving lessons.

My German was proficient enough but the language in the driving manual was a headache and I was struggling to learn the complicated phrases involved in the written test. Erik told me not to worry because if I didn't pass he would drive us. I learnt my stuff and passed the written and practical test with flying colors. Erik, who thought it would be a breeze, typically failed the written test because he hadn't bothered to study!

And so we set out on a journey with an old car, and me as the single driver on a brand new license with no experience. Within the first hour while we were on the motorway leaving Berlin, Erik said that my door wasn't closed properly and I should slam it shut. We were so naive that neither of us thought twice about opening the door at 80 kilometers an hour. The wind nearly took the door off. Shortly after that I put my foot on the brake and I could see the floor beneath me. It was rusted through so badly under the rubber mats that we could almost brake with our feet. So we ended up in Frankfurt at a sculptor's who had a metal workshop and made us a brand new aluminium floor for the 2CV. We spent weeks in Frankfurt to earn more money for the journey, Erik working for the sculptor; me in restaurants and strawberry-picking until we could move on to cross the Alps into what was then Yugoslavia.

The rest of the journey is for a future chapter! Suffice to say… we got to know each other claustrophobically well.

When we started to plan FontShop in 1988, I Ieft my job as office manager of an English design company in Berlin to concentrate on this new venture. Erik was working at MetaDesign and applying his time to both projects. We were both convinced that it was a great idea and much needed at the time. What neither of us could imagine was that 25 years later it would still be going strong and with many of the early employees still working there. We opened FontShop in February, 1989. In that year we witnessed the Berlin Wall falling and the thrill of closing our offices to go and stand at the Brandenburg Gate with thousands of others. Heady days indeed.

Although the intense working pressure and long hours at FontShop certainly contributed to the break-up of our marriage, I am proud of what we built up and of the fact that we managed to overcome our personal issues and have maintained a strong bond both privately and professionally over the years. Erik is family, along with his wife Susanna. I can't imagine not having him in my life and am richer through knowing him and having so many shared memories.

Joan Spiekermann was born in Leigh (Lancashire, England), which she left as soon as she could. She has lived in London, Berlin, San Francisco, and Zurich, and is still trying to settle down.

Designer

The Staff

We feel that you ought to know more about us than our names. **Ed Cleary** studied at Twickenham College of technology (for a very short period of time) before deciding that more could be learned outside the college, and worked in various commercial litho printing houses, on the origination processes, with particular concentration on setting and pre-camera techniques. After two years spent in a periodical house he moved to Letterform Limited in a make-up position. This was followed by a short spell at Apex Photosetting, before moving to the Typographical Workshop, where he stayed until Filmcomposition was formed.

Jim Kendrick served his apprenticeship at Eric Bemrose Limited, working on photo-gravure periodical make-up, and studied at Camberwell School of Arts & Crafts. After leaving Bemrose he worked for some time on a newspaper, before joining Daniel Greenaway & Sons as a monotype keyboard operator. From Greenaways he went to Rush Filmsetters, working in the first *real* filmsetting establishment. With the closure of Rush, he joined South London Typesetters, before returning to film with Letterform. TypeShop

was the last port of call before the formation of Filmcomposition.

Geoff Miller studied at Croydon Technical College and the London College of Printing, and served his apprenticeship with Wace Limited. His specialisation was monotype keyboard operation, which stood him in good stead when he left Wace for Rush Filmsetters where he operated Lumitype 540 machines and Photon 713's. From Rush he joined Letterform, but quickly ended up at Apex, operating diatype. He became one of the first Alphatype operators whilst with Apex, but soon saw the light and joined Conway Group Graphics operating diatronic. With the advent of Filmcomposition, Conway's had a vacancy.

These days the directors' responsibilities have evolved thus: Ed is involved with the general administration, printed publicity and certain areas of client liaison. Jim handles sales and client liaison operations as well as organising the Filmcomposition beanos. Geoff controls the financial administration but probably his most uncanny skill is his ability to repair most faults which occur on our equipment.

Dick Knight was our first employee. He worked for nine years at Charles Clarke, before gracing Conways' with his presence. Dick lives in Sussex and smokes a pipe.

He is our Production Manager, and spends all his free time digging his garden.

John Brundle is our Assistant Day Manager. He's about 26, a real flash bastard and drives a Scimitar. He worked at Rush until their closure, and then joined Telefotoset before joining TypeShop. He joined us from Alphabet Limited. Used to get very stroppy with the messengers, until he decided it made no difference!

Graham Saunders is our client contact. He used to be with Conways' until they discovered who it was. Graham is 21, and is known as the 'Blond Adonis'. He keeps going home early.

Dave Dubber is 28, but looks 22. He completed his apprenticeship at Rush, before joining Conways' who had another vacancy when he joined us. Used to be S.E. Area Squash Champion, now a would-be Gary Player, and doesn't let anyone forget the fact. He's awfully conceited, and generally boring. Hateful fellow. *Smashed a Bembo Grid!*

Sue Buzzard is 24 at time of going to press, and is our only full-time opposite sex. Sue answers the phones, types the invoices and placates uptight clients. She is a Rank Xerox Key Operator. She detests dogs, loves pigeons, and her nickname is 'chunky'. Super bit of crumpet, and her old man is 8' tall and built like the proverbial brick wall.

Peter Laxton is awfully old, and is our day diatype operator. He was apprenticed at C&E Layton, spending 9 years there. Later he worked at Eden Fishers, and was then with Art Repro for 6 years. After 2 years at TypeShop he joined Graphic Presentations, and then graced us with his presence. Pete knows *everybody* and has been *everywhere*. His hobby is the construction of model trains with which he taunts members of the NUR on his way in from Essex.

Malcolm Parham is very young. He's our night photographer. He drives like a bloody maniac and is always late. Pretty genned up. Formerly with TypeShop, but who's perfect?

Len Kenny is 25 and recently married. Used to be with Letterform, then joined Image. Now wields a scalpel. Is a fully paid up member of the Legion of Mary and won't eat hamburgers on Fridays. Works nights 'cos his wife works days.

Geoff Ludlow is our night diatype operator. He's refused to divulge his age. He's really old. Used to work at Laytons, Rush, then Apex. Leisure activities encompass wife-swapping parties, and reading medical directories.

Erik Spiekermann is our tame kraut consultant/fingerpoker. Erik is 27, mad, and a lecturer at London College of Printing. He has worked for Berthold in Germany, as well as the leading nazi adsetters. Nicknamed 'roadrunner' for his incredible ability to zoom his bifocals over ones' left shoulder, make a scathing comment about the immaculate quality of the work in progress and disappear again in a cloud of dust, multi 'miep, miep.' Has been to make comm... German... only... WWII, second due ...funds 'cos of ...is bill. *Censored!*

Terry Millard is our Night Production Manager. He was employed at Wace for 4 years, before joining Rush, and eventually ending up at Apex, via C&E Layton. Terry is a rather skilled make-up man, doesn't smoke or swear (much) but his vice-free life has made him sensitive about reference to his…

Mike Cavender is 26, and is our night copy preparation guy, with an open brief to help any area that is overloaded during the night. Mike was apprenticed at Nickeloid, and later had a three year stay at Apex. Quite a bouncy character. Very militant, but has a lovely wife. Spends a lot of time trying to phone-in to Capital. Doesn't often get through, but would probably get bleeped anyway. Wears slippers.

John Whitnell won't disclose his age. He's our client liaison man. He used to be an advertising whizz-kid, working at Bensons and a lot of other places before taking the easy way and joining Letraset International. Soon after joining Letraset a little man came along to his office and erected a chromed plate on the door which read *'John Whitnell/ Publicity for the Whole World'*. Wears a suit and gave up smoking 15 months ago.

Boris Kaufmann is our outstanding accounts settler. He was formerly with Sioux, Grabbit & Runne, before joining the UK amateur wrestling team. He makes sure that our clients don't forget to pay us. Eats Brillo pads for breakfast, and drives a JCB.

Hobbies: Botany (dissection) and weight-lifting. Aged 32. Won't speak to anybody on the telephone, but writes really *scary* letters.

Peter Drummond is the driver. 20 years old at the last count and stroppy with it. Idle, fat, ugly and quite likeable. No. 2 in the Filmcomp Sumo team. Wears frilly knickers (Size WX) when riding the bikes, very sensitive about his size, so please nobody take the micky…

Mike Russell is our handsome debonair other messenger. Although he used to work with Conways' he has adopted a far more benign attitude to life recently, and we are sure that very soon he will learn to smile again.

Paul Nicholls, our ex-night DC op, is rejoining us, but our illustrator refused to portray him on the grounds that artistic licence can only be taken so far.

Illustrations by Erik Spiekermann, von by Mick Manning

Pages from the ›JokeBook‹, the type specimen book by Filmcomposition, with caricatures of the staff by Spiekermann

Filmcomposition was the leading typesetter in London in the late 1970s. Spiekermann worked there as a typographer, setting type onto positive film, a method still unusual outside Germany: »Filmcomposition was very well known in the industry, and controversial, since we did everything differently. I drove with the boss, Ed Cleary to the ATypI congresses, where the whole type and typesetting manufacturers, scene was gathered. In those days to buy a typesetting machine one had to buy a few of their fonts, since there was no overall standard. That only changed with PostScript by Adobe in 1984.« Filmcomposition had Berthold photo-typesetting machines, and thanks to Spiekermann's good relationship with the Berlin type foundry, the Londoners gained an advantage over their competition by having the newest typefaces to work with, of which there were only a few hundred at the time.

With: Ed Cleary

In the late 1970s Erik Spiekermann was contracted by H. Berthold AG to redesign the ›Berliner Grotesk‹ typeface. The new family was created from ›Berliner Grotesk Light‹ from 1913, and ›Block Semibold‹ from the 1920s. The fonts, redrawn for phototypesetting, were released in 1979 as ›Berliner Grotesk Light‹ and ›Bold‹. A regular weight was added later when the fonts were digitized.

A page from the Filmcomposition loose-leaf edition advertising new typefaces showing Spiekermann's version of ›Berliner Grotesk‹ for phototypesetting

Berliner Grotesk Light

A 1913 house design from H. Berthold AG, Berlin, reworked for film by Erik Spiekermann. Now available for diatronic filmsetting from Filmcomposition.

Specimen setting/Berliner Grotesk Light/11 key on 12 feed/FC spacing

Excellence in typography is the result of nothing more than a n attitude. Its appeal comes from the understanding used in its planning; the designer must care. In contemporary advert ising the perfect integration of design elements often deman ds unorthodox typography. It may mean the use of compact spacing, minus leading, unusual sizes and weights; whatever is necessary to improve appearance and impact. Stating spe cific principles in typography is difficult. No rule is useful if it in hibits or restricts the ultimate purpose of the design. Fine typ ography is the result of nothing more than an attitude. Its ap

Specimen setting/Berliner Grotesk/11 key on 12 feed/FC plus setting

Excellence in typography is the result of nothing more than an attitude. Its appeal comes from the understandin g used in its planning; the designer must care. In contem porary advertising the perfect integration of design elem ments often demands unorthodox typography. It may m ean the use of compact spacing, minus leading, unusual sizes and weights; whatever is necessary to improve app earance and impact. Stating specific principles in typogra phy is difficult. No rule is useful if it inhibits or restricts the ultimate purpose of the design. Fine typography is th

We're Filmcomposition. It must look good.

Filmcomposition.

The original ›Lo-Type‹ was a hot metal typeface designed by Louis Oppenheim between 1911 and 1914 for the H. Berthold AG type foundry. Its name was derived from Louis Oppenheim's initials, LO. In 1977 Erik Spiekermann started to redesign the typeface, so that Berthold could update it for phototypesetting. He also completed missing characters, plus the ›LoType Regular‹ weight.

When looking through old type samples Spiekermann determined that each type size was drawn differently; he would have to begin by finding the typeface's ideal shape. Günter Gerhard Lange, Berthold's artistic director, was responsible for making corrections.

With: Günter Gerhard Lange

Typographer

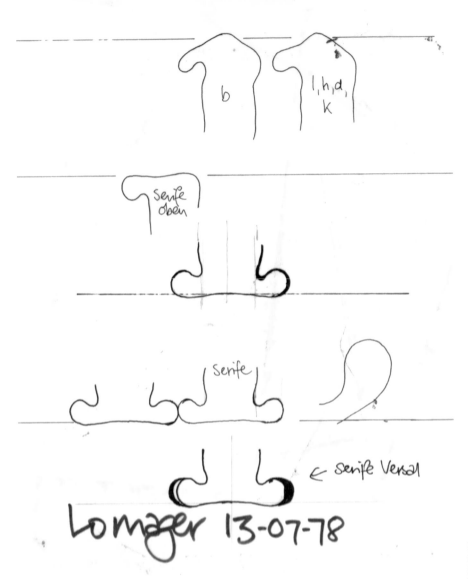

Left: Details of the serif ends as a sketch for the final artwork on tracing paper, 1978
Right: Sample proof of ›LoType Regular‹ in 36 point with correction notes by Günter Gerhard Lange, 1979

LEICHTER WIE ĔF

 zu FETT sh. O, VON INNEN AB

Å Ä B C D E F G

RUNDER & ZITTRIGER!

LINKE SEITE WIE GEKLEBT

ETWAS RUNDER

H IJ K L M N Ö P

AUFFÜLLEN

zu KRÄFTIG, VON INNEN AB
RAUHER
EINSTICH TIEFER

WESENTLICH
FETTER
VON LINKS
RAUHER VOLLER, RAUHER

Q R S T Ü V W X

IDEE UNTER DIE LINIE

ETWAS LEICHTER VON LINKS sh. A

GRUNDSTRICH
UM 2/3 SERIFEN-
STÄRKE NACH
RECHTS VERLEGEN

zu FETT
sh. A
VON
AUSSEN
AB

MAGERER
VON
AUSSEN AB

Y Z Ø Ç Æ Œ

ETWAS
BEGRADIGEN

VOLLER!
KONTUR
RAUHER

ETWAS zu LEICHT sh. bp

å ä b c d e fg h

zu KRÄFTIG sh. hb

ETWAS AUSGLEICHEN
AUFFÜLLEN

LEICHTER,
ETWAS GERADER

i j k l m n ö p q r s

zu FETT, SPUR RECHTS
NEIGEN

ETWAS zu FETT
sh. N

IDEE BEGRADIGEN

ETWAS zu FETT

bitte NEU

t ü v w x y z ß ø ç æ œ

BEGRADIGEN

GRUNDSTRICH ZUM QUERSTRICH HIN ETWAS KONISCH VERJÜNGEN

DIESE FORMEN
HARMONIEREN
NICHT MIT DEN
ANDEREN
GARNITUREN
konventionell

CO - TYPE NORMAL
13. 9. 79

KÜRZEN,
SCHRÄGSTRICH VON LINKS
ETWAS LEICHTER, STEILER

VW

In 1979 Erik Spiekermann drew the typeface
›Block Italic‹, part of the ›Block‹ font family for
the H. Berthold AG type foundry.
       »I began the sketches for it in late 1977, after
returning to London,« says Spiekermann.
A colleague in London used his pencil drawings
to cut a version on red repro film.

Notes on photographic proofs as a draft
for new drawings on tracing paper, 1977

Stahl
Hafen
Zink
Modlitwa

Max & Moritz
Hinz & Kunz
Kreti & Pleti
Castor & Pollux
Romeo & Julia

Für jeden etwas!
Volkshochschule Werl-Wickede-Ense
Kursbeginn 15.1.

Schall & Rauch

Rock & Roll

Kreti & Pleti
Max & Moritz,
Hinz & Kunz,
Alle kommen zur VHS.

Sport & Spiel.

Leben & lernen.
Aug' & Ohr.
Kind & Kegel.
Mann & Maus.

Left column: Pages from the documentation of the intensive seminar with Spiekermann ›For friends of Italian opera‹ from June 12–14, 1978
Right column: Extracts of the documentation of the project ›Kulturwerbung‹ in which designs for the Werl-Wickede-Ruhr adult education center program guide were developed

From 1978 to the early 1980s Erik Spiekermann gave one-week seminars on design at the Bielefeld University of Applied Sciences. Gerd Fleischmann, professor of typography there until 2003, recruited him. »We met at the ATypI working seminar in Reading in 1976,« says

who keeps silent consents! Reports and practical exercises for eye-catching type/ posters‹ and ›For friends of Italian opera‹.

Spiekermann sums it up: »It was fun, but I learnt that I'm not cut out to be a civil servant, and teaching isn't really enough for me.«

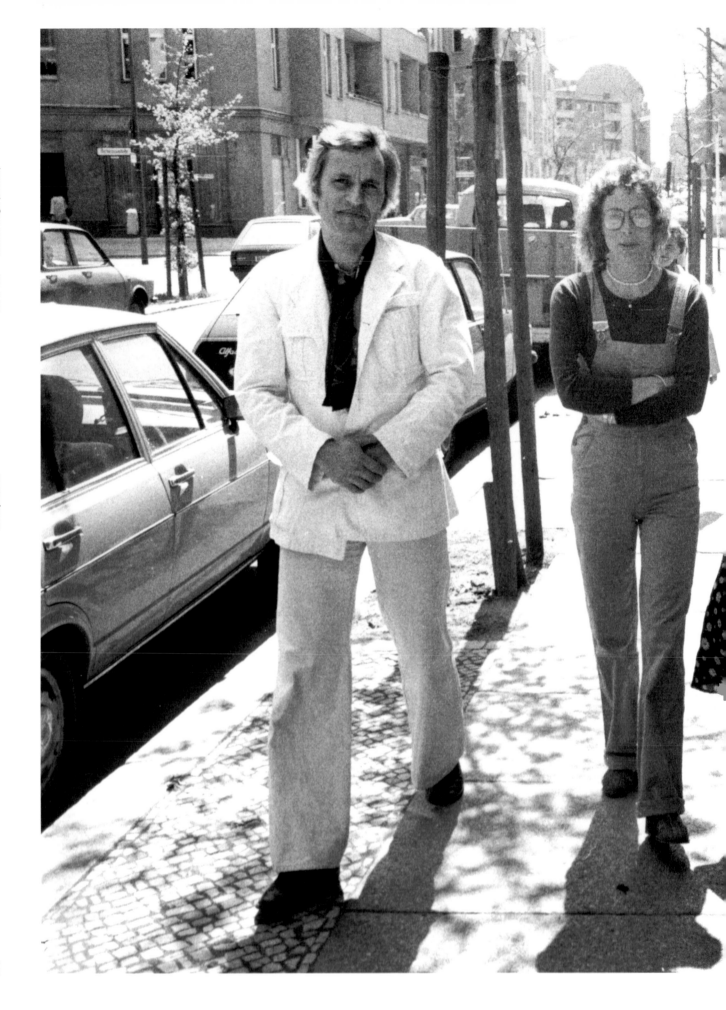

Since there were few large design studios in Germany capable of handling big projects, German businesses often went to design agencies in England. However, this collaboration was not without its problems. For example, British designers would often deliver final artwork and construction plans using inches instead of millimeters. So there was a need for good German design studios.

Erik Spiekermann founded MetaDesign in 1979 with Dieter Heil, with whom he had worked at Wolff Olins in London; Florian Fischer, his business partner in Berlin, and Gerhard Doerrié, a colleague of Fischer's. The first employee was Anna Berkenbusch. The name MetaDesign refers to the motto »design for design«.

Spiekermann traveled between London and Berlin, before moving back to Berlin in 1981. Since Florian Fischer wished to return to consultancy, and Spiekermann did not want to remain alone, MetaDesign »Mark One«

was bought in 1983 by Sedley Place Design in London, and renamed Sedley Place Design Berlin GmbH. The London company was founded in 1978 by former Wolff Olins employees. Dieter Heil became managing director of the Berlin branch.

With: Gerhard Doerrié, Florian Fischer, and Dieter Heil

From left to right: Florian Fischer,
Cornelia Bassenge, Anna Berkenbusch,
Erik Spiekermann

In der Handelsregistersache
der
Meta Design GmbH

- noch kein Aktenzeichen -

Fotokopie

melden wir hiermit die Gesellschaft
und uns als Geschäftsführer zur Ein-
tragung in das Handelsregister an.

Als im Gesellschaftsvertrag bestellte
Geschäftsführer der

    Meta Design GmbH

überreichen wir

1. Erste Ausfertigung des Gesellschafts-
   vertrages vom heutigen Tage - UR Nr.
   129   /1979 des Notars Dr. Werner
   Schettler in Berlin -,

2. Liste der Gesellschafter.

Die Kapitalverkehrsteuerunbedenklich-
keitsbescheinigung des Finanzamts für
Erbschaft- und Verkehrsteuern wird nach-
gereicht.

Wir versichern, daß die Stammeinlagen
zu einem Viertel eingezahlt sind und
daß sich die eingezahlten Beträge in
unserer freien Verfügung befinden.

Jeder der Geschäftsführer Gerhard
Doerrie, Florian Fischer, Dieter Heil
und Erik Spiekermann vertritt die Gesellschaft gemeinsam mit einem anderen
vorgenannten Geschäftsführer oder einem
etwaigen später bestellten anderen Geschäftsführer.

Amtsgericht Charlottenburg
-Registergericht-
Amtsgerichtsplatz 1

1000 Berlin 19

Wir zeichnen unsere Unterschriften wie
folgt:

- 2 -

MetaDesign certificate of incorporation,
listing Spiekermann as »Typographer
Hans-Erich Spiekermann«, the
official spelling of Spiekermann's name
at the time.

This project was the first commission for MetaDesign; it had started when Spiekermann was at Wolff Olins. MetaDesign took over the development of the concept and its implementation, and the production of the design manual. The team around Erik Spiekermann and Florian Fischer worked on a huge amount of forms, business documents, and publications. The sketches for the BfG: lettering were by Gerry Barney at Wolff Olins. Spiekermann made the artwork for phototypesetting at TSI in London (the type company had its own Ikarus system, and belonged to Letraset), and added several characters. He also supervised the production for Berthold and Linotype machines.

With: Gerry Barney, Anna Berkenbusch, Florian Fischer, and Dieter Heil

Page from the concept presentation for the new image design for Bank für Gemeinwirtschaft in Frankfurt.

In 1979 Erik Spiekermann installed a darkroom:
»Making one's own repro proofs was expensive
in those days, and most colleagues didn't really
know how. But I guess I was a technophile.«
In addition to a professional processing sink
unit and a photo exposure device, he had
a process camera by H. Berthold AG. The fk3
repromat was suitable for line and halftone work
on photographic paper or film up to 50 × 60 cm
in size. The motorized automatic focus worked
best with one foot on the baseboard.

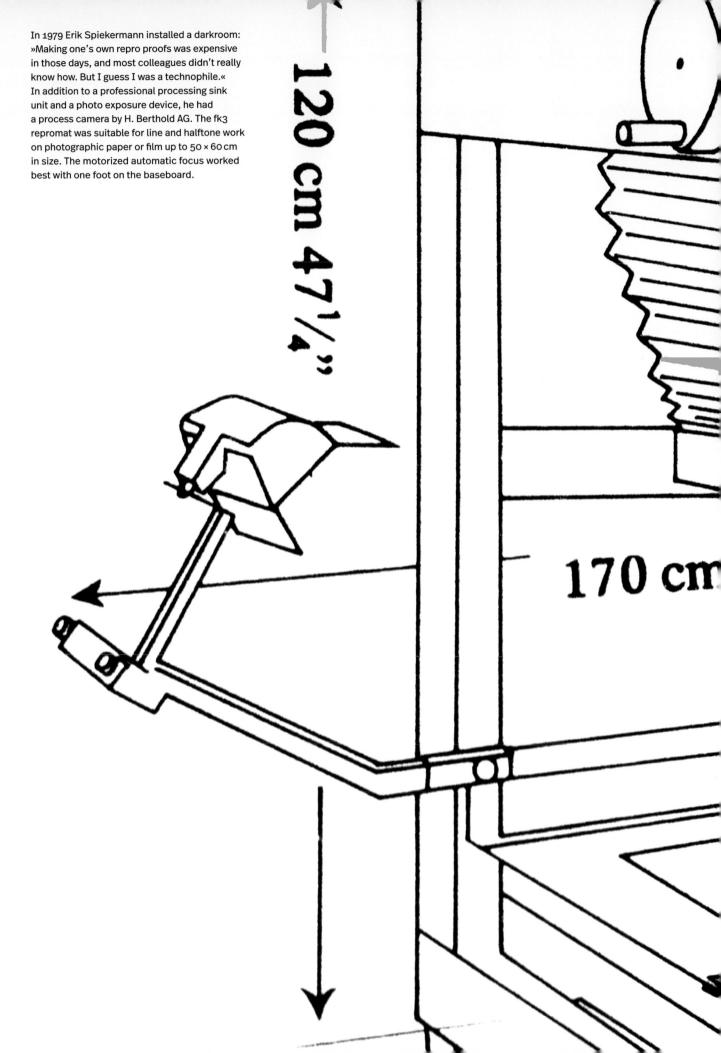

120 cm 47¹/₄"

170 cm

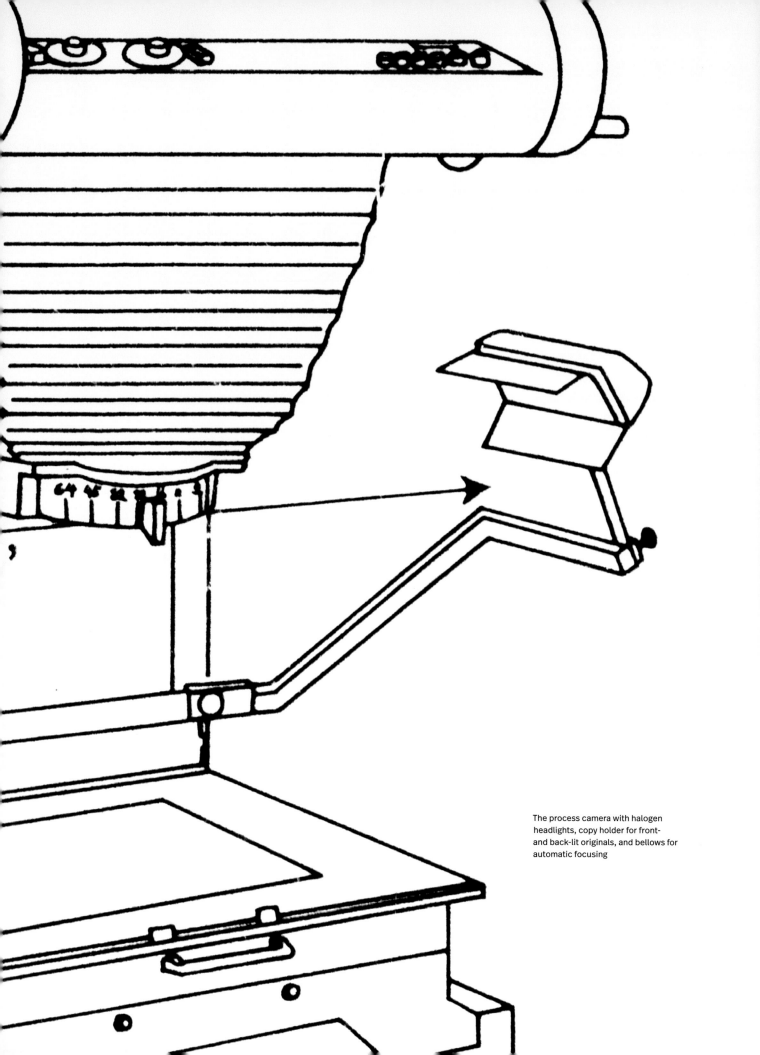

The process camera with halogen
headlights, copy holder for front-
and back-lit originals, and bellows for
automatic focusing

Spiekermann developed a system with Florian
Fischer for ›Berthold exclusive‹ brochures.
The first three jobs, designed and produced
by MetaDesign were: ›Comenius‹ (Hermann
Zapf), ›LoType‹ (Louis Oppenheim, later Erik
Spiekermann), and ›Poppl-Pontifex‹ (Friedrich
Poppl). The concept anticipated having future
brochures produced by other designers.

With: Anna Berkenbusch and Florian Fischer

Two booklets from the ›Berthold
exclusive‹ series in A4: type
specimen book for ›Comenius‹, left,
and ›LoType‹, right, 1981.

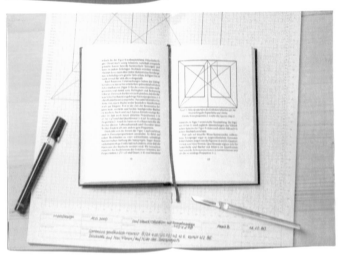

Person

After four years of traveling between London and Berlin, Erik moved back to Berlin with his wife Joan and their son Dylan in 1981. MetaDesign was doing well there, getting good jobs in.

The first office was a former children's day-care center. When MetaDesign moved to 18 Bamberger Straße in 1981, the old office became the legendary MetaCafé.

Spiekermann carrying a tripod on the corner of Bamberger Straße and Barbarossastraße, between MetaCafé and MetaDesign, 1981

65

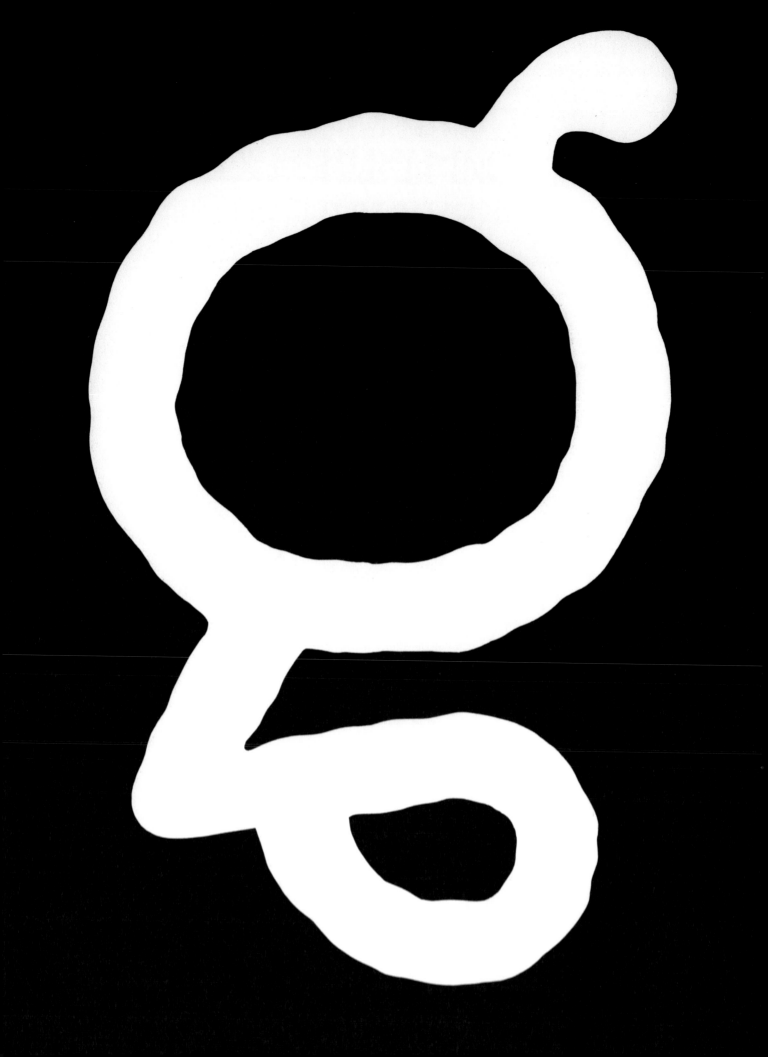

national Typeface Corporation (ITC) in 1981
was never used. On the other hand, his other
proposal for a text typeface was taken up:
›ITC Correspondence‹ (working title) later became ›ITC Officina‹.

Excellence in typography is
nothing more than an attitude
and has the quick brown fox
jumping over the lazy dog.
at last different weights
Excellence in typography is
nothing more than an attitude
and has the quick brown fox
jumping over the lazy dog.
at last different weights
Excellence in typography is
nothing more than an attitude
and has the quick brown fox
jumping over the lazy dog.
at last different weights
Excellence in typography is
nothing more than an attitude
and has the quick brown fox
jumping over the lazy dog.

›Studentenfutter‹, the first book Erik Spiekermann wrote about typography, refers in its sub-
title – ›Everything you always wanted to know
about typography but was afraid to ask‹ – to
the Woody Allen film about sex with a similar
title. It is about elucidation, inhibition, and tra-
ditions that must be broken in order to breathe
life back into them. The book is consistent

with Spiekermann's belief in typography as an
expression of language and communication for
everyone. ›Studentenfutter‹ is the perfect introductory work for anyone who wants to know
about the key functions of typography.

With: Hansjörg Stulle

Right: Spiekermann determined the
sequence and rough design of each
page in hand-drawn sketches.
Right page: Two double pages from the
chapters »Type is language's dress«
(top) and »The measure of all things«
(bottom)

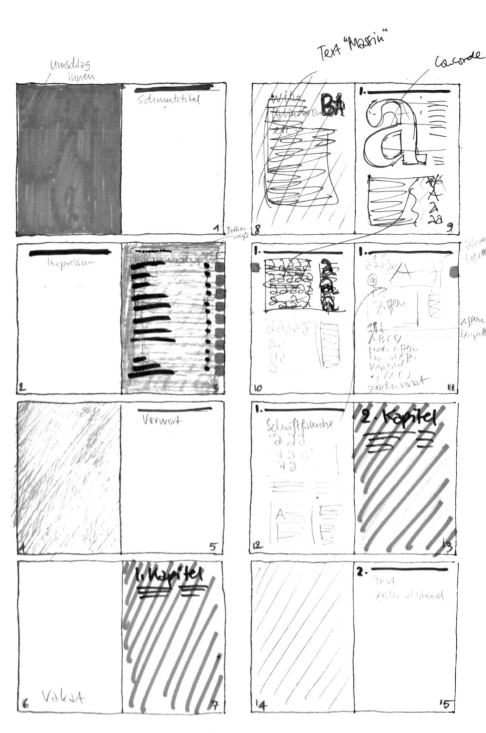

Page 98-99 spread

Adrian Frutiger:
für das Orientierungssystem
des Flughafens
Charles de Gaulle
in Paris entwarf
er die Schrift,
die heute als komplett ausgebaute
Schriftfamilie
seinen Namen
trägt.

Schriftentwurf als
geplantes System –
alle Garnituren der
Univers auf einen
Blick:

```
                    39
45 46 47 48 49
53 55 56 57 58 59
63 65 66 67 68
73 75 76
83
```

**Adrian Frutiger:
Schriften mit System.**

Ursprünglich wurde die Schrift, die heute den Namen ihres Entwerfers trägt, für das Orientierungssystem des Pariser Flughafens *Charles de Gaulle* gestaltet.

Betrachtungen zur optimalen Lesbarkeit führten zum Entwurf einer einfachen, vielleicht sogar etwas kahlen Grotesk, die in ihren *humanen*, individuellen Einzelformen der Antiqua verwandt ist und das Geschriebene noch durchscheinen läßt.

Dem Grundsatz, Schriftentwürfe in den Zusammenhang einer Planung zu stellen und nicht nur *künstlerischen* Impulsen zu folgen, entsprach Adrian Frutiger beispielhaft zuerst mit der Univers. Er sah die Schriftfamilie als geschlossenes System, innerhalb dessen normale, breite, schmale und kursive Garnituren in mehreren Strichstärken ohne

ästhetische Kompromisse miteinander kombiniert werden können.
Heute ist es für jeden Schriftanwender selbstverständlich, bei vielen Garnituren

innerhalb einer Familie alle nötigen Auszeichnungen vorzufinden; 1957 jedoch, als die ersten Bleisatzschnitte der Univers bei Deberny & Peignot erschienen, war es eine Revolution.

Ober- und Unterlängen sind ziemlich ausgeprägt, das macht die Wortbilder griffiger, also lesbarer. Großbuchstaben und Ziffern sind relativ klein und stören nicht den Zeilenfluß.
Die Rundungen zeigen Spannung zwischen kantiger und ovaler Form; Innenräume, die ja

zum Erkennen eines Buchstabens entscheidend sind, erscheinen besonders deutlich ausgeprägt, aber nicht übertrieben.

Acht verschiedene Frutiger-Schriften übereinander kopiert ergeben eine eindeutige gemeinsame Struktur.
Der Kern des Zeichens ist wie der reine Ton – individuelle Ausformungen sind der Klang.

Die Differenz zwischen horizontaler und vertikaler Strichstärke ist zwar vorhanden, doch genauso wie bei den schrägen Auf- und Abstrichen wird dieser Unterschied nicht *sichtbar*.
Wie alle Schriften von

Adrian Frutiger, ist auch diese Familie mit Ziffern für die verschiedenen Garnituren bezeichnet. Normal ist dabei immer die 5 – 55 bedeutet also normale Strichstärke in normaler Lage, will heißen geradestehend. 56 ist dagegen normale

Strichstärke in schräger Lage. Geringere Strichstärke wird mit einer niedrigeren Ziffer in der ersten Stelle bezeichnet, fettere Schnitte mit einer höheren, so daß Frutiger 75 die fette, geradestehende Garnitur ist.

98

99

Page 114-115 spread

Die Maße aller Dinge.

Das Normalformat A0 hat einen Flächeninhalt von 1 m² und die Proportion 1:1,414 = √2, das entspricht dem Verhältnis der Quadratseite zur -diagonalen nach dem pythagoreischen Lehrsatz.

A0	841 x 1189 mm
C0	917 x 1297
A1	594 x 841
C1	648 x 917
A2	420 x 594
C2	458 x 648
A3	297 x 420
C3	324 x 458
A4	210 x 297
C4	229 x 324
A5	148 x 210
C5	162 x 229
A6	105 x 148
C6	114 x 162

Die Formate der C-Reihe sind Umschläge für die A-Reihe.
Seite 115:
Nordisches Format
400 x 570 mm
Rheinisches Format
360 x 530 mm
Berliner Format
315 x 470 mm
Penguin 200 x 248 mm
dtv 108 x 180 mm
Reklam 95 x 155 mm

Flächen, gestürzten Zeilen und ganzseitigen Fotos ist die Kenntnis der Proportionen nützlich, die für unsere Wahrnehmung bestimmend sind, weil sie auch in der Natur ihre Entsprechung haben.

Das Format einer Drucksache ist oft von technischen und kaufmännischen Überlegungen bestimmt, was auf zunehmende Vorherrschaft der praktischen, aber langweiligen DIN-Formate hinausläuft.

Papierformate waren früher ungefähr im Verhältnis 3:4 und ergaben gefalzt dann abwechselnd die Proportionen 2:3 und wieder 3:4.

Der halbe Bogen heißt Folio (2:3), der Viertelbogen Quart (3:4) und der Achtelbogen Oktav (2:3). Den DIN-Formaten fehlt dieser spannungsreiche Wechsel der Proportionen, stattdessen wird das ursprüngliche Maß halbiert und das Verhältnis von 1:1,414 immer beibehalten.

Bei Zeitungen sind oft noch überlieferte alte Formate in Gebrauch. Als Norm gelten hierzulande nach DIN 16604 die drei oben abgebildeten Größen.
Bei Büchern herrscht große Vielfalt, weil die Normalformate der A-Reihe unhandlich sind und zu wenig Abwechslung bieten.
Vor allem Taschenbücher müssen handlich sein und die Formate der Druckmaschinen ausnutzen.

114

115

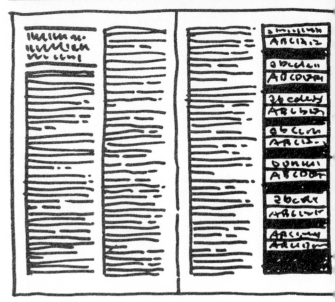

Einen Eindruck der Seitenaufteilung vermittelt die flüchtige Skizze, das Scribble. Das Zusammenspiel von Überschrift, Textspalten und Abbildungen läßt sich mit einigen Strichen anschaulich darstellen.

Der Klebeumbruch mit den gesetzten Spalten zeigt, wie der Text läuft, wo Zwischenüberschriften und Abbildungen eingefügt werden können.

Alle für den Satz wichtigen Positionen können als x- und y-Koordinaten angegeben werden. Ein Vordruck im Zeilenabstand des Textes (hier 3,00 mm) erleichtert die Zuordnung. Auch alle Satzangaben wie Schrift, Schriftgrößen, Linienstärken etc. werden hier festgehalten.

120

ROCKWELL DIE SCHRIFT IST EINE WARE

Gemeinhin denkt man sich vielleicht den Schriftentwerfer als einen etwas verschrobenen Künstler, der eines Morgens mit der Idee zu einer neuen Schrift aufwacht und nicht eher ruhen kann, bis er diese Vorstellung mit Pinsel, Feder oder gar Meißel zu Papier oder Stein gebracht hat.

Solche Schriftkünstler hat es sicherlich gegeben und gibt es wahrscheinlich heute noch, aber eine Druck- oder besser: Satzschrift mag wohl einer Laune entspringen, doch sie dient immer einem Zweck: nicht nur dem, gelesen, sondern zunächst dem, verkauft zu werden. Dazu muß sie nach dem Entwurf hergestellt, veröffentlicht, beworben und ausgeliefert werden, egal, ob es sich um Bleibuchstaben handelte oder jetzt um digitale Informationen auf Disketten.

Napoleon – und damit schlagen wir die Brücke zum Historischen – Napoleon hat einmal die Engländer als »Nation von Krämern« bezeichnet, darin lag Spott, aber auch Neid. Immerhin hatte er es trotz Konti-

Wie bei jeder anderen spiegelte sich auch diese wider in den Erzeugnisse mischen Schriftgießereie Katalogen erschienen Sch als *Egyptians* bezeichnet heute noch *Egyptienne* ge das an den Parallelen zu e dartigen Hieroglyphenze der massiv wirkenden äg Baukunst lag oder nur an Bestreben, auf der allgem ägyptischen Welle zu sch wissen wir nicht, einige U theiten gibt es jedoch: die erste serifenlose Sch Caslon-Verzeichnis von 18 ausgerechnet *Egyptian* ge während dagegen eine se tonte Schrift bei Figgins e vorher als *Antique* erschi

Alle Schriftgießereien von jeder Schriftart wenig eine Variante anbieten; al erst Linotype und danach type mit ihren Setzmasch den Markt kamen, mußte für sich auch diesen Anfo gen der Schriftkäufer an Bei der Entwicklung eine Schriftenprogramms grif meist auf historische Vorl rück, denn auch damals h alles schon einmal gegeb

Seit 1913 gab es bei M eine **Egyptian** mit der Se mer 173. Im gleichen Jahr

Double page from a hand-bound
proof with correction notes for the
final print

AV-Blatt 3mm

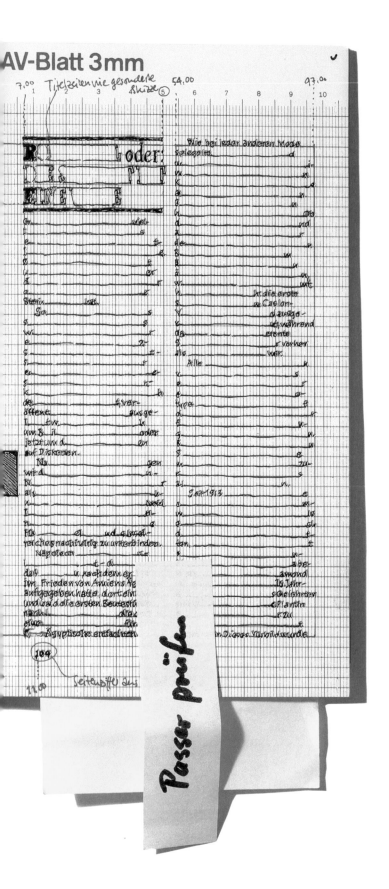

Spiekermann with friend and colleague
Steve S. Schmidt in MetaCafé

MetaDesign's first office was a small former day-care center on Barbarossastraße. When MetaDesign moved to Bamberger Straße in 1981, the old office became MetaCafé for two years.

»We didn't want to lose that nice little shop. There were no cafés close by, and an organic bakery had opened next door. Everyone who worked at Meta would have to do the odd shift at the café,« Spiekermann remembers. The café sold a daily menu of dishes, bread, cake, ice cream, coffee, wine, and much more. They placed a lot of importance on the use of natural organic ingredients. In 1983 the café was passed on to two private owners.

With: Anna Berkenbusch, Florian Fischer, Joan Spiekermann, and many others

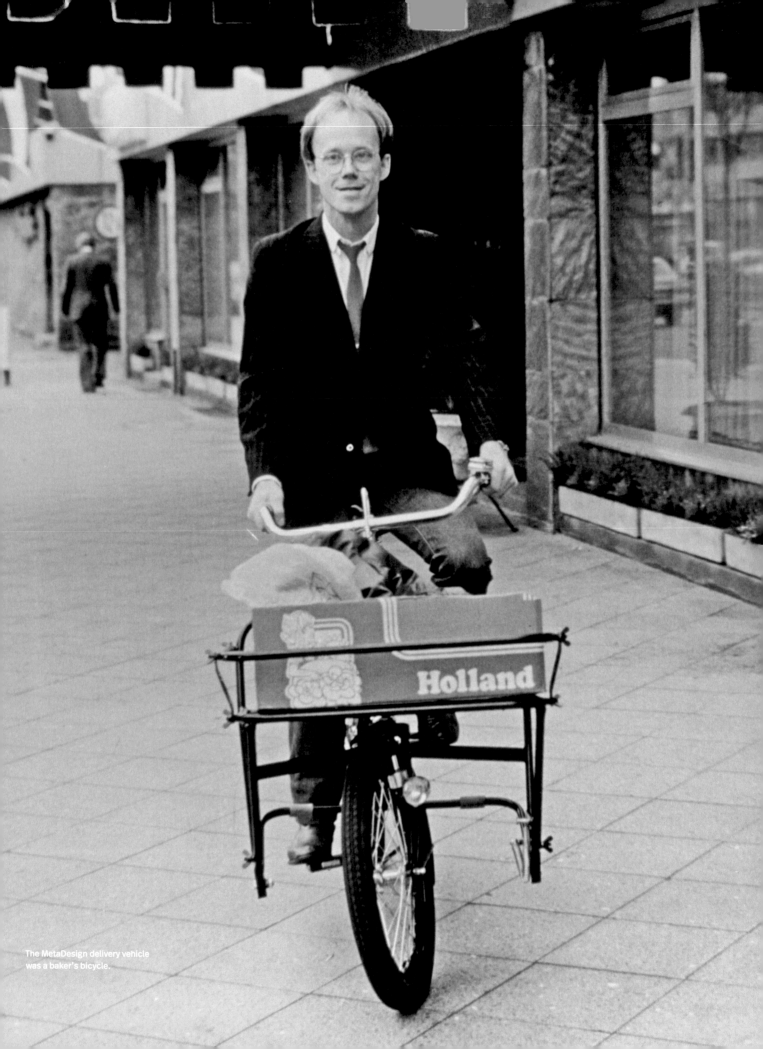

The MetaDesign delivery vehicle was a baker's bicycle.

Left: Sketches for a cover
Bottom: The final book cover, published
by Rotbuch in 1982

In 1982 Rotbuch-Verlag published the book
›Last train from Berlin: An Eye-Witness Account
of Germany at War‹ by Howard K. Smith. At the
time Spiekermann's sister was working as
managing director at the left-wing publishing
house in West Berlin. Normally, they would use
their own graphic designers, but Erik Spiekermann did the design for particularly tricky
publications every now and again. He designed
the cover for Smith's book, in addition to
the series that followed, ›Beiträge zur national-
sozialistischen Gesundheits- und Sozialpolitik‹.

Aussonderung und Tod
Die klinische Hinrichtung
der Unbrauchbaren

Rotbuch Verlag Berlin

**Feinderklärung
und Prävention**
Kriminalbiologie,
Zigeunerforschung
und Asozialenpolitik

Rotbuch Verlag Berlin

Reform und Gewissen
»Euthanasie« im Dienst
des Fortschritts

Rotbuch Verlag Berlin

**Herrenmensch und
Arbeitsvölker**
Ausländische Arbeiter
und Deutsche 1939–1945

Rotbuch Verlag Berlin

**Biedermann und
Schreibtischtäter**
Materialien zur
deutschen Täter-Biographie

Rotbuch Verlag Berlin

**Sozialpolitik und
Judenvernichtung**
Gibt es eine
Ökonomie der Endlösung?

Rotbuch Verlag Berlin

Six in a series of book covers designed
by Spiekermann, published between
1985 and 1991. Mounting the photo
on top of itself adds emphasis and does
justice to the delicate subject matter.

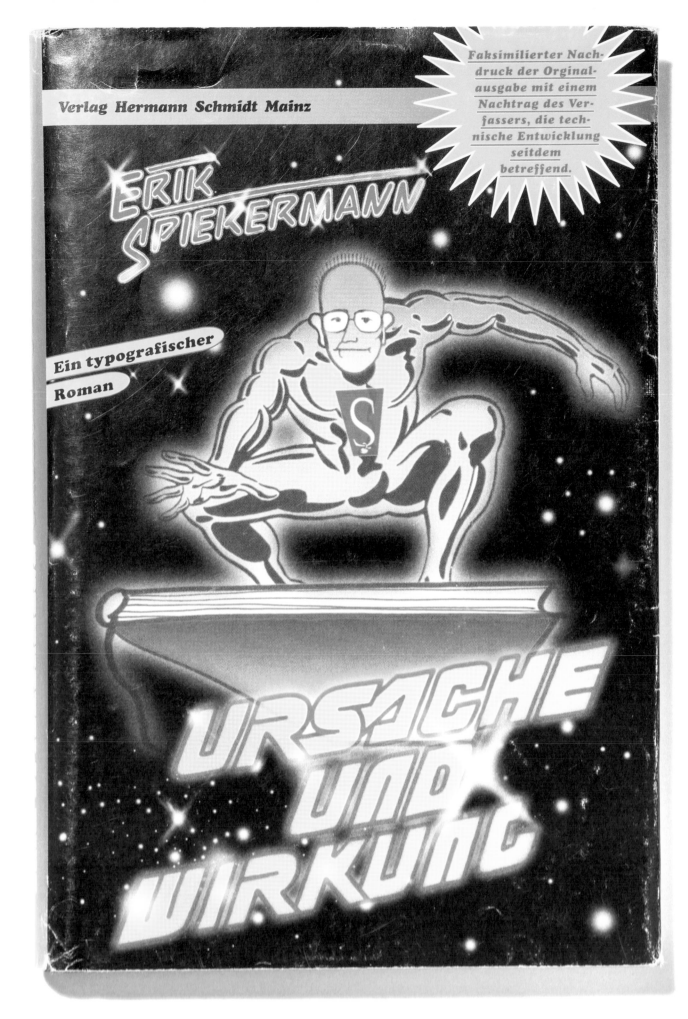

This book, of which new editions were continually published for twelve years, presents all the important typographic rules about typefaces, tracking, line spacing and length, word spacing, font size and weight, and methods of typesetting (phototypesetting) in the form of an entertaining novel. Spiekermann, who loves small sizes, packaged the nine chapters into a handy 18.4 × 12.8 × 1.8 cm. The book was proofread by Günter Gerhard Lange, and was published as ›Ursache und Wirkung. Ein typografischer Roman‹ in 1982 by Context,

then in 1983 by H. Berthold AG, and in English, translated by Spiekermann with Paul Stiff, in 1986. The English title was ›Rhyme and Reason: a typographic novel‹. In 1994 Hermann Schmidt Mainz published a facsimile edition with four ironic cover variations.

It received many accolades, among them the Typographic Excellence Award of the Type Directors Club (TDC), and the Black Pencil by D&AD in London. It was voted one of the »most beautiful books in the Federal Republic of Germany« by the Stiftung Buchkunst Frankfurt.

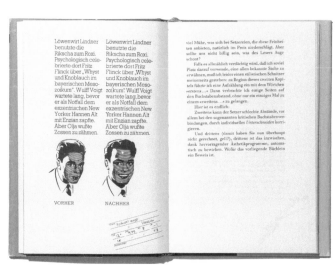

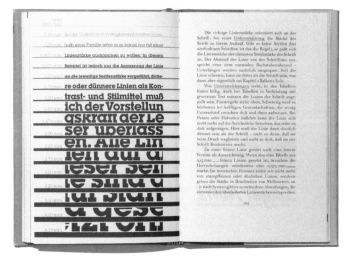

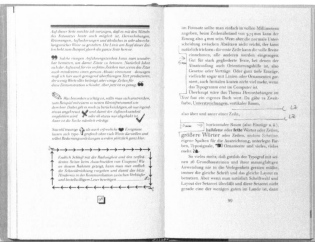

Es gibt eine Regel, die besagt, daß Unter- und Oberlängen sich nie berühren dürfen.

Es gibt für diese Regel die Ausnahme, daß Berühren erlaubt ist, wenn's besser aussieht.

Schrift LoType schmalhalbfett auf Mitte

SG ZAB WZ LW

Bemerkungen Titelsatz sehr eng

Wie schon beim Buchstabenabstand gibt es auch hier allgemeine, vom künstlerisch begabten Leser leicht nachzuempfindende Regeln und darüber hinaus wieder ein paar jener kleinen Tricks, deren Beherrschen auch an sonst trüben Tagen zu kleinen Erfolgserlebnissen führt. Besonders, wenn man den Vorher-nachher-Effekt den jüngeren, noch nicht so versierten Kollegen vorführt und dafür viele entzückte *ah*- und *oh*-Rufe erntet. Die Typografie ist eben unter den Wissenschaften nicht die geringste,* auch wenn der kritische Journalismus sie bislang nur benutzt, aber nicht würdigt.

Das Allgemeine zuerst. Die einfachste Regel ist ja wohl die, daß sich Unter- und Oberlängen nicht berühren sollen. Bei Titelzeilen tritt diese Grundregel natürlich mitunter außer Kraft, weil manchmal trotz Ober- und Unterlängen ein inniges Berühren in Kauf genommen werden muß, um den Zeilen optische Kraft und Entschiedenheit zu verleihen. Manchmal kommt nur eine Unterlänge in der ersten oder nur eine Oberlänge in der folgenden Zeile vor. In diesem Fall und sogar in dem extremen Fall, daß nur *eine* Unterlänge wiederum nur *einer* Oberlänge gegenübersteht, tritt der sogenannte 1. Spiekermannsche Lehrsatz in Kraft, der folgendes besagt:
»Gibt es bei zwei mit geringem Abstand nacheinander folgenden Zeilen auch nur jeweils eine *Unter- und Oberlänge, so treffen diese beiden in 99 Prozent der Fälle aufeinander und überlappen mehr oder weniger.«*

* *Inter scientias non minima est typographica.*

43

By 1983 Erik Spiekermann had made a name for himself as a consultant to many type companies – including Linotype. He worked for D. Stempel AG, a subsidiary of Linotype, proofing the designs for ›Neue Helvetica‹, and designing a brochure for the introduction of the typeface. »It was my idea to number ›Neue Helvetica‹ the same way as ›Univers‹. I insisted they produce a robust weight for ›Helvetica 65‹ that could be used in small sizes,« says Spiekermann.

Corrections by Spiekermann on a sample proof for the design of ›Neue Helvetica‹, here the thin weight

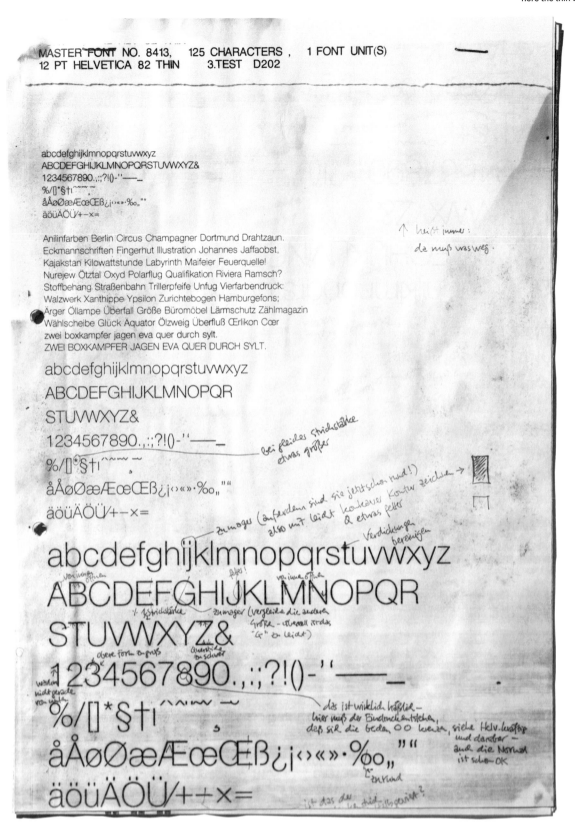

Double pages from the programs for
September '83, September/October '85
and March/April '86

In 1983 Erik Spiekermann was commissioned
to develop a cost-efficient template for the
programs of the Kunstamt Kreuzberg for their
contemporary group and themed exhibitions.
Spiekermann designed a simple layout for the
small format measuring a mere 7 × 10 cm, using
his typical colors red, black, gray, and white.

The texts were written on a typewriter by the
Kunstamt employees themselves. Spiekermann
then mounted them as a paste-up with the
headlines and repros on a single A4 sheet of
paper, which was then reproduced using cheap
high-speed printing.

According to the profile of the society founded in 1984: »Forum Typografie is a consortium of people who not only talk about improving typography, but actually do something about it.« It was intended as a counterpart to the American Type Directors Club. The idea originated on a trip to Ireland in 1983, to which Context GmbH, a consortium of German and Swiss typesetters, had invited trade journalists and specialists. In the tranquil village of Bunratty, nights were spent discussing the lack of exchange within the industry. Things became more concrete when they met at Frankfurt airport. Up until then they had specifically talked about an elite club. However, this idea was dropped once the society was founded. The first Forum Typografie meeting took place on October 12 – 14, 1984 in Berlin's Kreuzberg district. To this day, the Forum is not supposed to be an institute for further education, but an exchange for practicing specialists. The motto was devised by the late Hans-Peter Willberg: »It is not capital that unites us, but small capitals.«

Right page: Some of the speakers at the first Forum Typografie after the fall of the Berlin Wall. Berlin Weißensee School of Art, 1990

Aufruf zur Gründung eines Type Director Clubs Deutschland

Spontan hat die Context GmbH, Gesellschaft für Typografie und Satztechnik, auf ihrer Pressekonferenz am 21. 10. 1983 in Irland die aus Journalistenkreisen kommende Anregung zur Gründung eines Type Director Clubs Deutschland aufgegriffen und stellt eine Summe von 10 000 DM für dessen Gründung zur Verfügung.
Damit möchte Context eine Basis schaffen und interessierte Fachleute sind nun aufgerufen, diesen TDC Deutschland zu gründen.
Die vorläufige Kontaktstelle:
Hans-Peter Schmid,
8520 Erlangen, Falkenstraße 24C,
Telefon (0 91 31) 4 58 40.

Jens Kreitmeyer painted an enormous banner in the courtyard of 185 Oranienstraße for the first Forum in Berlin, 1984. However, it was only ready at the end of the event.

```
Verfasser: Erik Spiekermann,
Meta Design Berlin; typografischer Gestalter;
Ehrenpräsident des Type Directors Club London;
Präsidiumsmitglied des BDG.


Typografie

Noch 'n Verein!

Wer hierzulande meint, gute Typografie zu machen und
wem die Zähne stumpf werden beim täglichen Anblick der
Beispiele, wie man es nicht macht, der war bislang
heimatlos und kein richtiger Deutscher. Der ist nämlich
in einem Verein.

Für Typografie ist keiner der bestehenden
Berufsverbände zuständig; der BDG-Bund deutscher
Grafik-Designer - kann bei fast 1500 Mitgliedern
aus allen Bereichen der grafischen Gestaltung so
etwas Nebulöses wie "Gute Typografie" gar nicht
erst definieren, die Art Directoren im ADC haben
meist andere Sorgen und sehen oft Typografie als
Sache an, die man den Typostudios oder irgendwelchen
"freelance" Type-Freaks überläßt. Die Buchgestalter
und Hersteller schließlich haben zwar die Stiftung
Buchkunst als Mutter des guten Geschmacks im Rücken,
aber zur Kommunikation untereinander und zum Austausch
von Meinungen führt das auch nicht.

Immerhin aber gibt es anscheinend in allen eben
angeführten Bereichen Leute, die mehr wissen und
machen wollen. Diese typografisch Heimatlosen trafen
sich am 4. Februar während des Deutschen Designertages
in Berlin, um eine gemeinsame Strategie auszuhecken.

In einem Punkt aber man sich gleich einig:
noch einen Verein will keiner. Und Type Directors
Clubs wie London oder New York funktionieren nicht in
einer Republik mit vielen Zentren, wo Zeit und Geld
für Reisen draufgehen statt für typografische
Aktivitäten. Andererseits hat der Kampf gegen die
Windmühlenflügel der Dummheit und Borniertheit den
typografischen Einzelkämpfern in der Vergangenheit
wenig gebracht, so daß man doch gemeinsame Aktions-
und damit auch Organisationsformen finden muß.

Aber vor der Form steht der Inhalt und über diese
wurde teilweise recht kontrovers gestritten. Zwischen
Art Directoren, Setzern, Buchgestaltern, Grafik-Designern
und Typografen gibt es 1001 Definitionen, was Typografie
überhaupt ist und worin sich gute von schlechter
unterscheidet.
```

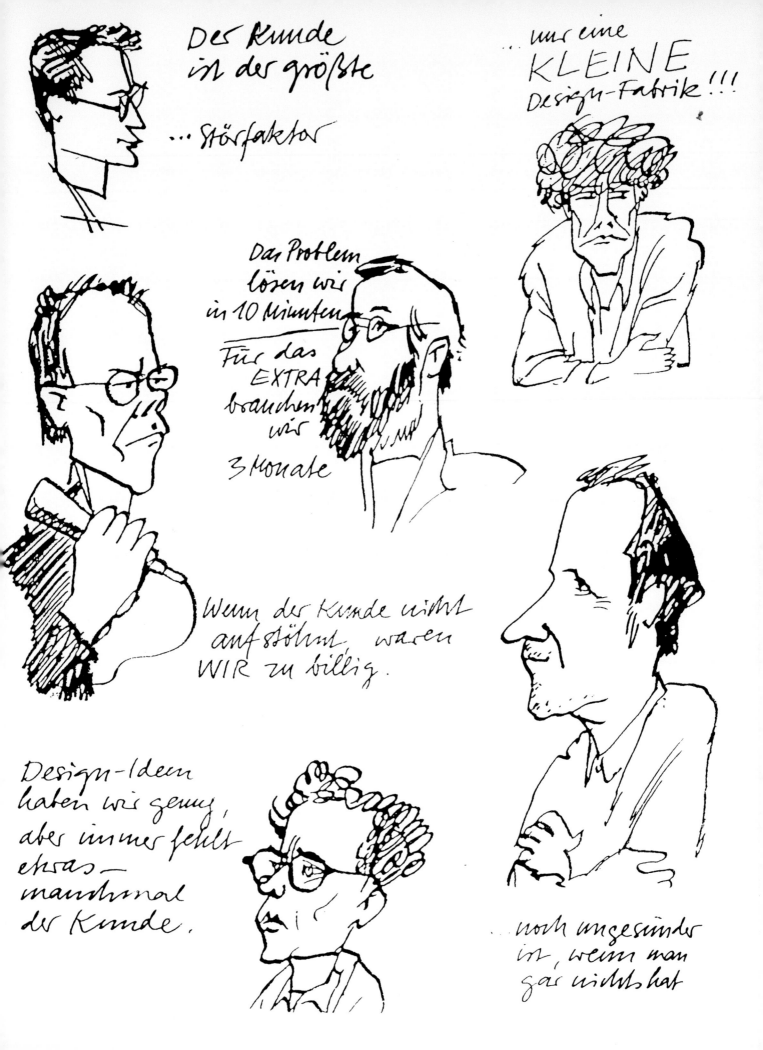

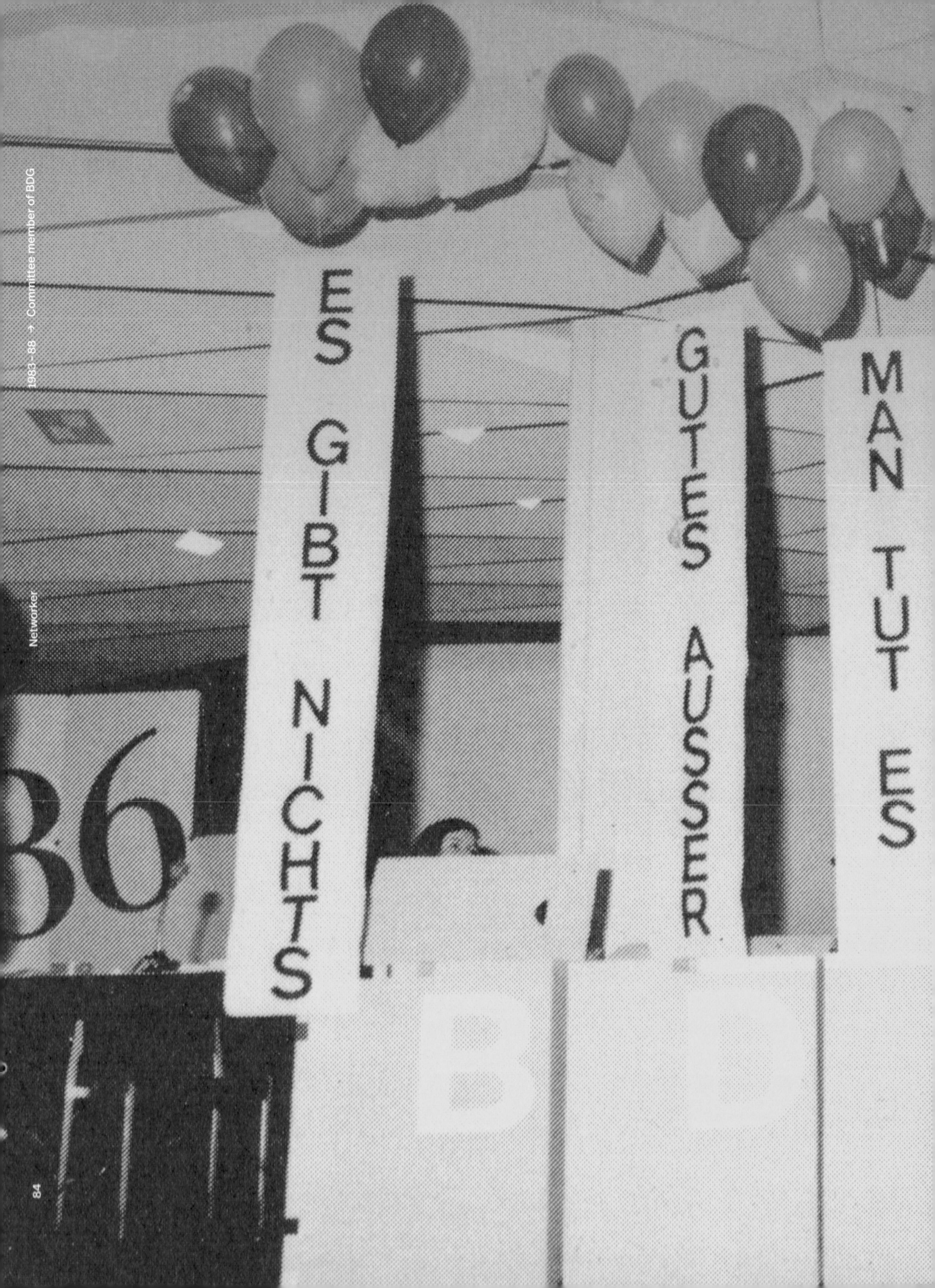

ES GIBT NICHTS GUTES AUSSER MAN TUT ES

86

BDG

In 1983 Erik Spiekermann was elected to the executive board of the Bund Deutscher Grafik-designer, and was named vice president in 1986. A year previously he was assigned the task of creating the corporate design for the professional association.

The association has a long history: founded on May 3 1919 as the Bund Deutscher Gebrauchsgrafiker (commercial artists) by, among others, Max Hertwig, Jupp Wiertz, and Hans Meyer, it was the first professional association in the industry. In 1968 its name was changed to ›Bund Deutscher Grafikdesigner‹, and changed once again in 2009 to Berufsverband der Deutschen Kommunikationsdesigner. Its remit is the advancement and protection of its members' professional and economic interests.

Newly elected vice president Spieker-mann and company lawyer Friedrich W. Siebeke at the annual meeting, 1983. The bearded gentleman on the right is Klaus Kuhn, president of BDG.

In the early '80s Deutsche Post contracted Sedley Place Design (who had taken over the contract from MetaDesign, with Erik Spiekermann as a consultant) to redo the entire graphic design for the German postal service, including forms and telephone directories. ›Helvetica‹ had previously been used as the corporate face, as it was by many other companies. However, Spiekermann argued against it, deeming it unfit for the purpose, and already overused by too many other companies, which would produce an incoherent and interchangeable image – »almost right« to »not quite right«. Instead, Spiekermann presented designs for an original typeface, still called ›PT55‹ at the time, which he had digitized in 1985 at Stempel AG on an Ikarus system. He wanted to use the early Apple Macintosh as a future typesetting machine, but the people in Bonn would not take it seriously, nor the typeface that was intended for the new system.

A few years later, as ›FF Meta‹, it would become one of the most successful of the new digital typefaces. Writing about it in ›PAGE‹ magazine Spiekermann said: »It's pretty disheartening. 550,000 people work for the postal service, yet nobody dares go out on a limb. That's why ideas are discussed until they're no longer recognizable, or they're simply shoved in a drawer so that nobody has to deal with anything that might actually change things.«

With: Florian Fischer, Dieter Heil, and Peter Scholz

Top: This was how many logos the German post office had in 1984. Bottom: A redesigned form; left, the printed version; right, the form set in the post office typeface ›PT55‹ that was never released.

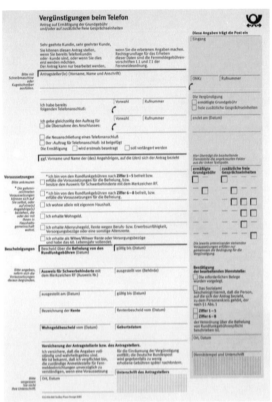

An advanced sketch by Gerry Barney for the new post office typeface with correction notes by Spiekermann. The next stage was the artwork for digitization.

Erik Spiekermann designed ›PT55‹, the forerunner to ›Meta‹, for the Deutsche Post corporate design; it was to replace the previously used ›Helvetica‹. The abbreviation ›PT‹ stands for ›PostType‹, and ›55‹ indicates the weight. After examining twenty existing typefaces, it was apparent that none of them was really suitable. The first sketches for the new typeface were undertaken with Michael Bitter from Bielefeld University of Applied Sciences, and the sketches for the first complete alphabet were produced by Gerry Barney and Mike Pratley (Sedley Place Design, London). This dedicated typeface was specially designed to withstand the many kinds of printing methods, some of them low-quality, used by the company – for example, different kinds of paper, high-speed printing, irregular ink application, and forms with very small type.

With: Gerry Barney and Mike Pratley

63 E*in*

209,5
mm

B3

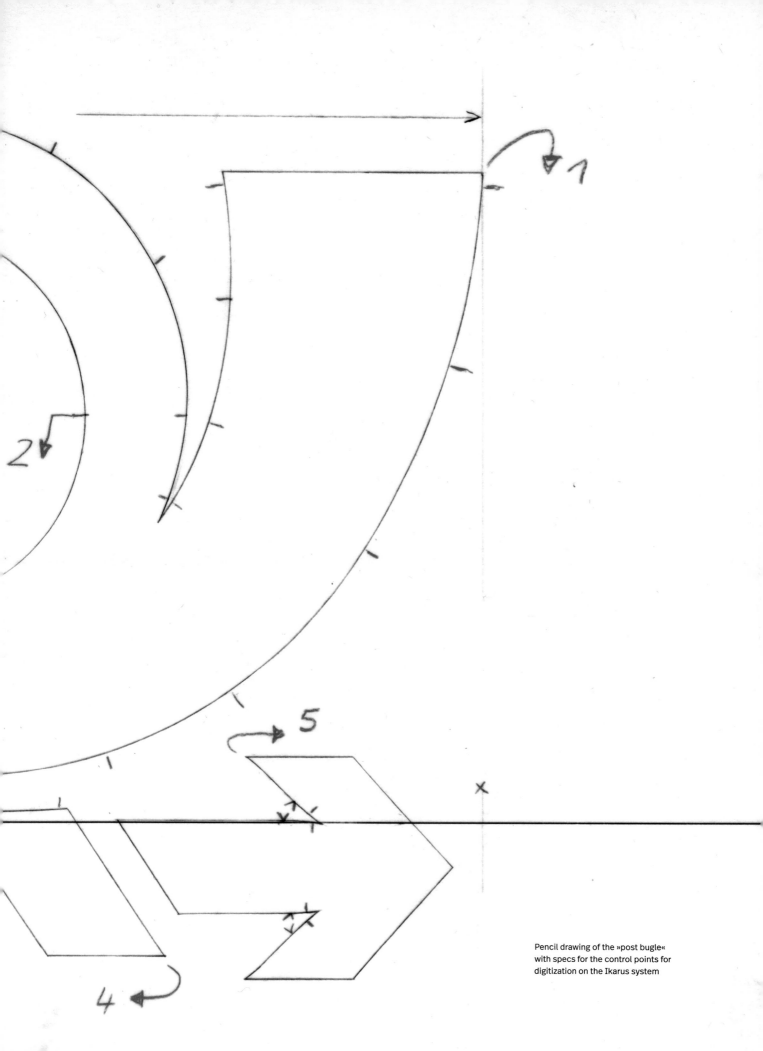

Pencil drawing of the »post bugle«
with specs for the control points for
digitization on the Ikarus system

The Studiengesellschaft für Nahverkehr (local transport research association) commissioned the design for a new city information system called ›Stadtinfo‹, a test route between Tegel airport and Budapester Straße. Passenger information needed to be improved; electronics, digital information transmission, and movement were the buzz words for designing the basic elements. Two information kiosks were introduced, plus bus stop announcements on the buses and an electronic display at one bus stop.

MetaDesign created the design system using a strong red color and rasterized type for displays in addition to ›Frutiger‹. The basic principles of the typographic design were clear arrangement and classification, and large type wherever possible. Diagrams showing all stops on the no. 9 bus line were stuck in the upper parts of the bus windows where they were clearly visible.

With: Hans Werner Holzwarth, Jens Kreitmeyer, and Theres Weishappel

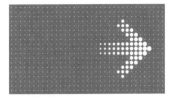

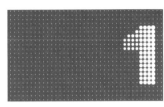

Top: Hand-drawn signs for the new information system. The dot screen was supposed to symbolize the electronic system, new at the time.
Left: A route 9 bus with old and new route numbers (the new sign shows the destination) and the new diagrams showing all bus stops inside the bus

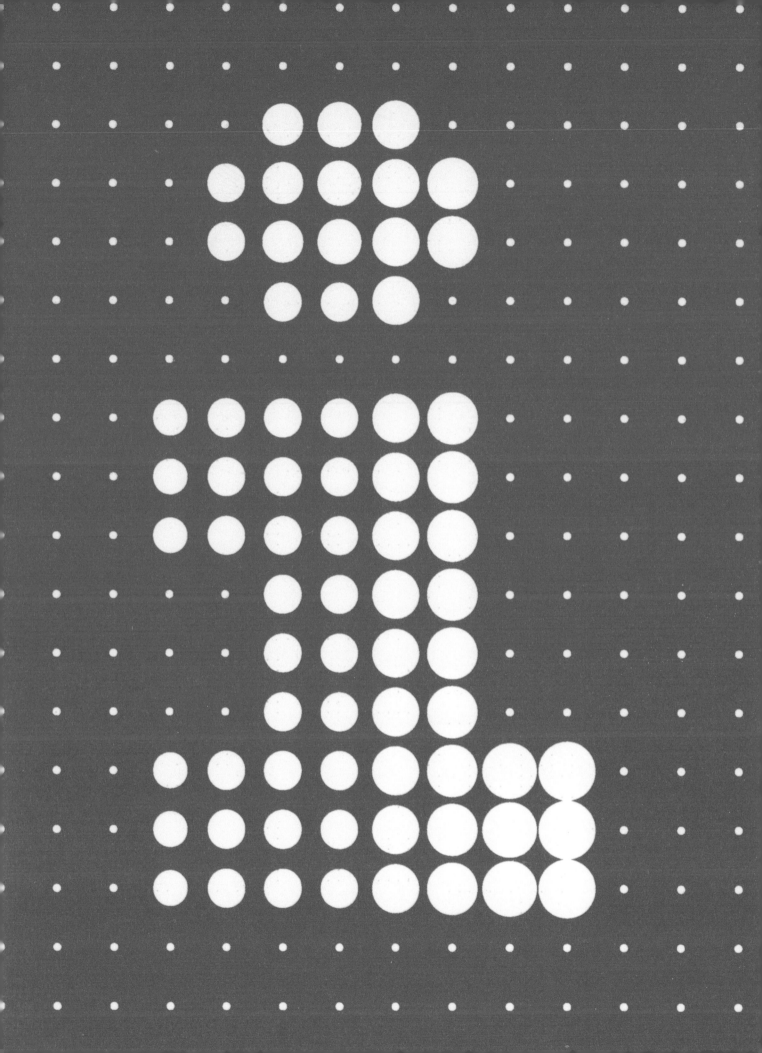

Designer

Satzmuster
Gesetzt und belichtet auf dem neuen digitalen CRT-Photosatz-system ›Scantext 1000‹.
Alle Arbeiten sind ohne Montage als ganze Seiten inklusive der Logos (Sonderzeichen) belichtet.

Examples of setting
Set and exposed on the new digital CRT-Phototypesetting system ›Scantext 1000‹.
All jobs were typeset as a whole page in position and composed without any paste-up.

Modèles de composition typographique
Photocomposé sur le nouveau système de photocomposition à tube cathodique ›Scantext 1000‹.
Tous les travaux ont été insoles en pages complétés sans aucun montage manuel.

SCANTEXT 1000.
THIS IS THE BEGINNING
OF A NEW GENERATION OF
TYPESETTING TECHNOLOGY.
HIGH STANDARDS
OF TYPOGRAPHIC QUALITY
AND SIMPLE OPERATION
COMBINED WITH FAST
OUTPUT SPEED.
A TOTALLY NEW APPROACH
TO DIGITAL TYPESETTING.
SCANTEXT 1000.

In 1984 MetaDesign designed an oversize type sample book (23.5 × 33 cm) for the typesetting machine manufacturer based in Wedel. All the typesetting was done without using paste-up artwork at all, which was sensational at the time, and required a lot of preparation.

Scantext systems were revolutionary in their day and are taken for granted today; starting in 1984, whole pages and fonts could be displayed and edited on a monitor, integrating text, images, and graphics.

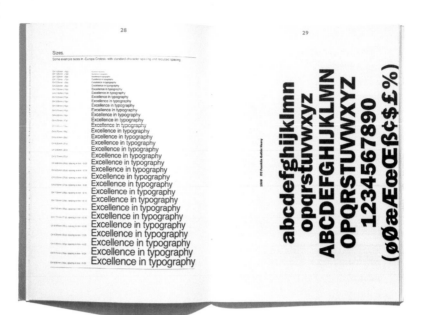

Left: Cover of the phototypesetting type specimen book
Right: Three double pages from the booklet introducing the digital CRT photo-typesetting system Scantext 1000

After Sedley Place Design Berlin GmbH bought MetaDesign, Erik Spiekermann continued working in 1984 as MetaDesign (not trade registered) – phase two of the company. He moved with around six colleagues into a house in Motzstraße, where Spiekermann himself lived on the top floor.

Shortly thereafter he founded HKSW GmbH with Hans Werner Holzwarth, Theres Weishappel, and Jens Kreitmeyer, its name being the founders' initials in alphabetical order.

Spiekermann in his studio on the top floor of 58 Motzstraße. The MetaDesign office was on the first floor.

Erik Spiekermann
MetaDesign
Motzstraße 58
1000 Berlin 30

Enlargement of an address label,
set in ›Berliner Grotesk‹, Spiekermann's
first typeface available for phototypesetting, 1984

In 1985 Erik Spiekermann created a new
corporate design for the Bund Deutscher
Grafikdesigner, of which he was a member and
later vice president. His approach was that of
a constructivist: make the syntax of one's own
work visible. The grid of the printed pages
was made visible by using dots and column
markers as design elements. The dots on the
letterhead mark all the other sizes contained
within A4.

Left: A4 sheet; the dots mark all
the sizes within A4; the type area and
columns have square marks.
Right: 20-page brochure for members
of the BDG, 1999
Right page: BDG newsletter, 1988

BDG
BDG

Telefon : BDG · BUND DEUTSCHER GRAFIK DESIGNER   : Gruppe Bremen e. V.
(04 21) 32 31 01 : Am Landherrnamt 8 · 2800 Bremen 1

Datum :

BDG
BDG

BDG:Intern

Informationen für die Mitglieder des BDG
Bund Deutscher Grafik-Designer e.V.

4 1999

Mit den besten
Wünschen für konkrete
und konstruktive
Ferienerinnerungen.

:Sich ein Bild machen!

Für den geplanten neuen Mitglieds-
ausweis, den **alle BDG-Mitglieder** erhalten werden, benötigen wir dringend Ihr Porträtfoto! Die Alternative
wäre ein weißes Feld auf Ihrem Ausweis – das wollen Sie doch nicht.
oder?

Alle Mitglieder, die ihren **Fragebogen**
noch nicht zurückgeschickt haben,
werden gebeten, dies möglichst bald
nachzuholen. Die Umfrage ist eine in
nerverbandliche Momentaufnahme
und wird streng vertraulich behan-
delt. Nur – das Präsidium ist zur Aus-
richtung von Verbandspolitik und
strategien dringend auf die Angaben
und Einschätzungen möglichst aller
Mitglieder angewiesen. Es macht z.B.
keinen Sinn, ein Sonderangebot für
„Word 2000" auszuhandeln, wenn alle
BDG Mitglieder dieses Programm
schon haben. oder keiner es haben
will ...

Geben Sie sich einen Ruck, senden
auch Sie den Fragebogen zurück. Um
so größer kann Ihr **Vorteil** ausfallen!

**:Gründer-TV mit der
Ausgleichsbank**

Ein neues Ratgebermagazin für Gründer und junge Unternehmer hat der
Nachrichtensender n-tv, wie uns die
Deutsche Ausgleichsbank mitteilt, je
den Donnerstag um 21.15 Uhr im Pro
gramm (Wiederholung jeweils am dar-
auffolgenden Samstag 17.35 Uhr)

Die Sendung gibt Gründern Rat und
Hilfe bei der Vorbereitung ihres Vor
habens, richtet sich aber auch an Fir
men hefs, die für ihr Unternehmen
einen Nachfolger suchen. Und natür
lich sollen auch Experten angespro-
chen werden, die Gründungswillige
auf ihrem Weg in die Selbständigkeit
unterstützen (z.B. Bankenberater,
Steuerberater, Wirtschaftsprüfer).

Die Deutsche Ausgleichsbank DtA
unterstützt Gründer TV, das auch aus
führlich über Förder- und Beratungs
angebote der DtA berichtet wird,
durch Hintergründe, Zahlen und Fak
ten

Grundsätzliche Informationen sind
auch im Internet unter der Adresse
www.gruender-tv.de zu finden

Inhalt

2 Begegnung Berlin-
   Ústi, Ústi–Berlin

4 Zdenka Zamany
   für den BDG

5 „Designer zeichnen"
   in Nienhagen

8 Besuch beim Design-
   Symposium in London

10 Next Generation
   Baden-Württemberg

14 Rechtsstreit „Problem-
   fall Aufkleber"

Gesetzt aus ITC Weidemann kursiv mit Kapitälchen von Headline Potsdam und gedruckt von Druckerei Rogaus, Bremen.

BDG : Intern 4 : 1999 :: Seite 1

BDG

PRO A4

BDG-Mitteilung
›Extraordinär‹
Februar 1988

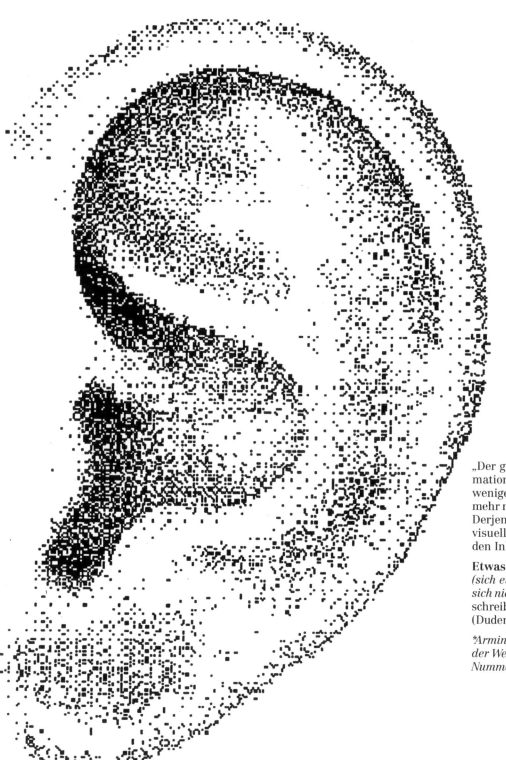

„Der gestaltende Mensch der Informationsgesellschaft muß sich immer weniger mit den Mitteln, aber immer mehr mit den Zwecken beschäftigen. Derjenige, der einer Botschaft die visuelle Form geben soll, muß auch den Inhalt verantworten können".*

Etwas hinter die Ohren schreiben
(sich etwas gut merken, damit man sich nicht wieder einen Tadel zuzieht): schreibt euch das hinter die Ohren! (Duden, Das Stilwörterbuch)

*Armin Hofmann, „Für eine Reform der Werbung", Basler Magazin, Nummer 37

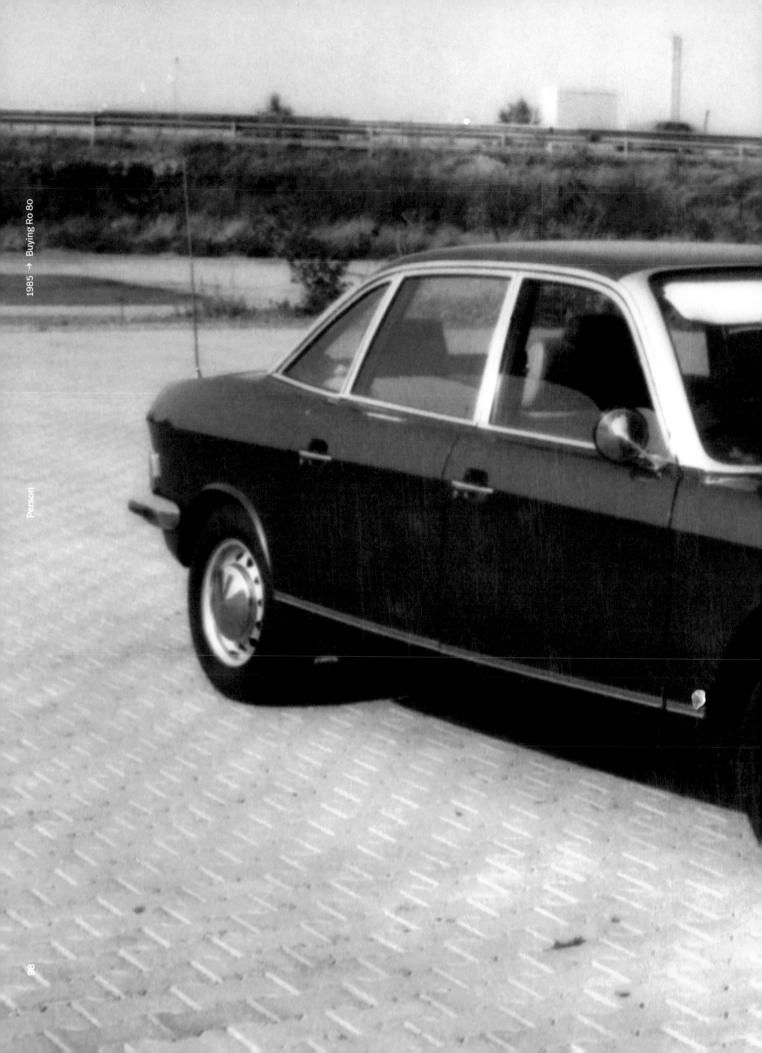

The Ro 80 was made in Heilbronn between 1967 and 1977 by NSU Motorenwerke AG, who were bought by VW in 1969 and later merged with Audi. Spiekermann bought the limousine with a streamlined metallic blue body in 1985: »When we lived in London in 1973 the Ro 80 was still being made. There were always a few parked near our house, because there was a garage around the corner that changed the Wankel engines to Ford V4s. That was a sin and totally unnecessary, but I liked the shape so much that I wanted one of my own. When Joan and I separated in 1985 I bought myself one as a consolation.«

Spiekermann's NSU Ro 80, made in 1977, Polaroid taken when he bought it in 1985

BASELINE

International Typographics Magazine Issue Six

SPECIAL FEATURE: TYPE FOR A PURPOSE

THE QUAY FAMILY

INTERNATIONAL STUDENT COMPETITION

ARABIC TYPEFACES

The first issue of ›Baseline‹, a magazine about typography, book illustration, and graphic design appeared in 1979 as a small-format booklet published by Mike Daines. The following publications varied considerably in size, publisher, and layout. MetaDesign did the design for issues 6 and 7 – the last ones not to be printed in full color.

Erik Spiekermann was the publisher, designer, and one of the writers; he decided the structure of the magazine and organized the contributions. Issue 7 contained a comprehensive article on Spiekermann's typeface design for Deutsche Post.

With: Hans Werner Holzwarth

Left: Cover of ›Baseline‹ 6, A4 format, phototypeset
Top: Cover and double pages of ›Baseline‹ 7 with an editorial by Spiekermann and an article on the planned Deutsche Post typeface

Franklin-Antiqua — BERTHOLD TYPES 174

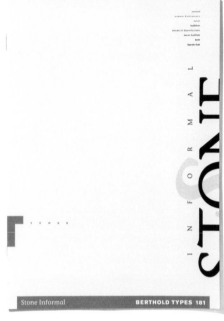

Stone Informal — BERTHOLD TYPES 181

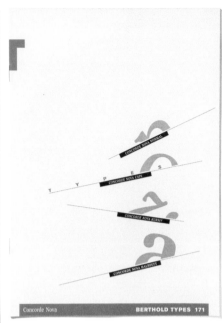

Concorde Nova — BERTHOLD TYPES 171

Agora — BERTHOLD TYPES 189

ITC Giovanni — BERTHOLD TYPES 188

Walbaum-Buch — BERTHOLD TYPES 186

Top: Type specimen books, each designed by different colleagues at MetaDesign, starting in 1985
Right: Front of an invitation postcard to an event (enlarged), 1988

Erik Spiekermann first started working in the mid-1970s for H. Berthold AG, who stood for high quality typesetting systems and typefaces. MetaDesign redefined their housestyle in 1985 and continued to develop it until the company ceased trading in 1993.

The corporate design was entirely in black and gray shades, red, and white. Type was often reversed out of a background. The red bars were particularly striking; MetaDesign also used them on stationery. They designed countless type specimens (at least 50), booths at trade fairs, and forms.

With: Alexander Branczyk, Inken Greisner, Hans Werner Holzwarth, Thomas Nagel, and Theres Weishappel

Type makes language legible.

In summer 1985 Erik Spiekermann saw the first
Apple Macintosh at Stempel AG in Frankfurt,
where he had gone to digitize the typeface
he designed for Deutsche Post. Only a little over
a year previously, Steve Jobs had presented the
first Macintosh 128k. Spiekermann borrowed
the computer in Frankfurt and took it to his presentation at Deutsche Post. For Spiekermann,
the fact that a font could actually fit on a disk
was the initial spark: here was the future of type!

Thus, he ordered his first Mac in 1986:
the follow-up model MacPlus with a built-in nine-
inch monitor and a price tag of 16,000 DM.

Spiekermann with his first Apple Mac
on the top floor of 58 Motzstraße

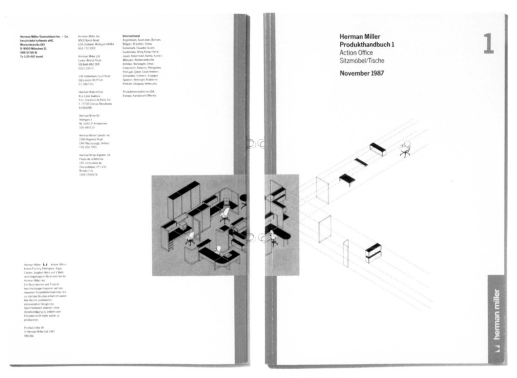

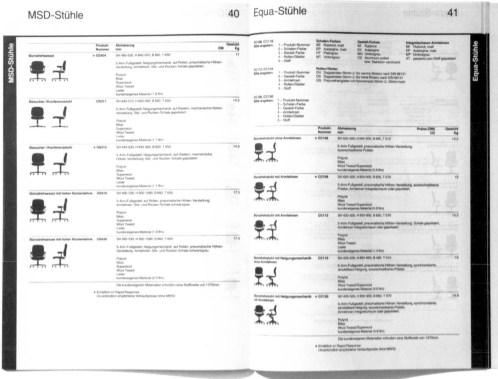

Product manual 1 from November 1987.
As usual for Spiekermann, without
horizontal lines, and with the newly developed product numbers emphasized in the
layout.

Herman Miller is one of the leading global manufacturers of office furniture. In 1987 Erik Spiekermann designed the German exhibition booths and various brochures and leaflets for the European branch in Britain. At the time, the logo was set in ›Helvetica‹, oft-criticized by Spiekermann. Ironically, Herman Miller now uses Spiekermann's ›FF Meta‹. The order forms for dealers were very confusing, since the order numbers were too complicated. Erik Spiekermann developed a new, more straightforward system, after which there were no more wrong product orders.

With: Hans Werner Holzwarth, Jens Kreitmeyer, and Theres Weishappel

In 1987 MetaDesign was one of seven European studios to develop business document templates for the PageMaker program, released by Aldus Corporation for Apple Macintosh in 1985. The program was the first – along with the first PostScript laser printer, Apple's LaserWriter – to make it possible to produce professional typesetting on a personal computer.

The manual was written in German, English, Spanish, French, Italian, Dutch, and Swedish – which is why seven design studios were contracted, each familiar with the »traditional design« of its country of origin. Templates for users were included on discs at the end of the manual.

With: Hans Werner Holzwarth, Jens Kreitmeyer, and Theres Weishappel

II

ALDUS PAGEMAKER STUDIO

Designer und Mustervorlagen

Diseñadores y Modelos

Concepteurs et Maquettes

Designers and Templates

Designer e Schemi

Ontwerpers en Sjablonen

Formgivare och Malldokument

Designer

The templates developed by MetaDesign were sent in a folder with floppy discs

Networker

In 1987 Erik Spiekermann gave a presentation
on the topic of »type and identity« at the Type
87 conference in New York, which the TDC
(Type Directors Club) had organized jointly with
the ATypI (Association Typographique Internationale). He spoke about the important effect
on identity that a typeface has for a business:
»The corporate design and the typeface it uses
says a lot more about a company than the
prophets of the ubiquitous ›Helvetica‹ would
have us believe.«

Other participants included Colin Banks,
Neville Brody, Roger Black, and Charles Bigelow.

Adobe was the first client of MetaDesign West branch, founded in 1992 in San Francisco. Spiekermann and his business partner to be, Bill Hill, had already developed this package for Adobe in 1987, as an aid for making forms – something of a speciality of Spiekermann's. The box contained a disc with the typefaces ›Lucida‹, ›News Gothic‹, and Univers, chosen by Erik, along with a couple of explanations

about why they were appropriate for forms. The box also contained an interview with Spiekermann, where he talks about his »obsession« for forms as important instruments for communication, in addition to some sample forms for a fictitious lighting manufacturer.

With: Gail Blumberg and Bill Hill

In 1987 MetaDesign underwent another metamorphosis and changed its name to Meta Gesellschaft für Design GmbH (Meta Design Company Ltd.). HKSW GmbH was dissolved because Hans Werner Holzwarth had left. The trade register would not allow the name MetaDesign on its own, since it is a technical term, and apparently not valid as a company name. Later it was allowed with the suffix ›plus‹.

MetaDesign in 1988, from left to right:
Inken Greisner, Robert Hummel,
Erik Spiekermann, Theres Weishappel,
Christoph Preussler, Jens Kreitmeyer,
Petra Mader, and Anke Jaaks

In the early 1980s Florian Fischer and Erik Spiekermann pointed out the lack of a consistent visual appearance for BVG, the Berlin public transport company. The varied architecture of subway stations and the inconsistent information system made it difficult to find one's way around. However, MetaDesign's proposals were repeatedly rejected.

In 1987 MetaDesign reanalyzed the state of the BVG image, showing its flaws. On its own initiative, MetaDesign produced a proposal for a consistent housestyle. Shortly thereafter, Spiekermann presented the results to BVG. In addition to an offset-printed and ring-bound presentation folder, the team built a small model of Zoologischer Garten train station. Unfortunately, the BVG company structure prevented its management from responding – the concept was never even discussed.

However, it was not forgotten: in 1990 after the fall of the Berlin Wall, the BVG approached MetaDesign. Konrad Lorenzen was now managing director, a man who recognized the importance of consistent signage for the reunified city.

With: Inken Greisner, Jens Kreitmeyer, Petra Mader, and Theres Weishappel

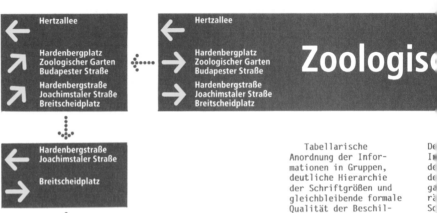

Tabellarische Anordnung der Informationen in Gruppen, deutliche Hierarchie der Schriftgrößen und gleichbleibende formale Qualität der Beschilderung vereinfachen die Selektion der angebotenen Informationen in einer hektischen Umgebung.

Farben werden rein funktional eingesetzt und unterstützen die schnelle Wahrnehmbarkeit.

This fictitious signage shows all the kinds of information one would find at a given subway station. Many of the elements represented here were used in the signage system that was actually produced after the fall of the Berlin Wall.

2.9 Leitsystem
(Bahnhofsbeschilderung)

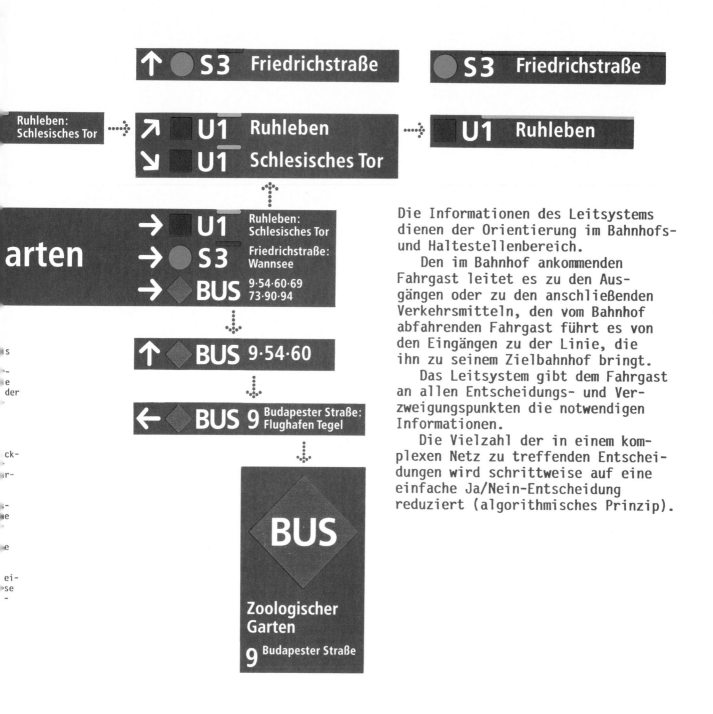

Die Informationen des Leitsystems dienen der Orientierung im Bahnhofs- und Haltestellenbereich.

Den im Bahnhof ankommenden Fahrgast leitet es zu den Ausgängen oder zu den anschließenden Verkehrsmitteln, den vom Bahnhof abfahrenden Fahrgast führt es von den Eingängen zu der Linie, die ihn zu seinem Zielbahnhof bringt.

Das Leitsystem gibt dem Fahrgast an allen Entscheidungs- und Verzweigungspunkten die notwendigen Informationen.

Die Vielzahl der in einem komplexen Netz zu treffenden Entscheidungen wird schrittweise auf eine einfache Ja/Nein-Entscheidung reduziert (algorithmisches Prinzip).

Erik Spiekermann

ITC - Typeface Review Board Meeting :
21 January, 1988

New concepts needed:

* Narrow, i.e. Sans-Serif with good definition for small sizes and modest resolution - not just 300 dpi-printers and bad printing in newspapers, etc.

More condensed than News Gothic, highly legible figures, well-defined counters and good weight for the book-weight-bolder than News Gothic regular. Look at Bell Centennial and Linotype's News Gothic family of 4 weights.

* Re-design of Gill Sans! Coordinate better weights - light is too light, bold is too bold. Only slightly larger x-height, about 5% condensed. Incorporate Gill Sans extra bold condensed, which is available from Letraset - a condensed version in 4 weights.? Get a European designer for the job - i.e. Gerard Unger, Bram de Does.

* Re-design, or rather re-define Syntax, the world's most underrated typeface! The regular weight is too light, the extra-bold too bold and not in keeping. There's only one italic. Very good name= ITC Syntax. Most legible figures around. Very suitable for a few condensed weights.

* Grotesk No. 215, 216, / No. 9, 9a , 9b, / No. 7. Related , but uncoordinated family of faces, representing the " grotesg " style - i.e. slightly awkward shapes, reminiscent of stonecut early sans serifs. Very distinct Anglo-American feel and totally under--represented. Could do with a complete re-appraisal.

* Missing from the ITC-Range is a "curly" face, just like I have revived for Berthold. A complete family with that rugged look could be made out of Berliner Grotesk and Block families. Very successful for wholemeal, " alternative " applications and nostalgic, " handmade " applications. Could also be a range of related sans-serif and roman faces - i.e. LoType and Block all in one. There are some historical models which would serve as guides - eg. Holland Mediaeval and Nova by Berthold.

* My favorite idea = a correspondence face, on the same lines of thinking as Stone Informal; a face for business correspondence that reads better, takes up less space than Courier or Pica, but still doesn't look too much like a proper "designed" typeface - because once you're using a real typeface, the whole page wants to be laid-out, to be designed. A business letter, an estimate, an invoice should be more neutral, not making a comment about it's content. So we need something between Courier and American Typewriter, again perhaps both with and without serifs . Also the present versions of Courier or Letter Gothic available for LaserWriters by Adobe and Bitstream are too light to withstand more than one copy stage. (ITC - Officina).

* Finally what about a hand-written correspondence face, eg. Snell Roundhand, Berthold Script, Kunstler schreibschrift? A new face within the genre needs to reproduce under modest resolution conditions and should be almost mono-linear, see Poppl-College.

Erik Spiekermann was on the advisory board of the International Typeface Corporation (ITC), who were bought by Letraset in 1986. He had to make regular trips to New York for it. The Typeface Review Board selected which typefaces to publish from those presented to them by external designers. It would also identify gaps in the ITC range of typefaces, and commission new ones to fill them.

»As far as I know I owed that job to my knowledge of the type scene, since the Americans didn't really know what was happening elsewhere,« says Spiekermann. He presented his concept for ›ITC Officina‹, still called ›ITC Correspondence‹ at the time, at an ITC Typeface Review Board meeting on January 21, 1988.

Suggestions for new or re-issued typefaces at the ITC Typeface Review Board in New York, including one for a new correspondence face, 1988

First print of a new correspondence
face conceived as a replacement
for traditional typewriter faces, 1989

ITC Correspondence

abcdefghijklno123456
abcdefghijklno123456
abcdefghijklno123456
abcdefghijklno123456
abcdefghijklno123456

In 1988 Spiekermann suggested to the International Typeface Corporation (ITC) that he design a new typeface with the working title ›ITC Correspondence‹ to replace typewriter fonts that were no longer practical for laser printers. The typeface was released in 1980 as ›ITC Officina Sans‹. This sans serif version was narrow like ›Letter Gothic‹. A wider serif face à la ›Courier‹ was supposed to follow. Gerard Unger created a preliminary design for it, after which he had to drop out of the project. Another Dutch typeface designer, Just van Rossum (an intern at Meta-Design at the time), quickly drew serifs on the Sans, creating ›ITC Officina Serif‹. Ole Schäfer,

still a student in Bielefeld at the time, suggested designs for further weights in 1995. Seizing the opportunity, the font family was expanded to include small caps and old style figures. ›Officina Display‹ was created in 2001 for the redesign of ›The Economist‹ in London, first by Ole Schäfer exclusively for ›The Economist‹, before being reworked by Christian Schwartz for its release by ITC. ›ITC Officina‹ currently comprises 25 different fonts and stands at number eight in the list of the hundred most successful typefaces ever.

Mirjam van Blokland, Ole Schäfer, Christian Schwartz, and Just van Rossum

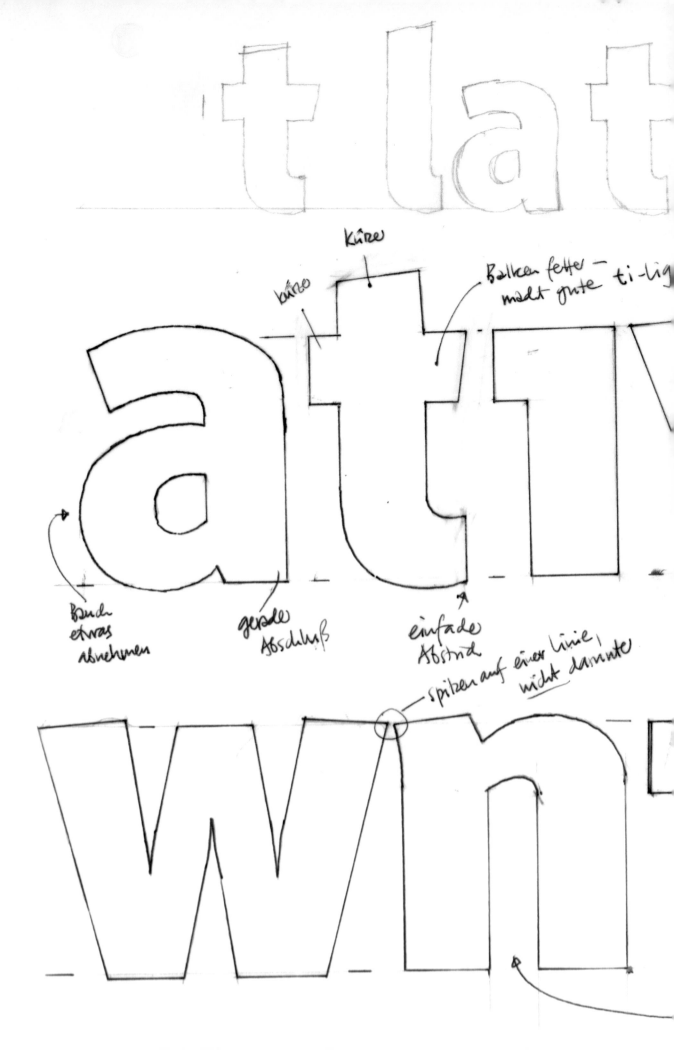

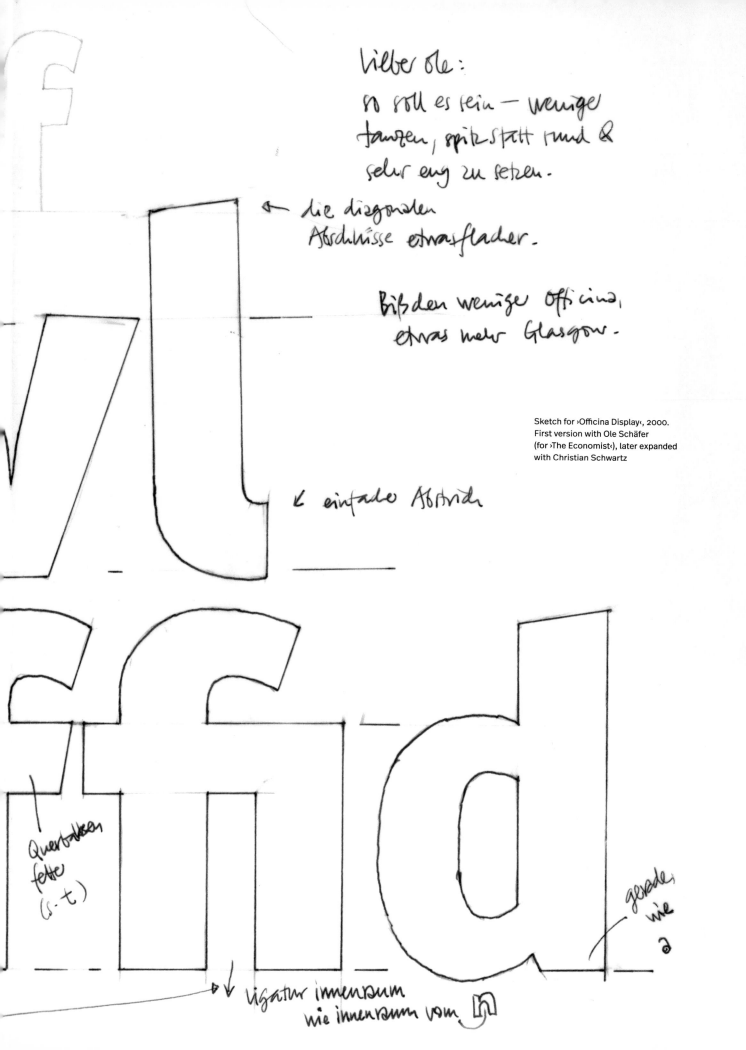

Lieber Ole:

so soll es sein — wenige
tanzen, spitz statt rund &
sehr eng zu setzen.

← die diagonalen
Abschlüsse etwasflacher.

Bißchen wenige Officina,
etwas mehr Glasgow.

← einfache Abstrich

Querbalken
fette
(s-t)

gerade
wie
ə

Ligatur innenraum
wie innenraum vom ſ

Sketch for ›Officina Display‹, 2000.
First version with Ole Schäfer
(for ›The Economist‹), later expanded
with Christian Schwartz

Have you ever thought about the amount of type you read in a day? How many different typefaces you encounter? How does a day in your life read?

So where do all these typefaces come from? Why don't we all use one typeface? Why are there so many different typefaces? Because we are different. We're shaped by different cultures.

So you see, type is civilization.

»Most people take the way words look for granted.« This is Erik Spiekermann's opening quote from ›Typomania‹, a one-off program he made for the BBC in 1988, which attempted to make viewers aware of the significance of typography. He uses type on restaurant signs, magazines, trains, and book covers as examples of the presence of typography in everyday life. Spiekermann asserts that type is culture. To support this, he uses typefaces such as ›Caslon‹, ›Century School Book‹, and ›Cheltenham‹ as examples of Anglo-American culture; ›Garamond‹ and ›Bodoni‹ as French or Italian, and ›Futura‹ and ›Helvetica‹ as German. It was written and directed by Mary Sprent as part of her series ›Into Print‹.

With: Mary Sprent

The publishing house for digital fonts was founded by Joan and Erik Spiekermann in 1989. The concept for its corporate design was to show a lot of different FontShop typefaces, but only three colors: black, white, and yellow.

Spiekermann writes on his blog: »I have never used many colors, apart from the basic typographic black and red. Twenty years ago, however, Alex Branczyk and myself designed the logo etc. for FontShop. We thought light and dark would nicely represent the digital process of one and zero, as well as the process inside the laser printer. Black and white was too plain, so it became black and yellow. That color scheme has become synonymous with FontShop and its products, to the point where we couldn't possibly change it for a rebrand. We recently made the FontFont website nearly all black and white in order to distinguish it more from the dominantly black and yellow FontShop.com site.«

With: Alexander Branczyk

Right page: Order form from the era before online sales, 1991

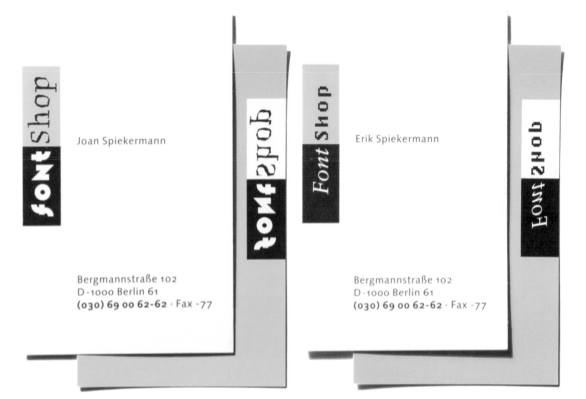

Joan Spiekermann

Bergmannstraße 102
D-1000 Berlin 61
(030) 69 00 62-62 · Fax -77

Erik Spiekermann

Bergmannstraße 102
D-1000 Berlin 61
(030) 69 00 62-62 · Fax -77

Lieferanschrift

Firma ▶ ....

Name ▶ ....

Straße ▶ ....

PLZ / Ort ▶ ....

Telefon ▶ ....

Fax ▶ ....

Bitte immer angeben, wenn schon vorhanden:

Kunden-Nr. ▶ ....

Rechnungsanschrift (falls abweichend)

....

....

....

Freiwillige Angaben, mit denen Sie uns helfen und sich vor unerwünschter Post von FontShop schützen.

Wir haben
- ☐ Macintosh
- ☐ PC
- ☐ andere

Wir sind
- ☐ selbständig
- ☐ Handel / Dienstleistung / Behörde
- ☐ Verlag
- ☐ Werbung / Design
- ☐ Setzerei / Belichtungsstudio
- ☐ Azubi / Student
- ☐ Sonstiges

Bestellung Hiermit bestelle ich zu den allgemeinen Geschäftsbedingungen des FontShop

Anzahl	Artikel	Bestell-Nr.	Mac	PC	NeXT	Preis inkl. 15% Mwst. Bücher 7% Mwst.
▶	▶	▶	☐	☐	☐	▶
			☐	☐	☐	
			☐	☐	☐	
			☐	☐	☐	
			☐	☐	☐	
			☐	☐	☐	
			☐	☐	☐	
			☐	☐	☐	

FontShop-Katalog(e) à DM 69,-

Sonstiges ....

Versandkosten (s.u.) ....

Auslandszahlung zuzügl. Bankspesen von DM 15,– (außer bei Kreditkarten) ....

Gesamtpreis DM ....

Zahlweise Inland

1. per Kreditkarte

☐ Eurocard ☐ Visa

Karten-Inhaber ....

Karten-Nr. ....

Gültig bis ....

2. per UPS-Nachnahme

☐ Verrechnungs-Scheck ☐ Bar / Euro-Scheck

3. per Lastschrift

Bank ....

BLZ ....

Konto-Nr. ....

Konto-Inhaber ....

Versand

	Bestellungen bis 1000,-	über 1000,–
Alte Bundesländer	DM 12,– (UPS) 2 Werktage DM 18,– (AirService) 1 Werktag	Entfällt Entfällt
Neue Bundesländer	DM 20,– (UPS) 2 Werktage DM 35,– (AirService) 1 Werktag	DM 10,– (UPS) DM 17,50 (AirService)
Ausland	nach Vereinbarung	

Hier falzen und im Fenster-Umschlag verschicken

FontShop GmbH

Bergmannstraße 102

D-1000 Berlin 61

Tel. 030 / 69 00 62 62 • Fax 69 00 62 77

Zahlweise Ausland

1. per Kreditkarte (s.o.)

2. Post Nachnahme zuzügl. DM 15,– Bankspesen

Datum, Unterschrift:

Datum ▶ ....

Unterschrift ▶ ....

Geöffnete Schrift- und Software-Pakete sind vom Umtausch ausgeschlossen.

Advertisement for the first independent font publisher. Distorted typefaces were a new thing at the time and virtually impossible to produce using old typesetting methods.

The publishing house for computer typefaces and design conference organization was founded in 1989 by Erik Spiekermann and his wife Joan in Kreuzberg, Berlin. Since November 1990 FontShop has published new fonts several times a year on its own label FontFont. Since 1995 the company has also hosted the annual typography and design conference TYPO Berlin, which now has offshoots in London and San Francisco.

Erik Spiekermann still sits on the company board. It has become the world's largest manufacturer-independent publishing house for typefaces, with over 100,000 fonts from over 100 libraries.

With: Neville Brody and Joan Spiekermann

FontShop

Nichts als Schrift

MetaDesign für MetaDesign

Originalschriften im PostScript-Format direkt von Adobe und anderen Herstellern.

Alle Fonts für Mac & PC.

Alle Fonts original & verpackt.

Alle Fonts direkt & ab Lager.

Alle Fonts jetzt & sofort.

Alle Fonts per Mailorder & über Nacht.

Alle Fonts im FontShopKatalog.

Jürgen on Erik

I have never done it... but I am sure of it: if one were to ask Erik Spiekermann what his five best traits were, I guarantee he would list punctuality as one of them. After all, it makes sense for someone like him who travels around the world a lot. The worst outcome of poor timekeeping for businessmen is an unscheduled wait. For that reason alone they will do what it takes to be at airports and railway stations on time. Let us call this area vital or primary punctuality.

Then there is secondary punctuality, for simple appointments; in Berlin, for example. As chance would have it, I happened to have three meetings last December, all of which Erik was also invited to. Although... invited is not really the right word; after several days of emailing back and forth, eventually everyone settled on one of the precious few windows in Erik's diary.

Four weeks later the meetings drew close: the FontShop annual general meeting at a hotel in Moabit, plus the board of directors meeting and the FontFont typeboard, both in the company conference room. To cut it short, Erik was 30 minutes late for the first one; he completely forgot about the second meeting – he was not even in Berlin that day –, and the third conference clashed with an unmissable partners' meeting, so he missed that too.

To help pass the time while we were waiting, we made up a fun game: guess the excuse. While we waited for Erik yet again, everyone was allowed to have one guess at his excuse for being late. One guessed a flat tire on his bicycle, another guessed there were too many red lights, our guest from Belgium plumped for road works. Erik's former wife Joan won by guessing, »He goes by bike but it starts to rain, so he goes back home to get the car.« Which is exactly what he said.

Even though calendar technology has progressed mightily over the last 25 years, I became concerned about it at the end of 2013, after Erik clean forgot about two meetings. His explanations were impressively complicated; a series of uncontrollable synchronization blips, coupled with Cloud-incompatibilities that even managed to stump the digital natives at Erik's studio. In a way it's nice when the guy who founded one of the most successful German communication companies tells you why the calendar on his smartphone keeps missing appointments. At least the battery was charged.

Edenspiekermann still have a human fire department, of the kind formerly called »secretariat« or »management assistant«. However, these colleagues now have more important things to do than check appointments on a self-monitoring digital calendar. Like, for instance, keeping the analog espresso logistics moving – the very heart of a creative studio, according to Erik's own office philosophy. Good mood instead of boring meetings... what is there not to like?

Jürgen Siebert studied physics before founding the publishing magazine ›PAGE‹ in 1986. In 1991 Erik Spiekermann brought him to Berlin to organize projects such as FUSE, ›FontBook‹ and the TYPO conference at FontShop International (FSI). Today Siebert is chairman of FontShop and program director of the TYPO conferences.

In 1989 MetaDesign joined other European design companies in Amsterdam, Copenhagen, Stockholm, and Milan to form EDEN – European DEsigners Network in order to pool their knowledge of design and acquire international clients. Erik Spiekermann explains: »I'd known the colleagues at BRS in Amsterdam since 1983. When the British and American design companies entered the European market, Jan Brinkman thought we needed a counterbalance in Europe. And seeing as none of our companies was big enough, he suggested a union.«

Spiekermann himself contributed the name, which the people at BRS Premsela Vonk eventually chose for themselves after many name changes. Later still, Spiekermann would found Edenspiekermann with them. The European DEsigners Network became superfluous a few years later, since not only had MetaDesign become big enough to tackle the foreign competition alone, it had also opened branches in San Francisco in 1992 and London in 1995, thereby becoming an international player itself.

Meeting of the European DEsigners
Network at MetaDesign in Berlin, 1990:
Hannes Krüger, Jan Brinkmann,
Perry King, Santiago Miranda, Steffen
Gullman (behind Erik Spiekermann)

As soon as the Wall was opened up, many friends came to Berlin to grab a piece of concrete as a souvenir. One of them was Neville Brody, in the photo above carrying a hammer in a plastic bag, 1990.

Shortly before German reunification Erik Spiekermann visited East Berlin on two occasions: once for the opening of Grappa's offices in Berlin Mitte in 1989, and once to visit Wolfgang Geisler, whom he had met at the Forum Typografie in Hanover in 1988. After the fall of the Wall in November 1989 Neville Brody, a friend of Spiekermann's for years, visited Berlin and wanted to see the changes for himself. »Everyone wanted to go to the Wall, and, since we'd moved to our office in Weinhaus Huth on Postdamer Platz at Christmas 1989, we were only a stone's throw from the Brandenburg Gate and all the goings-on there. Our office was right next to the Wall, about two meters away,« Spiekermann recalls.

Neville on Erik

Erik is one of those people. Everywhere you look, you come across him, better not cross him :)

I love him dearly!

Writing this, I'm shocked to realize that I have known Erik for nearly thirty years. He is like an older brother to me, and we certainly have a chequered history. He sways gloriously from inspiring to infuriating, from impatient to incredibly interested, interesting, and impassioned. A heart of gold, beneath that tough exterior lays the reason why Erik has always fallen short of his dream to become a global corporate executive! Let's hope it never happens to him!

We originally met at Type 87 in New York at the Grand Hyatt Hotel, I think my very first conference speech. I don't remember much about it except meeting Erik and Joan and Roger Black and David Berlow and Pinky in the lobby bar, and then getting really excited about this FontShop idea Erik was enthusing about. That, and the fact that I had been mistaken for the electrician by the conference desk on arrival and taken to the electrics cupboard behind the stage, a chastening experience that did little to help my confidence levels. I hated giving talks then, they terrified me, but Erik was so calm and confident and still is, completely at ease in front of an audience, the showman in him revelling on a stage like an MC.

We instantly became long-lost friends. I would join Erik and Joan frequently in Berlin, staying at Erik's wonderful flat in Motzstraße high above the first Metadesign studio, and we joined forces. I partnered them in FontShop, later launching FontWorks in the UK, and together we created FontFont. FUSE evolved from there, something I consider one of the most key ventures I've ever been involved in, leading to conferences and twenty years of really exciting commissions, collaborations, and design innovation.

Erik and myself are like left and right brain hemispheres. To Erik's structural engineering precision and detailed obsession, I was the chaotic and messy painter. Where I would invent stuff Erik would regulate it. Well, although

that's how it seemed, the reality was far different – in fact we are very similar – underground rebels (sometimes above ground too!), and coming from a background of alternative culture and left-leaning politics. In fact, Erik ended up teaching typography at the LCP not long after I graduated from there. We both share a love of systems, and exercise the same diagrammatic approach to design, despite appearances and outcomes. Our working relationship was perfectly matched through this balance, and we really did become like family members.

Gosh, if I think about it, Erik has been instrumental at so many key points in my professional life. Things that stand out include Erik MC-ing at FUSE conferences we put on. The very first one, held in London in 1994 at the Royal College of Art was a key event, the first live broadcast workshop in FuseLab, and the introduction to the wider design community of a whole raft of young designers who have since gone on to become household names, well, if you live in a design household that is.

Memories of that event include Vaughan Oliver terrified to speak at his first public lecture, getting drunk, and having a chaotic discussion on stage with an equally-drunk Graham Wood to the background of holiday films, as his slides had got lost en route. The other striking memory I have of the conference is of Erik running screaming across stage toward me red-faced at the end of my lecture looking like he was about to hit me. The crime I had committed was to say that I thought no one cared about kerning and that in that case it didn't matter to the public: a blasphemy in Erik's mind and worthy of dis-communication!

Equally strong was Erik's joy and excitement at the fall of the Berlin Wall and his love and mad knowledge of all national quirks and peculiarities. Our paths intertwined many times: FUSE Berlin 1995, San Francisco in 1998, both amazing events; type panels, conferences, just hanging out. Always passionate, obsessive, difficult, and a best friend, I owe him loads.

Neville Brody was art director of magazines ›The Face‹ and ›Arena‹, and has created record covers, typefaces, and corporate designs. In 1994 he founded Research Studios. In 1998 he initiated FontShop International with Joan and Erik Spiekermann, and the FUSE conference in 1995, which later became TYPO. He is also a dean at the London Royal College of Art.

TYPO·thek

TYPOthek ist eine neue PAGE-Serie, in der Erik Spiekermann regelmäßig eine Schrift portraitiert. In der ersten Folge stellt er die Futura vor, das nächste Mal folgt die Helvetica.

Eine Schrift entsteht aus dem Zeitgeist, jeder Entwerfer ist Einflüssen ausgesetzt, die sich – bewußt oder unbewußt – in seiner Arbeit niederschlagen.

1925 erschien das Sonderheft der Typografischen Mitteilungen mit dem Titel *elementare typographie*, herausgegeben von Jan Tschichold, in dem dieser zum ersten Male die Bestrebungen zusammenfaßte, eine Neue Typografie zu schaffen.

Zur gleichen Zeit waren die Entwürfe von Paul Renner zu einer neuen Grotesk-Schrift nach konstruktiven Prinzipien schon recht weit gediehen. Der eine wußte vom andern wahrscheinlich nichts, doch hatte der Zeitgeist dafür gesorgt, daß beide das gleiche wollten.

Was war und was wollte die Neue Typografie? Tschichold hat es in einem Aufsatz 1930 aus der Distanz von ein paar Jahren zusammengefaßt; daraus einige Zitate:

„Zur Erreichung einer typografischen Gestaltung können ... alle historischen und nichthistorischen Schriften, alle Arten der Flächengliederung, alle Zeilenrichtungen angewandt werden. Ziel ist allein die Gestaltung: Zweckmäßigkeit und schöpferische Ordnung der optischen Elemente. Daher sind Grenzen, wie die Forderung nach Einheit der Schrift, zulässige und verbotene Schriftmischungen, nicht gezogen. Auch ist es verkehrt, etwa Ruhe der Erscheinung allein als Ziel der Gestaltung aufzustellen – es gibt auch gestalterische Unruhe."

Zur Schrift für diese Art der Gestaltung hatte Tschichold auch Vorstellungen, die ähnlich großzügig gehalten waren:

„Von den zur Verfügung stehenden Schriften steht der Neuen Typografie die Grotesk oder Blockschrift am nächsten, da sie einfach gestaltet und gut lesbar ist. Die Verwendung anderer gut lesbarer Schriften, auch historischer Schriften im neuen Sinne ist durchaus möglich, wenn die Schriftart gegen andere zugleich auftretende Schriften gewertet ist, d.h. die zwischen ihnen auftretenden Spannungen gestaltet sind."

Aus diesen Zitaten ist zu erkennen, daß es für die Neue Typografie zwar rigorose Vorstellungen gab, aber keine Doktrin.

Paul Renner war schon 46 – also kein jugendlich-revolutionärer Heißsporn mehr –, als er 1924 damit begann, eine neue Schrift zu entwerfen. Die Idee eines Verlegers von der Schrift unserer Zeit hatte ihn dazu bewegt.

Bei der Bauerschen Gießerei in Frankfurt am Main kamen die ersten Schnitte 1928 heraus. In Frankfurt war Renner auch mit den Arbeiten des Architekten Ferdinand Kramer bekannt geworden, der für die Drucksachen des Neuen Frankfurt eine konstruktive Grotesk-Schrift entworfen hatte. Die Kramer-Grotesk war nicht verbissen geometrisch, aber auch keine historische Schrift im Sinne Tschicholds. Diese Verbindung abstrakter Formenstrenge mit edler, klassischer Anmutung zeichnet auch die Futura aus. Der Name stammt von Fritz Wichert, einem Kunsthistoriker und Direktor der Frankfurter Kunstschule, der Paul Renner 1925 als Leiter der Abteilung Werbegrafik und Typografie berufen hatte. Die Vorproben der neuen Schrift waren erstmals auf einer Ausstellung der Kunstschule im Herbst 1925 zu sehen; bei einigen Zeichen war der Kampf zwischen Geometrie und gewohnter Form noch nicht entschieden.

1925 wurde Renner Leiter der Meisterschule für Buchdrucker in München, der er in den folgenden Jahren zu internationaler Anerkennung verhalf. Seine kompromißlose Haltung zur Ausbildung und zur gesellschaftlichen Aufgabenstellung des Künstlers machte Renner bei den neuen Machthabern acht Jahre später untragbar. Schon 1933 mußte er daher die Schule – als Kulturbolschewist diffamiert – verlassen.

Er zog sich an den Bodensee zurück, malte gegenständliche Bilder und bereitete sein Buch *Ordnung und Harmonie der Farbe* vor, das 1947 erschien, zur gleichen Zeit wie die Neuauflage seines 1938 erstmals erschienenen Buches *Die Kunst der Typografie*.

Renners andere Schriftentwürfe – Plak (1928), Ballade (1937) und Renner-Antiqua (1939) – konnten nicht annähernd an den Erfolg der Futura anknüpfen.

Die Schrift ihrer Zeit – die Futura von 1928 – dagegen ist zu einem Klassiker geworden, dem man seine 60 Jahre auch heute nicht ansieht.

1928

DIE SCHRIFT DER NEUEN ZEIT

abcdefghi
jklmnopqr
stuvwxyz

Herbert Bayer: Druckschrift, 1926; g und k sind noch als unfertig zu betrachten. Komposition in den primären Formen Kreis und Quadrat.

Joost Schmidt: Konstruktionsschema einer Grotesk, 1925; Grundlage des Schriftunterrichts im Rahmen des Vorkurses am Bauhaus.

EINLADUNG zum Vortrag des Herrn Paul Renner aus München: TOTE ODER LEBENDE SCHRIFT? am Freitag, den 3. Juli abends 8 Uhr im großen Saale des Löwenbräu Große Gallusstraße 17 Bildungsverband der deutschen Buchdrucker Ortsgruppe Frankfurt

Die Einladungskarte zeigt die Urform der Futura mit Mediävalziffern.

aaaa ggg

Die heutige Zeitungsillustration
Die heutige Zeitungsillustration
1234567890 1234567890
Arbeitsgemeinschaft
Arbeitsgemeinschaft

Die geometrischen Buchstabenformen waren nur ideologisch vertretbar, für eine Textschrift jedoch nicht gerade geeignet.

Mies van der Rohe: Stuhl aus Stahlrohr 1927; lackiert oder vernickelt. Der erste Stuhl, der nicht nur hinterbeinlos, sondern auch federnd war. Während Marcel Breuer und Mart Stam die kubische Grundform vorzogen, sind es hier nach vorn ausgreifende Halbkreise: der Futura-Stuhl.

Paul Renner um 1930; fotografiert von E. Wasow.

PAGE 3/89

PAGE 3/89

»TYPOthek« was the name of the column in ›PAGE‹ magazine in which Erik Spiekermann regularly wrote a portrait of a typeface, starting in 1989. In the first issue he introduced ›Futura‹ by Paul Renner, and explained in an interview why he was fascinated by the type as a bulk commodity: »It's about time that type stopped being subordinate to the cartel of availability. I remember well when the first Letraset letters appeared. It was wild, the freedom – the typographic freedom to work with letters.«

In late 1990 the Potsdam transport company VIP was the first »East German client« to contract MetaDesign to create a new corporate design. MetaDesign had impressed with their work for the BVG in Berlin, something of a »big brother« for the Potsdam company.

»In Potsdam they had very similar problems to the BVG, and wanted to draw on our experience. Also, they were joined (and still are) with BVG in a transport association, so common information elements and rules of design made sense,« Spiekermann explains.

ViP with Thomas Nagel
BVG-Kursbuch with Anke Martini and Priska Wollein

Top: Cover of the schedule guide from 1991 for Potsdam city and environs
Bottom: Double page from the Berlin schedule, 16 × 23 cm

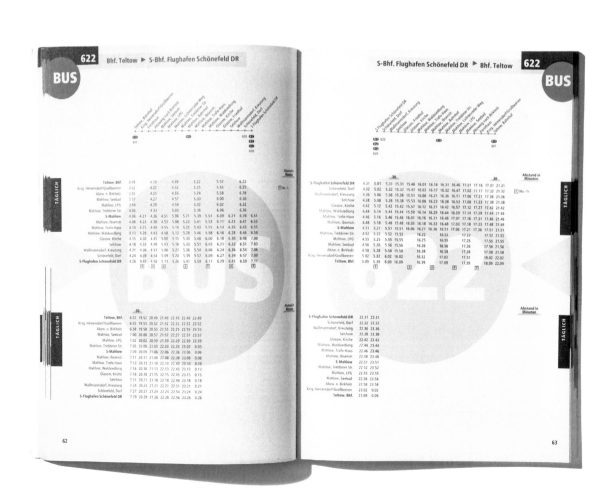

After the reunification of Berlin in 1990 there was no unified information system for public transport. Right after the fall of the Berlin Wall MetaDesign designed the first standardized schedule book for East and West Berlin with new city and route maps.

Starting in 1991 the team led by Erik Spiekermann was commissioned to develop a new signage system for the Berlin public transport company BVG, from which the new corporate design emerged with its main parameters: fonts, symbols, layouts, and company colors.

The new information system was tested at the transport hub Alexanderplatz before being installed in the entire subway system. Previously, vehicles had been colored white, gray, beige, lemon yellow, orange, or red. Spiekermann introduced yellow as the sole color. The typeface ›Transit‹ was created exclusively for BVG signage, based on ›Frutiger Condensed‹, and published commercially in 1997 as ›FF Transit‹.

The signage still works well today, but is being watered down in a few areas.

With: Rayan Abdullah, Charly Frech, Brigitte Hartwig, Karsten Henze, Henning Krause, Anke Martini, and Bruno Schmidt

This is what the BVG signage looked like before MetaDesign stepped in. Spiekermann had already tried to alert the company in the 1980s with pictures like these.

Ausgang →
Leipziger Straße
Kronenstraße
Gendarmenmarkt

mitte

U2 →
BUS

2057

The new signage had to be installable with simple means in historic stations. The workmen did not always go about this in the most subtle way, as one can see from the holes in the ceiling, still visible in 2014.

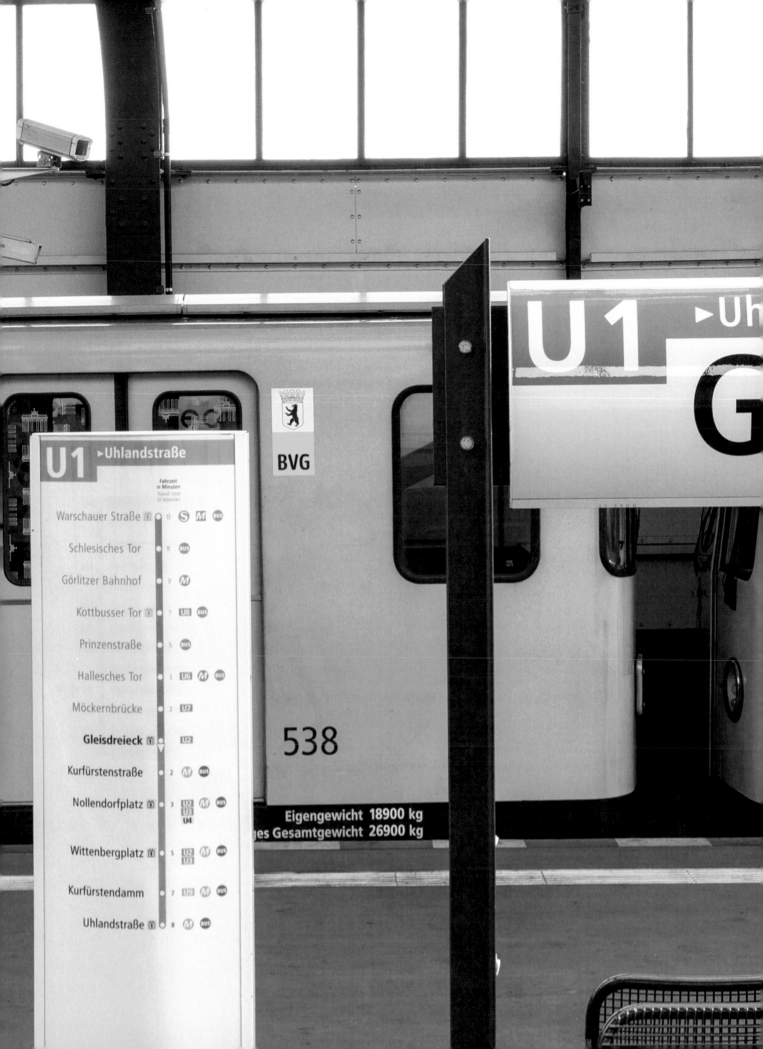

Right: Hand-drawn sketch by Brigitte Hartwig for the new transport network diagram beside a detail from the printed map from 1994

Bottom: In late 1988 Konrad Lorenzen became director of the Berlin public transport company. Unlike his predecessors, he understood the importance of a unified signage system, and so offered the contract to Erik Spiekermann and MetaDesign. Here he proudly shows the first of the new large-size network maps, now hanging behind the tracks at all stations.

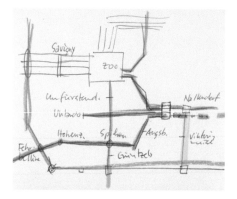

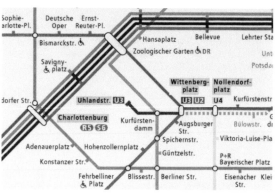

The new signage typeface ›Transit‹ included pictograms, easy to use as fonts.

Designing political themes is very close to Erik Spiekermann's heart; in 1990, together with Alex Branczyk and Michael Etter, he was responsible for the parliamentary election campaigns of Alliance '90 / The Greens, before they merged. On the poster for the Alliance '90 founding assembly in 1991 the typical Spiekermann arrow played a key role. Spiekermann designed a new image for The Greens parliamentary group in 1995. He remembers that, »All the printed matter had titles such as ›short & sweet‹ in different DIN sizes, which in turn contained the next size down as text box.«

With: Alexander Branczyk and Michael Etter

A1 poster by Alex Branczyk for
the inaugural meeting of Alliance '90/
The Greens political party, 1991

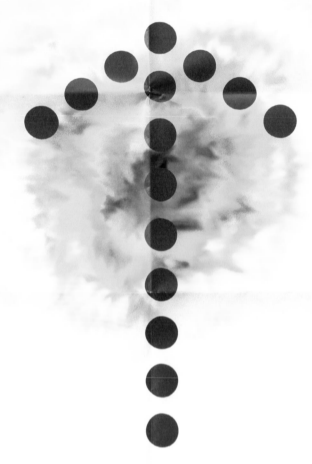

Vollenden und *aufbrechen*

Gründungsversammlung
21. und 22. September 1991
Potsdam
Am Neuen Garten

BÜNDNIS 90
Bürgerbewegung

Alex on Erik

Everything has already been written about Erik Spiekermann. What has not been said about him in umpteen magazines and books or on the web, has been blogged or tweeted by the man himself. So I am going to say something about myself instead! From back then...

Back then was from 1988 to 1994 – first in the »bicycle shop« in Motzstraße, then in the »First toilet in the West« on Potsdamer Platz. And finally, perched under the roof in Berg-mannstraße in Kreuzberg, with an open door to FontShop, whose black and yellow image I developed with Erik. We also designed their first font samples, together with Inken Greisner and Theres Weishappel, after we had delivered the very last ones for dear old H. Berthold AG.

My story is not at all about how he taught me the ropes when I had finished my studies. He didn't »teach« me anything – at least, not in the usual sense of showing me. But Erik Spieker-mann has a way of extracting something out of people for himself when he speaks to them. Nobody can touch him in that respect!

As I say, Erik did not actually »teach« me anything; he prodded me into giving something useful. At some point we had a contract to develop a design catalog, perhaps the first ever. It required copy, but instead of writing it himself (as he was more than capable of) or sending me off to find a copywriter, he simply told me, »Write it yourself!« Erik knew I could do it, even though I did not know it myself at the time. So I wrote it. And today, looking back at over 25 years of »designdesign« (as we used to call it), I

have probably written more than I have des-igned. From that point on I wrote most of the things I was working on. It was Erik's idea...

Shortly after we left our Western pad in Schöneberg to share the first floor of Weinhaus Huth on Potsdamer Platz with FontShop, the Berlin Wall fell. Our undisturbed little design environment at the most deserted end of the Western world came to an abrupt end. We liter-ally were the first toilet in the West! We waited just long enough to see Pink Floyd's ›The Wall‹ performed on our rabbit patch, before leaving it to investors...

In 1990 there was the first general election since German reunification. My wonderful friend and colleague, the late Michael Etter, asked us whether we would conceive and design the corporate identity and election campaign for Bündnis 90 (Alliance 90), an alliance of four opposition political parties from the former East. Erik's partners were not especially keen on doing advertising for the protagonists of the popular movement that had pressured the East German government in 1989. Was Helmut Kohl better? However, Erik pushed it and loaned me to Michael Etter. We did the project with a small external team that consisted of myself and production manager Peter Stumpe, Berlin cartoonist Detlef Surrey, and the painter and illustrator Michael Sowa. Two great artists, one production manager, and one greenhorn assis-tant director named Branczyk, plus a brilliant Michael Etter; we did the campaign. Incidental-ly, the election result in the East has only been trumped once, in 2009. After the success-ful election campaign I went on to do the design for the founding congress of the Alliance '90/The Greens, before an agency from the West took over, and my nice, pure typo-logo was giv-en a stupid sunflower border...

Erik Spiekermann made sure »his« designers had all the creative space they needed. When he could not make it for them, he made sure they had a way of making their own. After the Wall fell, a new music scene emerged, particu-larly in the former East: techno! Before long much of the techno scene image was being designed under Erik's roof, on his Mac. My colleagues Heike Nehl (now at Moniteurs) and Tina Frank (now professor at Linz University of Art) designed the corporate identity and flyers for the legendary techno temple E-Werk. Sibylle Schlaich fitted out the Bunker. At night I

designed the music magazine ›Frontpage‹, and the corporate identity for big raves, such as Mayday or LoveParade. In the evening when most colleagues had left, we would change the CDs and our rooms in Bergmannstraße were transformed from a design studio into a techno joint. Each night those who stayed behind discovered all the things that could be done on those new computers...

Erik's office turned into an experimental lab-oratory at night, where the new club culture was taking shape. Many ideas were tried out that found their way into our daytime work. Other colleagues also used the night for professional experiments; I fondly recall Luc(as) de Groot, for example, tinkering with his type dissertation, even though we did not exactly share a taste in music...

I mean, where would you find something like that? In the post-reunification years at Erik Spiekermann's!

We would almost certainly have stayed to-gether longer than 1994, when I founded xplixit with my colleagues who are now my partners, Thomas Nagel and Uwe Otto. When we left, we asked Erik whether he wanted to come with us – we knew things would not end happily with his partners at the time. A few years later Erik Spiekermann was kicked out himself, and had to start afresh with good friends.

There are a few things I am proud of in my life as a designer – and all of them have to do with Erik Spiekermann, one way or another. That does not merely apply to the old days; I am still happy to walk in his footprints today. The good thing is, they are never too small...

Alexander Branczyk (born 1959) worked at MetaDesign from 1988 to 1994. He created the FontShop image and the legendary techno magazine ›Frontpage‹. He runs the xplicit design agency with Thomas Nagel and Uwe Otto. Branczyk lives in Berlin with his family.

Entrepreneur

All the members of the FontShop
network at their annual meeting in Berlin

One year after the foundation of its parent company in Berlin, an independent foundry was started, directed by Erik and Joan Spiekermann with Neville Brody. The first typeface to be published was ›FF Beowolf‹ by Dutch designers Erik van Blokland and Just van Rossum. It was described as a »living« typeface, since it used a function of the page description language PostScript to change the letter shapes at random with each print.

    Numerous new releases meant the library grew to become one of the largest collections of original contemporary typeface designs. Today FontShop International is the licenser for four FontShops: Benelux, Germany, Austria, and the USA. The branch in San Francisco is the only one hundred percent subsidiary company.

With: Neville Brody, Jürgen Siebert, Joan Spiekermann, and Petra Weitz

When fonts were still sent
on floppy discs: ›FF Info Office‹,
ready to send with envelope
and user booklet

The main focus of FontShop International is
looking after and expanding the FontFont
typeface library. Fonts it publishes itself are
indicated by the prefix FF. Incidentally, the
logo, consisting of two slanted, intertwined Fs,
was devised by Neville Brody. Alongside text
and headline faces such as ›FF Dax‹, ›FF DIN‹,
›FF Meta‹, ›FF Quadraat‹, and ›FF Scala‹, there
are also more outlandish designs such as
the »dirty« typewriter face ›FF Trixie‹, the
»living« face ›FF Beowolf‹, and the first digital
handwriting faces ›FF Erikrighthand‹ and ›FF
Justlefthand‹ (›FF Hands‹).

The library comprises over 4,000 fonts
within over 400 different font families, as of
the start of 2014. Designers may submit their
own designs for inclusion in the library. A board
composed of international experts chaired
by Erik Spiekermann decides what typefaces
to publish every six months.

With: Neville Brody and Joan Spiekermann

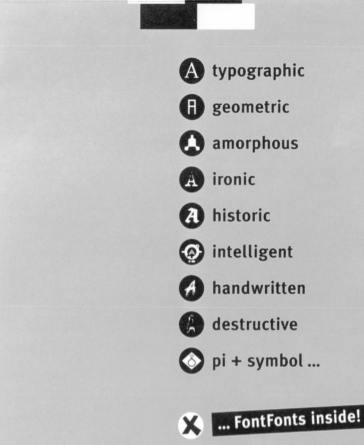

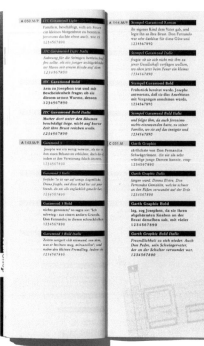

This brochure was the precursor to ›FontBook‹. The cover is by Theres Weishappel, the inside layout by Erik Spiekermann, 1989.
Half A4 size; that proportion is still typical of FontShop today.

From 1990 to 2008 FontShop International published this printed manufacturer-independent reference work of all the fonts sold by the company. The booklet ›All FontShop Fonts‹ was the forerunner to the publication. The first version of ›FontBook‹ was released in 1990 as a ring binder. Even the very first hardcover edition had to be revised and republished three times due to the rapidly growing FSI range.

The fourth edition from September 2006 displayed over 32,000 fonts from 90 international libraries and manufacturers on 1,760 pages –

the most comprehensive printed typeface compendium. In addition to samples of typefaces, the reference work also contained information about each designer, the year of publication and style category, plus language versions and cross-references to alternative typefaces.

Since 2011 ›FontBook‹ has appeared exclusively in digital form as an app for iPhone and iPad.

With: Ed Cleary, Jürgen Siebert, Mai-Linh Thi Truong, and Petr van Blokland

A 564 Mac
Banco

THE QUICK BROWN FOX JUMPS OVER A DOG. ZWEI BOXER JAGEN EVA DURCH SYLT PORTEZ CE VIEUX WHISKY BLOND QUI FUME UNE PIPE 01234567890

German Display 2: Banco, Charme, Flyer Black Condensed, Flyer Extra Black Condensed, Wilhelm Klingspor Gotisch

C 468 Mac
Barnum Block

The quick Brown fox jumps over a Dog. Zwei Boxkämpfer jagen Eva durch Sylt 01234567890

Headlines 82S: Broadway, Davidsonzip Black, Trophy Oblique, Benguiat Frisky Bold, Neon Extra Condensed, Futura Maxi Bold, Futura Maxi Book, Barnum Block, Fiedler Gothic, Ritmo Bold

C 595 Mac
Basilica

The quick Brown fox jumps over a Dog. Zwei Boxkämpfer jagen Eva durch Sylt portez ce vieux Whisky blond qui fume une pipe aber echt über die Mauer the big 01234567890

Basilica, Floridian Script, Jasper & Liberty

M 551 Mac/PC
Baskerville Expert

▶ Regular

ABCDEFGHIJKLMNOPQRSTUVWXYZ
fiflffffiffl ŽŠÁÝÇȘȩŁÆŒÞSˢᶜ&?!
½ ⅓ ¼ ⅛ ⅔ ¾ ⅜ ⅝ ⅞ 01234567890
01234567890 01234567890 abdeilmnorst

▶ Italic

fiflffffiffl seSˢᶜ ½ ⅓ ¼ ⅛ ⅔ ¾ ⅜ ⅝ ⅞
01234567890 01234567890 01234567890
abdeilmnorst

▶ Semibold

fiflffffiffl seSˢᶜ
½ ⅓ ¼ ⅛ ⅔ ¾ ⅜ ⅝ ⅞
01234567890 01234567890
01234567890 abdeilmnorst

▼

▶ Semibold Italic

fiflffffiffl seSˢᶜ ½ ⅓ ¼ ⅛ ⅔ ¾ ⅜ ⅝ ⅞
01234567890 01234567890
01234567890 abdelmnorst

▶ Bold

fiflffffiffl seSˢᶜ
½ ⅓ ¼ ⅛ ⅔ ¾ ⅜ ⅝ ⅞
01234567890 01234567890
01234567890 abdeilmnorst

▶ Bold Italic

fiflffffiffl seSˢᶜ
½ ⅓ ¼ ⅛ ⅔ ¾ ⅜ ⅝ ⅞
01234567890 01234567890
01234567890 abdeilmnorst

C 467 Mac
Behemouth Semi Condensed

The quick Brown fox jumps over a Dog. Zwei Boxkämpfer jagen Eva durch Sylt 01234567890

Headlines 81S: Futura Maxi Light, Behemoth Semi Condensed, Benguiat Frisky, Quirinus Bold, Egiziano Black, Section Bold Condensed, Tower Condensed, Stratford Bold, Woodblock, Futura Maxi Demi

M 515 Mac/PC
Bell

▶ Regular

The quick Brown fox jumps over a Dog. Zwei Boxkämpfer jagen Eva durch Sylt portez ce vieux Whisky blond qui fume une 01234567890

▶ Italic

The quick Brown fox jumps over a Dog. Zwei Boxkämpfer jagen Eva durch Sylt portez ce vieux Whisky blond qui fume une 01234567890

▶ Semibold

The quick Brown fox jumps over a Dog. Zwei Boxkämpfer jagen Eva durch Sylt portez ce vieux Whisky blond qui fume une 01234567890

▶ Bold

The quick Brown fox jumps over a Dog. Zwei Boxkämpfer jagen Eva durch Sylt daarbij verschillende zwaar gapen 01234567890

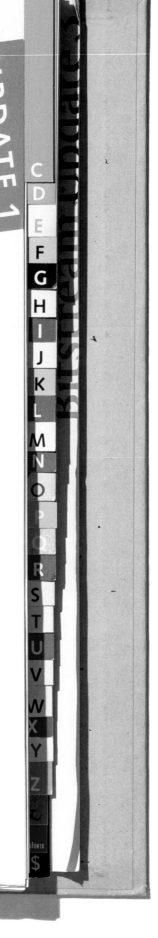

C D E F G H I J K L M N O P Q R S T U V W X Y Z & FONTS $

The first »real« FontShop catalog appeared in 1990 as a loose leaf folder measuring only 32 × 18 cm. The alphabetical separator sheets were each designed by a different colleague – from Neville Brody's A to Phil Bicker's Z and Theres Weishappel's extra page for Letrafonts.

›FontBook‹ from 1998. Cover and inside
layout by Erik Spiekermann.
The catalog displays 32,000 fonts on
1760 pages.

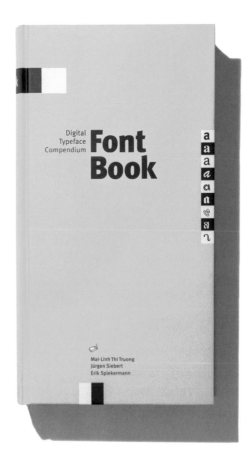

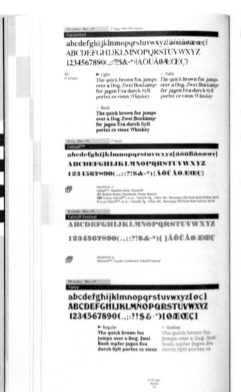

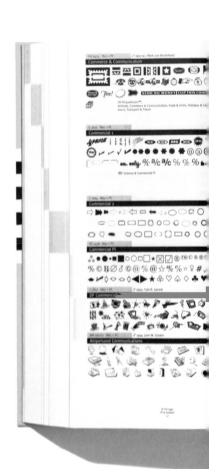

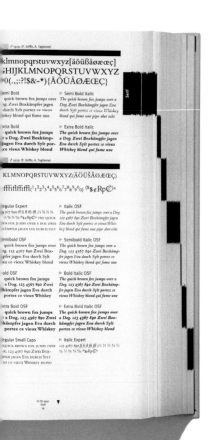
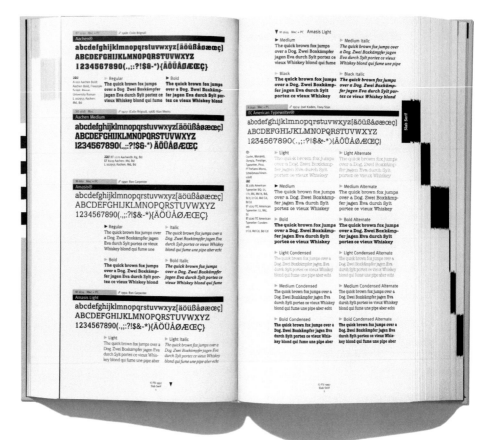

MetaDesign self-profile from 1992,
layout with Libby Carton.
80 pages with transparent separator
sheets, clothbound in red, 13 × 18.5 cm

Erik Spiekermann founded MetaDesign GmbH in 1979, together with the late Gerhard Doerrié, Florian Fischer, and Dieter Heil. In 1990 it became MetaDesign plus GmbH. The two new partners were the graphic designer Uli Mayer and the businessman Hans Christian Krüger, who were represented by the »plus« in the name. The change of name was followed by a move to Potsdamer Platz before settling in Bergmannstraße, along with CitySatz and FontShop. Over the following years the company mushroomed from eight to 170 employees, and the office space from 150 to 2,000 square meters. In 2001, Spiekermann left the company which had been renamed Meta-Design AG by then.

With: Hans Christian Krüger and Uli Mayer

Bruno on Erik

I have often experienced Erik – unlike many other people I know – as someone who not only gets along with people, but also lets them grow and encourages them. He lets us share his virtually encyclopedic knowledge, and that is always a good thing!

However, sometimes it can nearly go wrong, like in the following scene that I will never forget.

There was this management committee meeting at a large schoolbook publishing house in summer 1997. MetaDesign was presenting designs for the new catalogs. The previous evening I had met the publisher, who had found MetaDesign's proposal the most bold and convincing of the three pitches that had been chosen. The committee approval was but a mere formality. After a brief introduction Erik opened by saying that he had something fundamental to address before the presentations began. He continued by pointedly reminding the publishing committee of their responsibility towards the quality of typography in their schoolbooks, which he assured them was in a truly sorry state. The more Erik got into his stride, the longer the faces on the management committee grew. I wished he would just stop. MetaDesign got the contract, but the publisher did say to me afterwards, »A minute longer, and I would have thrown him out.«

Bruno Schmidt studied German and Romance philology, and geography. He was a teacher before joining Cornelsen schoolbook publishers, where he was in charge of advertising. In 1992 he switched to MetaDesign. Since 2000 he has been co-managing Meta-Design Zurich.

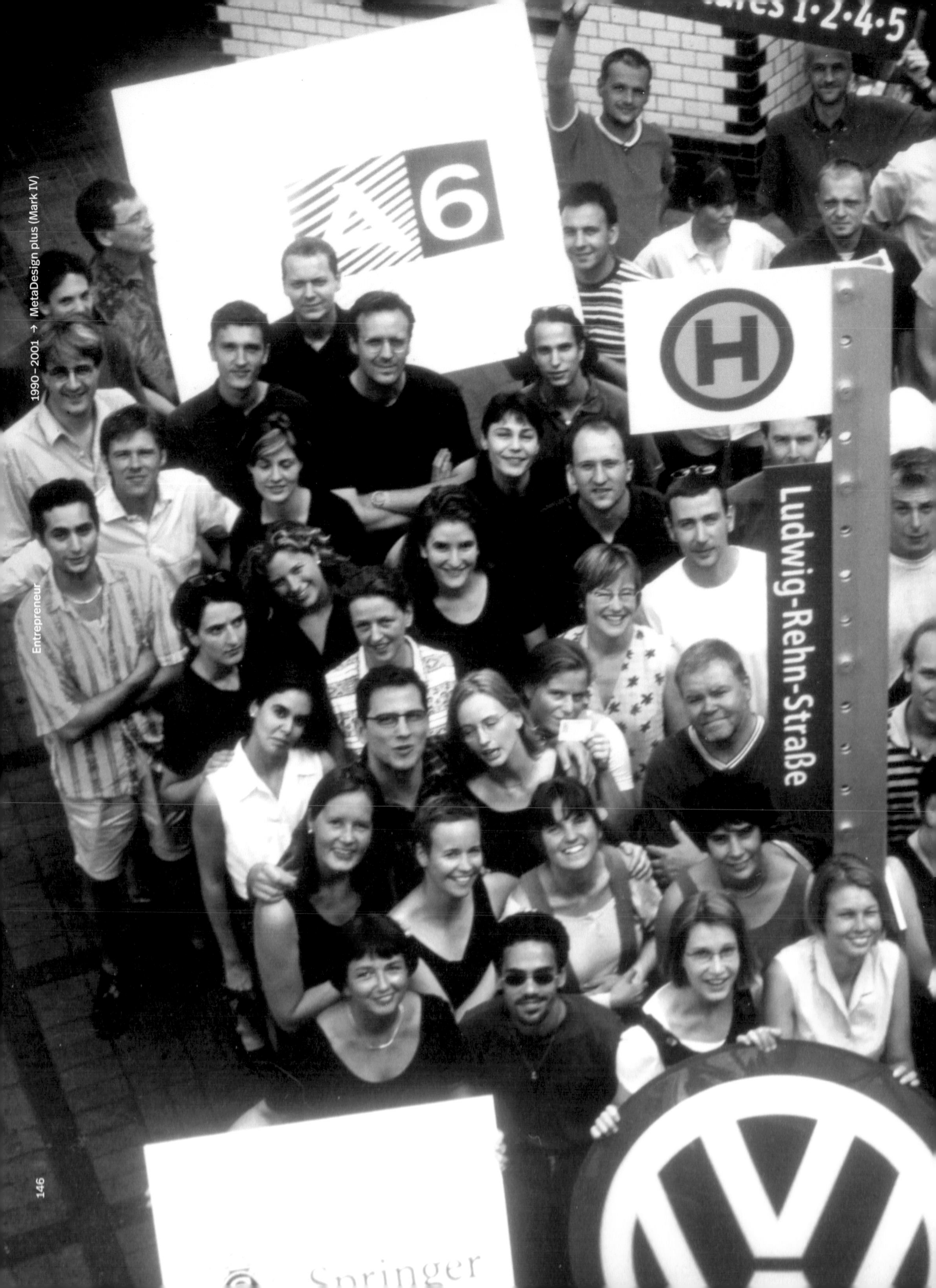
Ludwig-Rehn-Straße
Springer

All staff except Erik Spiekermann
in the courtyard of 102 Bergmannstraße
in Kreuzberg, Berlin, MetaDesign
headquarters from summer 1990 to 2000

Studiengang Grafik - Design   Bremen, den 28.5.90

Vereinbarung über die Erteilung
einer Gastprofessur

Für 1990 erhält   Erik Spiekermann
                  Motzstr. 58
                  1000 Berlin 30

eine Gastprofessur im Studiengang Grafik - Design an der
Hochschule für Künste (gegenwärtig noch: Hochschule für
gestaltende Kunst und Musik).

Vereinbart worden ist ein Einsatz von 160 Stunden im Semester.

Das Honorar beträgt DM 75,-- je Stunde (einschließlich
Mehrwertsteuer), es wird in einer Summe zum Abschluß der
Lehrveranstaltungen aufgrund einer entsprechenden Abrech-
nung des Gastprofessors gezahlt.

Das Thema und die Durchführung der Lehrveranstaltung/en
(regelmäßig wöchentl. oder Kompaktseminare) sind der
Hochschule rechtzeitig aufzugeben, da es im Lehrveran-
staltungsverzeichnis ausgewiesen werden soll.

Zusätzlich ist die Erstattung von Reisekosten, Tage- und
Übernachtungsgeld in einer Pauschale von DM
vereinbart worden.

_____   _____
Sprecher des Studiengangs   Unterschrift des Gastprofessors

Spiekermann was made honorary professor
at the University of the Arts Bremen in 1990,
where he had held workshops for many years.
The corporate design for the university came
from one such workshop, and is still used today.

Later he became a full professor at Berlin
University of the Arts (UdK) for two years,
after he had initially stood in for a colleague
during a term. Many of his former students
are now themselves professors, for example
Ulysses Voelker and Robert Paulmann in Mainz,
Victor Malsy in Düsseldorf, or Ralf Weißmantel
in Aachen.

Left: Before becoming an honorary
professor Spiekermann was a visiting
professor at the University of the Arts
Bremen. An honorary professor is so
called because there is honor but no fee.
Bottom: 1987 diploma thesis by Victor
Malsy, published in 1990 by Hermann
Schmidt Mainz – ›El Lissitzky: construct-
er, thinker, pipe-smoker, communist‹.
Spiekermann wrote a text titled ›Against
the rules of craft, but according to the
rules of Art‹.

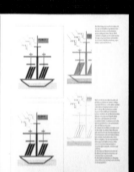

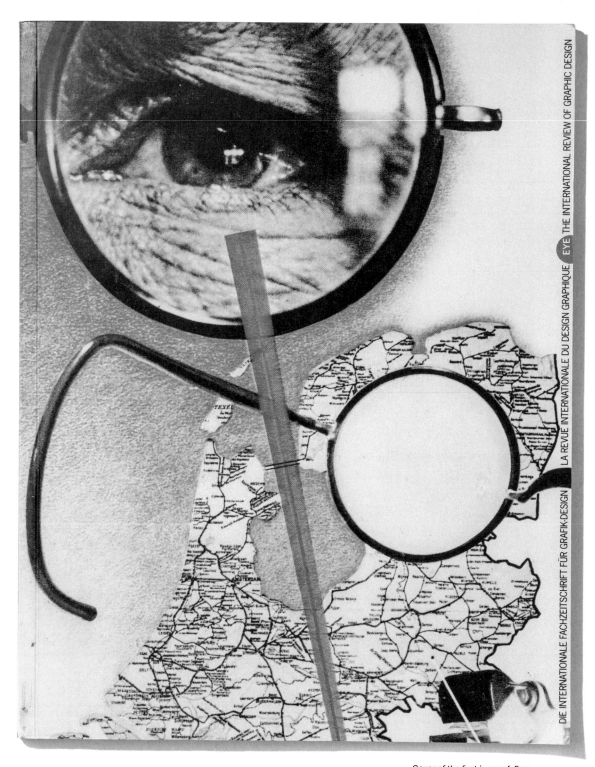

DIE INTERNATIONALE FACHZEITSCHRIFT FÜR GRAFIK-DESIGN
LA REVUE INTERNATIONALE DU DESIGN GRAPHIQUE
EYE THE INTERNATIONAL REVIEW OF GRAPHIC DESIGN

Cover of the first issue of ›Eye‹,
1990, showing a detail from ›Het boek
van PTT‹ by Piet Zwart.

The quarterly magazine about graphic design
and visual culture was founded in 1990 by Rick
Poynor. Erik Spiekermann was onboard from
the first editorial conference, and was credited
in the multilingual debut issue as »acting
chief editor (German issue)«. Later, ›Eye‹
appeared only in English, with Erik Spiekermann
on the editorial board. He left after issue 12.

With: Stephen Coates, Simon Esterson,
and Rick Poynor

Eerste dag
van uitgifte ·
First day
of issue

Olympische
Spelen '92

VOLLEYBA

80c

Steun onze olym
Koop en verzamel de
olympische wens

FERSTE DAG VAN UITGIFTE
4-2-1992 DEN HAAG

OLYMPISCHE
SPELEN'92

In 1990 Erik Spiekermann was the first foreigner commissioned to design a series of Olympic stamps for the Dutch postal service. The challenge was to show five sports on four stamps: volleyball, athletics, rowing, skating, and field hockey. The Olympic rings were an important design element.

Since Spiekermann himself admits he is a typographic designer rather than an illustrator, he developed a typographic picture created from the white markings typical of each sport against gray playing fields. The names of each sport were on the margin on a colored strip. Without perforations the picture appeared to represent five separate stamps – however, with the word »Netherlands« and the postage value, four stamps emerged, each one in two of the five Olympic colors. This design was a little too »Teutonic« and lacking in color for the client, so pictures of athletes were added.

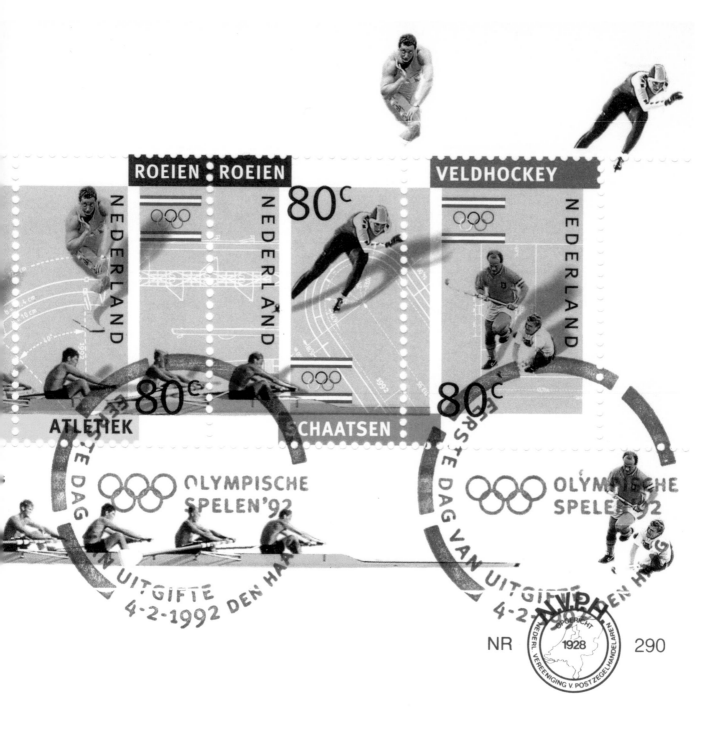

The four stamps on an envelope also designed by Spiekermann, stamped on the first day of issue

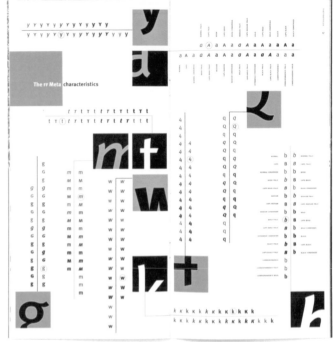

The ›FontFont Focus‹ series introduced the most popular fonts from the library in their own brochures. This edition was designed by Wim Westerveld.

In 1991 FontShop International published ›FF Meta‹, previously the exclusive Deutsche Post typeface ›PT55‹ until the project was ended, whose success soon led to it being dubbed the »Helvetica of the 1990s«. It has been expanded several times over the years: ›FF Meta Plus‹ (1993), ›FF Meta Correspondence‹ (1996), ›FF Meta Condensed‹ (2001), ›FF Meta Headline‹ (2005), and ›FF Meta Serif‹ (2007). In 2011 it was placed in the permanent collection of MoMA as one of the first digital typefaces. ›FF Meta‹ is particularly good for guaranteeing readability in small type sizes, even when the print quality is poor. »Have a look at the a in FF Meta Bold and Black. Isn't it cute? It looks as though it's sitting there with a fat belly saying: ›I'm the little fat a and I've eaten too much‹,« Spieker-mann wrote in his book ›Stop Stealing Sheep‹.

With: Oded Ezer, Lucas de Groot, Ole Schäfer, Christian Schwartz, Jay Rutherford, Kris Sowersby, Erik van Blokland, and Just van Rossum

Mirko on Erik

Nobody believes me now when I say it: I designed my entire dissertation using ›Meta‹! Because I like the typeface so much, as much as I appreciate the man behind it. Back then he was already a reason for the world to look respectfully at German design. I imagined he would have to be quite a strict man – that is how I understood his typefaces, and I imagined the person to be the same. However, he is not. I have known that ever since I got to know him personally. To me, Erik actually seems modest, and very amusing! A clever fellow! Even though there are few parallels between his work and mine (as he would probably point out), I am always happy to meet him and chat. Erik, we clearly do not see each other often enough!

Mirko Borsche is one of the most influential German editorial and graphic designers. He developed the magazines ›Jetzt‹ and ›NEON‹, and was for a long time art director of ›Süddeutsche Zeitung Magazin‹ before becoming creative director of ›ZEIT‹ and ›ZEIT Magazine‹. His Bureau Mirko Borsche in Munich designs editorials and images.

The making of ›FF Meta Serif‹

By Yves Peters. FontShop 2007

Since it was tentatively announced on Erik Spiekermann's Spiekerblog in February, the prospect of a serif counterpart to ›FF Meta‹ – the most influential sans of the digital revolution – sent out a ripple of trepidation through the (typo)graphic design community. Last week it was finally confirmed in the FontShop News e-mailing: ›FF Meta Serif‹ is available in all its OpenType goodness. By the way, I do hope you subscribed to those e-mailings, because that is where you can find out about new typeface releases and new foundries added to the FontShop catalog. And don't forget to read The FontFeed as well. I consider Unzipped to be complementary to both FontShop News and The FontFeed, so I won't be retreading stuff that has been written about there. If you don't read those, you're missing out!

Waiting for ›Meta Serif‹

The first thing that crossed my mind when I saw ›FF Meta Serif‹ announced was »Why now and not ten years ago?« Erik Spiekermann had made several attempts to design the serif companion to ›FF Meta‹ throughout the nineties. Yet he never got across the hurdle of making it just like the sans, albeit with serifs on. In Erik's own words: »I kept sketching it, but it sucked.« Then of course there were all the other type families he created, like ›FF Info‹, ›ITC Officina Display‹, ›FF Meta Headline‹, ›FF Unit‹ …

Erik had been talking to Christian Schwartz about ›Meta Serif‹ for a few years. They met at the end of the previous millennium, when Christian went to Berlin to work at MetaDesign, straight out of college. Erik directed his work on a couple of projects, but he wasn't around all that much. Their collaboration started in earnest around 2002, when Christian moved to New York after leaving The Font Bureau, Inc, with ›Unit‹ and ›MetaHeadline‹. (A little anecdote: at first Erik and Christian thought that ›Unit‹ could be a headline face for Deutsche Bahn. They made just a bold weight to suggest it for the advertising department in 2001/2002. It turned out a bit like ›Meta‹ and ›Bundespost‹. When the client didn't want it, they took it for the studio, which was United Designers at the time.) »Christian Schwartz has as much talent as Jonathan (Hoefler) and Tobias (Frere-Jones), as much historical knowledge as older designers, and is technically pretty turned-on. He has an output more prolific than most of us – his body of work is tremendous, ranging from novel headline faces to hard-working text families and corporate type he has developed with me and other clients.«

Yet it was precisely their work together on corporate type that delayed ›Meta Serif‹ even

longer. First they did ›Bosch Sans‹ and ›Serif‹ for Robert Bosch GmbH, then the ›DB Type‹ family for Deutsche Bahn AG which won them a gold medal from the German Design Council in early 2007. Like Erik says: »Work is always in the way of projects.«

Close collaboration

Regarding his collaboration with Christian, Erik told me they have been working like this for years. The development of a type family consists of roughly three stages. Initially Erik may make sketches or send rough files, but sometimes they just sit together and look at other stuff to say »a bit like this, and a little like that, but not quite like that. Let's look at the Scottish stuff and mix in some of the Fuller Benton approach…«. Then Christian thrashes out a word or two and Erik comments or sketches details or alternatives.

At that point Christian produces a complete base font which serves as a basis for evaluation. A number of parameters are decided on, like contrast, widths, weight, x-height, special features, significant characters, things like terminals, counters. Erik and Christian look at the range of weights, then perhaps sketch out the extremes. When they're satisfied with the results, Christian designs both of those extremes or perhaps even three, depending on the range. Different sample settings are compared and more details are settled. All this is done with just a basic character set, without kerning, but with pretty good fitting.

Once the weights are satisfactory and Erik and Christian have decided on things like figures and all the other stuff besides the basic letters, Christian draws the extremes with a full character set before interpolating. That may involve Erik van Blokland's Superpolator or writing Python scripts. Christian has sometimes had other designers like Tal Leming or Christian Acker help him finish large character sets, go over the interpolated weights, add accents, help with kerning.

To Erik this division of labor makes perfect sense and hails back from the day when type production was a collaborative effort by necessity: »Type design involves a lot of different disciplines, from sketching to production, and when you're making hundreds of weights and versions, four or more eyes see more than two and a lot of the boring work gets shared.«

»We enjoy our online discussions and e-mail exchanges, and the finished product doesn't suffer from the sort of blindness that comes from being too close to your own creation.« Erik's role is largely that of the art director. »I try and give a brief and I comment on the results, but I hardly touch anything myself. Because Christian and the others are so much quicker than me it would be a waste of my time to draw actual outlines. But I generally know what I want – or what the client wants – and I can sell it.«

Tackling ›Meta Serif‹

As he realized that his own efforts to design ›Meta Serif‹ didn't amount to anything, Erik felt he needed a second opinion and some distance. This was where Christian came in. Erik explains: »The original ›Meta‹ owes a lot of its idiosyncrasies to the fact that the first versions never really got finished by today's standards, they were cobbled together over time and the expansion of the family then involved many other designers. That is probably just as well because perfection can be dangerous and make a face slick and impersonal. My own sketches for ›Meta Serif‹ never got anywhere and it took Christian to take a step back and design a serif companion that is more than an extrapolation.« Once they had made up their minds about which way the design should go, the development of the ›Meta Serif‹ family »only« took two years. At some point ›Unit Slab‹ – currently in progress – entered the equation, as they used that typeface to define how slabby and straight ›Meta Serif‹ should get. More on ›Unit Slab‹ soon. ;)

A third designer came on board to help with ›Meta Serif‹. In an e-mail to Erik Spiekermann late September 2006, Christian announced: »I've finally found a brilliant young designer to work with – the incredibly talented Kris Sowersby in New Zealand.« I asked Christian how he had stumbled upon Kris, as he was relatively unknown. »By clicking a banner he had designed for typographi.ca several years ago. I bookmarked his site because he seemed to be an uncommonly talented young designer with enormous potential – which, luckily for all of us, he has been living up to, both in his own work like ›National‹, and his work with me and Erik.«

By then Christian and Kris had already spent a bit of time throwing ideas around for ›Meta Serif‹. »Kris was involved much earlier than my previous collaborators had even been, in that he had input on the first round of sketches. He and I threw very rough sketches back and forth on the italic for several days, and the final product was really a 50/50 combination of our respective ideas.« Kris was more inclined to turn ›Meta Serif‹ into a slab – a pretty literal take – basically ›Meta‹ with ever so slightly trapezoidal serifs tacked on. Christian's sketch took it firmly into Antiqua territory (Antiqua being the common German name for serif faces, as opposed to Grotesk which means sans serif) by increasing the contrast and adding bracketed serifs. Christian tried to keep as many of the salient features intact as he could, yet his design was definite departure from ›Meta‹. The slab was closer to what Erik and Christian had discussed in the past, but Christian's grand plan (and the underlying reason why he thought ›Meta Serif‹ should be an Antiqua) was to draw ›Unit Slab‹ as well, and let that one be a real Egyptian. That way they would end up with a serif and slab that could be used together and be compatible with both ›FF Meta‹ and ›FF Unit‹.

Top: Sketches by Spiekermann for ›Meta Serif‹

Bottom: Erik van Blokland's picture, produced using programing, of all the characters in ›Meta Serif‹

Redrawing from the ground up

After discussing the project at ATypI Lisbon, ›Meta Serif‹ was redrawn from the ground up. It was starting to look like a credible, sturdy news face, and had the warmth and seriousness of ›The Economist‹ text face, so it could work well for magazines or corporate design too. This made Erik think about eventually adding a specific magazine set of dingbats, bullets, arrows, and symbols. Christian suggested they should also make sure to have some 5-pointed stars, cap-height boxes, and bullets, and some simple triangular arrows pointing in all four directions, for newspaper customers.

By January 2007 it was decided to add more weights to the planned book and bold. They were already hesitating about a medium or semibold for captions, sidebars, subheads. Christian explains: »European newspapers always want this weight, and magazine designers can use it for text that reverses out of a picture. And the medium was really easy to make using Erik van Blokland's Superpolator, which even interpolates the kerning.« Christian and Kris also proposed a black weight, which Erik thought wouldn't work. Nevertheless they persevered and Kris drew the Black from the ground up. This caught Christian completely by surprise: »I got up one morning intending to sketch out a few characters in the black for Kris, only to find he'd already drawn the entire upper and lowercase while I was sleeping.« By playing up the increased contrast they succeeded in proving Erik wrong – it did end up working.

When it finally came to filling out all those glyph slots and finalizing the fonts, Kris did everything from finishing character sets to interpolating weights to drawing extra characters to trying out alternate shapes to kerning thousands of pairs. Regarding drawing the numerous alternate shapes and additional ligatures Christian reassured Erik: »No problem. Kris seems to enjoy drawing silly ligatures. His ›Feijoa‹ family gives ›Mrs Eaves‹ a run for its money.«

Family matters

One major concern was that – although ›Meta Serif‹ was more of a departure from the original ›Meta‹ than initially intended – the typefaces still needed to work perfectly well together. Erik and Christian deliberately didn't want to make ›Meta Serif‹ as stylish and novel as ›Meta‹ was when it was first designed in 1985. It was supposed to be an ordinary, legible typeface for all purposes. They never intended each single character to be the exact seriffed equivalent of its sans original.

Making ›Meta Serif‹ 100% compatible with ›Meta‹ meant that they could be alternated in the same line and they would work together without having to adjust the size or the tracking of either one of them. Users often have to mix sans and serif faces in one document, like an annual report where the text would be set in a serif face while the number section would be a sans. Or a sans is used for captions, subheads,

listings etc. as a contrast to a more traditional serif text face. This helps navigation, adds interest, and makes typographic hierarchies obvious.

Erik explains his position in this matter: »I have always liked to add a sans headline to serif text, but doing that in the same paragraph or even line was only possible with either a lot of adjustments or within one of the mega-families. Some of those – like ›Rotis‹ – are simply clones of each other with bits removed or stuck on, providing noise instead of contrast. The whole ›Meta‹ system is supposed to solve separate typographic problems while keeping a family resemblance. This is not a family of identical triplets (there is also ›MetaHeadline‹), but sisters and brothers or even nieces and nephews.

In the end Christian was pretty excited about how this family came together: »I think it transcends being just a companion serif face for ›Meta‹.« Erik was satisfied with the end result. »›Meta Serif‹ feels like ›Meta‹, and they look good together. That was our brief and I think we have achieved that. Which doesn't mean that certain characters couldn't look different or may even be improved. I have learnt that there comes a time when things are best left alone. After many years at trying to get it right, I now look forward to actually using ›Meta Serif‹. Only that will determine whether we did well.«

›FF Meta Serif‹ is a full OpenType family in book, medium, bold, and black, plus their italics and small caps, with oldstyle, lining and tabular figures.

Yves Peters is a graphic designer / rock drummer / father of three who tries to be critical about typography without coming across as a snob. His talent for identifying most typefaces on sight is utterly useless in daily life.

»I am ›Helvetica‹, your typeface. You must not use any other typefaces besides me,« writes Erik Spiekermann about the dominance of the popular sans serif face in the book ›Type and Typographers‹. In this classic, Manfred Klein, Yvonne Schwemer-Scheddin, and Erik Spiekermann introduce readers to the history and characteristic features of the most commonly used typefaces: ›Helvetica‹, ›Baskerville‹, ›Caslon‹, ›Bodoni‹, ›Gill‹, ›Times New Roman‹, ›Univers‹, ›Futura‹, ›Stone‹, ›Rockwell‹ and the typographers responsible for them. The original English edition was published by SDU Uitgevers in 1991.

With: Manfred Klein and Yvonne Schwemmer-Scheddin

Three double pages from Spiekermann's contribution »When in doubt, set it in ›Caslon‹«. ›Caslon‹ was drawn by William Caslon in 1725. The title refers to the fact that ›Caslon‹ was the typeface of choice for many English language authors for decades.

Top spread — left page

When in doubt, set it in Caslon

Biographical notes:
William Caslon was born in Cradley, Worcestershire in 1692, a traditional metalworking area. At 13, he was apprenticed to an engraver in London, presumably because his talents had come to a teacher's eye. In 1717, he became a citizen of London, and was thus entitled to practise a craft or trade. In 1718, he set up as an independent engraver. Two years later, he opened his first type foundry. In 1749, King George II made him a Justice of the Peace for the County of Middlesex in recognition of his services. He retired from business soon after and left his successful foundry to his son. He died at his country house in Bethnal Green on January 23rd 1766, aged 74.

44

The period after the invention of printing with moveable type was initially governed by scientists and publishers of Venetian origin, followed by French and Dutch typographers. These were men of the spirit rather than of money; they took Gutenberg's invention further and designed types which we still use as models today. The early punch cutters and type founders were not exactly outstanding as commercially-minded businessmen. It was not until the 18th century that the English came on the scene and created their own independent styles, although their ideas were initially largely based on those of the Dutch and French. Many of them saw themselves less as artists than as craftsmen, and showed that the craft of typecasting could even be profitable.

We know that William Caslon, too, used a Dutch model in designing his first typeface: the Roman of Christoffel Van Dyck (1607-1669). Whether Caslon was familiar with the ideas of the Enlightenment, which came to England from Holland at the end of the 17th century, we do not know, but true to English empiricism (one of the tenets of the philosophy of the Enlightenment, which uses simple ideas as building blocks which understanding can combine, compare and abstract to form new composite ideas) he used Van Dyck's principles to create his own typeface - the first genuine English Roman.

* Note:
The philosophy of the Enlightenment was critical of institutions and tradition, and wanted to show Man as a 'rational' being the 'way out of his self imposed immaturity' (Kant).

Given that Caslon was aware of Van Dyck's typefaces, he must have known of the French efforts to produce a royal style for their Sun King, Louis XIV. A committee of the Académie Française had carefully prepared the Romain du Roi by analysing and measuring other styles and seeing how they looked in print. Jaugeon, one of the three experts involved, developed a grid of 2304 small units as a model for the large original, from which Grandjean, an experienced punch cutter, then cut the punches freehand, adding the necessary judgement and experience. This pragmatic approach must have impressed Caslon, for he was neither a calligrapher nor an artist, but had trained as an engraver with a gunsmith.

Technology transfer

The advantages of Van Dyck's Roman over the French and, even more so, the Venetian Renaissance designs lay in the pragmatic way in which he increased the x-height in lower-case letters, straightened the serifs and filed off exaggerated points to make the type more resistant in printing and distribute the ink more evenly.

Nowadays, we would probably call using proven Dutch ideas 'technology transfer'.

Top spread — right page

the top margin if
The demy quarto pag
ABCDEGHJKM

An extra prize for
The object was to a
ABCDEGHIJKM

Comparison of Van Dyck's Antiqua (left) and that of William Caslon, shown in Monotype's display version.

From gunsmith to type founder

William Caslon had already built up a successful business engraving all kinds of designs in rifles for wealthy customers. This also involved script, in this case the names of the owners of the rifles engraved in cursive style. In addition to his main business, he undertook other work, such as silver casting - another craft which might have been useful later in typecasting. Caslon's first encounters with the graphics business were the embossing stamps which he cut for bookbinders, and which they used to decorate and inscribe the spines of their books. Like the steel punches used in casting matrices, these were cut as embossed letters, whereas the designs on rifles were engraved in metal.

In fact, it was a bookbinder, John Watts, who engaged Caslon to design and cast type for book covers. One of these books then caught the eye of William Bowyer, a well-known London printer, who asked his bookseller who the talented engraver of the title was and so was given Caslon's name. The two Williams quickly became friends. Bowyer showed Caslon around some London printers. At some stage, he also showed him a type foundry, a business which was completely new to Caslon. After this visit, Bowyer asked Caslon whether he could imagine himself pursuing both the art and the business of typecasting. Caslon asked if he could sleep on it (at least, that's what the sources say). The next day saw the start of the career of one of England's most successful type foundries.

Initially, Caslon was supported financially by Watts, Bowyer and his son-in-law, James Bettenham, also a London printer. The initial capital enabled Caslon to survive the first few months until the quality of his products had proved itself and he could hold his own alongside established businesses. In 1720, his first year of business,

Caslon's contacts with his backers brought him an invitation to supply a new typeface to the Society for the Propagation of Christian Knowledge for printing a Bible in Arabic. Caslon had no experience to recommend him for the job, but he got it anyway.

Having finished the Arabic script, he printed a sample page so that he could sell it to other printers. At the foot of this sheet stood his name, 'William Caslon', in Roman letters designed specially for the purpose. Perhaps he had not given it much thought, but these few letters in themselves were enough to make a respected contemporary so enthusiastic about the new style that Caslon felt encouraged enough to actually create it. The result was the popular style we now know as Caslon Old Style.

Following this style, the first to bear his name, Caslon next cut a number of non-Roman and exotic styles, such as Coptic, Armenian, Etruscan, Hebrew and others. Caslon Gothic was his version of Old English, or Black Letter. All these typefaces had appeared before Caslon published the first extensive catalogue for his type foundry in 1734. This was a large sheet divided into four columns, with a total of 38 faces. Even

45

Design drawings for Romain du Roi.

Construction de la lettre A. *Construction de la lettre B.*

Bottom spread — left page

DIT fyn de KEUREN der Stede van Oud-Hollandt ghelyck defe fyn vaft ende ftadigh ghemaect by *Schout ende Schepenen* van voorfz. ftede opten elffden maius v. d. Jaere onfes Heere dufent achthondert ende vyfendetnegentich

46

if you have never seen this sample, you will know the text Caslon used to display his alphabets. It is the extract from Cicero's speech against Catilina, which was used in almost all English type specimens and which Giambattista Bodoni made famous in his *Manuale Tipografico*: 'Quosque tandem abutere, Catilina, patienta nostra?'

In 1727, Caslon's type foundry moved into larger premises. Once his styles were used by virtually all major English printers and the royal printing works used nothing else, the business moved to the famous Chiswell Street Foundry, where Caslon's son and several generations after him ran the family business for 120 years.

The second type specimen appeared in 1742, this time with twelve types by the son, William Caslon II, who had just been made a partner in his father's business.

Good style from bad letters?

Caslon's success was certainly not due to any stylistic elegance or particularly exciting details; on the contrary, it was due to its pragmatism, which was more interested in overall appearance, technical suitability and legibility.

This suitability made Caslon more or less the English national style, and also won

friends in the American colonies. Despite the anti-British feeling prevailing during the War of Independence, it was used for setting both the Declaration of Independence and the Constitution.

After the founding of the United States, Caslon gradually sank into obscurity until, in 1858, Laurence Johnson, the owner of a Philadelphia type foundry, visited the Caslon works in London. He persuaded the director to cast him a complete set of Caslon, which he took back to the USA, where he made matrices by the galvanic process and marketed the result as Caslon Old Style. Sales were slow, however, until 1892, when a new magazine, *Vogue*, discovered it and made it an overnight success.

At about the same time, the American Type Foundry was established by the merger of 23 smaller foundries, including the one in Philadelphia which had imported the original Caslon some years before. ATF renamed this Caslon 471 and included it in its successful product range.

The popularity of the Caslon revival shows in the host of imitations which appeared in the years that followed. In its catalogue of 1923, ATF alone had over 12 different families called Caslon. The American Lanston Monotype brought out a copy of

Caslon Series 60 with two-colour initial, displayed by Joh. Enschede & Zonen in 1910 University Library Collection, Amsterdam.

* Footnote:
'How long, Catilina, will you abuse our patience?'
As Roman consul in 63 B.C. Marcus Tullius Cicero discovered Lucius Sergius Catalina's conspiracy against the Senate and presented it without resorting to arms. His four Catiline speeches became famous.

Bottom spread — right page

CASLON versus BASKERVILLE

CASLON'S only rival as a typefounder was John Baskerville, of Birmingham. Benjamin Franklin, in the following letter to Baskerville, explains in an amusing manner the difficulty even connoisseurs find in comparing the work of the two typefounders: 'Let me give you a pleasing instance of the prejudice some have entertained against your work. Soon after I returned, discoursing with a gentleman concerning the artists of Birmingham, he said you would be the means of blinding all the readers of the nation, for the strokes of your letters, being too thin and narrow, hurt the eye, and he could never read a line ...

JKLMNOPQR
ABCDE
FGHJK
MNTP
kVRUQu
abcdefghjkm
prstuwxyzh
?ABCDEFGHI STUVWXYZ!

SHOWN HERE: CASLON 128 ITALIC IN 24 PT.

DIE DIREKTION DES ERZIEHUNGSWESENS
DES KANTONS ZÜRICH
BESTÄTIGT, DASS

HERR MAX BERHOLZER
VON SCHAFFHAUSEN, GEBOREN 1906
NACH ORDNUNGSGEMÄSSER ABSOLVIERUNG DES KANT. TECHNIKUMS
IN WINTERTHUR UND NACH BESTANDENER FÄHIGKEITSPRÜFUNG DAS

DIPLOM
DER ABTEILUNG FÜR MASCHINENTECHNIKER MIT „GUT" ERLANGT HAT.
ZÜRICH UND WINTERTHUR, DEN 8. APRIL 1930.

FÜR DAS KANT. TECHNIKUM: FÜR DAS ERZIEHUNGSWESEN:

DER DIREKTOR: DER SEKRETÄR:

47

Three Caslons: Linotype (top left), Monotype (top right) and H. Stempel A.G.

In 1992 MetaDesign West was founded in San Francisco. Erik Spiekermann's partners were Bill Hill (IDEO) and Terry Irwin (Landor Associates). The up-and-coming technology companies in Silicon Valley soon approached MetaDesign West: Adobe was their first client, commissioning the team to design and produce ›Stop Stealing Sheep‹, written by Erik Spiekermann. Contracts from Apple followed for the ›Newton‹ fonts and ViZability. In 1995 they designed the first webpage for IDEO, and in 1998 a homepage with information about the FUSE98 conference »Beyond Typography« for FUSE98.com.

With: Bill Hill and Terry Irwin

Bill Hill and Terry Irwin (obscured) in the first MetaDesign SF office at 300 Broadway, summer 1992.

Bill on Erik

As soon as I heard his voice, I knew – as clearly as the British inflection on his German accent – that I was going to be connected with Erik Spiekermann in some important, meaningful way. »How« was not clear and »Why« was not revealed in the moment, but has continued to be revealed from that moment on a Saturday morning in 1988, on the 4th floor of the David Kelley Design offices on University Avenue in Palo Alto.

As he got off the elevator, my office was out of site visually, the connection launched by his voice, penetrated the walls. We were meeting for the first time after a few weeks of reading articles – a piece in ›Blueprint‹ entitled »Sex, Drugs, Rock and Roll« comes to mind – and through conversations with my friend and client, Gail Blumberg. We were meeting to discuss a marketing project for Adobe, at a time when the total number of PostScript was less than my age, and Erik was, in his words, »the token German amongst us American designers.«

For a week we talked, designed, ate sushi on the lawn in front of Adobe, and began a friendship that bubbled like one of his Indian curries in balmy – he may have said wimpy – California winter. While driving to the airport at the end of the week, I casually asked: »Why don't you open an office here? Frog and ID Two have both brought European industrial design to the Bay Area, why not graphic design?« His response: »Why don't we do it together?« Four years later, we did.

MetaDesign West was conceived that day as a dream that formed into words in the international terminal at SFO, inspired by his comment that he considered himself a »visual engineer« not a designer. It was a picture that fit perfectly then – as a graphic designer surrounded by engineers – and now, presciently predicting the roles of information architecture and experience design forming in the online tsunami that was not yet visible to the design community at large.

Finally, in the spring of 1992, on a Sunday bike ride across the Golden Gate Bridge with Erik dapper in his then trademark bow tie – one always wears a tie on Sunday he noted – we stopped for an espresso at Café Trieste in Sausalito. »Ok Bill, when do we do this? You know, we are not getting any younger.« Pondering for the rest of the ride to Tiburon and then fueled by margaritas for the ferry ride home, I made the commitment. It was time to leave IDEO and give form to the concept of being a designer and an entrepreneur.

Things moved quickly and spontaneously, beginning with a chance – really? – meeting in NYC between Erik and Terry Irwin. »What are you doing in New York?« he asked. »Interviewing for a new job,« Terry replied. »You need to meet my friend Bill Hill. We are going to start a MetaDesign office in San Francisco.« And with that, Terry and I »got married« without dating, trusting Erik with what turned out to be an 18-year adventure for me in creating the space of possibilities that was MetaDesign, a noun and, more importantly, a verb.

The first year was a blur, driven by a combination of fear, excitement, and synchronicity. We rented a furnished design studio at 300 Broadway that had belonged to my friend Julie Christensen, circumventing the need to buy furniture and phones, and managed to negotiate a rental agreement with no credit history. Adobe was our first client, commissioning the design and production of ›Stop Stealing Sheep‹ which Erik was writing in real time. Apple commissioned us to create a custom handwriting font for Newton, necessitating the learning of Fontographer and late nights of not-always-successful bit fiddling. And a host of clients from our collective connections seemed to arrive just before payroll was due.

Meta's CFO in Berlin, Hannes Krüger, told me one day as I struggled to make sense of spreadsheets, »Bill, the first year will be really hard.

You will work long hours, not know what you are doing, get frustrated with your colleagues, and wonder why you ever did this. But the second year, it get's even harder.« Truer words were never spoken and then promptly ignored…

Our first employee was Jeff Zwener, who had applied to be an intern in Berlin until Erik convinced him to join us in San Francisco. Then we »borrowed« Jens Kreitmeyer from Berlin for help with a complicated information design project for HP – he stayed for 5+ years. The idea of a designer exchange with Berlin was great from our side, but no one wanted to go back to Berlin after living in SF. And I will never forget a call from Robin Richmond, an unknown Brit from London, informing us that we were now partners and Union Design was now MetaDesign London. The perpetrator in this stealth display of organic growth: Erik.

Always the consummate connector, Erik complemented his typographic and technologic visions with an uncanny ability to attract talented, slightly weird, and occasionally psychopathic, designers, writers, and sys ops named Andy. The clients came too, many that appreciated his insights until his irreverence and candor resulted in a call to me for intervention.

The spark that connected us was always present even in the discord of growing too fast, or promising too much, or just simply being so driven by design that we neglected to keep our hands on the expense throttle. ›Stop Stealing Sheep‹ nearly killed me trying to make the deadline and keeping everyone focused over the Thanksgiving holiday, FUSE 98 nearly bankrupted us unbeknownst to the 1,500 people who attended, and on occasion, likely in the presence of Tim and Robin and fueled by wine, beer and/or glühwein, I approached the angle of repose on what had been, earlier in the evening, the flat streets of London or Berlin.

Too many memories to paint in the 1,000 words that Johannes asked for two weeks ago, so I will end with thanks from my heart, light from my soul, and humor from my lips to you Erik, the token German who was anything but token in my life for these past 26 years. And, God willing, I believe will be an integral part of the next 26 years or as long as we can still turn the crank of a Vandercook proof press without spilling our beer.

Bill Hill has been a FOE (friend of Erik) for half of his life and counting. He has been blessed to have worked with some of most influential designers in the world. As a visual engineer, he appreciates the rhyme and reason of typography when served with a dash of humor.

A4 versus 8½ by 11

By Erik Spiekermann

Why would a German design company open a branch in San Francisco? Is it because of the weather, the landscape, or simply as a business opportunity? We – MetaDesign – took the plunge, and we know a song about it.

California Dreaming

Everyone loves California: magnificent landscapes, a superb climate, friendly people, and fantastic wine. However, a leisurely vacation driving up and down Highway 1 in a rented convertible is not quite the same as a serious business venture. Ultimately, our decision was a mix of all these »soft« factors plus the fact that we are a high tech-oriented design company. After all, there is nowhere more high tech than Silicon Valley, that peninsula south of San Francisco. On the other hand, even the best business plan would not have worked without the help of good friends. One cannot run a business at such a huge distance without partners one can trust unconditionally. We were lucky – friends became partners.

Go East!

For decades it was a very different story: American design companies followed American business and opened branches in Europe, normally in London, where there were fewer language problems. European designers, on the other hand, had a history of emigrating to the USA – albeit as artists, and never as businessmen and women. A few of them built up very successful design companies that, in turn, founded branches in Europe. The most well-known example must be Walter Landor, who emigrated to the USA from Munich in 1938, and whose company now has branches throughout the world.

»Small« may be »beautiful«, but big is successful

Over the course of the twenty years in this business, I have learnt that large companies prefer to deal with other large companies when it comes to the big stuff. Thus, design companies in the States have long behaved and felt like big companies. That's why they got contracts from their business partners at the major companies who were after safe, evolutionary solutions, rather than creative surprises.

Corporate identity and corporate design were global buzzwords in the 1980s, which shows how both language and business practice had become very Anglo-Saxon. German clients looking for designers with a strategic approach were more or less forced to go to London. Most designers in Germany still worked like good old-fashioned artists, and were therefore not in a position to take on big projects.

Or they still thought (and still do) that all they needed to do was give their clients a new logo. So while graphic designers were sleeping, advertising agencies jumped at the chance, and quickly put up a couple of signs on doors saying »CI Department«, and released statements full of redundant copy in marketing gobbledygook. It's no surprise then that Zthe actually perfectly serious world of corporate design soon got itself a bad reputation.

The important design projects still got snapped up by the major design companies in the USA, England, and Switzerland, while Germany stuck to exporting what we are much more famed for: products and, consequently, product design. Hartmut Esslinger's Frogdesign took German thoroughness to the West Coast and added a touch of Californian lifestyle and entrepreneurship. The combination proved irresistible, yet curiously it was never imitated by graphic designers in Europe, let alone Germany.

Desktop design

Then, about ten years ago the prospects for graphic design changed overnight, and Silicon Valley was to blame. A desktop computer was from then on supposed to enable every housewife to become an independent designer. She could work from her apartment in the country, send data over vast distances, and produce great design at a fraction of the previous cost – at least, that's what the manufacturers' advertising slogans had us believe. A few designers, however, understood that these new tools would not separate designers from clients; they could, in fact, bring them much closer together. The same computer systems would exist both in design studios and company offices, thereby forcing designers to rethink their roles. It was not only about delivering perfect final artwork or corporate design handbooks as gigantic but stillborn print works. If design was to be truly effective in the long term, we had to make the clients' problems our very own. It was no longer enough to simply produce individual solutions, even if they looked great, won prizes, and were fun to do. Now it was more about developing flexible but systematic solutions for current and future communication demands. Since we now used the same tools as our clients, we were forced to think about how to implement our ideas, instead of delegating all the responsibility to the clients' data processing or sales departments. We had to learn to see ourselves as visual engineers, and develop knowledge of computers, in addition to using our traditional artistic skill. Otherwise we would soon be incapable of meeting all the demands of our clients.

The fusion of communication design and computer science required large investments in hardware and software for design companies that had previously had nothing but a couple of drawing tables and maybe a process camera. Many of the traditional major design studios did not keep up with these requirements. Most of them are run by marketing people who keep their designers as far as possible from the cli-

ents. Consequently, it did not take long for new companies to emerge that were founded by a younger and hungrier generation of designers who enjoyed working with computers, and were neither afraid of nor dominated by them.

The grass is greener on the other side of the fence...

This atmosphere of sudden change in Silicon Valley influenced me considerably when I visited colleagues and friends there in the late 1980s. I returned to Berlin with projects from clients who wanted our »cool« European style and our problem-oriented approach. An obsessive attention to detail and a healthy knowledge of analog and digital production methods soon earned us the respect of our American clients, who bought a piece of German workmanship every time they gave us a contract.

On the other hand, over here we were still very frustrated because there was a scarcity of clients who understood the complexity of the design process, not to mention the business opportunities connected to it. It seemed as though our services received more recognition in the States than in Europe. At the same time, however, our American colleagues complained that there were so few quality-oriented design studios over there, and that the clients' marketing people were only interested in short-term results, instead of seeing the big picture. It looked as though we had a product that nobody realized they needed.

MetaNew

In 1990 we founded our new office in Berlin with a strong emphasis on a systematically integrated design philosophy. We wanted to be involved in the design process right from the beginning – defining the problem, developing surprising solutions, and finally converting our ideas into daily business. We wanted to be a high tech company that used up-to-the-minute computer systems. And we wanted to develop complete, independent design systems that could be further developed by our clients and applied to future projects. The maxim was »design for design«. Metadesign is the technical term for that, so that is what we called our company.

MetaWest

As soon as we had a grip on the German office, we started thinking about California again. We still had a few American clients, and it seemed as though there were many other high tech companies in America that urgently needed the MetaMethod, unknown on their own design scene. It had also become apparent to us that we could not supervise design projects at a distance of 12,000 km. Conversations with friends in Palo Alto and San Francisco reinforced my original impression that we had a lot in common. Rational German thinking, thoroughness, and reliability were qualities that were not only to be expected of cars and other products, but

were also needed in communication design. Of course, our German clients also had expectations of California; they wanted the latest technological developments, the hottest unreleased software, and a loose, colorful design language.

After we opened our office in San Francisco in 1992 with two partners who were based there, we sent designers from Berlin to San Francisco to learn how our American colleagues did things, as well as to show them our own methods. It didn't take long before a designer from Berlin was ready to work in a San Francisco studio. We had the same computers, the same software, the same printers and other equipment, and an idea is an idea, just like a client is a client. It was very difficult for German designers to distinguish a 1 dollar bill from a 100 dollar bill, while our American guests in Berlin could never understand why the shops were always shut whenever they had time to go shopping.

Selling design

After four years as an international design company, we know where the real difference between the two design cultures lies: not in the creative approach, but in the business of corporate design. This can be demonstrated in the way we write and design pitches in the USA.

In Germany we present ourselves – our design approach, our case studies, our people – to clients who normally don't know exactly what they really need nor what to expect of us. Thus, we lose the odd client to advertising agencies that promise a quick, painless solution, whereas we might present a project as a potentially complex problem that requires a good deal more than a new logo and a couple of double page ads in financial magazines. However, as soon as we have convinced a client that we can work together, and that we demand nothing but a reasonable fee, a long-standing working relationship often ensues. We don't always get all the design contracts that are going (we don't necessarily want all of them), but so far we're getting new clients without losing our old ones.

In America, on the other hand, clients appear to be a lot better informed about our business. They are more demanding, and much more hard-nosed to deal with. They know the difference between design companies and advertising agencies, and know precisely which of them to offer contracts. After all, there are a few dozen large reputable design companies there, whereas in Germany there are hardly any studios that can handle more than one big project at a time. They have several advertising agencies with more than 100 employees, but MetaDesign is the only company we're aware of that employs over 110 people.

New clients in the States don't tend to be satisfied with a little live presentation about our skills and our references, together with a few basic figures, a schedule, and an outline of the various phases of the project – that will only suffice in Germany. Over there they demand a good deal of effort and, more than anything, a document they can hold in their hands.

Such a document has to explain who we are, why we're the right choice for the project, what we've done in the past, how we will tackle this specific problem, who will work on it, how we'll structure it, how long it will take, what it will cost, and what we expect of them.

If we get a contract due to such a pitch, the trouble we go to can form a good basis for work in the future. Unfortunately, most of these pitches have to be written out without knowing the clients well, let alone their design problems. That's why these elaborate print works are often very impressive, but not necessarily particularly useful.

Informal formalities

It's strange that in the USA everyone calls each other by their first name, even on big, formal occasions. Nevertheless, they still expect a very official presentation before committing themselves. In Germany a client may address us as Mr or Mrs so-and-so for many years, but will still give us a job based purely on trust, instead of a piece of paper. That doesn't mean we don't have contracts, sales departments, or lawyers. Quite the contrary: it's simply because design is still not regarded as a proper business. Our tradition of artist-designers, who feel and behave more like architects than engineers is a good thing for us, even if it is responsible for the fact that we barely have a professional design scene. The combination of American technology and a tough sense of enterprise with our German love of free-thinking inventors (who are even allowed to be a little crazy) and problem-oriented solutions would appear to be a recipe for success.

The international language

We have learnt from one another that design really is an international language. It transcends cultural differences without destroying them, and in doing so represents a powerful tool for communication. Increasingly, companies are grasping the necessity and potential of having a designed company image, the usefulness of sensible information, and an integrated approach to all types of media. We need more designers who can take care of these clients. But they must be international design companies with a vision that goes beyond their own front yard.

One day even the USA will join the international community and finally change its paper size from 8½ by 11 inches to A4.

Spiekermann wrote this article in 1996, four years after MetaDesign opened its offices in San Francisco. Some things have changed in the meantime, but the US paper size is still eight-and-a-half by eleven inches.

Author

Erik Spiekermann wrote the book on typography ›Stop Stealing Sheep & Find Out How Type Works‹ with help from editor E.M. Ginger. The title refers to a quote by the typographer Frederic Goudy (1865-1947): »Anyone who would letterspace lowercase would steal sheep.« The first edition was published by Adobe Press in 1993; the second, revised edition in 2003, and a further improved and completed third at the end of 2013.

The German edition with the title ›Über-Schrift‹ was published in 2004 by Hermann Schmidt Mainz, and has become something of a collector's item. By showing lots of easy to understand comparisons, Spiekermann succeeds in his efforts to make type less complex and more experienceable. He compares choice of font to choice of clothing, and the tonality of type with the sounds of different musical instruments.

With: E. M. Ginger

Left: Soft sheep cover by Shoko
Saito, Tokyo
Double pages from the first edition of
›Stop Stealing Sheep‹, 1993

Cover of the second edition, 2003
Cover of the German edition, ›ÜberSchrift‹,
2004, Hermann Schmidt Mainz
Cover of the third edition, 2014

Good Times, Better Times

"Inglorious here he lays."

Frances Franklin

Be ashamed to catch yourself idle. When you have so much to do, be up by the peep of day. Handle your tools without mittens; remember, that the cat in gloves catches no mice. There is much to be done, and perhaps you are weak-handed, but stick to it, and you will see great effects, for constant dropping wears away stones; and by diligence and patience, the mouse ate in two the cable, and allow me to add, little strokes fell great oaks. If you want a faithful servant, and one that you like, serve yourself. Be circumspect and caring, even in the smallest matters, because sometimes a little neglect breeds great mischief.For want of a nail the shoe was lost, for want of a shoe the horse was lost, being soon overtaken and stolen by the enemy, all for want of care of a horseshoe nail.

New! So much for industry, and attention to one's own business, but we must add frugality to these if we want to make our industry more successful. A person may, if she doesn't know how to save as she gets, keep her

Wishing and hoping for better times? We can make these times better if we bestir ourselves. Industry need not wish, and if you live upon hope you will die fasting. If you have a trade, you have an estate, and if you are lucky enough to have a calling, you have an office of profit and honor. But the trade must be worked at and the calling well followed. Though you have found no treasure, nor has any rich relation left you no legacy, remember that diligence is the mother of good luck, and all things are given to industry. Work while it is called today because you don't know how much you may hindered tomorrow: one today is worth two tomorrows, and don't forget: if you have something to do tomorrow, do it today.

Many of the examples in the first edition from 1993 were designed by colleagues at MetaDesign San Francisco, including Thomas Nagel and Jeff Zwerner.

Today's counterculture lifestyle has one thing going for it: it provides tomorrow's nostalgia; as soon as things are far enough down memory lane, we invariably start looking at them with enchanted eyes.

The other good thing about nostalgia is that you can recycle the ideas without being accused of petit larceny; people might even admire your interest in things historical. Frederic Goudy once said "The old guys stole all our best ideas" – we could certainly do worse than look to the past for typographic inspiration. After all, most of the typeface styles we now see have been around for a few hundred years, or at least several decades.

Old advertisements are always a source of amusement, and today we have access to digital versions of the typefaces our predecessors used. We can re-create early ads almost faithfully. A note of caution: if you imitate that old look too well, people might not realize that you're actually trying to tell (or sell) them something new.

The fonts used in our nostalgic ad all come from the days of hot metal typesetting, when one typeface would have to serve the printer not only for setting advertisements, but also for things like invitations and stationery. Type was neither cheap nor as easily available as it is today, so a printer's investment had to go a long way.

Berliner Grotesk was designed in Berlin around 1913 as a narrow, fairly light face. What is now the medium weight started out as Block Medium, and was redrawn to match weights and shapes of Berliner Grotesk Light. A bold version is still outstanding.

The Block family is thus related to the Berliners. This relationship is seen not only in the wobbly outlines, but also in some of the idiosyncratic lettershapes.

.Handgloves

BERLINER GROTESK LIGHT

.Handgloves

BERLINER GROTESK MEDIUM

.Handgloves

BLOCK REGULAR

.*Handgloves*

BLOCK ITALIC

.Handgloves

BLOCK CONDENSED

.Handgloves

BLOCK EXTRA CONDENSED

.*Handgloves*

BLOCK EXTRA CONDENSED ITALIC

.**Handgloves**

BLOCK HEAVY

Susanna aged 32, when Spiekermann met her for the first time in her Chicago studio.

Erik Spiekermann met his future wife Susanna Dulkinys on May 15, 1992. Spiekermann was due to travel to New York after being invited to Chicago to give a talk at the AIGA (American Institute of Graphic Arts) design conference. Jan Abrams, a client of Dulkinys's and editor of ›Blueprint‹ magazine, who knew Spiekermann from London, happened to bump into him on the street and introduced him to the designer. After this initial encounter they began corresponding and a regular exchange about design ensued, at first by postcard, later by letter and fax. »Erik has wonderful handwriting, as you'd expect of a typographer, and his messages were short, original, and full of humor,« Dulkinys recalls.

Both of their marriages broke up over the course of the following year (Spiekermann had been separated from his wife Joan since 1985). What had started as a common interest in design turned into love. The couple moved back and forth across the globe between Berlin and Chicago for the next few years before setting up home in San Francisco.

Susanna on Erik

Boy Meets Girl in Chicago 1992, Boy Loses Girl in Berlin 1994, Boy Gets Girl a couple times thereafter, until marriage in 2007.

In our 22 years together one discovers that it's the little things that make life a rich one. So here I can provide a short list of little personal things that make Erik truly happy.

A perfectly set breakfast table
Dark bread and hard cheese
Hot tea with a little sugar and milk
Two eggs in a glass, with chives
Coffee black
Espresso perfect: piping hot, short, with crema
Guacamole
Bourbon vanilla quark from Butter Lindner, Berlin
Sorbet, but only lemon or cassis
Kaffee und Kuchenzeit
A glass of Montrachet
Hot chocolate made from molten chocolate, preferably TCHO
The Tuesday ›FAZ‹ for ›Technik und Motor‹
White shirts with narrow collars
White handkerchiefs
Briefs vs. boxers
Handmade shoes
Thin ties
Narrow suits
Socks that don't slip

Susanna Dulkinys, Erik's wife and founding partner of Edenspiekermann, SpiekermannPartners, and the United Designers Network.

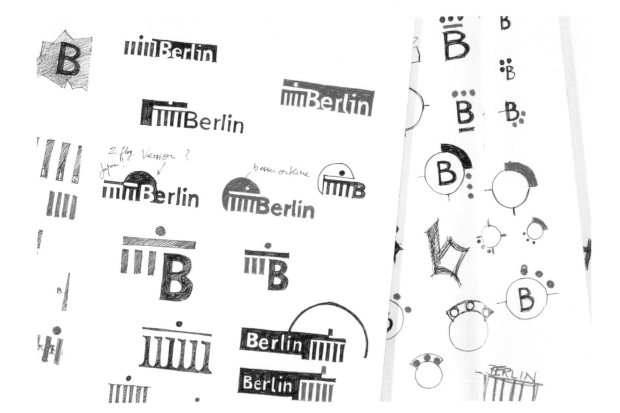

Without Erik Spiekermann, Berlin would look different. In the early 1990s at MetaDesign he was responsible for the design of a passenger information system for BVG, the Berlin transport authority, plus the image for the reunited city. Ever since, all buses and trains in the capital have been yellow, and a stylized Brandenburg Gate is used as the symbol of the city's new image. The logo was used for official correspondence by the public authorities. Today it is used throughout the city, including for ›visitBerlin‹, the emblem of Berlin Tourismus & Kongress GmbH.

With: Pia Betton, Lucas de Groot, and Thomas Nagel

Thomas Nagel drew the stylized Brandenburg Gate, and Lucas de Groot manipulated the letters of his typeface ›Thesis‹ into an unmistakable logo.

MetaDesign West developed a CD-ROM for the educational book publisher PWS Publishing of Boston. It explained the basics of design in six chapters – anything from design culture and the production of prototypes to creative inspiration. The CD-ROM also had games, puzzles, 3D exercises, Quicktime films, and graphics to inspire the students to draw, learn, and do practical work.

Spiekermann's partner Bill Hill sums it up: »It really was about helping the students trust their instincts, understand visual language, and focus their own visual senses.«

With: Gayle Curtis, Bill Hill, Kristina Hooper Woolsey, Terry Irwin, Scott Kim, and Jeff Zwerner

In 1993 CD-ROM was still the format of the digital future. Spiekermann's ›ITC Officina‹ was already on the road to becoming »the« typeface for information design.

Author

VOLKSWAGEN
Werk Braunschweig

Erik Spiekermann had already done the final art-work for the old V.A.G. logo, among other things, for VW in the late 1970s when he was at Wolff Olins in London, where the future founders of Sedley Place worked.

The work for VW and Audi began at Meta-Design at the end of 1994; Lucas de Groot and Erik Spiekermann thought about how to reduce the new 3D logos by Sedley Place, from whom MetaDesign had taken the job, from several

megabytes to more manageable file sizes. The circular VW logo, reminiscent of a wheel, was redrawn to look three dimensional. This apparently minor change required further changes in the entire company image.

From 1995, MetaDesign developed a globally consistent corporate design system for VW, completed by the house typeface ›Volkswagen Headline‹. It was originally intended for head-lines only, based on ›Futura Dreiviertelfett‹

(three-quarters bold). Lucas de Groot also drew the light and regular weights at MetaDesign, even including old style figures. Spiekermann later recommended to VW they use ›Utopia‹ as a second typeface for longer texts.

With: Gerald Christ, Axel Kolaschnik, Eva Walter, and Harald Welt

Emblems that appeared three-dimensional became fashionable in the mid-1990s. Since then the VW symbol is redesigned every once in a while in order to move with the times.

Four programs in leporello fold with the typical blue box, which the other elements are subordinate to

In 1994 MetaDesign Berlin created an extensive design concept for WDR, the radio and television broadcaster, that allowed room for product- and target group-specific solutions. The corporate typeface was the sans serif ›FF Meta‹, complemented by ›Minion‹, a serif face for long texts. Spiekermann selected ›Pantone 293‹ as the corporate blue, with

›Pantone 108‹ as the accent color. In particular, the blue corner logo from the WDR word mark plus the tectonic element help achieve a high recognition value. The new corporate design from 2013 is based on the original design by MetaDesign.

With: Pia Betton and Anke Martini

Left: Asymetrically joined frames defined the new layout system for Audi. It also works on metal columns.
Bottom: The brochure page elements were eye-catching; white and aluminum were the new corporate colors, with red highlights.

In 1993 Audi registered a deficit of 89 million German marks. One year later MetaDesign received the contract to redo the brand's corporate design, including a logo tweak, literature concept, new website, and 3D design. Erik Spiekermann recalls: »In summer 1994 we drove in my Ro 80 to Audi in Ingolstadt to introduce ourselves. At the end of that year I worked with Lucas de Groot on getting the 5 MB Audi logo down to a few KB, and rede-

signing it. In January 1995 Audi had a meeting in Hong Kong, where we already presented the basic concept of the new corporate design.«

This basic concept was to make the design grid visible here and there by using a few lines or boxes. »I sold it by arguing that the new A8 was constructed on a ›space frame‹ module, and that this was also the impetus for the graphic design. I worked on it over Christmas with Anke Martini and Pia Betton, turning it

from a granny brand to a design brand.« The colors were also changed by the »red« team, who worked exclusively on the concept for Audi at MetaDesign Berlin: black disappeared, claret was replaced by a more vibrant red, silver was adapted to the actual material aluminum.

With: Pia Betton, Lucas de Groot, Charly Frech, and Anke Martini

Jürgen on Erik

At the beginning of the '90s I was responsible for global brand communication for Audi. Those were revolutionary times, in which Audi wanted to change from being a brand for middle class squares to being a rival competitor to BMW and Mercedes. Everything was supposed to be »premium«, so who better as a partner for the new corporate design than Erik Spiekermann, who also just so happened to drive an NSU Ro 80, which really impressed the car geeks at Audi. We poached the Hamburg advertising agency Jung von Matt, still new at the time, from their first car client Porsche – altogether an excellent combination to give the brand a completely new image that still applies today.

So Spiekermann was part of the team that set the course for the future. Unlike the less strategically-minded advertisers who often had nothing but their own grand ideas to go on, he was almost dogmatic in his approach; as a typographer he was much more precise than all the others. It is exactly this approach to precision and consistence that is required for such tasks, and it is what makes him successful. During the course of a huge branding process there are plenty of pragmatists who use various constraints as an excuse for circumventing laws of design and working messily, so it is vital to think thoroughly, argue strongly, and defend energetically, all of which are traits of Spiekermann's. He creates design-oriented brand foundations that can be built upon securely.

He does all this arguing and defending in his own unique way: lippy and direct like a Berliner, without any airs and graces. This made me like him right away.

I only got to know Erik properly later on a trip to California. Our job was to convince the American subsidiary company to go with our globally-consistent brand image for Audi, which we managed to do in one day, instead of the four we had set aside. Erik used the unexpected free time to introduce me to his wife and drive me around places that were important to him in a pretty ugly Chrysler Stratus. We had a wonderful time in Palo Alto, Chinatown, and Sausalito! It was like a short road movie. We drove on and on as we chatted, and it felt as though we had known one another for a long time. His was not the usual »look after your clients« sort of behavior; it went deeper, and showed me how open and curious Erik was about people. We have remained friends ever since those four days.

We see each other infrequently. However, our relationship has not changed, and each time we do meet it is as if we had seen each other the previous week. A long-distance emotional relationship that started as a business client relationship.

Erik is a man with rough edges. Although he is by now very experienced, he keeps himself up to date, which makes him seem ageless. He remains relaxed when dealing with his team and other people, and is always straight-talking. He does not merely tell people what they want to hear, and he makes his point clearly. This can take time to get used to, both in business and in private, but it is worth it in order to get to know him since he is one of the best in his business, and also a great human being.

Jürgen Korzer, has over 20 years' experience in global marketing and communications in the auto and motorcycle industries at Audi, smart, and BMW. He has been a consultant since 2009, first with his own brand consultancy before joining one of the major networks. Jürgen lives with his wife and three children in Munich.

Technik-Zeitschriften

Musterseiten im neuen CI-Konzept
Gestaltung für 16 Zeitschriften ab 1994

Springer-Verlag
Berlin, Heidelberg, New York,
London, Paris, Tokyo,
Hong Kong, Barcelona,
Budapest

A4

Herausgeber · Editors
- Berufsgenossenschaftliches Institut für
  Arbeitssicherheit – BIA
- Hauptverband der gewerblichen Berufs-
  genossenschaft e.V., Sankt Augustin
- Kommission Reinhaltung der Luft (KRdL)
  im VDI und DIN Düsseldorf

Redaktion · Editorial board
Bereich Gefahrstoffe am Arbeitsplatz:
Dr.-Ing. Joachim Lambert
Dipl.-Geol. Wilfrud Kopp
Dipl.-Ing. Lothar-H. Engeln, Sankt Augustin
Bereich Reinhaltung der Luft
Dr.-Ing. Klaus Grefen
Dr.-Ing. Klaus Jüstel, Düsseldorf

Staub Reinhaltung der Luft · Air Quality Control
ist die Fachzeitschrift der Gefahrstoffe in der Luft
am Arbeitsplatz und für die Reinhaltung der
Außen luft. Sie berichtet über Schadstoffentste-
hung, -ausbreitung, -erfassung und -abscheidung,
Probenahme- und Meßverfahren, Wirkung von
Luftverunreinigungen, Sicherheitstechnik, über
Gefahren durch Stäube und Gase am Arbeitsplatz
einschließlich der Diskussion über Grenzwerte
aus technischer und arbeitsmedizinischer Sicht
sowie über technische und persönliche Schutz-
maßnahmen und arbeitsmedizinische Vorsorge.

Staub Reinhaltung der Luft · Air Quality Control is
an Export journal dealing with pollutants in
workplace air and in the atmosphere. It reports on
the generation, dispersion, capture and separation of hazardous substances, as well as on sampling and measuring techniques, effects of air pollution, safety technology and on hazards due to
dust and gases in workplace air; it also provides
information on technical and medical aspects of
limit values, on technical and personal protective
measures and medical check-ups.

Inhalt · Contents

Band 1, Heft 1, Januar 1994 · Volume 1, Number 1, January 1994

Originalarbeiten · Originals

129 D. Steinhoff
Grenzwertsetzung für die Luft am Arbeitsplatz in Deutschland
Determination of atmospheric limit values for workplace exposure in Germany

135 W. Karl
Gesetzliche Grundlagen der Kalibrierung von Immissionsmeß-
einrichtungen
Legal basis for the calibration of ambient air measuring equipment

139 U. Schlink
Die Definition der Immissionskenngrößen nach Bundesrecht und
DDR-Recht
*The definition of air pollution characteristics in Federal- and in GDR-
law*

143 D. Kuchenbecker, H. Grau, H. Schaffernicht
Vergleich zweier Probenahmemethoden zur Konzentrations-
bestimmung von Formaldehyd in der Luft am Arbeitsplatz
*Comparison of two sampling methods for determining
formaldehyde concentrations in workplace air*

147 J. von Czarnecki, C. Loipführer, G. Renk
Mustererkennung zur Identifizierung faseriger Stäube im Rahmen des
Immissionsschutzes
*Pattern recognition techniques applied to the identification of airborne
man made mineral fibres*

153 S. Sollinger, K. Levsen
Parameter zur Charakterisierung von Adsorptionserscheinungen bei
dynamischen Emissionsprüfungen nach der Prüfkammermethode
*Parameters for characterizing adsorption phenomena occuring during
dynamic emission tests in accordance with the test chamber method*

Zum Titelbild · Cover page information
Forschung und Entwicklung für die Reinhaltung der Luft und den Schutz der Umwelt
FFF tamsfelt Filtermedien sind solche langzeit-, praxisorientierten Problemlösungen
für alle industriellen Filtersysteme, als Schlauch- oder Taschenfilter für Druck- oder Saug-
betrieb sowie mechanische Abreinigung. Sie bewähren sich seit Jahren bei der Abscheidung
von Pulvern, Stäuben, Mahlgütern feinster Körnung auch im Mikrometerbereich sowie bei
der Heißgasentstaubung im Dauerbetrieb.
FFF tamsfelt Filtermedien werden aus hochwertigen Nadelfilzen gefertigt. Das Bild zeigt
einen Blick in das Labors, in denen die Auswertungen entwickelt und erprobt werden.
(Werkfoto: Filzfabrik Fulda GmbH & Co, D-6400 Fulda, Deutschland)

Zahnradgetriebe, Kupplungen, Wälzlager, Antriebstechnik
Trends in der Antriebstechnik

H. Muno

Zusammenfassung Getriebe und Antriebselemente gehören ebenso wie Wälzlager zu den klassischen Maschinenelementen. Ihre
technologische Weiterentwicklung hat wesentlichen Einfluß auf
ihre internationale Konkurrenzfähigkeit sowie diejenige der
Maschinen, in die sie eingebaut werden. Der Autor nennt vor dem
wirtschaftlichen und konjunkturellen Hintergrund überblickartig
technische Weiterentwicklungen bei Zahnradgetrieben, Kupplungen und Wälzlagern.

Anwendungen aus der Sicht des Herausgebers Der Geschäftsführer
der Fachgemeinschaft Antriebstechnik im Verband Deutscher
Maschinen- und Anlagenbau e. V. (VDMA), Frankfurt a. M. belegt
die internationale Wettbewerbsfähigkeit der deutschen
Antriebstechnik mit Zahlen. Gerade mit Blick auf der derzeitige
konjunkturelle Flaute muß dies Anlaß sein, die weltweite Herausforderung jetzt erneut durch technische Weiterentwicklungen
anzunehmen.

1
Wirtschaftliche Aspekte

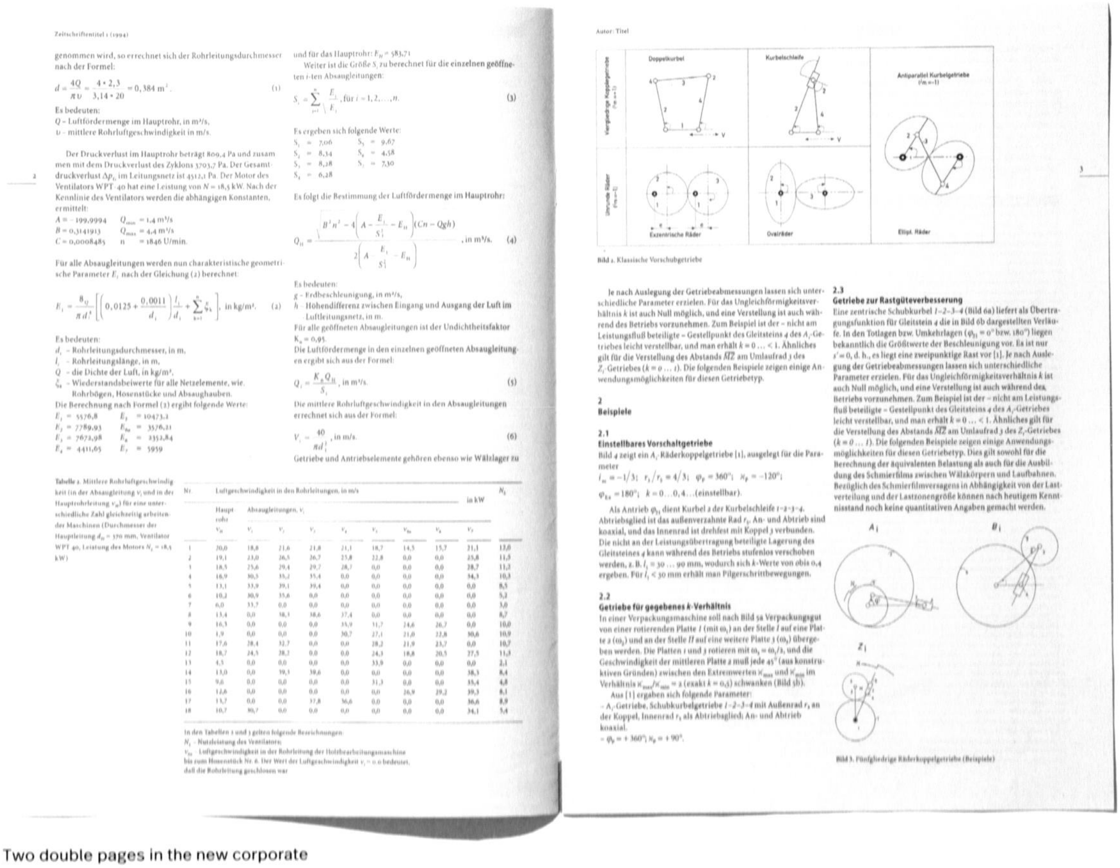

Der Maschinenbau versteht unter dem Begriff „Antriebstechnik"
die Produktgruppen Getriebe und Antriebselemente (z. B. Zahn-
räder, Getriebe, Riemen- und Kettentriebe, Kupplungen, Gleitla-
ger) und Wälzlager – im wesentlichen also die klassischen Ma-
schinenelemente. Die Branche gehört damit zur Zulieferindustrie
– der Maschinenbau ist zur Zulieferindustrie – des Maschinenbaus und die Zulieferindustrie selbst.

Die Größe dieses Fachzweigs wird häufig falsch eingeschätzt,
mit einem Produktionsergebnis von fast 12 Mrd. DM lag die
Antriebstechnik 1991 mit an der Spitze der Fachzweige des
deutschen Maschinenbaus. An diesem Ergebnis war der Sektor
„Getriebe und Antriebselemente" mit einem Ergebnis von
7,34 Mrd. DM beteiligt, während auf die Wälzlager 4,52 Mrd. DM
entfielen.

Die Antriebstechnik ist – wie der Maschinenbau – mittelstän-
disch strukturiert: 80% der Betriebe gehören in die Größenklasse
„bis 500 Beschäftigte". Eine große Zahl der kleinen und mittleren
Unternehmen ist im Markt mit einer Palette unterschiedlicher
Produkte präsent. Neben den „Spezialisten" mit gewollt schma-
lem Programm steht der „Mehrkämpfer" mit breit angelegter Pro-
duktpalette.

Die mittelständische Struktur war für die Antriebstechnik kein
Hindernis, sich im Laufe der Jahre zunehmend dem Exportge-
schäft zuzuwenden. 1991 wies die Statistik ein Exportvolumen von
6,22 Mrd. DM auf (Getriebe und Antriebselemente 3,51 Mrd. DM,
Wälzlager 2,71 Mrd. DM), d. h., der direkte Export betrug 52,4%.
Anders ausgedrückt: Jedes zweite Getriebe, jede zweite Kupplung,
jedes zweite Wälzlager wird in Deutschland für den direkten
Export gefertigt.

Diese Zahlen belegen nicht zuletzt die internationale Wettbe-

werbsfähigkeit der deutschen Antriebstechnik. Die internationale Exportstatistiken bestätigen diesen Eindruck: Rund 30% der
Exporte der westlichen Industrieländer gingen 1991 auf Rechnung
deutscher Antriebstechnik. Dies bedeutet wie in den letzten zwei
Dekaden Platz 1 in der Export-Rangliste.

Für Zulieferbranchen kommt neben dem direkten Export noch
der indirekte Export hinzu, also der Anteil der im Inland abge-
setzten Produktion für Erzeugnisse anderer Hersteller, die für den
Export bestimmt sind. Die indirekte Exportquote der Antriebstechnik liegt bei 50% bis 60% des Zuliefergeschäfts im Inland.
Damit liegt der Gesamt-Exportanteil (direkt + indirekt) in einer
Größenordnung von 75% bis 80%. Produktion und Beschäftigung
der Antriebstechnik sind damit in sehr stärkerem Maße export-
abhängig, als dies auf den ersten Blick in den Statistiken deutlich
wird.

Die augenblickliche Lage ist gekennzeichnet durch eine weltweite Konjunkturflaute. Die Antriebstechnik ist direkt abhängig
von der Entwicklung ihrer Abnehmerbranchen. Dabei spielt der
Maschinenbau eine besondere Rolle.

Der wenig positive Konjunkturverlauf, den der Maschinenbau
in wichtigen europäischen Ländern (Großbritannien, Frankreich,
Italien, Skandinavien) im letzten Jahr genommen hat, blieb
bereits 1991 nicht ohne entsprechende Auswirkungen auf die
Zulieferindustrien. Auch wichtige inländische Abnehmerbereiche
(z. B. Werkzeugmaschinen, Papier- und Druckereimaschinen,
Landmaschinen, Hütten- und Walzwerkeinrichtungen) hatten
negative Entwicklungen zu verzeichnen, so daß die Zuwachsraten
des Auftragseingangs und der Produktion in der deutschen
Antriebstechnik 1991 im Minus rutschten. Für 1992 zeigt der Auf-
tragseingangsstatistik sowohl im Inlands- als auch im Auslands-
geschäft im Vergleich zu der schlechten Situation des Vorjahres
wieder moderate Zuwachsraten an. In der Produktion kam es aber
auch 1992 zu einem Rückgang.

Es ist nicht das erste Konjunkturtal, das die Branche zu durch-
schreiten hat. Die tägliche Herausforderung seitens der Abneh-
mer, die sich häufig durch „Technologie-Führerschaft" in ihrer
Branche auszeichnen, haben die deutsche Antriebstechnik im
Laufe der Jahre ziemlich viel Schmerz gemacht. Getriebe und
Antriebselemente gehören ebenso wie Wälzlager zu den klassischen Maschinenelementen. Ihre technologische Weiterentwicklung hat wesentlichen Einfluß auf ihre internationale Konkurrenzfähigkeit sowie diejenige der Maschinen, in die sie eingebaut
werden. Der Autor nennt vor dem wirtschaftlichen und konjunkturellen Hintergrund überblickartig technische Weiterentwicklungen bei Zahnradgetrieben, Kupplungen und Wälzlagern.

Getriebe und Antriebselemente gehören ebenso wie Wälzlager
zu den klassischen Maschinenelementen. Ihre technologische
Weiterentwicklung hat wesentlichen Einfluß auf ihre internationale Konkurrenzfähigkeit sowie diejenige der Maschinen, in die
sie eingebaut werden. Eine augenblickliche Lage ist gekennzeichnet durch eine weltweite Konjunkturflaute. Die Antriebstechnik
ist direkt abhängig von der Entwicklung ihrer Abnehmerbranchen. Dabei spielt der Maschinenbau eine Rolle. Dies bedeutet wie
in den letzten Dekaden Platz 1 in der Export-Rangliste.

Fachverband Antriebstechnik VDMA, Lyoner Straße 18, D-60528 Frankfurt a. M.

---

genommen wird, so errechnet sich der Rohrleitungsdurchmesser
nach der Formel:

$$d = \sqrt{\frac{4Q}{\pi U}} = \sqrt{\frac{4 \cdot 2,3}{3,14 \cdot 20}} = 0,384 \text{ m}^2. \qquad (1)$$

Es bedeuten:
Q – Luftfördermenge im Hauptrohr, in m³/s,
v – mittlere Rohrluftgeschwindigkeit, in m/s.

Der Druckverlust im Hauptrohr beträgt 800,4 Pa und zusam
men mit dem Druckverlust des Zyklons 3703,7 Pa. Der Gesamt
druckverlust Δp_{ges} beträgt insgesamt 12 4511,1 Pa. Der Motor des
Ventilators WPT-40 hat eine Leistung von $N = 18,5$ kW. Nach der
Kennlinie des Ventilators werden die abhängigen Konstanten,
ermittelt:

$A = -199,99994 \quad Q_{max} = 1,4 \text{ m}^3/\text{s}$
$B = 0,314913 \quad Q_{opt} = 6,4 \text{ m}^3/\text{s}$
$C = 0,0008485 \quad n = 1846 \text{ U/min}.$

Für alle Absaugleitungen werden man charakteristische geometri-
sche Parameter E_i nach der Gleichung (2) berechnet:

$$E_i = \frac{8v_i}{\pi d^2} \cdot \left[\left(0,0125 + \frac{0,0011}{d_i} \right) \frac{l_i}{d_i} + \sum_{l}^{n} \xi_k \right], \text{ in kg/m}^4. \quad (2)$$

Es bedeuten:
d_i – Rohrleitungsdurchmesser, in m,
l_i – Rohrleitungslänge, in m,
Q – die Dichte der Luft, in kg/m³,
ξ_k – Wiederstandsbeiwerte für alle Netzelemente, wie,
Rohrbögen, Hosenstücke und Absaughauben.
Die Berechnung nach Formel (2) ergibt folgende Werte:

$E_1 = 5570,8 \quad E_5 = 10473,1$
$E_2 = 7789,93 \quad E_{05} = 3576,21$
$E_3 = 7075,98 \quad E_6 = 1351,84$
$E_4 = 4411,65 \quad E_7 = 3939$

Tabelle 2. Mittlere Rohrluftgeschwindig
keit (in der Absaugleitung v_i und in der
Hauptrohrleitung v_H) für eine unterschiedliche Zahl gleichzeitig arbeiten-
de Maschinen (Durchmesser der
Hauptleitung $d_H = 370$ mm, Ventilator
WPT-40, Leistung des Motors $N_i = 18,5$
kW)

und für das Hauptrohr: $E_8 = 583,71$
Weiter ist die Größe S_i zu berechnet für die einzelnen geöffneten i-ten Absaugleitungen:

$$S_i = \sum_{i=1}^{n} \sqrt{\frac{E_i}{E_i}}, \text{ für } i = 1, 2, \dots, n. \qquad (3)$$

Es ergeben sich folgende Werte:
$S_1 = 7,06 \quad S_5 = 9,67$
$S_2 = 8,34 \quad S_6 = 4,58$
$S_3 = 8,28 \quad S_7 = 7,30$
$S_4 = 6,28$

Es folgt die Bestimmung der Luftfördermenge im Hauptrohr:

$$Q_H = \frac{\sqrt{B^2 n^2 - 4 \left(A - \frac{E_i}{S_i^2} - E_n \right)(Cn - Qgh)}}{2 \left(A - \frac{E_i}{S_i^2} - E_n \right)}, \text{ in m}^3/\text{s}. \quad (4)$$

Es bedeuten:
g – Erdbeschleunigung, in m²/s,
h – Höhendifferenz zwischen Eingang und Ausgang der Luft in
Luftleitungssystem, in m.
Für alle geöffneten Absaugleitungen ist der Undichtheitsfaktor
$k = 0,95$.
Die Luftfördermenge in den einzelnen geöffneten Absaugleitung
en ergibt sich aus der Formel:

$$Q_i = \frac{K_S Q_H}{S_i}, \text{ in m}^3/\text{s}. \qquad (5)$$

Die mittlere Rohrluftgeschwindigkeit in den Absaugleitungen
ergibt sich aus der Formel:

$$V_i = \frac{4Q}{\pi d_i^2}, \text{ in m/s.} \qquad (6)$$

Getriebe und Antriebselemente gehören ebenso wie Wälzlager zu

in den Tabellen 1 und 3 gelten folgende Bezeichnungen:
N_i – Nutzleistung des Ventilators,
v_H – Luftgeschwindigkeit in der Rohrleitung der Hauptabsaugeinrichtung
bis zum Hosenstück No. 6. Der Wert der Luftgeschwindigkeit $v_i = 0$ bedeutet,
daß die Rohrleitung geschlossen war

N_1	\multicolumn{10}{c}{Luftgeschwindigkeiten in den Rohrleitungen, in m/s}	N_2
	Haupt rohr	\multicolumn{9}{c}{Absaugleitungen, v_i}	in kW
	v_H	v_1	v_2	v_3	v_4	v_5	v_6	v_7	v_8		
1	20,6	18,8	21,6	21,8	21,1	18,7	14,3	15,7	21,3		13,0
2	19,1	23,0	26,3	26,7	21,8	22,8	0,0	0,0	25,8		11,3
3	18,3	23,6	29,4	29,7	28,7	0,0	0,0	0,0	28,7		11,3
4	16,9	30,3	35,2	35,4	0,0	0,0	0,0	0,0	34,3		10,3
5	15,1	33,9	39,3	39,4	0,0	0,0	0,0	0,0	0,0		9,5
6	19,2	16,9	35,0	0,0	0,0	0,0	0,0	0,0	0,0		10,0
7	6,0	33,7	0,0	0,0	0,0	0,0	0,0	0,0	0,0		7,2
8	13,4	0,0	38,1	38,6	37,4	0,0	0,0	0,0	0,0		8,7
9	16,3	0,0	0,0	0,0	35,9	11,7	14,6	26,7	0,0		9,0
10	1,9	0,0	0,0	0,0	30,7	27,1	21,8	12,8	30,6		10,8
11	17,0	28,4	0,0	0,0	0,0	28,2	21,9	23,7	0,0		10,7
12	18,7	24,3	38,7	0,0	0,0	24,2	18,8	20,5	27,5		11,3
13	4,5	0,0	0,0	0,0	0,0	33,0	0,0	0,0	0,0		3,1
14	13,0	0,0	39,1	38,0	0,0	0,0	0,0	0,0	38,3		8,4
15	18,3	0,0	0,0	0,0	0,0	31,3	0,0	0,0	0,0		4,8
16	16,6	0,0	0,0	0,0	0,0	0,0	26,9	28,7	39,3		8,1
17	13,1	0,0	0,0	17,8	36,6	0,0	0,0	0,0	0,0		4,3
18	16,7	16,7	0,0	0,0	0,0	0,0	0,0	0,0	34,3		5,4

Bild 2. Klassische Vorschubtriebe

Je nach Auslegung der Getriebeabmessungen lassen sich unterschiedliche Parameter erzielen. Für das Ungleichförmigkeitsverhältnis ist es auch Null möglich, und eine Verstellung ist auch während des Betriebs vorzunehmen. Zum Beispiel ist der – nicht am
Leistungsfluß beteiligte – Gestellpunkt des Gleitsteins 4 des A_3-Ge-
triebes leicht verstellbar, und man erhält $s = 0 \ldots < 1$. Ähnliches
gilt für die Verstellung des Abstands $\overline{MZ}$ am Umlaufrad 3 des
Z_2-Getriebes ($k = 0 \ldots 1$). Die folgenden Beispiele zeigen einige An-
wendungsmöglichkeiten für diesen Getriebetyp.

2
Beispiele

2.1
Einstellbares Vorschaltgetriebe

Bild 2 zeigt ein A_3-Räderkoppelgetriebe [1], ausgelegt für die Parameter
$i_{m} = -1/3; \quad r_1/r_2 = 4/3; \quad \varphi_p = 360°; \quad \aleph_p = -120°;$
$\varphi_{24} = 180°; \quad k = 0 \ldots 0,4 .$ (einstellbar)

Als Antrieb φ_p dient Kurbel 2 der Kurbelschleife 1-2-3-4.
Abtriebsglied ist das außenverzahnte Rad r_2. An- und Abtrieb sind
koaxial, und das Innenrad ist drehbar auf Koppel 3 verbunden.
Die nicht an der Leistungsübertragung beteiligte Lagerung des
Gleitsteines 4 kann während des Betriebs stufenlos verschoben
werden, z. B. $l_i = 30 \ldots 90$ mm, wodurch sich k-Werte von obis 0,4
ergeben. Für $l_i < 30$ mm erhält man Pilgerschrittbewegungen.

2.2
Getriebe für gegebenes k-Verhältnis

In einer Verpackungsmaschine soll nach Bild 3a Verpackungsgut
von einer rotierenden Platte 1 (mit ω_1) an die Stelle 2 auf eine Platte 2 (ω_2) umd an der Stelle 1 auf eine weitere Platte 1 (ω_1) übergge-
ben werden. Die Platten 1 und 2 rotieren mit $\omega_1 = \omega_2/3$, und die
Geschwindigkeit der mittleren Platte 2 muß jede 45° (aus konstruktiven Gründen) zwischen den Extremwerten x_{max} und x_{min} im
Verhältnis $x_{max}/x_{min} = 6$ (exakt $k = 0,5$) schwanken (Bild 3b).

Aus [1] ergaben sich folgende Parameter:
– A_3-Getriebe, Schubkurbelgetriebe 1-2-3-4 mit Außenrad r_2 an
der Koppel, Innenrad r_3 als Abtriebsglied; An- und Abtrieb
koaxial.
– $\varphi_p = +360°; \aleph_p = +90°.$

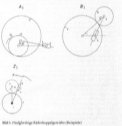

Bild 3. Fünfgliedriges Räderkoppelgetriebe (Beispiele)

2.3
Getriebe zur Rastgüteverbesserung

Eine zentrische Schubkurbel 1-2-3-4 (Bild 6a) liefert als Übertra-
gungsfunktion für Gleitstein 4 die in Bild 6b dargestellten Verläu-
fe. In den Totlagen bzw. Umkehrlagen ($\varphi_p = 0°$ bzw. 180°) liegen
bekanntlich die erforderliche der Beschleunigung vor. Es ist vor
$s' = 0$, d. h., es liegt eine zweipunktige Rast vor [1]. Je nach Auslegung der Getriebeabmessungen lassen sich unterschiedliche
Parameter erzielen. Für das Ungleichförmigkeitsverhältnis k ist
auch Null möglich, und eine Verstellung ist auch während des
Betriebs vorzunehmen. Zum Beispiel ist der – nicht am Leistungsfluß beteiligte – Gestellpunkt des Gleitsteins 4 des A_3-Getriebes
leicht verstellbar, und man erhält $k = 0 \ldots < 1$. Ähnliches gilt für
die Verstellung des Abstands $\overline{MZ}$ am Umlaufrad 3 des Z_2-Getriebes
($k = 0 \ldots 1$). Die folgenden Beispiele zeigen einige Anwendungs-
möglichkeiten für diesen Getriebetyp. Dies gilt sowohl für die
Berechnung der äquivalenten Belastung als auch für die Ausbildung des Schmierfilms zwischen Wälzkörpern und Laufbahnen.
Bezüglich des Schmierfilmvorsagens in Abhängigkeit von der Last
verteilung und der Lastzuneigrolle können nach heutigen Kennt-
nisstand noch keine quantitativen Angaben gemacht werden.

Bild 3. Fünfgliedriges Räderkoppelgetriebe (Beispiele)

**Two double pages in the new corporate
identity concept for the technology
magazines by Springer International**

»When we asked to see an existing corporate design, they all nodded. We had to point out to them that all their business cards looked different, and it meant the corporate design wouldn't work,« says MetaDesign Berlin partner Pia Betton, describing the first meeting with the leading international scientific book publisher Springer. MetaDesign began by developing sample pages for the technical magazines, redesigning the logo and the new corporate typeface, a slight adaptation of ›Minion‹. In reference to the publisher's name (Springer translates as knight, the chess piece), the cover design of the various book series is based on the knight's move in chess, with the ratio 2:3, and with a defined color code.

According to Spiekermann the best idea was to print the Springer logo on the book spines – despite different book sizes – at the same height from the bottom, so that they appear perfectly aligned on the bookshelf. The titles on the spine were adapted to the English standard to run top to bottom, so that the titles can be read when the books are laid flat.

With: Pia Betton, Lucas de Groot, Uli Mayer, and Frido Steinen-Broo

The knight's move (»Springer«) in chess was the idea behind the cover design using the proportions 2:3 and 3:2.

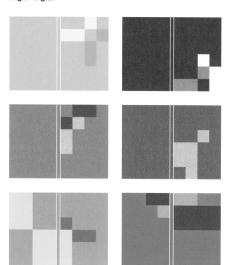

Gerhard Mustermann

Molekularbiologie

Gerhard Mustermann

Molekularbiologie

Gerhard Mustermann

Molecular Biology

116 mm
120 mm
124 mm
144 mm
148 mm

150 mm
155 mm

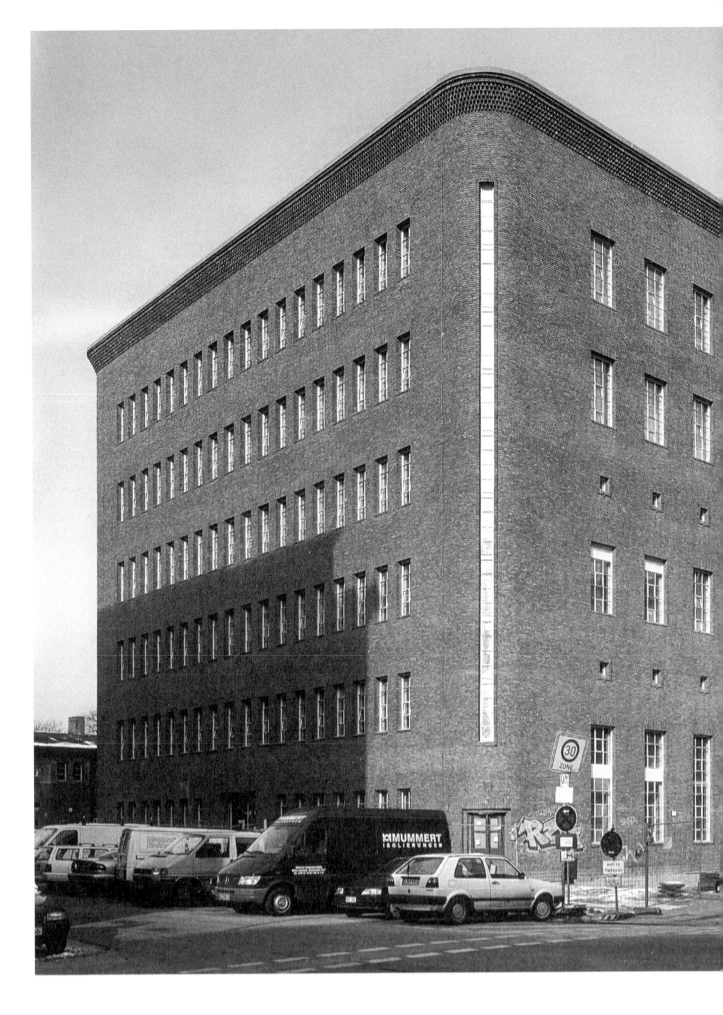

In the mid-1990s MetaDesign's office in Berg-mannstraße was becoming too cramped for the ever-expanding design company. They decided to move, and discovered the red brick building at 65 Leibnizstraße built by the architect Hans-Heinrich Müller in 1928 as a substation to supply electricity to the Charlottenburg district.

Between 1999 and 2001 the old building was thoroughly renovated and adapted to the particular requirements of a design company by architects Petra and Paul Kahlfeldt.

Erik Spiekermann was in charge of the house plans on behalf of the MetaDesign management, and brought the interior architect Christa Fischer onboard, with whom he had previously undertaken several projects. However, he never got to see the completed ›MetaHaus‹, as it was called, since he left MetaDesign shortly before the move. Rainer Köble, who was in charge of financing and supervising the building work, is now controller at Edenspiekermann.

With: Christa Fischer, Paul Kahlfeldt, Petra Kahlfeldt, Rainer Köble, and Sylvia Robeck

View of the unrenovated MetaHaus on the corner of Leibnizstraße and Niebuhrstraße in Charlottenburg, Berlin

1995 – 99 → MetaDesign London

Entrepreneur

Three years after the branch in San Francisco
was founded in 1992, MetaDesign opened
an office in London. Tim Fendley and Robin
Richmond (previously Union Design) joined as
partners. The team specialized in corporate
identities and digital projects early on, including for The Economist Group, Skoda, Lexus, and
Ferrari. MetaDesign London also developed
the ›Legible City initiative‹ for the city of Bristol,
with new signage for pedestrians, in addition
to design for Glasgow when it was ›UK City
of Architecture and Design‹. In 1999 the London
branch left the MetaDesign group and was
acquired by Icon Medialab, who merged with
Michael Mol's Lost Boys in 2002.

With: Tim Fendley and Robin Richmond

Robin on Erik

The Spiekermann, Erik Spieksalot, The Kaiser, »Guv«. Mostly informal, hugely engaging, and never neutral, Erik always leaves an impression. It's hard to put a context on a person who is as fêted as Erik. He is a breath of fresh air in the often-stuffy confines of a small pond industry that can get lost in its own value. He's therefore not everyone's cup of tea, deliberately gauche and irreverent at the altar of high design. He is undoubtedly an important figure – his companies and typefaces have defined the way a global industry developed, reshaping the way German agencies approached design and putting a visual mark on the way his home city was re-organized at the end of the Cold War.

Erik is both big picture and in the details. A contrarian (he reasons his birth date is responsible), who is one minute this, the next that, but a force for good, and above all, for the art of communicating well. For Erik this starts with words. The true mark of a bi-linguist is the ability to find humor in a second language. Erik loves word play and wit. A favorite text by Mark Twain berates the »awful German language«, which despite its author's many prejudices proves that a culture can only be appreciated through its language. Some of his love of British English was colored by his time working on the shop floor, teaching at the London College of Printing and contracting as a proof reader and comp at one of London's best typesetters, rubbing shoulders with an array of characters with links as varied as connections to Jan Tschichold and the London underworld, while also designing typefaces for Wolff Olins. This leads me to suspect that

Erik is better equipped in his second language than I am in my first. He has after all, mastered three languages, cultures and humors: German, English, and American. This fascination with communication and the use of words is clearly manifest in his day jobs, which must be somewhere in the back of his mind when shaping the bowl of a non-aligning numeral or the x-height of a new transitional humanist typeface.

Erik stands as a German design icon, somewhere in the mix between a Weltempfänger T1000 and Ro 80. But when I think of him, I think of spontaneous laughter, word play, a collection of pompous oxymoronic phrases (think »military intelligence«), a love of dialect and local slang terms (»bap, barm, or cob«). I think of his diatribes against mannerist and cliquey adherence to design norms, his dislike of the ›Rotis‹ typeface as a text, the cult of ›Helvetica‹ and the spacing of lower case typography.

I also think of the warmth of Erik's hospitality, weekends in his Wilmersdorf gaff and buying wurst at the Winterfeldt Markt, »brown German food«, and book hunting in Savignyplatz. I remember with a smirk his palpable relief at escaping from a faux-spiritual management brand values workshop set deep on the German-Polish border, using the excuse of having to drive the »Brits« back to Berlin, and the spontaneous outcry of British football terrace invective fuelled chanting and Derek and Clive monologs as we drove back along Karl-Marx-Allee. Professor Erik Spiekermann, acknowledged intelligent typographic raconteur and cunning linguist, you made the work fun.

Robin Richmond works as a design consultant on bespoke projects, mostly in London, sometimes in America, and lately in Japan. He teaches as a visiting lecturer at undergraduate level and has organized and curated the odd design conference. Robin worked with Erik, officially between 1995 and 1999, as a fellow founding director of MetaDesign London.

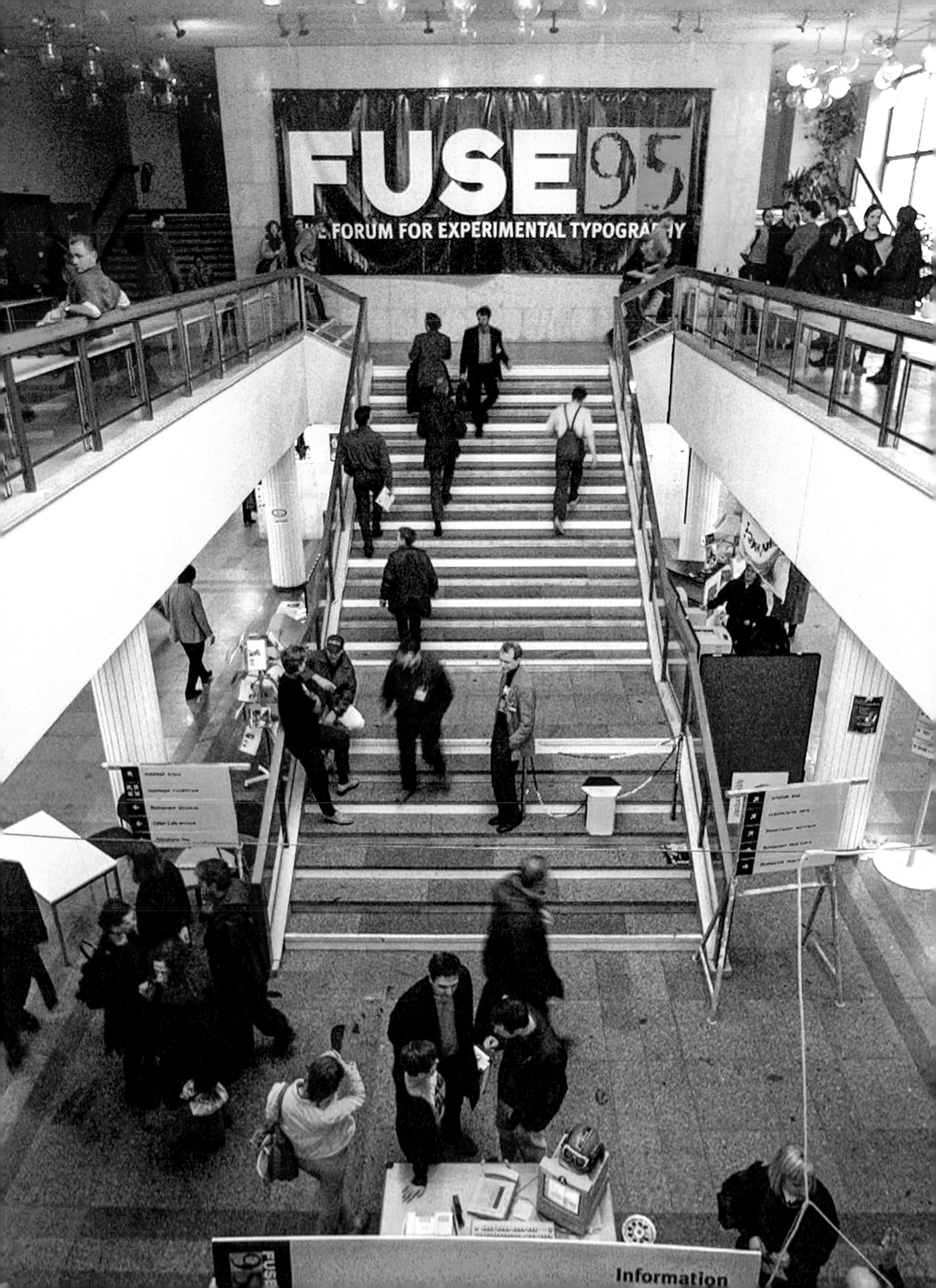
FUSE95
FORUM FOR EXPERIMENTAL TYPOGRA
Information

Between 1990 and 2000, FontShop International and Neville Brody published 18 issues of the experimental typographic magazine ›FUSE‹, in addition to initiating the first FUSE conference in 1994 in London, which was a runaway success. Graphic designers, typographers, and experts met again in 1995 in Berlin's Mitte district for a symposium. Around 30 experts gave insights into their work: Spiekermann and Brody were joined by Günter Gerhard Lange, Gerard Unger, Ian Anderson, and David Berlow, among others. The occasion marked Spiekermann's first time as conference »Master of Ceremony«.

With: Neville Brody and Jürgen Siebert

From left to right: David Carson, Roland Henß, Jürgen Siebert, Erik Spiekermann, Neville Brody
Bottom: The big hall in the Haus am Köllnischen Park, Berlin Mitte

Poster for the first TYPO at the Kongresshalle in Berlin, designed by MetaDesign

FontShop

Barbara und Gerd Baumann · Manfred Becker
Anna Berkenbusch · David Berlow · Axel Bertram
Pia Betton · Alexander Branczyk · Neville Brody · Matthew Butterick
Matthew Carter · John Critchley · David Crow · Wim Crouwel
Friedrich Friedl · Adrian Frutiger · Franz Greno · Lucas) de Groot
Jonathan Hoefler · Peter von Kornatzki · Henning Krause
Günther Gerhard Lange · Zuzana Licko · Hans-Rudolf Lutz
Just van Rossum · Yvonne Schwemer-Scheddin
Eckehart SchumacherGebler · Erik Spiekermann
Gerard Unger und Angela Zumpe

← eingeladene Sprecher

Idee versus → Ideologie

2. internationale FontShop Konferenz

Typo Berlin 96 → Typografie & Grafikdesign

Veranstalter
↓
FontShop Berlin
Bergmannstraße 102
D-10961 Berlin
Tel +49 (0) 30 69 58 95
Fax (030) 692 88 65
http://www.fontshop.de

Subskriptionspreis
bis 15.08. (790.-)
danach 980.-

Studenten
bis 15.08. (290.-)
danach 390.-

TYPO Berlin 96

3.–5.10.96

→ Haus der Kulturen der Welt
→ Berlin

MetaDesign Berlin

Since 1996 TYPO has continued the concept of FUSE in Germany, but without Neville Brody as joint organizer. Today the design conference is the largest of its kind in Europe, and is organized by FontShop. Every year more than 1,500 designers, teachers, marketing people, scientists, artists, journalists, and many more meet to discuss a different theme in the Haus der Kulturen der Welt in Berlin. The conference deals with trends in society, as well as personal ideas, technical innovations, and applicable rules of good design. TYPO has also been going in London since 2011, and San Francisco since 2012 – a truly successful German export.

With: Jürgen Siebert

Kate Moross appearing at TYPO 2013
in the ever well-attended TYPOhall at the
Haus der Kulturen der Welt in Berlin

1996. Berlin. Idee versus Ideologie.

Erik Spiekermann

Erik van Blokland, Just van Rossum

Inaugural press conference

Günter Gerhard Lange

David Berlow at the TYPOdrome

1998. Berlin. Type is money.

TYPOdrome

ART DIRECTORS CLUB BRIEFING
Wolfgang Behnken, Lo Breier,
Veronika Claßen, Ivica
Maksimovic, Markus Rasp,
Helmut Rottke, Uwe Loesch
ADC Talkshow

Erik Spiekermann with Roger Pfund

1999. Berlin. Image and language.

Johannes Erler

Kai Krause, Erik Spiekermann

The first TYPO was difficult to plan. Nobody knew whether it would work. But soon after it all seemed simple and first legends were born. Erik Spiekermann, 1998

House Industries

2000. Berlin. Style.

Bazon Brock

Stefan Sagmeister

2001. Berlin. Brands.

Stefan Sagmeister

Lunchtime

2002. Berlin. Information.

Ken Garland

Jürgen Siebert with students from Bremen

Richard Saul Wurman

2003. Berlin. Humor.

Tom Rielly

TYPO editorial office

Stefan Sagmeister

2004. Berlin. Schrift.

Grafitti workshop

Tobias Frere-Jones, Jonathan Hoefler

TYPOhall

Evert Bloemsma

Matthew Carter

2005. Berlin. Change.

Saki Mafundikwa

Dylan and Erik Spiekermann

Chip Kidd

2006. Berlin. Play.

Liza Enebeis, Donald Beekman

Mai-Linh Thi Truong, Erik Spiekermann, Jürgen Siebert

2007. Berlin. Music.

Wolfraam (Band)

Hans Reichel

Berliner Congress Center

Gerrit Terstiege, Klaus Voormann

2008. Berlin. Image.

Kurt Weidemann, Susanne Zippel

Dieter Telfser

2009. Berlin. Space.

Henning Krause   Erik Spiekermann
Erik Spiekermann

Ebon Heath

Florian Fischer

2010. Berlin. Passion.

Oliver Reichenstein

Eike König

Jürgen Siebert

2011. Berlin. Shift.

April Greiman

FontShop Lounge

2011. London. Places.

Lawrence Weiner

Lecture by Dale Herigstad

Erik Spiekermann, King Bansah

2012. Berlin. Sustain.

Kirsten Dietz

FontShop Lounge

Andreas Uebele

2012. London. Social.

Erik Spiekermann, Ken Garland

Paula Scher, Erik Spiekermann

2012. San Francisco. Connect.

Participants' registration

Erik Spiekermann, Tina Roth-Eisenberg

2013. Berlin. Touch.

Drury Brennan

Print workshop

TYPO is the largest design event in Europe. Leading designers, teachers, scientists, artists, and journalists speak at TYPO.

Simone Wolf, Petra Weitz, Neville Brody

Simon Manchipp

2013. San Francisco. Contrast.

Peter Biľak, Greta Fischer

Jürgen Siebert, Kali Nikitas

Stefan on Erik

Some years ago Erik gave a presentation at the Typographic Circle in London, where, due to all sorts of technical difficulties, the entire group of typefaces he designed and had planned to show reverted to ›Arial‹.

This apparently could not be fixed and eventually the projector was turned off. Erik made up a talk on the spot right there and then. A number of people told me it was the best talk about type and design they had ever heard.

Herr Spiekermann is the only person in design who can pull this off.

Stefan Sagmeister (born 1962 in Bregenz, Austria) is a graphic designer, artist, and writer. He runs Studio Sagmeister & Walsh in New York. He became famous for work he did for the Rolling Stones, Talking Heads, Lou Reed, etc. His work has been exhibited in New York, Paris, Tokyo, and Berlin, among other places.

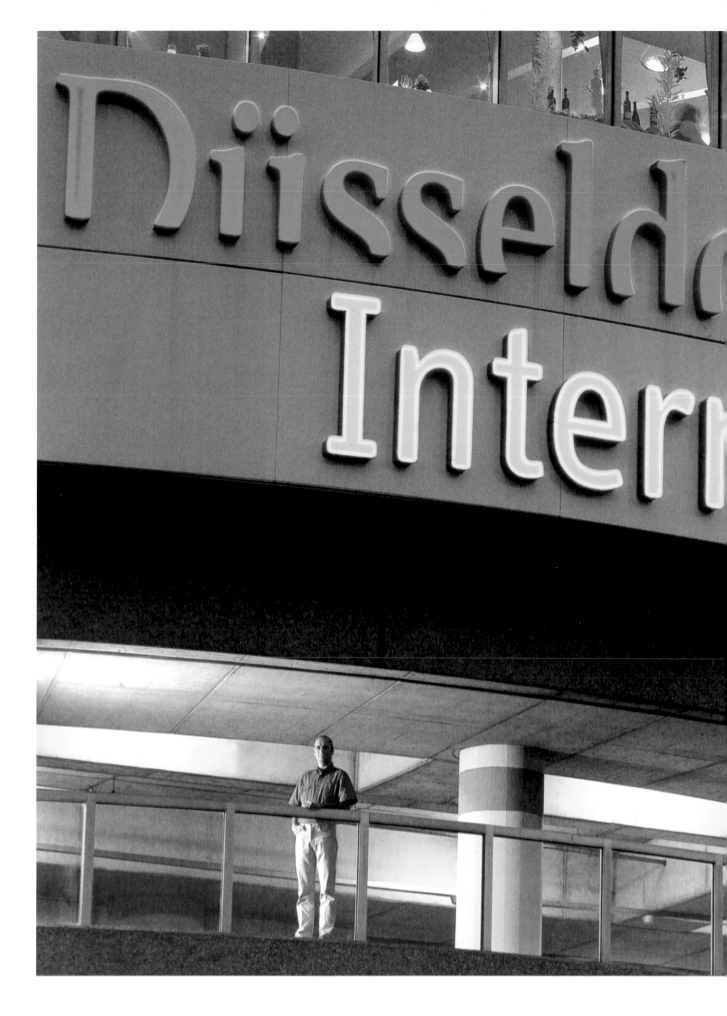

After a devastating fire in April 1996, a new signage system had to be developed for Düsseldorf airport within six weeks. There were several challenges facing MetaDesign: the short amount of time, the lack of a test phase, the approaching holiday season, and the fact that each day around 70,000 passengers would be guided between makeshift tents and provisional lobbies by 2,500 signs. Being responsible for the project at MetaDesign, Erik Spiekermann insisted on one condition: in order to speed things up, the airport would have to keep two people capable of making decisions available round the clock to answer any questions the eight designers might have.

The typeface used for the signage was based on a design that Erik Spiekermann devised for the Italian pharmaceutical company Fidia in 1988: the easy to read and economic ›FF Info‹. Along with a dark opal green color, it has been been the hallmark of the airport ever since. A redesign of the logo followed, and the name was changed to Düsseldorf International.

With: Brigitte Hartwig, Bruno Schmidt, Oliver Schmidthals, and Uli Mayer

The new lettering derived from a cut-off ›Concorde Nova‹ and ›FF Info‹ on the building, guarded by Karl-Heinz Morawietz, then project manager at Düsseldorf airport.

The new signage using ›FF Info‹ had to be installed during ongoing building works, right in the middle of the new terminal building site, 1996.

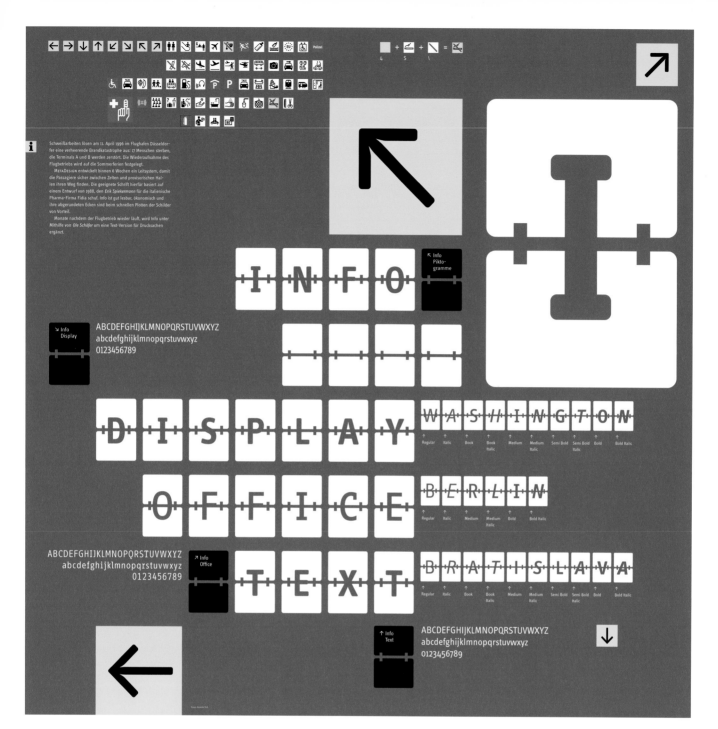

›FF Info‹ with its pictograms and the colors yellow, white, and dark green were the principal design elements of the new signage for Düsseldorf International airport after the fire in 1996.

In 1988 the Italian pharmaceutical company ›Fidia‹ contracted Erik Spiekermann to design a new information typeface that would also be easy to read in 6-point print, and that would contain various expressive aspects from serif to slab (headlines). Unfortunately the job came to nothing. However, in 1996 there was a fire at Düsseldorf airport, and new signage was needed within six weeks; Spiekermann based ›FF Info‹ on the ›Fidia‹ typeface, and had it ready within four weeks. The typeface was perfectly suited to the task: it is easy to read both in print and on illuminated signs; it is compact – it takes up up to 12 percent less space than ›Helvetica‹ or ›Univers‹, for example – and its stroke ends are slightly rounded, which helps avoid a halo effect on backlit signs. This also makes it easier to produce using a cutting plotter. It has negative and positive versions for specialized signage use (e.g. the stroke width of regular in negative corresponds to medium in positive).

With: Albert Pinggera and Ole Schäfer

Originally designed for a competition, this type-face is the chief element of the corporate design for the Scottish city of Glasgow, named ›UK City of Architecture and Design‹ in 1999. Spiekermann's concept was to visualize the peculiarities of the English language and its differences in pronunciation, particularly the Glasgow dialect.

Many alternative letter combinations can be made using ›Glasgow‹, since it offers the choice of over- and underlines for vowels and ligatures for consonants. Spiekermann made three versions in total: one where the most-used letters are accentuated by over- or underlines, or connected by a stroke; a second with a co nventional character set, plus a third with symbols and both parts of the »Glasgow 1999« and »UK City of Architecture and Design« logos.

In 2002 Ole Schäfer created a commercial version based on ›Glasgow‹ called ›FF Govan‹, named after an area of Glasgow.

With: Ole Schäfer

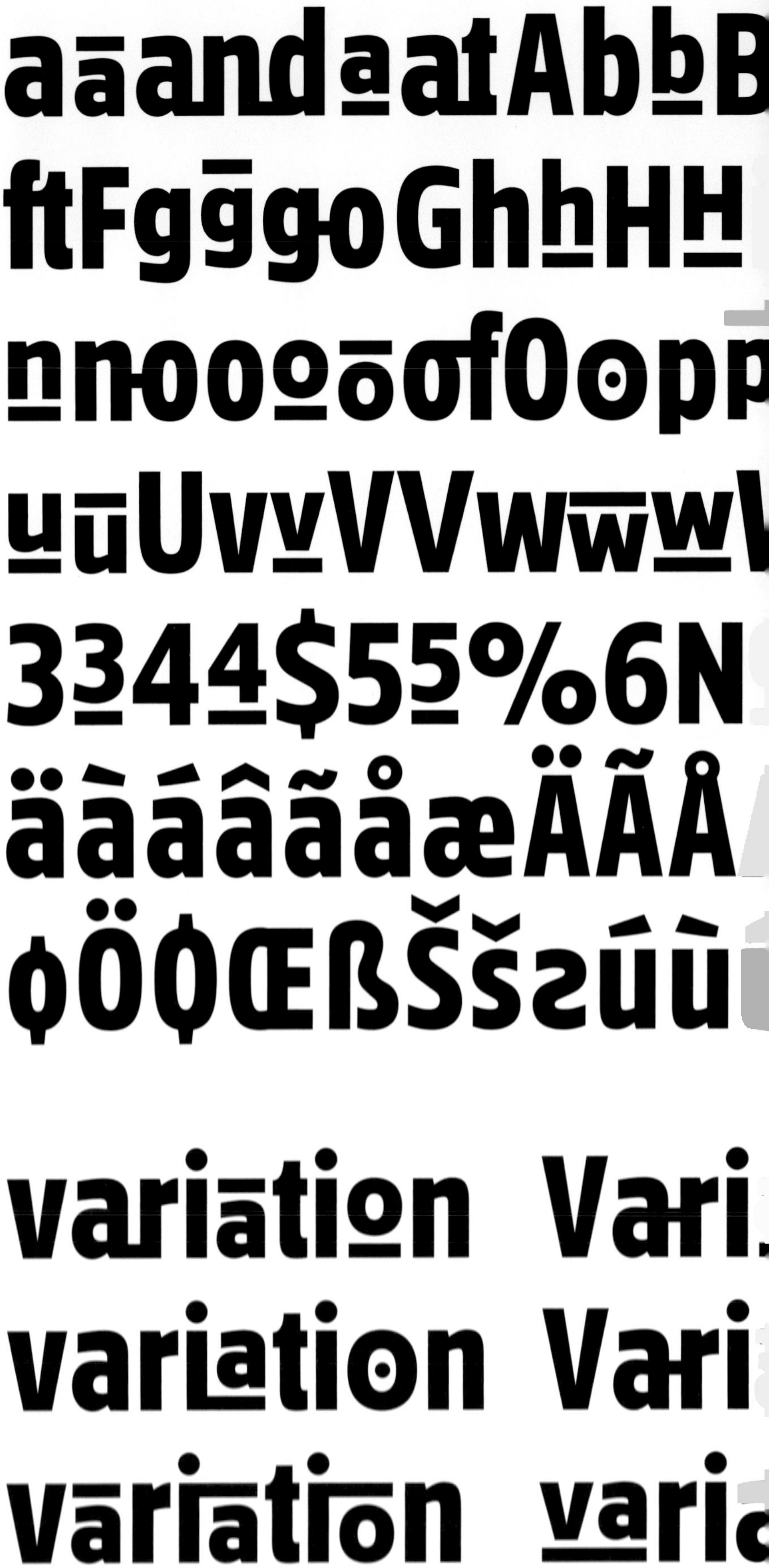

When designers set ›Glasgow‹ intelligently, every word can find its own voice.

a ā and a at A b b B

ft F g ḡ g o G h h H H

n n o o o ō o f O o p p

u u U v v V V w w w W

3 3 4 4 $ 5 5 % 6 N

ä à á â ã å æ Ä Ã Å

ọ Ö Ọ Œ ß Š š ʒ ú û ù

variation Vari

variation Vari

variation varia

cCddoDeeEffffififlfl

ngitIjJkkKllLmmMMnN

qQQrrRssssstStttththeT

xxXyesyouYzzZ11!2?@

¶&88*99(00).,:/¿?»«"

çëèéÊËÈÉIïñÑóôôöõœ

ùÿž©™ÓÓ☯!☯☯←↓!⊗

on variation variation

on Variation variation

on variation variation

Glasgow is Scottish in its stone, European in its urban pedigree, and American in its gridiron plan.

In 1997 MetaDesign London developed the corporate design for the City of Glasgow, which was due to be »UK City of Architecture and Design« in 1999. The concept was based on the ›Glasgow‹ typeface, previously designed by Spiekermann for a competition, and whose overlines, underlines, and many alternative character shapes reflect the work of Charles Rennie Macintosh.

The design's distinguishing features were its logo, large colorful type, and stylized street grid of the city, placed as a motif at an angle

of 9.99 degrees on note paper, posters, and programs. Both parts of the logos »Glasgow 1999« and »UK City of Architecture and Design« are composed of one of the three ›Glasgow‹ fonts; a total of 99 different combinations are possible – 99 being a reference to the year. The typeface was used exclusively for headlines; Frutiger was used as a smaller text face. A palette of 12 different colors indicates different activities during the festival year.

With: Tim Fendley and Robin Richmond

The city of Glasgow is really constructed on a grid at an angle of nine degrees: a good model for a layout grid for 1999

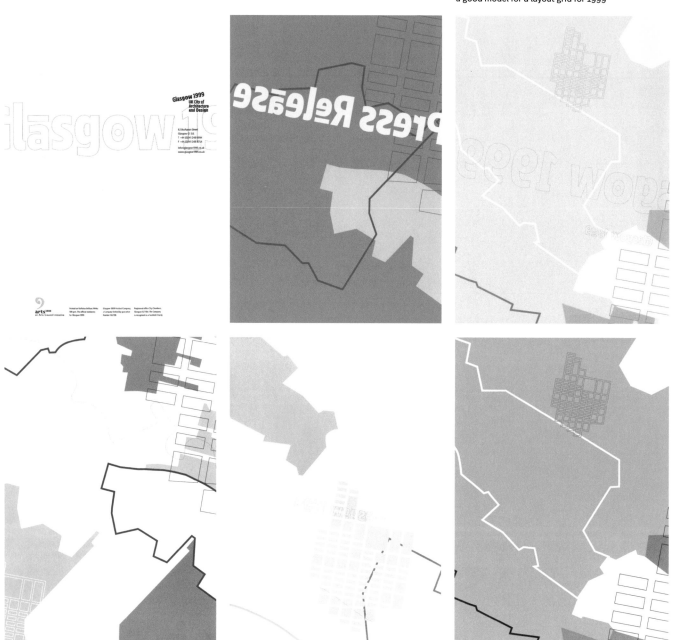

Person

The little house in San Francisco is
barely 3.60 m (12 ft) wide.

In 1996 Susanna Dulkinys bought the narrow-
est town house in the middle of San Francisco.
In 2003 the couple had the 84 square meters
of living space converted. Dark wooden floors,
white furniture (some of it custom-made),
practical fitted wardrobes, and reduced fittings
(e.g. a projector instead of a television) gave
the house a sense of spaciousness. In 2012
the couple moved into a house on the lagoon
in Belvedere.

With: Susanna Dulkinys

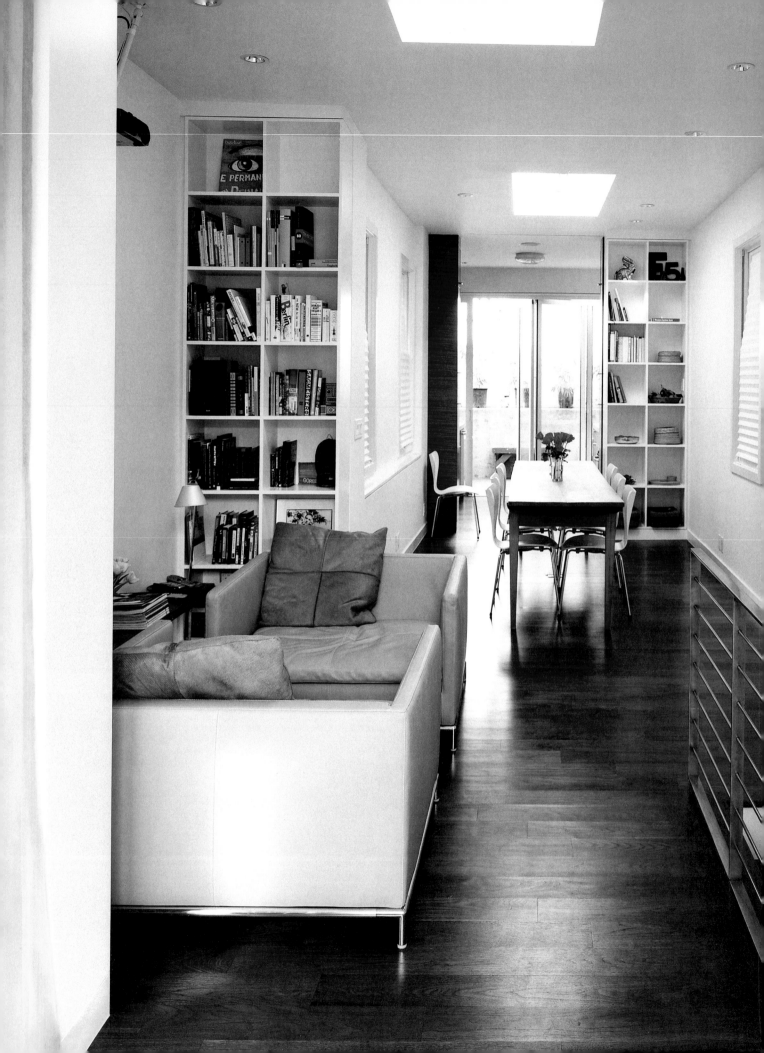

Erik Spiekermann was voted vice president of the German Design Council on November 20, 1997. The nonprofit organization promotes design in Germany. It currently has over 170 members comprising economists and designers, and representing associations and institutes. According to the organization's manifesto:

»We encourage and pursue exchange between nations and cultures, media and politics, businesses and designers, and also between teaching, research, and practice. (…)
We strive to reinforce design as an international economic factor. Our aim is to encourage innovation in design.«

Guests of Nils Holger Moormann's in Aschau, Chiemsee are »arrested« and photographed. The German Design Council meets there once a year for a weekend workshop.

Andrej on Erik

Erik Spiekermann simply knows everything. A lot of the time he knows everything better too. Just recently, for instance, he knew that the design enfant terrible Luigi Colani's father was a master tailor in the Imperial Navy, where he invented the Colani – a warm, midnight blue, double-breasted uniform jacket – which, after the fall of the empire, mutated into a generic term also used in civilian menswear. To be honest, Erik Spiekermann was wrong in this case, but only slightly: he was not Luigi Colani's father, but it is the same family.

Usually someone who knows everything, and more importantly, who knows best about everything, also has an irrepressible urge to communicate. With Erik it is different. Spiekermann goes further. He is a communication machine. He once told me, »If I don't post for 24 hours, my friends (editor's note: 290,000) will think I'm dead.« I don't know whether Erik Spiekermann was born on Whitsun, the day of the Pentecost, but his birthdate, May 30, 1947, might well fall on it. He certainly has the inspiration to inform. He talks at 223 words per minute on a bad day. It is no coincidence that his greatest successes as a designer have involved type, maps, or signs – always information, always through means of imparting knowledge. It is also no coincidence that he was, among other things, president of the International Institute of Information Design.

What drives him? His deep-felt passion for explanation. He could be the last true humanist. I mean that quite seriously, with the greatest respect for Erik Spiekermann. Titans like him tend to tell people directly what they think of someone. He once described me as »diplomatic, but with no slime«. He liked that and so did I.

Andrej Kupetz (born 1968) studied industrial design, philosophy, and product marketing in Berlin, London, and Paris. Since 1999 he has been managing director of the German Design Council in Frankfurt. The German Design Council was founded in 1953 to support German design as an economic and cultural factor.

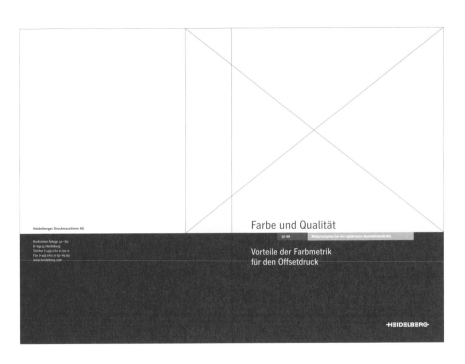

In 1998 MetaDesign was commissioned to do a new corporate design for Heidelberger Druckmaschinen AG. The reason for the redevelopment was the print media trade fair drupa 2000, at which the company wanted to make a reappearance.

Erik Spiekermann explains how they got the commission: »In 1998 our colleagues at BMW Design in Los Angeles asked me to help them talk to Heidelberg, because they were not communicating well with the German engineers. That's where they did the product design for the printing machines. At the same time, Dirk Grosse-Leege, assistant to Hartmuth Mehdorn, who was the director at Heidelberg, was charged with getting the corporate design together. He asked his brother, a product designer in Darmstadt, for a useful address, and he mentioned my name. So I went to Heidelberg with two recommendations.«

With: Oliver Schmidthals and Carolyn Steinbeck

Specially designed ›Heidelberg Gothic‹ is the exclusive house face; a comprehensive grid displays planes of color, reflecting the precision of the printing machines, and arranges products, markets, and themes.

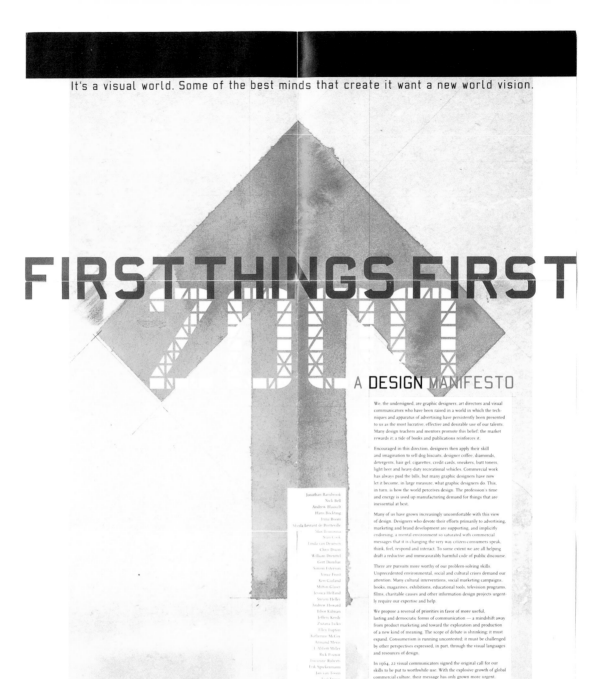

Poster measuring 45.5 × 60.5 cm.
Poster design: Chris Dixon, as an insert
in ›Adbusters‹ (Vancouver, Canada)

In 1999 ›Adbusters‹ magazine revised its manifesto, written in 1964 by Ken Garland. The original version addressed the excessive consumer
society of Great Britain in the 1960s and the
design industry that depended upon it, characterized as lazy and uncritical. The idea behind
it was that design does not play a neutral role
free of value in society, and that it must pose
political questions. The 1999 relaunch also
reanimated this debate. Erik Spiekermann was
the only German designer to lend his signature.

»I am 50 percent guilty, like in a marriage.«
About Erik Spiekermann's separation from MetaDesign

By Johannes Erler

Erik Spiekermann would surely count leaving MetaDesign as his most serious and painful occupational experience. In summer 2000 the news of his departure was like a bombshell in the industry; many wondered how Meta-Design could exist at all without its founder and guiding spirit.

Much has been speculated about what happened at the time. What is certain is that not everybody at MetaDesign was happy, least of all his partners Uli Mayer (as Uli Mayer-Johannsen was still called) and Hannes Krüger, at the way Spiekermann interpreted his position at the company. Previously, numerous important employees had left the company to become independent. This was not due solely to Spiekermann's dominant role, but also to Mayer and Krüger, who increasingly made use of Spiekermann's regular business trips to alter the company course.

The three of them had forged the company into an international design agency that no longer had much in common with the peaceful designer community MetaDesign had started off in. By the turn of the millennium MetaDesign was working for multinational corporations, and its staff had grown to over 200. It was by far the biggest design studio in Germany and, with branches in London and San Francisco, one of the most important in the world.

Mayer and Krüger did not much care for Spiekermann's casual style of leadership. They wanted what they called a »proper company«. They saw Spiekermann as a sort of patriarch who would not allow this to happen, and who clung to his spontaneous approach and public role at the company – a role he lived, since it suited his character perfectly and had got Meta-Design to the successful position it was in.

It is likely that Mayer and Krüger decided together at some point to oust Spiekermann from the company. It was not working out with the three of them, and in situations like that an alliance tends to form with one person losing out.

At the time business was stalling. It was the height of the »new economy« and the huge stock market bubble that had formed around the many startup companies was threatening to burst. MetaDesign's business suffered, since company marketing budgets are the first things to be capped during uncertain economic times.

Spiekermann saw, as his partners did, how there were problems in store for MetaDesign. He anticipated that pure corporate design alone would not be enough. So he contacted several international networks and agencies – on his own, like he usually did – and hatched plans to merge MetaDesign with Frog Design (Hartmut Esslinger's famous product design company), among other things. The rift widened.

And there was more trouble. The overseas branches in San Francisco and London wanted more independence from Berlin and were inclined towards siding with Spiekermann. A few of the original Berlin employees suddenly found themselves in the crossfire; Spiekermann offered them the prospect of a share for their work in building the company in the '90s, which

Mayer in particular was against. Things like that soon strain the breaking point of a company, since they erode trust in the leadership.

In summer 2000 the situation escalated. It emerged that MetaDesign's capital base had become extremely thin. At the same time there were high expenditures for the Spiekermann-initiated move to the MetaHaus in Leibnizstaße (a project he had pursued since the mid-'90s, largely responsible for funding and planning it).

The situation was made trickier when their bank refused a loan, since MetaDesign could not pay their own demands. Mayer and Krüger countered Spiekermann's plans with a proposed merger with the Dutch internet agency Lost Boys. However, the negotiations took so long that any other possible partners dropped out. Supposedly MetaDesign was close to insolvency at that point.

What followed was a bitter divorce that Spiekermann today describes as »straight out of a financial thriller«. According to him things came to a head at an explosive board meeting in summer 2000, during which Spiekermann's lawyer had advised him to leave the company immediately or face the threat of being found guilty of delayed filing for insolvency. With gritted teeth Spiekermann signed his departure, and was no longer managing director. The merger with Lost Boys nevertheless took almost a year. When MetaDesign, with the promise to continue as a brand and company, was practically swallowed up in August 2001, Spiekermann also had to give up his positions as a supervisory board member and shareholder. There was not much money left from the takeover for MetaDesign and its partners, since the bank took most of it. Spiekermann unsuccessfully sued over what he considered the undervaluation of company shares and for the right to continue using the name MetaDesign, and had to pay the court costs. It was the end of his relationship with MetaDesign, the company he had founded 22 years earlier, a relationship that could not have been more productive. Spiekermann was banned from competition and from the company offices. He never entered the completed MetaHaus.

Speaking to him today about that time it is evident that he was left scarred by it, even though he has been back in business for a long time. He still thinks ill of Uli Mayer, and accuses her of coldly plotting the whole thing behind his back. Nevertheless, he said in a 2002 interview in the financial magazine ›brand eins‹: »I am 50 percent guilty, like in a marriage. I didn't behave well; I wasn't clear about what I wanted, because I didn't know myself what it was.« In the same article Mayer says MetaDesign needed stable structures and less improvisation: »Erik wasn't prepared for that, and as a result we had to separate.« The pair are unlikely to make up and be friends.

Shortly thereafter, Hannes Krüger also had to leave MetaDesign. The alliance against the third partner lasted precisely as long as it took to go from three to two. Only Uli Mayer remained. She still leads MetaDesign to this day –

and is successful. MetaDesign has risen once again to well over 200 employees, with branches in Düsseldorf, Zurich, Geneva, San Francisco, and Beijing. For years it has been by far the largest design agency in Germany. On the other hand, the shine from the early years has worn off. MetaDesign might have some big accounts, but creatively it is something of a spent force. Perhaps this is not Mayer's intention, but she favors the really big clients who prefer popular design over brave design.

Today Spiekermann's relationship with Meta-Design is somewhere between relaxed and divided. He still places trust in the brand, and attaches a lot of value to the fact that Meta-Design was founded by himself and two partners in 1979 and not, as sometimes claimed, by Uli Mayer 11 years later. He has no contact with its head office in Berlin, but in Zurich and San Francisco he is still welcome and considered the founder. Quite a few former MetaDesign employees now work at Edenspiekermann.

And then there is of course »RealMeta«, a loose group of former colleagues who occasionally meet in Berlin – their website lists 412. All this proves that MetaDesign is more than just a company, it remains to this day a great idea.

Montage by Jens Kreitmeyer (for Meta-Design's 25th anniversary). Spiekermann liked to make little red books.

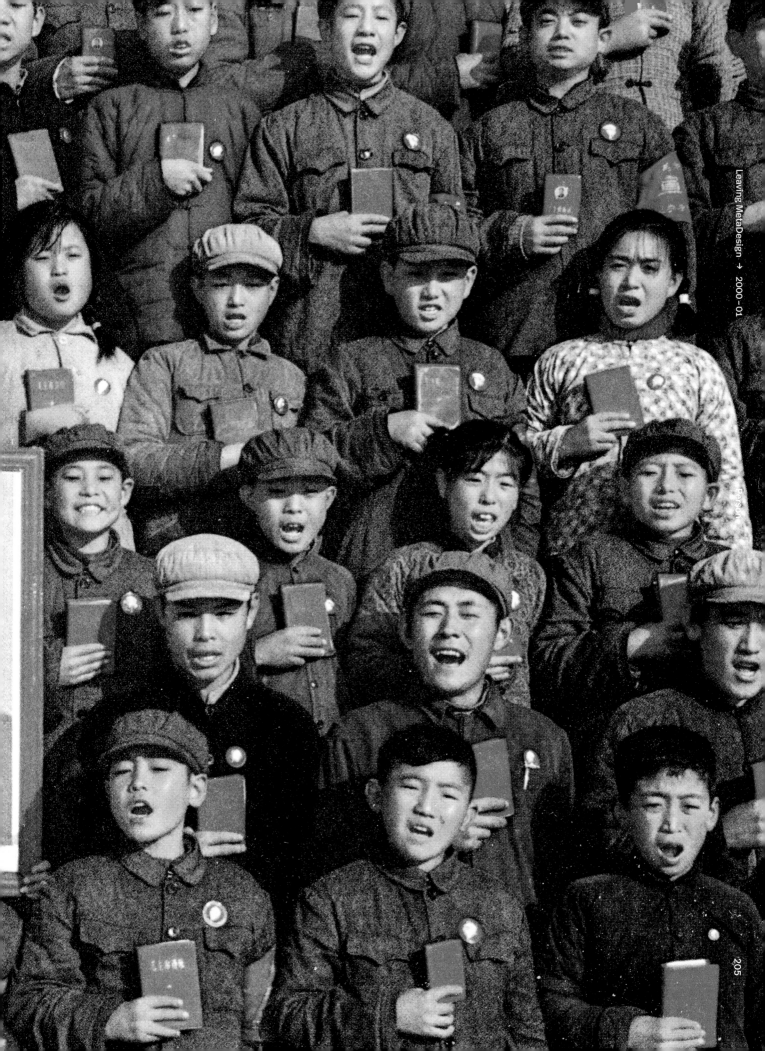

»I am officially unemployed.«

Interview: Petra Schmidt. ›Form‹ 2/2001

Erik Spiekermann is the living legend of corporate design. The dedication with which he built MetaDesign up into an international network proved to be trend-setting for the industry. Now, however, Spiekermann is turning his back on MetaDesign. The branches in San Francisco and London have cut loose and are going their separate ways. Does revolution consume its children?

You are Germany's best known graphic designer, and yet you are unemployed. How come? Actually, I am not a graphic designer, nor therefore the best known. I would sooner describe myself as Germany's most notorious typographer. I'm unemployed because since last year my livelihood no longer depends on MetaDesign; in other words, I don't receive a salary anymore. However, I still own a third of the company, and I'm still on the board of directors. But because I haven't taken on any freelance work since then, I'm officially unemployed.

Did they kick you out? I wasn't kicked out; I resigned from my position as managing director by mutual consent. After that, we were unable to agree on a new way of working together.

Is it true that your partners at Meta wanted to change from being a design studio to a consultancy, and that you were against it? In late 1999 we began talking about the famous New Economy. The idea was that we had to offer more »valuable« consultancy work, since dessign was regarded as inferior by customers anyway. My colleagues wanted to form sub-brands such as Metacom, Metaconsult, and so on. They decided not to after my big protest. My concerns were reinforced by some advice from a colleague in branding. He warned me that the sub-brands would have no content of their own, whereas MetaDesign represented a strong brand.

Why were you against this idea? I'm a designer, not a consultant. Consulting is a subset, as far as I'm concerned. My colleagues went and called our business »Integrated Identity«, using bad English. Nobody could understand what that was supposed to mean, so it didn't work. Now all the talk is about how design ought to return to being top priority. In other words, we've turned 360 degrees and are right back at the starting point.

Are these internal quarrels also the reason why the branches in London and San Francisco fell by the wayside? That's due to a misconceived birth. We only owned a third of the shares of both the London and San Francisco offices.

We were the third partner for both of them. All we could do was stop things by veto from being designed, instead of designing them, and stopping things is no way to run a business.

Up until now it has looked as though San Francisco and London were one hundred percent children of Meta. Were you conning us? No. That was no con. It was one of those typical Spiekermann constructs. I like to put people together, but I'm not so interested in the details. And I still work with those people in England and America.

MetaDesign was the forerunner in the formation of large design networks. Now the company is among the first to have to deal with local interests and cultural differences. Will this also happen to other design companies such as Frog or Ideo? No. Frog is a good example. Content-wise, Hartmut Esslinger is the absolute dictator. The clients want Esslinger. He comes to Germany once every four weeks and takes care of everything. That was supposed to have been the model for Meta, but it didn't work out. We ended up learning a banal lesson: politics is always a local affair. The tiniest details can upset everything. The people on the second floor run things differently from the people on the third floor. And in San Francisco it's different anyway.

Is it true that the San Francisco office wanted to take control themselves? The boys in San Francisco suggested forming a company together. No doubt it would have been based in America, and the managing director would probably have been an American. Sure. I don't really see it being about taking control; it's about management. But it seems that some of my former colleagues would not have been happy with someone else ruling over them. I myself ruled over MetaDesign without ever having wanted to rule. And most importantly, without wanting to exercise power. I had no desire for it, because I'm an old revolutionary student from the late sixties. Today I see things differently.

So you learnt from it? Yes, not to be so afraid of being called power hungry. Things just don't work without authority. Effectively, I was the sole ruler until my colleagues got sick of always having to realize my ideas.

Is it a case of patricide? Absolutely. I unwittingly played the father role, but not consistently enough. On the one hand I was their buddy, and on the other their father. People didn't know where they stood with me.

Are you in favor of hierarchies? We don't need bureaucratic hierarchies, but if I'm responsible for something, then I also have the right to make decisions. It's not important whether the design I'm presenting to the client is my own or not. I don't have to have drawn a single stroke myself, nor written a schedule in order to make decisions. I certainly don't see myself as

a great designer. Designing a company named Meta is my lifetime achievement, of which I'm proud. Motivating co-workers is also a creative endeavor. I once had the idea of buying an Italian village or monastery. At its peak there were 300 people at Meta. If 150 of us had invested 10,000 marks, we could have spent the 1.5 million on real estate. As a cooperative, the company would have been obliged to put some money aside for maintenance from its turnover, not from its profit. That means that when Meta Berlin was doing well, the fountain would get fixed; when San Francisco was doing well, the road would get resurfaced, and if London was doing well, the church would get repaired.

Is there still a chance that Erik Spiekermann will make up with MetaDesign? Yes, as far as I'm concerned. But there's so much pride and jealousy at stake. They squeezed me out with the excuse that it was time to finally make some money. But business was always just fine, and I'd like to see whether it really will be more profitable in future.

How have the clients responded now that you've left? A lot of clients ask about me, and on the last New Year's card my name had suddenly reappeared.

Is it true that you want to start a new company? Competition for Meta? If at all, I'd like to start a virtual company. I have an idea, which I would call Band of Bandleaders, as suggested by Jochen Pläcking, head of the DDB ad agency in Düsseldorf. The concept for it is based on the fact that many companies only find their designers through pitch presentations. A pitch can cost up to half a million marks. My new company would perform a sort of preliminary screening. We know what the tasks involve, and can recommend what agencies the company needs. We also make concrete recommendations. This company would, however, not be a real company – more a network of friends. I'm thinking of top people like Jochen Pläcking, Michael Wolff, founder of Wolff Olins, or other clever folk at Razorfish, Frog, IDEO, or Meta. It should be a case of people having fun and spending a few days together, paid for by a little commissioned work. I imagine us meeting in a nice hotel or villa in Siena, for instance, and working out recommendations. It won't cost the earth for customers, and in exchange they receive expert analysis. From genuine bandleaders, no less! It would be more useful than the expensive stack of papers they'd get from McKinsey and their ilk. But that's just one of many ideas – it may turn out very differently. Whatever happens, I'll work with some of the many people throughout the world whom I've grown fond of over 21 years of MetaDesign, both professionally and privately.

Petra Schmidt was chief editor of the design magazine ›Form‹ from 1999 to 2007. Today she works as a journalist, book author, and design consultant in Frankfurt.

the news magazine regarded as gray and impenetrable by many of its readers almost doubled its weekly readership from 500,000 to nearly a million after its relaunch in May 2001. Spiekermann and three colleagues at MetaDesign London were responsible for the new design. »We reworked the text face, introduced another new typeface for navigation and information hierarchies, improved the access to content via a more clearly designed, two-page table of contents, and, above all, introduced color throughout the publication, which until then had been seen as totally impossible,« Spiekermann says of the most important alterations. All the design and production parameters are documented in detail in a comprehensive handbook, and remain unchanged since 2001.

With: Ben Acornley and Timon Botez

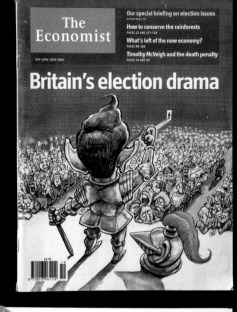

Left: First issue after the redesign from May 12, 2001
Top: Other covers after the redesign

China

Don't worr

BEIJING

The government introdu

THE pursuit of happin
the most consequenti
penned, is an unalienable
sonian sentiment seem

be happy

As part of ›The Economist‹ relaunch, MetaDesign London also reworked the text face EcoNewtype, the magazine house typeface. Spiekermann explains: »The original typeface was designed by Gunnlaugur Briem, the only Icelandic typographer. Then Aurobind Patel changed the typeface in the late 1980s. The first time I saw it, it didn't look too inviting. It was set too tightly, and there was too much noise in the letters, too much stuff. Pages blurred into a very dense gray.«

Spiekermann concentrated on a clearly defined concept: »The design became cleaner in order to counterbalance the weight of the bold a little. The italic wasn't changed so much. Ole Schäfer digitized it in a matter of weeks.«

In 2013 Ole Schäfer once again reworked the typeface for screen use.

With: Ole Schäfer

The new text face for ›The Economist‹ is more open and simple than its predecessor. Less noise in the detail makes it easier to read.

s the country's new mantra

s, runs one of
entences ever
ght. That Jeffer-
o have influ-

unco-ordin
The id
spread ove
early this

──Names──	──Carreido, Elena──	──Names──	──Menu── 2	──Call settings── 2
Aaltonen, Satu	+491235512344	**Jimmy-George**	**Messages**	**Summary after call** On
ADM	@ Elena@mango.com	**Harrison**		**Alarm clock** Off
Erika Svenson	+491665445667	+491235512344		**Language** Nederlands
Eric Svenson	+496787346849			
	+491178364866			
Select Back	Options Back	Options Back	Select Back	Select Back

──Message── 1	──Message── 1	──Message── 1	──Message── 1	──Message── 1
When having (19) pixel high font, it is possible to have more rows	When having 16 pixel high font, it is possible to have more rows and small font text fitted in one …	When having 12 pixel high font, it is possible to have more rows and small font text fitted in one view. Though it requires …	When having 12 pixel high font, it is possible to have more rows and small font text fitted in one view. Though it requires better eyesight…	When having 12 plain pixel height font, it is possible to have more rows and a small font text fitted in one view. Thus it requires even better eyesight to have a look also on the
Select Back	Select Back	Select Back	Select Back	Select Back

Top: Every pixel counts in bitmap fonts on small, simple displays.
Bottom: Nokia's new house face grabs the features of the pixel font and in doing so creates brand recognizability in all kinds of media.

The exclusive ›Nokia‹ corporate typeface was created as part of a project for which Spiekermann had to produce bitmap fonts separately in many different sizes for screens. What they all had in common was the marked contrast between vertical and horizontal strokes. This design principle is what characterizes the typeface, used for the brand until recently.

Spiekermann describes the decision-making process: »It seemed easy to simply draw an outline around the larger bitmap fonts in order to see how the typeface would work as an outline font. The bitmaps all measured 2 pixels in height by 1 pixel in width, with no extra small pixels at the foot of the round letters such as e, c, or s, to simulate round, closed shapes.«

He turned Ole Schäfer's first one-word sketch into rough digital fonts, including a serif version. Finishing touches and production was carried out by Jelle Bosma at Monotype, who also expanded ›Nokia Sans‹ to include other weights, and in so doing created an extensive font family.

With: Jelle Bosma and Ole Schäfer

The first sketch for the print typeface originally consisted merely of an outline around the bitmap font with a few extra details, 2001.

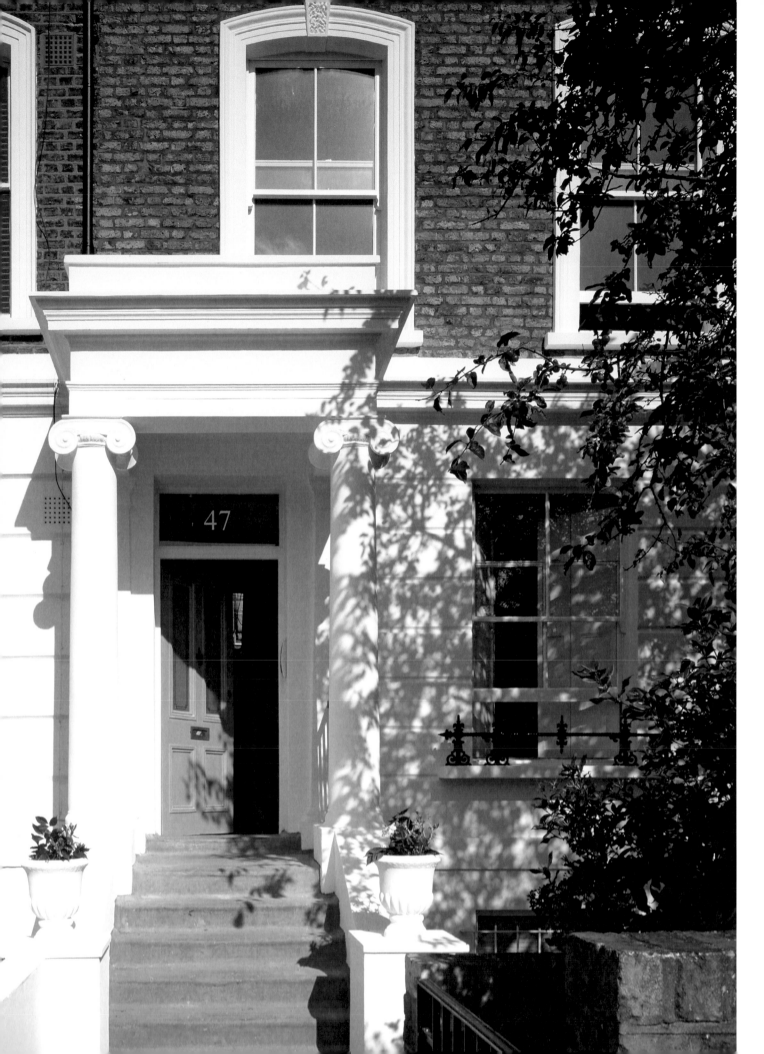

In 2002 Erik Spiekermann bought a typical Victorian-style house in London, which was converted in 2006 by the Anglo-German architects ullmayersylvester. His son Dylan lived there with his family Emi and Luke, along with Dylan's old school friend Joely Hegarty, who rented a room. The loft was converted for Erik and his wife Susanna to use as their London base.

The spatial structure was largely retained, but adapted to modern requirements. The rooms were partially opened up to give them more space. The interior design was intended to be multifunctional – for living and working – like it was in the narrow house in the middle of San Francisco. Also like the house in San Francisco, the dark wooden floors create a charming contrast with the white fitted furniture. The German contractor attached a lot of importance to an environmentally friendly method of construction that retained most of the original stylistic elements.

With: Andreas Lohmann, Cornelia Reckleben, Allan Sylvester, and Silvia Ullmayer

A surprisingly modern loft conversion was added to this classic London terraced house.

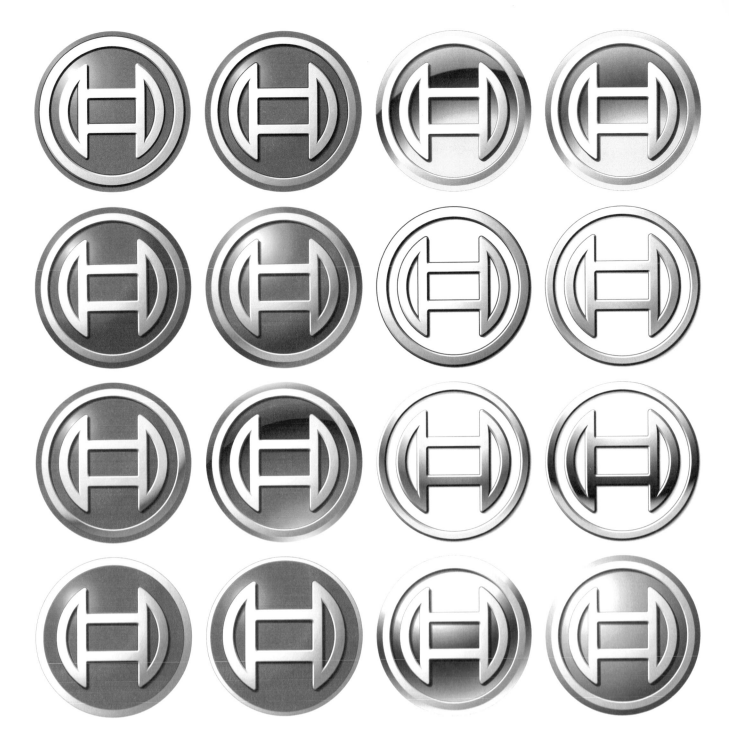

Creating the corporate design for a global corporation such as Bosch presents an appealing challenge. »It encompasses everything from enormous lettering for the head office, through to labeling for precision components. The attention to detail never stops, whether defining the right shade of metal for the symbol, or documenting the control system in dozens of style guides. Charles Eames said: ›The details are no details, they make the design‹,« Erik Spiekermann explains. The armature symbol,

showing an »ignition coil in a circle« was drawn by Bosch head of development Gottlob Honold in 1918. It was reworked by United Designers and combined with the word mark. The new typefaces ›Bosch Sans‹ and ›Bosch Serif‹ by Spiekermann and Christian Schwartz complete the new design nicely.

With: Fabian Rottke, Oliver Schmidthals, and Ralf Weißmantel

The path to depicting the new Bosch
armature symbol led through many
stages: glass, chrome, stainless steel,
in process color printing where required.

BOSCH

Invented for life

›Unit‹ was based on ›Meta‹ as a first draft of a bold headline face that Erik Spiekermann had proposed for Deutsche Bahn in 2002. At the time, however, the company was not interested in a new corporate typeface. So Spiekermann and Christian Schwartz developed the typeface and renamed it ›Unit‹ – as a house typeface for the newly formed United Designers Network.

In 2003 »Meta's grown up, sensible sister,« as Spiekermann described it, was released as ›FF Unit‹ by FontShop. Spiekermann says it is free of puppy fat: »Whereas ›Meta‹ was always a bit unruly and never over-engineered, ›FF Unit‹ is more direct and disciplined. But like ›Meta‹ it's good for small and large type sizes. ›Unit‹ does have fewer of the diagonal strokes and curves that give ›Meta‹ its slightly informal touch.« The family was expanded to include ›FF Unit Rounded‹ in 2008 with help from Erik van Blokland, and ›FF Unit Slab‹ in 2009 with Christian Schwartz and Kris Sowersby.

With: Christian Schwartz, Kris Sowersby, and Erik van Blokland

›FF Unit‹ has seven weights: thin, light, regular, medium, bold, black, ultra.

Christian on Erik

I met Erik when I was a shy and serious first year design student at Carnegie Mellon University. He had come to give a talk on campus, and when it was over one of my professors grabbed me by the arm and said, »You're really into all of this type stuff. You should meet Erik.« I protested that I had no idea what to say, and he said »I'm sure you'll think of something.«

Erik meets a lot of students, so he knew how to keep the conversation going and short. As luck would have it, Erik had a short gap in his schedule the next day, so he agreed to look at my five or six embryonic attempts at type design. I could tell he wasn't expecting much; maybe ›Helvetica‹, or worse, ›Meta‹, with the points pushed around. He flipped through the pages while I braced myself for the worst. Finally he said, »These are not nearly as bad as I thought they would be! Maybe you won't believe me, but I actually like this Hanna-Barbera kind of shit. And you're seventeen? Fuck me. You'll have plenty of time to make serious typefaces, so it's good that you're making this cartoon shit now. You need to learn how to space, though.« I was stunned, and not just by his language. His genuine excitement about letterforms got him past the bumps and uneven spacing, and his advice to learn about spacing was exactly what I needed right then.

Erik and I ran into each other at a few more design conferences before I graduated, and I tried to get his feedback on my typefaces without being annoying or wasting too much of his time. I ended up interning for him at MetaDesign in Berlin during the summer of 1999, right after I graduated. Erik was on the road most of the time, but he was very generous with the limited time he had in Berlin. The biggest lesson I took from watching him deal with both clients and our graphic designer colleagues that summer was that the story that frames a typeface is nearly as important as the typeface itself. A good story gives non-type designers a reason to get as excited about letterforms as a type designer does.

Christian Schwartz (born 1977) is a partner in the type foundry Commercial Type, together with London-based designer Paul Barnes. He has published fonts with many respected independent foundries and designed proprietary typefaces for corporations and publications worldwide. His work has been honored with many international awards. Schwartz lives in New York.

>FF Unit Slab‹ type specimen as a plastic template requires a few adjustments to the letter shapes so that the counters do not fall out. Alexander Roth for FSI

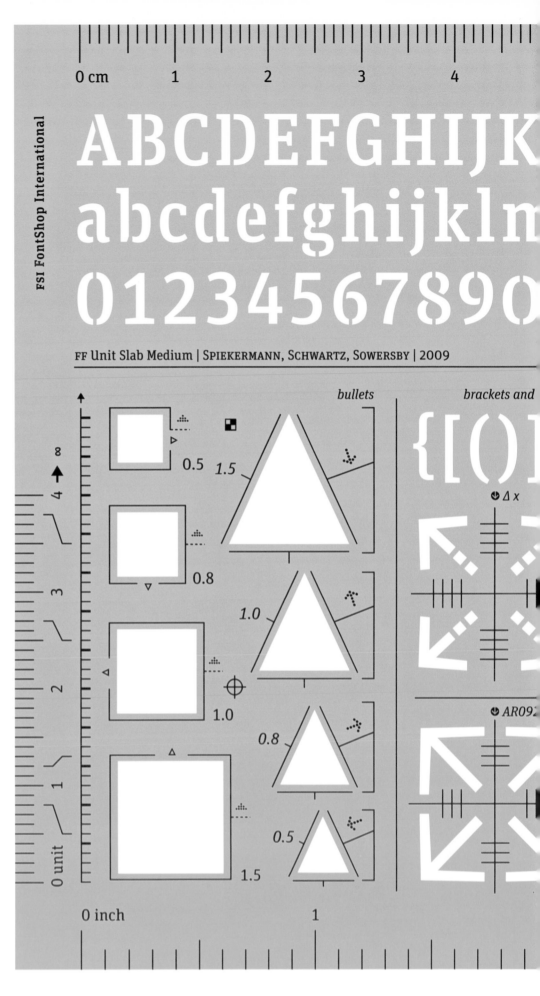

FSI FontShop International

0 cm   1   2   3   4

ABCDEFGHIJK
abcdefghijklm
01234567890

FF Unit Slab Medium | SPIEKERMANN, SCHWARTZ, SOWERSBY | 2009

bullets   brackets and

{[()]

0.5   1.5

0.8

1.0

1.0

0.8

0.5

1.5

0 inch   1

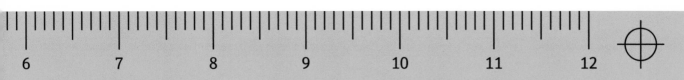

MNOPQRSTUVWXZY

opqrstuvwxyz.:,;-!?

3456789/0123456789

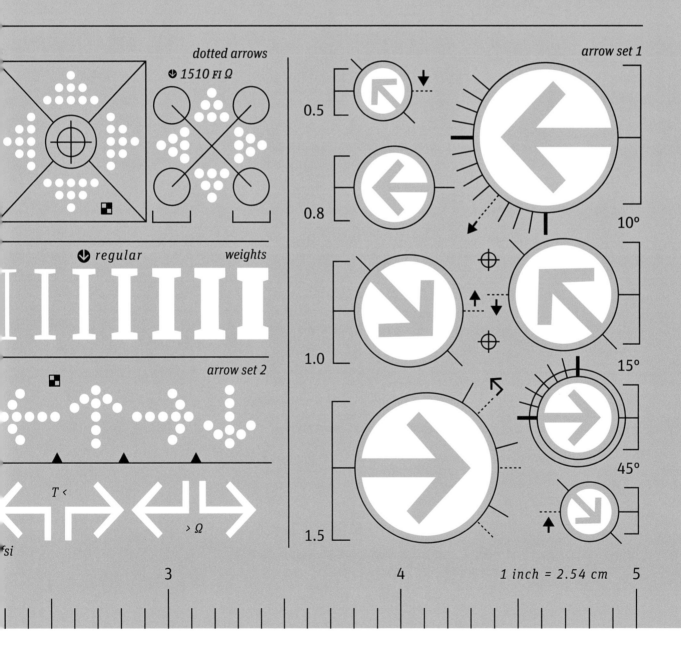

How does United Designers Network work?

After leaving MetaDesign, Erik Spiekermann and his wife Susanna started United Designers Network with an initially small group of freelance designers in 2002.

By Erik Spiekermann

When running a design company, design and business have to go together. Unfortunately these two disciplines often contradict one another. Designers do not want to be told that their work is subject to the need to make money. Nor do they want to be told that customers, not moods, determine deadlines, and those customers do not care to argue about taste. Sales people do not see why ideas for a pitch should not come free, why designers always think a little more than they have to, and why the consumer is not intrinsically stupid.

During the course of our design experience we learn not to see any contradiction in this fundamental conflict. Instead, we see completion. Whoever chooses to become a designer must know that they will be doing commissioned work, and must recognize commercial obligations. But they should also insist that the customer's requests are not set in stone; they are merely requests. Our job is not necessarily to do what the customer wants, but to find out what they really need.

A few decades' experience in design studios – the last of which had a staff of almost 200 – have taught me that it is easier to apply this philosophy with colleagues who have already drawn these conclusions themselves. For this reason we only have designers at our office in Berlin with many years' experience behind them. Not that that makes them all mellow with age and eager to compromise. But all of them know when not to contradict a customer, and when it is time to show some results without back-chat. We also know that in every design studio across the world most jobs disappear in dusty archives once they are completed, and are not entered into competitions.

That does not mean that we do not want to show what we can do. It simply means that every studio first has to work the costs, then work on pleasing the customer, and only then maybe try to probe the boundaries of our profession, and even gain approval from our colleagues and competitors. Vanity is certainly a motivating factor when it comes to pushing the boundaries, and pragmatic assessment of possibilities in the context of a paid project must not stand in the way of the desire to do things better than last time. In the end, however, we should agree that we bear responsibility not only for ourselves, but also for our customers and their clients and users.

The United Designers Network in Berlin consists of ten people at the moment: four male and two female designers; a programmer and a design intern, both men; an office intern and a communications specialist dealing with project planning, both women. Business cards printed »An associate of United Designers Network« also list another programmer and a designer in London, who do not work together in the same office.

This is the core. Around the core are colleagues who work alone or have their own studio. We do projects with these people. What they all have in common is that I like them, I appreciate their work and their experience, and I have worked with them previously, so I know who can do what. Almost all of them have worked at MetaDesign at some point – whether in Berlin, London, or San Francisco.

The new office in Berlin has been going since fall 2002; a small office will open in San Francisco in fall 2003, and London will follow soon after. At most there will be 256 United Designers, but always in a network free of bureaucracy and titles. And they all take responsibility for themselves.

Up to now we have mainly worked on projects with the focus on typography. The product literature for Deutsche Bahn – i.e. the guidelines for the design of all printed matter – was completed in late 2002, as version 1.2. Now we are updating to 2.0, which includes such tasty morsels as the design of business graphics and tables. A new typeface is also being planned. I myself designed a new typeface for our office, called ›Unit‹. We are working on a dealer identification system for a car manufacturer; a quarterly magazine is due a new edition; a website for a small printing company is underway; a large Japanese car manufacturer rang the other day, and a daily newspaper wants to do a relaunch in September. We have plenty to do. It will be difficult to spread the work among everyone while maintaining an overview, having fun, and remaining small. And one day we will even have our own website.

Since we all sit in two rooms within calling distance of each other, there is no separation into teams. Everybody works on the projects with one or more partners, and everybody is free to join in on a discussion. Even though we are a small company, we can take on commissions that would normally go to much larger companies, since we all have experience of big projects. However, we have also learnt that a few people without hierarchies deliver more than twice as many people in a bureaucratically run company where performance is judged by controllers looking at time sheets, rather than by designers looking at content. Interns are as involved in work as they choose to be, and according to their ability. There is no typical drudge work such as copying, scanning, or making coffee.

Everyone does what they are best at. I write most of the time.

With: Susanna Dulkinys as co-founder. Fabian Rottke, Oliver Schmidthals, Marianne Schuler, Julia Sysmäläinen, and Ralf Weißmantel joined later.

The shop in Motzstraße was spacious at first, since it was sparsely furnished with specially made furniture, but it soon became too small.

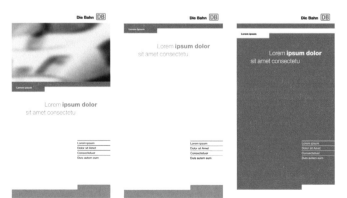

Die Bahn

Niedersachsen-Ticket Single
Pro Nase, pro Tag

15
EUR

Die Bahn macht mobil. Mit dem Niedersachsen-Ticket Single. Und für Familien und Gruppen bis 5 Personen gibt es nach wie vor das Niedersachsen-Ticket für 21 Euro. Beide Tickets gelten montags bis freitags von 9 Uhr bis 3 Uhr des Folgetages in der 2. Klasse in den Nahverkehrszügen der Deutschen Bahn (S, RB, RE) und weiterer Bahnen (EVB, eurobahn, metronom, NordWestBahn) in Niedersachsen, Bremen und Hamburg. In den Verbünden GVH, HVV (Großbereich Hamburg), VBN, VRB und VSN können alle übrigen Busse&Bahnen benutzt werden. Erhältlich in Niedersachsen an DB Fahrkartenautomaten, im Internet unter www.bahn.de/fahrkarten, beim ReiseService über 11 8 61* sowie in DB ReiseZentren und DB Agenturen.

*Einmalig 25 ct/15 Sek., danach 36 ct/15 Sek., ab Vermittlung zum ReiseService 6 ct/7,3 Sek. (Blocktarife inkl. USt. aus dem Festnetz der Deutschen Telekom)

Regio Niedersachsen | Bremen

Spiekermann was able to draw upon his experience with Deutsche Post for the concept of the new corporate design for Deutsche Bahn, the German railway company. When he began working on the concept it was still using the old house face, the ubiquitous ›Helvetica‹. The layouts were later simply reset ›DB Type‹, which remains clear and distinct even in tiny point sizes – on-screen as well as in print.

This approach guaranteed typographic consistency within the system, from the elaborate brand manual through to everyday timetables and advertising posters. The logo strip (umbrella brand with free space) was successfully introduced as another constant element.

Everything by Deutsche Bahn is designed throughout the world by many different agencies according to the same rules based on the ›DB Type‹ typographic system.

With: Fabian Rottke and Ralf Weißmantel

Media for trans-regional (left) and regional (right) transport are important elements within the corporate design system.

Top: Left, an advertisement in the new design still set in ›Helvetica‹, next to it the same motif in the new ›DB Type‹. Bottom: Company-related (left) and internal (right) communication

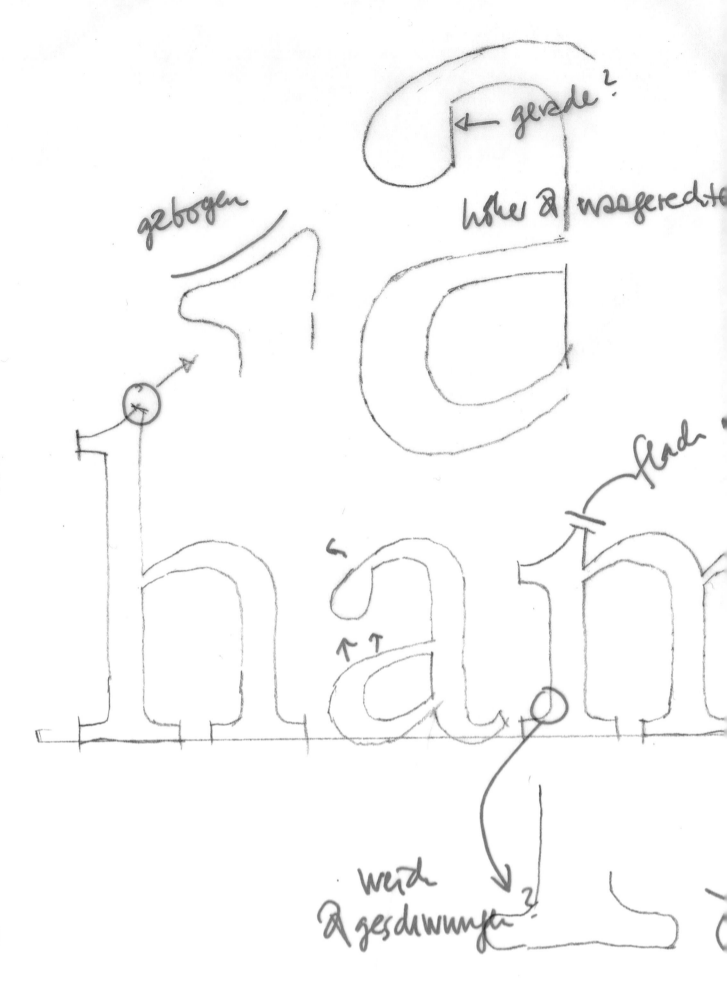

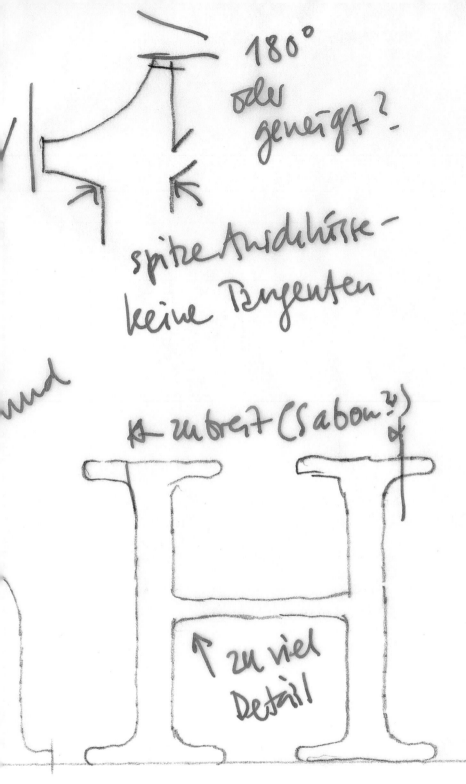

180° oder geneigt?

spitze Anschlüsse – keine Tangenten

zu breit (Sabon?)

zu viel Detail

einfache Steigung

gerade Abschluß?

When one realizes quite how much effort it took to persuade the Deutsche Bahn managing board to accept this typeface, the development of the exclusive ›DB Type‹ becomes an even greater achievement.

It is based on a serif face, from which the sans version is derived, and it replaced the previously used ›Helvetica‹ and ›Stinnes Sans‹. The DB typeface comprises six font families in total: ›DB Sans‹, ›DB Head‹, ›DB Sans Condensed‹, ›DB Sans Compressed‹, ›DB Serif‹, and ›DB News‹. This system satisfies all the company's technical and communications requirements, whether forms and schedules, newspapers and magazines, or advertisements, on-screen or in print. Moreover, it gives a global corporation like Deutsche Bahn a recognizably independent and friendly look of its own.

›DB Type‹ received Gold, the biggest prize at the German Design Award in 2007. Spiekermann describes the project as one of his favorites, since it is »rooted in our own culture – in the most visible way, with the greatest influence«.

With: Christian Schwartz

Spiekermann made these sketches after Christian Schwartz proposed a new serif face.

Typographer

DB BAHN

20 Jahre Einheit.
Euro-Ticket.

Für 20 Euro durch ganz Deutschland. Nur am 2. und 3.10.2010 erhältlich. Gültig vom 3. bis 23.10.2010, einfache Fahrt, 2. Klasse, auch im ICE. Solange der Vorrat reicht. Gleich hier kaufen.

Die Bahn macht mobil. Seit 175 Jahren.

175 Jahre Eisenbahn in Deutschland

www.deutschebahn.com/175

The railway typeface ›DB Type‹ should look as striking as on the poster top left, and be readable in tight spaces with a lot of text in small point sizes, for example on the train schedule, enlarged on the right.

		weiter in Richtung **Köln Hbf**	
10:09	RE 10118	Mülheim (Ruhr) Hbf 10:14, weiter in Richtung **Aachen Hbf**	Gleis 2
10:11	Ⓢ 9	Sa, So | Essen-Borbeck 10:18, **Bottrop Hbf 10:28**	Gleis 7
10:14	IC 2013	**„Allgäu"** Mülheim (Ruhr) Hbf 10:20, 2. bis 30. Sep | weiter in Richtung **Oberstdorf**	Gleis 1
10:15	Ⓢ 1	Mo–Fr | Mülheim (Ruhr) Hbf 10:25, weiter in Richtung **Solingen Hbf**	Gleis 7
10:16	Ⓢ 3	Mo–Fr | **Hattingen (R) Mitte 10:35**	Gleis 11
10:18	RB 11219	Gelsenkirchen Hbf 10:25, weiter in Richtung **Münster (Westf) Hbf**	Gleis 21
10:18	Ⓢ 6	Sa, So, nicht 1. Sep | Kettwig 10:33, Ratingen Ost 10:44, weiter in Richtung **Köln Hbf**	Gleis 12
10:21	Ⓢ 9	Mo–Fr | Essen-Borbeck 10:28, **Bottrop Hbf 10:37**	Gleis 7
10:22	Ⓢ 2	Sa, So | Gelsenkirchen Hbf 10:33, weiter in Richtung **Dortmund Hbf**	Gleis 22
10:23	🚌 SEV	1. Sep | **Kettwig 10:51**	
10:26	Ⓢ 3	Mülheim (Ruhr) Hbf 10:34, **Oberhausen Hbf 10:43**	Gleis 7
10:31	NWB 75348	Essen-Borbeck 10:36, Bottrop Hbf 10:43, Gladbeck West 10:50, Dorsten 11:01, **Borken (Westf) 11:27**	Gleis 8
10:35	Ⓢ 1	Mülheim (Ruhr) Hbf 10:45, weiter in Richtung **Solingen Hbf**	Gleis 7
10:36	Ⓢ 3	**Hattingen (R) Mitte 10:55**	Gleis 11
10:37	IC 131	1. Sep | Wanne-Eickel Hbf 10:49, Recklinghausen Hbf 10:57, weiter in Richtung **Emden Außenhafen**	Gleis 6
10:41	Ⓢ 9	Essen-Borbeck 10:48, Bottrop Hbf 10:57, Gladbeck West 11:05, **Haltern am See 11:27**	Gleis 7
10:42	IC 2421	Fr | Königswinter 12:46, Linz (Rhein) 13:19, Bad Hönningen 13:26, Neuwied 13:38, Rüdesheim (Rhein) 14:38, **Eltville 14:55**	Gleis 1

▼ Duisburg Hbf   Gleis 4

an 10:10
ab 10:12

BahnCard-Kunden erhalten mit "City-Ticket" eine kostenlose
Anschlussfahrt im Stadtgebiet Duisburg + City (Tarifgebiete 23 und 33).

10:20	RE 10510	Oberhausen Hbf 10:26, 2. bis 30. Sep | Dinslaken 10:40, Wesel 10:55, **Emmerich 11:25**	Gleis 13
10:21	RB 31568	**Duisburg Entenfang 10:31**	Gleis 1
10:23	RE 10118	✈ Düsseldorf Flughafen 10:31, weiter in Richtung **Aachen Hbf**	Gleis 4
10:25	Ⓢ 1	Sa, So | Angermund 10:37, ✈ Düsseldorf Flughafen 10:41, weiter in Richtung **Solingen Hbf**	Gleis 5
10:26	IC 131	2. bis 30. Sep | Oberhausen Hbf 10:31, Gelsenkirchen Hbf 10:43, weiter in Richtung **Emden Außenhafen**	Gleis 12
10:30	IC 2013	**„Allgäu"** ✈ Düsseldorf Flughafen 10:38, 2. bis 30. Sep | weiter in Richtung **Oberstdorf**	Gleis 4

Spiekermann Condensed

Illustration: Christian Borstlap

Erik Spiekermann ist Schriftentwerfer und typografischer Gestalter. 1979 gründete er *MetaDesign*, dessen Geschäftsführer er bis August 2000 war. 2003 gründete er das Büro *United Designers* in Berlin.
Erik Spiekermann is type designer and information architect. He was founder (1979) and Managing Director of MetaDesign. In 2003 he founded the studio United Designers in Berlin.

Wie man spricht, so denkt man

Meine Mutter hat mir eingeprägt, auf saubere Schuhe zu achten. Und sie hat mir immer gesagt, dass eine unsaubere Ausdrucksweise auf unordentliches Denken schließen lässt. Vielleicht habe ich meiner Mutter daher die Einsen in Deutsch zu verdanken. Jedenfalls achte ich seitdem auf Wortwahl und Grammatik, oft genug so sehr, dass meine penible Kritik den Kollegen gelegentlich auf den Geist geht. Man kann schließlich nicht erwarten, dass ein Gestalter auch noch schreiben kann. Wenn sich jedoch große Design-Firmen „Agentur" nennen und ihre Auftraggeber als „Kunden" bezeichnen, muss ich annehmen, dass sie sich entweder keine Gedanken über ihre Wortwahl gemacht haben oder dass sie diese Begriffe ernst meinen. Beides wäre gleich schlimm. Ein Kunde kommt in einen Laden und will etwas kaufen, das es schon gibt – ein Produkt oder eine Dienstleistung. Das Adjektiv „kund" ist zur Silbe verkommen (verkündigen, erkunden, kund tun); es war einmal das Partizip jenes germanischen Verbs, aus dem „können" und „kennen" entstanden. Kund ist demnach, was bekannt ist. Ein Kunde weiß also, dass er etwas will, was es schon gibt und was man prinzipiell auch dem nächsten Kunden verkaufen kann. Deshalb haben alle Werbeagenturen bezeichnenderweise Kunden, Anwälte und Berater hingegen Klienten.

Im Englischen gibt es den Unterschied zwischen „customers" und „clients", wie dort die Auftraggeber bei Agenturen, Designern und Anwälten heißen. Leider wurde diese Unterscheidung von unseren sonst so anglophilen, aber offensichtlich nicht ganz so anglophonen Werbern nicht übernommen. Auftraggeber sind Leute, die mir den Auftrag geben, ein Problem für sie zu lösen und dabei zu einem Ergebnis zu kommen, das so neu und ungewöhnlich ist, wie es die Aufgabenstellung, der Zeitrahmen und das Budget eben zulassen. Agenturen heißen so, weil sie ursprünglich nur für das Vermitteln von Anzeigenschaltungen bezahlt wurden. Die fällige Gebühr nennt man heute noch „AE-Provision", wobei AE die traditionelle Abkürzung für Annoncenexpedition ist. Eine Design-Firma kann sich frei entscheiden, ob sie als Agentur, als Büro, als Studio, als Atelier und sogar als Unternehmen in Erscheinung treten will. Aber Vorsicht: Jede dieser Bezeichnungen steht für eine Herkunft, eine Haltung, einen Anspruch.

Speak what you think

My mother always insisted that I cleaned my shoes. And she also impressed upon me the notion that untidy language signifies untidy thinking. My good marks in German (and later: English) at school may owe a lot to her: I certainly have become a stickler for words and grammar; so much so that, occasionally, my colleagues get a little bored with my constant attention to linguistic detail. After all – nobody could possibly expect designers to be able to write as well.

When, however, large design companies refer to themselves as "agencies" and to their clients as "customers", I have to presume that they have either not given this any thought or – worse still – that they mean to use both these labels. A customer walks into a store, wanting to buy something that exists, a product or a service. (I cannot, here, follow the same etymological path that I did in the original German version of this column, where the word "Kunde" – customer – actually means "knowing".) The customer knows what he wants, what there is and what the next customer will also get. Not surprisingly (at least not for the cynic), advertising agencies in Germany have customers, whereas lawyers and consultants have clients.

Our very anglophile, but obviously not so anglophone friends in advertising must have overlooked that fact that in English-speaking countries there are only clients, for agencies, designers and lawyers alike. A client gives me a problem to solve. The result will be as new and unprecedented as budget, time frame and briefing permit – my talent notwithstanding. Agencies are called thus because originally they would only buy advertising space for a fee, for a cut. The creative work was done by the newspapers and magazines themselves. A design company can decide whether it wants to refer to itself as a firm, an office, a studio, or even an atelier. But beware: each of these labels stands for a history, a future, an attitude. You may just be judged by what you say about yourself.

Michael on Erik

My first encounter with Erik Spiekermann occurred more than 20 years ago. Although I had just met him, he immediately seemed like an old friend. In that first conversation, he mentioned to me how much he disliked designers who were so eager to please their clients that they would compromise their designs before they were asked to. He gave this syndrome a name: preemptive acquiescence. I'm not sure how that would translate into German, or even if it can be translated into German. But hardly a week goes by that I don't think of those two words, usually in silent self-admonishment.

I would like to think I am a slightly better designer as a result, or perhaps only a slightly more guilty one. In any case, the ability to reduce complex ideas to unforgettably simple forms is a remarkable gift. Erik can do it with typefaces, or images, or words, and – seemingly – in any language. That is the mark of a great designer, and that is what Erik Spiekermann is.

Michael Bierut (born 1957) is a partner in the New York office of Pentagram, a teacher at the Yale School of Art, co-founder of DesignObserver.com, and author of 79 ›Short Essays on Design‹.

The redesign of ›Bauwelt‹, a weekly architectural publication with a circulation of 12,000 was undertaken by Erik Spiekermann with Fabian Rottke and Eva Schekkor at United Designers Network in 2004. The first newly designed issue appeared on October 1, 2006. The typefaces employed were ›Unit‹, an uncomplicated sans serif by Spiekermann; and a more traditional serif face, ›Proforma‹.

Felix Zwoch, the chief editor, wrote on page 2: »The layout is more severe, the pictures are arranged in a more block-like manner and form their own story alongside the text, set apart from it by white islands. We agreed on an ambivalent formula for the redesign: cautious radicalization.«

With: Fabian Rottke and Eva Schekorr

Three double spreads from the second issue after the redesign from October 6, 2006. Magazine size: 23.5 × 29.7 cm

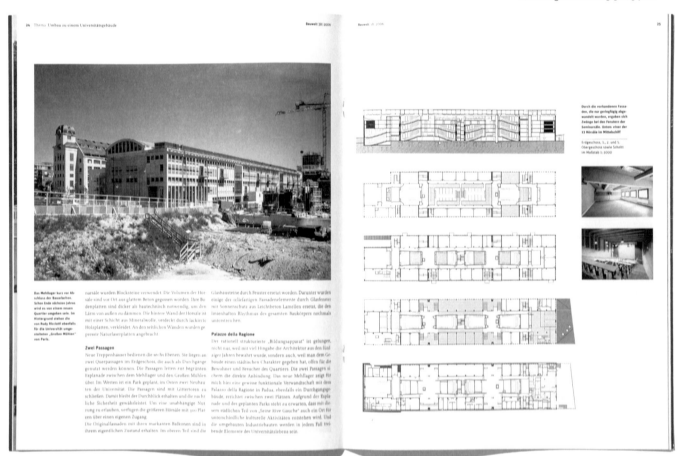

Theaterschaden in Potsdam

Text: Michael Kasiske Fotos: Dieter Leistner

Am 22. September wurde das Hans Otto Theater Potsdam mit der Uraufführung von Thorsten Beckers Schauspiel „Katte" eröffnet. Das neue Haus an der Schiffbauergasse ist ein Werk von Gottfried Böhm und seines Sohns Paul. Die aufdringlichen Dachhauben erklären sich weder räumlich noch konstruktiv. So sind sie als Produkt des Augenblicks zu verstehen und leben allein von der Idee eines Zeichens.

Wer weiß schon, dass der italienische Industrielle Gianni Agnelli fast zwanzig Jahre lang Juror der seit 1979 verliehenen Pritzker Architecture Prize gewesen ist. Trotz dieser Konstante wurde die als „Nobelpreis der Architektur" apostrophierte Auszeichnung so unterschiedlichen Protagonisten wie Richard Meier, Christian de Portzamparc, Oscar Niemeyer und Gordon Bunshaft verliehen. Die zweite Entscheidung, an der Agnelli beteiligt war, fiel zugunsten eines deutschen Architekten. Das war 1986, und der Ausgezeichnete hieß Gottfried Böhm. Bis heute wurde kein anderer Vertreter unseres Baukultur so reichen Landes wieder mit dem Preis geehrt. Eine Tatsache, die anlässlich der Eröffnung von Böhms jüngstem Projekt, dem Hans Otto Theater in Potsdam, stets erwähnt wird.

Jung, so muss präzisiert werden, ist lediglich das fertiggestellte Bauwerk. Auf den Zeichentischen der Familie Böhm – neben seiner Frau sind die Söhne Stephan, Peter und Paul fakultativ Projektpartner des inzwischen 86-Jährigen – geisterte das Vorhaben seit über zehn Jahren herum. Das ist keinesfalls salopp gemeint, erst recht nicht für das Potsdamer Theatervolk, dem der Neubau jahrzehntelang wie eine Schimäre erschienen sein muss.

Ein Rückblick

Das im Zweiten Weltkrieg zerstörte Schauspielhaus von 1795, laut Giebelinschrift „Dem Vergnügen der Einwohner" gewidmet, wurde trotz Diskussion um den Wiederaufbau 1966 gesprengt. Somit musste sich das Landestheater, das nach dem von den Nationalsozialisten in den Selbstmord getriebenen Schauspieler Hans Otto benannt ist, weiterhin mit einem ehemaligen Tanzsaal begnügen. Erst in den achtziger Jahren wurde ein Neubau am Alten Markt beschlossen, der im Rohbau stand, als die Mauer fiel. Wegen der unglücklichen städtebaulichen Disposition verfügten Stadt und Land den Abriss, gegen den Widerstand des Theaters.

1995 kam Böhm ins Spiel

Beim Wettbewerb um einen Neubau an der Schiffbauergasse, unweit des heutigen Standorts, setzte sich Böhm gegen 13 Konkurrenten durch. Drei von hohen Pylonen abgehängte Fächer unterstreichen die Orientierung des Entwurfs zum Wasser. Das Preisgericht gab dem Architekten mit auf den Weg, „die gewählte, übertrieben expressive Gestaltung des Baukörpers im Hinblick auf seine Fernwirkung zu anderen stadtbildprägenden Gebäuden zu überprüfen".

Es folgen mehrere Einsparungsrunden, desgleichen ein Gutachterverfahren für den Umbau und die Erweiterung des bis her genutzten einstigen Tanzsaals in der Innenstadt, das Böhm erneut für sich entscheiden konnte. Freilich wurden immer wieder Stimmen laut (und eine war die von Böhm), zur Schiffbauergasse zurückzukehren, wo sich inzwischen die Sparten Kinder- und Jugendtheater, das Tanztheater, die Kulturinitiative und das Theater T-Werk angesiedelt hatten. Schließlich

---

en neues Entree der Universität von Süden und Osten her. Es ist davon auszugehen, dass trotz aller Unterschiede – der andere Standort, die andere Bauaufgabe – der Neubau ohne Koolhaas so nicht entstanden wäre.

Die Fassade von Périphériques kann ohne Wenn und Aber als modisch bezeichnet werden. Es wurde wieder eine doppelte Haut gewählt, bei der die äußere Schicht aus perforierten Aluminiumelementen mit unterschiedlich großen runden Öffnungen zusammengefügt ist. Diese Haut ist als Spielerei zu sehen, da sie sich im Vergleich zum klar gegliederten Fassadenaufbau von Albert nicht erklärt. Hinter der über alle Obergeschosse reichenden Musterwand verbergen sich eine im Aufbau einfache Stahlkonstruktion mit schmalen Wartungsgängen und eine Glasfassade ohne Besonderheiten. Bei hell erleuchteter Fassade hat dieser Aufbau einen besonderen Reiz. Das Gebäude wirkt dann extrem leicht und scheint sich sogar aufzulösen. Mit Geschick wurden in die Fassaden über zwei und drei Geschosse reichende Loggien eingeschnitten, die bis zur zentralen Halle reichen. Die Architekten bezeichnen sie als „grandes Fenêtres urbaines". Dadurch wird die Käfigartigkeit der gleichförmigen äußeren Haut aufgebrochen. Bei näherer Betrachtung wird deutlich, dass die Fassaden nicht präzis dem Gitter von Jussieu folgen, sondern leicht abgewinkelt wurden. Damit bekommt das Gebäude eine eigene Dynamik.

Die Qualitäten des Baus sind die einzigartige Raumgestalt und die Organisation des großen geschlossenen Atriums, wo sich durch die Farben Violett, Grün, Orange und Rosa unverkennbar die einzelnen Ebenen mit ihren unterschiedlichen Funktionen voneinander absetzen. Die Erschließungsebene dient der Anmeldung und Betreuung der Studenten im ersten Semester. Es folgt die Ebene der Verwaltung, darüber stapeln sich fünf Ebenen Seminarsäle, Labore und Computerräume.

Die Studenten erreichen komfortabel per Rolltreppe die Seminar- und Laborräume. Auch die Rückfront der Betonfertigteile der Atrium-Fassade und die Böden erhielten die Farbe der jeweiligen Ebene. Oben: der große Saal für die Prüfungen im Sockelgeschoss. Längsschnitt durch das Atrium mit den Brücken, in denen sich auch Arbeitsplätze befinden. Unter dem Neubau verläuft die Metro-Linie 7.

Schnitt im Maßstab 1:1000

Possessing chara
is everything.

A person with *chara*
or deceive, and kee
a sense of duty tow
his family and hims
a salesman popula

Robert Bosch

ter

The ›Bosch‹ corporate typeface is a contemporary interpretation of ›Akzidenz Grotesk‹ that works well on headlines, due to the contrast between the light and bold weights.

ter does not lie
s his word. He has
rds his client,
f, and that makes
and respected.

The impetus for the new ›Bosch‹ corporate typeface was ›Akzidenz Grotesk‹, which was released at the end of the 19th century by the type foundry H. Berthold AG in Berlin. It had long been used as the company typeface. The plan was to modernize it for modern reading habits. The question was: what might a warmer Grotesque look like? With this in mind, ›Scheltersche Grotesk‹ was, to a certain degree, crossed with ›Akzidenz Grotesk‹ and expanded to include all language systems, including Greek and Cyrillic. A serif face was added later to replace ›Baskerville‹, which had previously been used. Thus, two font families were created:

›Bosch Sans‹ and ›Bosch Serif‹. Christian Schwartz, who drew the typefaces and expanded the families, recalls that »Bosch had a long history with Akzidenz Grotesk, but the typeface was slowly getting old. As part of the new corporate design program United Designers were working on, Erik Spiekermann asked me how I would imagine a rounder ›Akzidenz‹.« The result was ›Bosch Sans‹, a simple but pleasant sans with a characteristic semi-cursive italic.

With: Christian Acker, Joshua Darden, and Christian Schwartz

Jubiläumsausgabe: 10 Jahre Le Monde diplomatique auf Deutsch

Deutsche Ausgabe
Mai 2005
05/11. Jahrgang
Deutschland: 3,60 EUR
Ausland: 3,90 EUR

LE MONDE
diplomatique

05

Die Europäische Union diente lange als Ersatzideal einer desillusionierten Linken. Mit der europäischen Verfassung ist das vorbei.
▶ Seite 4/5

Die einstigen Kolonien von einst arbeiten zusammen. China investiert zunehmend in Afrika – und schafft selbst neokoloniale Strukturen
▶ Seite 14/15

Das deutsche Kaiserreich war weniger ein Nationalstaat, als ein Imperium: in seinen ostmitteleuropäischen Gebieten lebten viele Völker
▶ Seite 16/17

Die ungarische Nation bildete sich auf Grundlage der von ihr selbst erzählten Mythen. Die Bedeutungen sind wie bei allen Nationen veränderlich
▶ Seite 18/19

Das Imperium der Star-Wars-Filme ist nicht nur ein politischer, sondern auch ein religiöser Mythos: Taoismus trifft Kapitalismus
▶ Seite 21

Künstler dieser Ausgabe: ZWELETHU MTHETHWA (siehe Kasten S. 2) hier: Detail aus der Serie: Ticket To the Other Side, 2003

Der irakische Untergrund – aktiv und blind

von David Baran und Mathieu Guidère

Die UNO reformieren

von Ignacio Ramonet

Vor 60 Jahren, am 25. April 1945 – der Krieg war noch nicht zu Ende –, begann auf Einladung der Vereinigten Staaten, Großbritanniens und der Sowjetunion die Konferenz von San Francisco. Dort wurde am 26. Juni die Charta der Vereinten Nationen unterzeichnet, die am 24. Oktober 1945 in Kraft trat. Damit begann eine neue Ära.

Tatsächlich war die Gründung der UNO von Roosevelt, Churchill und Stalin schon im Februar 1945 auf Jalta beschlossen worden. Man wollte damit die Vormachtstellung des im Krieg gegründeten Direktoriums auch zu Friedenszeiten aufrechterhalten. Zweck der neuen Organisation war nicht die Gründung eines „Tribunals der Nationen", sondern die Schaffung einer neuen Weltordnung, deren Bestand die drei Supermächte garantieren sollten.

Sehr bald jedoch beendete der Kalte Krieg das ehrgeizige Projekt. Die tiefen Differenzen zwischen den Siegermächten und der wiederholte Rückgriff auf das Vetorecht führten schließlich zu einer Lähmung der UNO. Die Nord-Süd-Problematik äußerte sich in zahlreichen lokalen Konflikten, in die sich die Supermächte auf der Seite ihrer jeweiligen Verbündeten einmischten. Im Laufe der 1980er-Jahre kam es immer häufiger zu „Kriegen geringer Intensität", die eine Art internationale Anarchie zur Folge hatten. Der Niedergang der UNO schien unaufhaltsam.

1989, als mit dem Fall der Mauer der Kalte Krieg zu Ende ging, entstand neue Hoffnung. Da Ost und West sich nicht mehr feindlich gegenüberstanden, schien nun die Anwendung der Charta von San Francisco möglich. Die Veto-Waffe wurde begraben. Im November 1990 billigte die UNO den Einsatz von Gewalt gegen den Irak, der in Kuwait einmarschiert war. Doch bereits seit März 1999, als die Nato in Kosovo intervenierte – und erst recht seit dem Einmarsch der englisch-amerikanischen Koalition im Irak im März 2003 –, steht die Autorität der Weltorganisation, die beiden Interventionen nicht zugestimmt hat, erneut in Frage.

Während George W. Bushs erster Amtszeit drängten die USA die UNO mehr und mehr an den Rand und reduzierten sie auf die Rolle einer humanitären Organisation. Die USA sind mit ihrer militärischen Schlagkraft in der Lage, überall effizienter einzugreifen als die Blauhelme. Und ihr Mitgliedsbeitrag ist so hoch, dass die USA den Bestand der Organisation ernsthaft gefährden könnten. Heute hängt das Handeln der Vereinten Nationen vom Goodwill der Vereinigten Staaten ab.

Eine Reform der UNO scheint daher unerlässlich. Kofi Annan hat eine grundlegende Umgestaltung der Organisation angekündigt, die noch immer zu stark vom Klima der unmittelbaren Nachkriegszeit geprägt ist. Wir brauchen ein „San Francisco II", eine neue konstituierende Konferenz. Zu den drei wichtigsten Veränderungsvorschlägen gehört eine Aufstockung der Zahl der ständigen Mitglieder des Sicherheitsrats. Deutschland und Japan müssen in dem Weltdirektorium ebenso ihren Platz finden wie die regionalen Mächte: Indien für Asien, Brasilien für Lateinamerika, Südafrika für den Schwarzen Kontinent, Ägypten für die arabische Welt. Denkbar wäre auch eine Einbindung der regionalen Großorganisationen: der Afrikanischen Union, der Organisation der amerikanischen Staaten sowie einer noch zu gründenden asiatischen Organisation. Bei einer Erweiterung des Sicherheitsrats muss man auch über die Zukunft des Vetorechts neu reden.

Zweitens wird die Schaffung eines Wirtschaftssicherheitsrats ins Auge gefasst, der sich mit Entwicklungsfragen und der Verschuldung der armen Länder befasst. Und drittens soll eine zweite, beratende Versammlung mit Vertretern der Zivilgesellschaft geschaffen werden, von Bürgervereinigungen, Gewerkschaften, sozialen Organisationen aus Wissenschaft, Kultur, Umweltschutz usw. Diese drei Maßnahmen wären ein entscheidender Schritt, um die UNO aus ihrer Erstarrung zu lösen. Sie würden ihr die Autorität und Effizienz verschaffen, die sie so dringend braucht. ◀

Bei uns gelten die Attentäter im Irak als Killer, die nichts erklären, sondern nur terrorisieren. Doch viele der bewaffneten Widerstandsgruppen betreiben im Internet intensive Öffentlichkeitsarbeit und rechtfertigen ihre brutalen Aktionen. Darüber, dass sie keine politische Perspektive haben, schweigen sie lieber.

Die Gruppen des bewaffneten Widerstands im Irak haben ihre Politik des Terrors seit langem durch eine Propagandastrategie ergänzt. „Medienkommunikation" ist das Schlüsselwort – es wäre ein Fehler, nur auf die besonders brutalen und drastischen Bilder und Texte zu schauen. Denn unter den unzähligen Äußerungen dieser Gruppen finden sich nicht nur einschüchternde Deklarationen, sondern auch erstaunlich viele intelligente und nüchterne Analysen, die detailliert darlegen, wie man den Gegner besiegen könnte.[1]

Die abscheulichen Videoclips sollten also nicht den Blick auf die zahlreichen Beiträge verstellen, die – oft in Spielfilmqualität – anschaulich machen, was den Gruppen wichtig ist. Da gibt es „Konferenzen" in Koran-Arabisch über die Herstellung von Sprengkörpern, aber ebenso professionelle Werbespots von neuen Gruppierungen, die sich der Öffentlichkeit präsentieren wollen.[2] Manche Gruppen setzen stark auf Öffentlichkeit; sie unterhalten „Informationsabteilungen", deren Verlautbarungen auf zahlreichen Internetseiten erscheinen. Einige Homepages fungieren wie Online-Presseagenturen und werden mehrmals täglich aktualisiert.[3] Auf einer Website rief kürzlich ein Aktivist dazu auf, „mit allen Mitteln gegen die Missachtung des Widerstands in den Medien vorzugehen"[4].

Warum unternimmt der bewaffnete Widerstand so große publizistische Anstrengungen? Stellt diese Form der Propaganda tatsächlich eine wirksame Waffe dar? Nur weil sie im Westen nicht gut ankommt oder gar kontraproduktiv wirkt, muss diese Propaganda nicht ungeschickt oder schlecht gemacht sein.

In den Debatten über den Irakkonflikt dominieren heute die Wortmeldungen der Regierungen in Washington und in Bagdad. Ihre Gegner werden zunehmend unhörbar und machen fast noch mehr durch die Detonation ihrer Sprengsätze und die Aufregung um Entführungen auf sich aufmerksam. Was sie verbal mitteilen, erscheint uns eher nebelhaft.

Vieles davon ist Flüsterpropaganda, oder es wird nur in Form von Flugblättern, Videos oder Verlautbarungen unter häufig wechselnden Internetadressen verbreitet, und zwar fast ausschließlich auf Arabisch, bleibt also für ein anderssprachiges Publikum so gut wie unzugänglich. Die Rezeption dieser Äußerungen ist deswegen stark eingeschränkt. So sind die Videos meist bar aller Argumente. Sie enthalten nur bestimmte Schlüsselbilder, denen eine dauerhafte Wirkung zugeschrieben wird. Die Auswahl, die im Ausland getroffen wird, entwertet die Beiträge: Man nimmt sie nur als Äußerungen eines „fanatischen" und „blutrünstigen" Feindes wahr, der keine Interessen vertritt oder Einschätzungen verbreitet, sondern nur bestrebt ist, seine blinde Gewalt zu rechtfertigen. Wenn, so die Folgerung, der Gegner nur die Sprache des Terrors spricht, darf man ihm gar nicht erst zuhören – denn sonst hätte er schon gewonnen.

Irhab, der Terror, gehört unbestreitbar zu den Instrumenten des politischen Widerstands im Irak. Einige Gruppen distanzieren sich von diesen Methoden, andere halten ihn für religiös legitimiert und politisch angemessen. So hat ein anerkannter sunnitischer Korangelehrter zwar deutlich zwischen „erlaubtem" und „nicht erlaubtem" Terror unterschieden – aber zugleich befunden, dass die Aktionen nicht unter die erste Kategorie fallen.[5] Und der angesehene irakische Scheich Muhammad al-Alusi hat 2003 in einer Fatwa, einem Richtspruch, sogar geäußert, dass der *dschihad*, der heilige Krieg, ohne *irhab* nicht zu denken sei.[6]

Militärisch gesehen erscheint der Terror als Teil einer psychologischen Kriegführung. Im Internet werden mittlerweile ausgesprochen differenzierte Analysen verbreitet. Hier legen offensichtlich erfahrene Kämpfer dar, wie Terrorakte gegen „Kollaborateure" einen Keil zwischen die irakische Regierung und die Bevölkerung treiben können oder wie man mittels Entführung von Ausländern auch entfernte Länder unter Druck setzen kann.

Mit dem Feind und seinen potenziellen Bündnispartner kommunizieren die bewaffneten Gruppen also – mit ganz wenigen Ausnahmen[7] – in der Sprache des Terrors. Doch mit der Verbreitung ihrer Bilder und Texte verfolgen sie auch noch andere Ziele, weil sie diese offenbar eher an die eigenen Kämpfer und das Lager der Sympathisanten richten. Ihre Inhalte sollen demnach der Verständigung innerhalb eines dynamischen Netzwerks von Gruppen dienen, die immer wieder neue Bündnisse schließen oder sich voneinander abgrenzen – ohne die Wirksamkeit des Terrors aus dem Blick zu verlieren. Jede Gruppierung braucht ein eigenes Image und muss sich mit allen anderen auseinander setzen.

Die Propaganda der Terroristen verfolgt also großenteils die Absicht, ihre Aktionen bekannt zu machen und um Anerkennung zu werben – bei Verbündeten, Konkurrenten oder potenziellen

▶ Fortsetzung auf Seite 8

Left page: Title page of the first German
edition after the relaunch, May 2005
Top: Other double pages from inside the
first edition

›Le Monde diplomatique‹ is a French monthly
newspaper with analysis and comments on international politics and culture. The newspaper
has appeared in French since 1954. Thirty-eight
editions in a further 16 languages add up to a
total print run of around 2.2 million worldwide.

The German edition first appeared in 1995.
United Designers Network designed a relaunch
for its tenth anniversary in 2005. Unlike its

French counterpart, the German version's graphics
are highly structured and tidy. However, one
French feature has been retained for Germany: Most articles are illustrated with drawings,
paintings, or artistic photographs. UDN used the
typefaces ›Benton Gothic‹ and ›Arnhem‹, which
were specially adapted for the job.

With: Fabian Rottke, Eva Schekorr, and Ralf Weißmantel

Typographer

Linz A1

221

Wiental

Gürtel-West

The Austrian authorities introduced
›TERN‹ as the standard typeface for all
transport signs in the country. Unfortunately they used the condensed version,
which is not as easy to read as the
regular weight, specially designed for
the purpose.

As part of the sixth European Union research framework program in 2005, the Trans European Road Network, TERN for short, decided to commission a new typeface for signage on European highways. The aim was to harmonize the use of pictograms and written information on standard transport signage and dot matrix displays throughout Europe.

Erik Spiekermann recalls: »My task was to make the ›VMS fonts‹ (Variable Message Signs) – fonts for electronic displays on highways. I compared all the fonts used by the various highway operators in Europe, including DIN 1451, the British Transport alphabet, etc.« In addition to the characters for electronic displays, consisting of dots only, the client later decided that they also wanted a typeface for

print, i. e. an outline version. The first version of the typeface now called ›TERN‹ still consisted merely of an outline around the bitmap shapes. Ralph du Carrois was brought onboard when an italic, condensed, and narrow version were requested.

›TERN Condensed‹ has since become standard on all roads in Austria. The project was very complex and time-consuming, lasting until 2010. A total of 3,000 symbols or pictograms were designed, and several test series produced. »We wanted to expand the family properly, and while we were at it improve the ugly characters we made for the tests that weren't up to scratch,« Spiekermann explains.

With Ralph du Carrois

Author

The signs at Düsseldorf airport lit up the building, displaying themselves but not the content.

I use different typefaces because I want them to give places an identity.

Like all airports, Düsseldorf faces competition; in Europe there is an airport every 100 kilometers, so Düsseldorf needs to sell itself as a brand.

›Im Reich der Schilder – Wie Leitsysteme uns durchs Leben führen‹ (›In the realm of signs – how signage guides us through life‹) was a documentary about symbol and pictogram development for intercultural communication through signage at airports, railway stations, or on regional public transport. The program, produced by TV broadcaster ARTE, included an interview with Erik Spiekermann about his information and signage system for Düsseldorf airport: »After five or six years, a system tends to become a little untidy, a bit like one's wardrobe at home. Every now and again one has to go in and tidy it up. (…) In the '60s and '70s interiors were often dark, comfortable spaces, so the idea was for signs to stand out by becoming lamps. (…) In other words, if I put black type on a light green background, and then make the green backlit, I have a lamp – and I don't like looking straight at a lamp. Adding type to a lamp creates more distraction than information.«

The numbers from ›FF Meta Bold‹
consist of sand-blasted cast aluminum,
10 cm high.

Designer

Rob Forbes, founder of the American furniture and design company Design Within Reach (DWR), commissioned Spiekermann to design four different exclusive series of house numbers. The results were ›Classic‹, Spiekermann's translation of ›Bodoni‹ (designed in 1788 by Giambattista Bodoni); ›Contemporary‹, with ›Meta Bold‹ as its model; ›Industrial‹, as a negative stencil shape, and finally ›Tech‹, Spiekermann's crack at constructing numbers without diagonals.

The house numbers had different colors and materials, from enameled brass to extruded anodized aluminum, laser-cut painted steel, and water jet-cut polished stainless steel. The numbers were sold with drill templates, to make it easier to space them properly. The stencil face ›Industrial‹ is now available as house numbers exclusively through mail order from MAGAZINE in Germany.

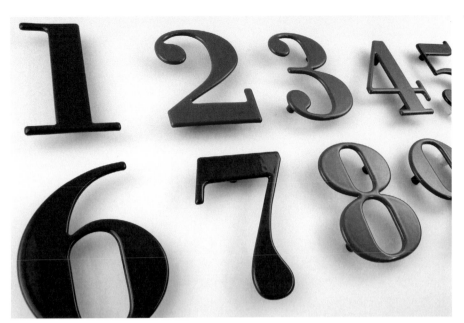

The »classic« house numbers are en-ameled from Spiekermann's version of ›Bodoni‹; the polished stainless steel numbers with visible screw heads are a new set of numbers without diagonal shapes, and the painted steel stencils are reminiscent of industrial labels.

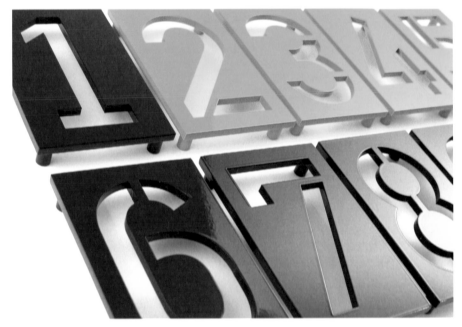

BIRKHÄUSER

BIRKHÄUSER

Michael Erlhoff
Tim Marshall
(Hg.)

BIRKHÄUSER

BIRKHÄUSER

Designer

ɔ)ⲥ GUTE GESTAL

The logo of this Swiss book publisher revokes the classic reading band. Birkhäuser specialize in architecture and design, and the ribbon appears in white on red, the Swiss national colors.

When the designers discovered that the syllables BIRK and HÄUSER related to each other as 5:8 in length, the next design element was established. This is the proportion of the Golden Section, as in the Fibonacci series 5:8:13:21, etc. All elements of the cover design are thus related: images, headlines, text areas.

The typeface used in the logotype is ›Akkurat‹ by Swiss designer Lorenz Brunner. It is complemented by ›Arnhem‹.

With: Eva Schekorr and Ralf Weißmantel

To coincide with the FontFont label's fifteenth anniversary, Jan Middendorp and Erik Spieker-mann published the book ›Made with FontFont‹ in 2007. It demonstrates what can be done using the foundry's typefaces, and contains contributions by Akira Kobayashi, Rian Hughes, Emily King, Ellen Lupton, and Reza Abedini,

among others. Its 368 pages are divided into five chapters that tell FontShop's story with pictures. Many illustrations depict FontFonts used for anything from instructions for wearing Indian saris to packaging for Viagra.

With: Jan Middendorp

Right: Pages from the book. The type specimens are mostly by the typeface designers themselves.
Overleaf: Henning Wagenbreth designed this page for his typeface ›FF Prater‹.

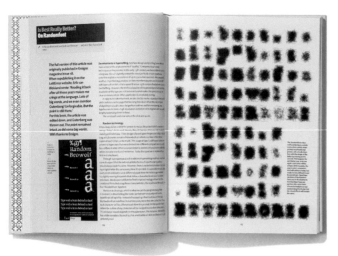

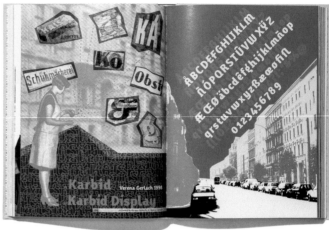

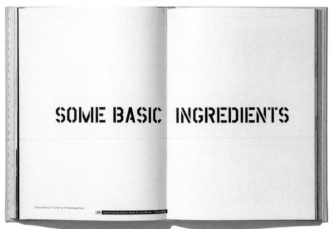

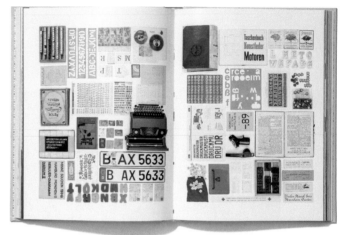

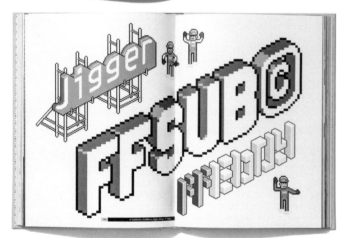

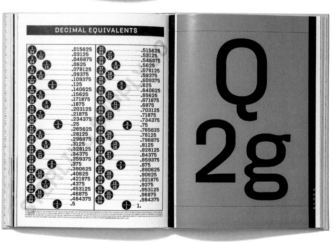

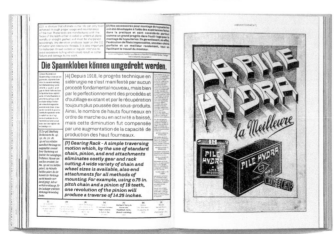

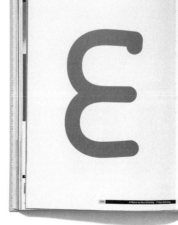

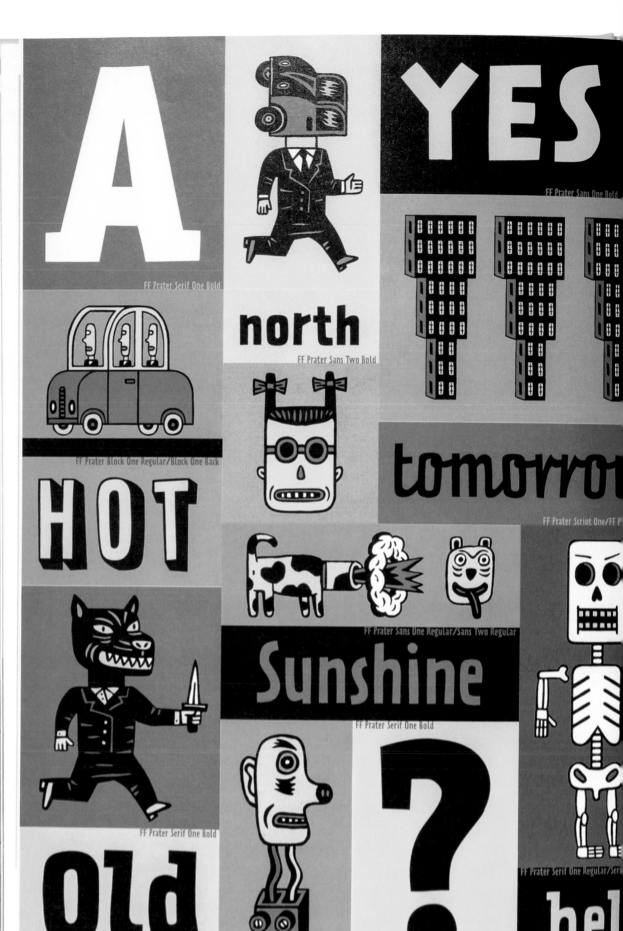

A
FF Prater Serif One Bold

YES
FF Prater Sans One Bold

north
FF Prater Sans Two Bold

tomorro
FF Prater Script One/FF P

FF Prater Block One Regular/Block One Back

HOT

Sunshine
FF Prater Serif One Bold

FF Prater Sans One Regular/Sans Two Regular

FF Prater Serif One Bold

old

?

FF Prater Serif One Regular/Seri

hel

eaven

FF Prater Serif One Regular/Serif Two Regular

FF Prater Script One Regular/Script Two Regular

!

, Two Regular/Block Two Back

FF Prater Sans One Bold

yesterday

COLD

FF Prater Sans One Regular

Thunderstorm

FF Prater Serif One Bold

New

FF Prater Sans Two Bold

south

FF Prater Serif One Bold

Z

NO

FF Prater Sans One Bold

all illustrations: tobot-automated illustration systems

font design: Steffen Sauerteig, Henning Wagenbreth

g +  =

In 2006 United Designers Network created a new corporate design for this German Apple distributor. The logo and typeface symbolize the connection between analog and digital. The g is analog at the bottom and becomes digital towards the top, which illustrates the motto: »experience digital ideas«.

A vivid green is the new company color. Bright and cheerful orange, blue, and light gray colors indicate prices, news, and other offers. Susanna Dulkinys devised the logo and, with Julia Sysmäläinen developed the icons for ›Gravis Hybrid‹, one of the two exclusive fonts. Spiekermann and Christian Schwartz created ›Gravis Rounded‹ (the new headline font), based on ›FF Unit‹, which also works for body text.

With: Susanna Dulkinys, Tina Schoepflin,
Christian Schwartz, and Julia Sysmäläinen

GRAVIS

The Gravis logo was the impetus for a complete typeface with pictograms in the same style.

In September 2007 Spiekermann and his wife Susanna Dulkinys moved into their new town house in Berlin Mitte, virtually next door to the Foreign Office. Like their house in San Francisco, the shape of the building is tall and narrow – just 6.5 meters wide. The interior is entirely made of concrete, and is as modern as its thermally insulated glass facade.

The garage is at street level, with offices on the floors above it. The private office is on the fifth floor, with the couple's grand Leica camera collection. There is a mechanical hoist for those brave enough to fetch a book from the top shelf of the two-storey-high bookshelf. The showpiece of the sixth floor is the stainless steel kitchen by bulthaup. The bedroom is on the top floor.

With: Susanna Dulkinys

The printing press in his house has since moved to a workshop (see page 280).

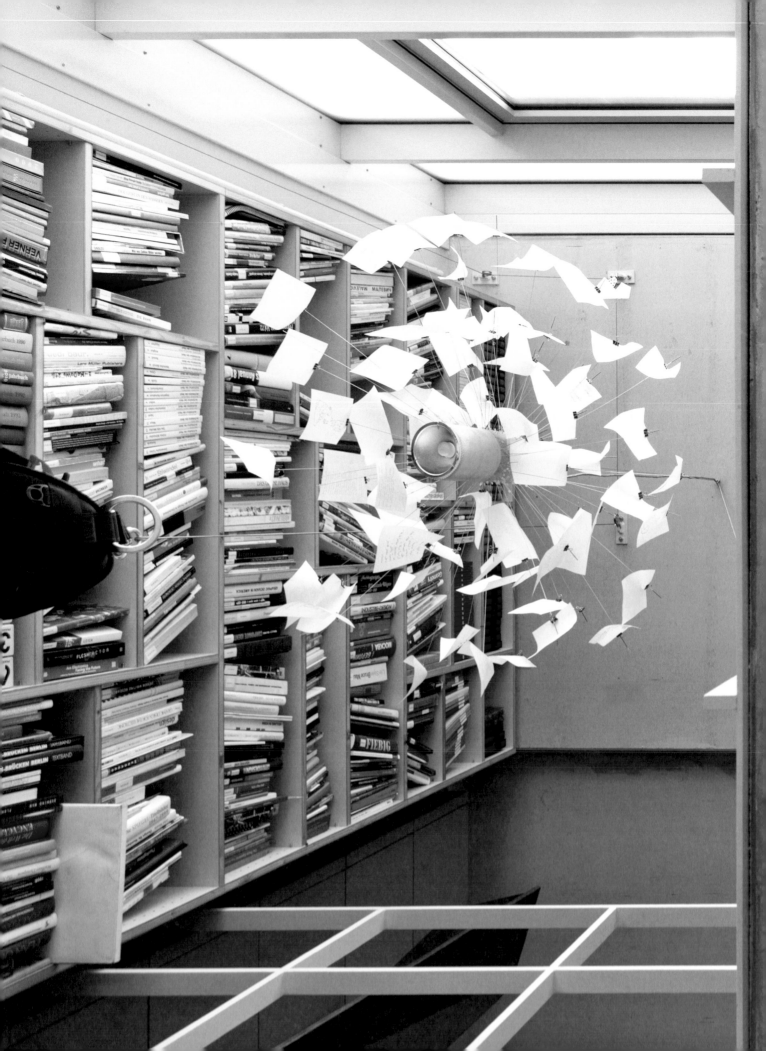

The top of the six-meter-high bookcase can only be accessed with a mechanical hoist (the Zettel lamp is moved to one side), which can just be seen on the left.

I'm obviously a typomaniac – an incurable if not mortal disease.

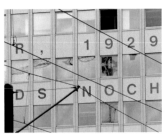

I just love, I just like looking at type. I get a total kick out of it: they are my friends. Other people look at bottles of wine or whatever, or, you know, girls' bottoms. I get kicks out of looking at type. It's a little worrying, I admit, but it's a very nerdish thing to do.

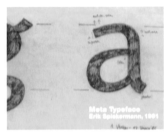

A real typeface needs rhythm, needs contrast, it comes from handwriting, and that's why I can read your handwriting, you can read mine. And I'm sure our handwriting is miles away from ›Helvetica‹ or anything that would be considered legible, but we can read it, because there's a rhythm to it, there's a contrast to it.

The crème de la crème of the design world get to speak in Gary Hustwit's documentary about the history, spread, and use of ›Helvetica‹: Mattew Carter, Massimo Vignelli, Wim Crouwel, Hermann Zapf, Neville Brody, Stefan Sagmeister, Michael Bierut, David Carson, Paula Scher, Jonathan Hoefler, Tobias Frer-Jones, Experimental Jetset, Michael C. Place, Norm, Alfred Hoffmann, Mike Parker, Bruno Steinert, Otmar Hoefer, Leslie Savan, Rick Poynor, and Lars Müller all talk about their experience with the omnipresent typeface.

Erik Spiekermann confirms his dislike of it: »Most people who use ›Helvetica‹ use it because it's ubiquitous. It's like going to McDonald's instead of thinking about food.«

**Erik, the Spiekermann
of SpiekermannPartners**

Friedrichstraße
Berlin, Germany

Make this my default location

With contracts for well-known clients plus
a growing number of employees, United
Designers Network kept expanding. Thus, the
structure and character of the branding and
design agency needed to be changed – it was
renamed SpiekermannPartners and went
from being a limited liability company (GmbH)
to a stock corporation (AG).

Furthermore, Erik Spiekermann was tired of
clients still thinking he was with MetaDesign.
His name had long since become a brand. »The
partners suffix is important: I'm not alone
after all, like I wasn't alone before. Since I'm not
such a great designer I need people with
other talents around me. Perhaps that's my
real talent: finding good people and motivating
them,« he explains.

With: Robert Stulle, Fabian Rottke, Marianne Schuler,
Susanna Dulkinys, Ralf Weißmantel and
Oliver Schmidthals

The staff at SpiekermannPartners in Friedrichstraße, Berlin. From the company brochure, 2007

Designer

DARK
CHOCOLATE
"FRUITY"
Peru
70 % Cacao
Organic
Fair Trade Beans
60 g (2.12 oz)

In 2007 Susanna Dulkinys and Erik Spieker-mann developed the corporate design for the chocolate manufacturer TCHO in San Francis-co – from the name to the logo, website, and packaging.

First they tackled the logo. It was supposed to be simple but strong: »As though it were stamped on the side of an oil tanker,« says Dulkinys. Whereas the »T« is as straight-lined as possible, the remaining letters give the impression of having been broken off a chocolate bar.

The inspiration for the design came from European banknotes. The different patterns were printed in gold on the packaging. The ›flavor wheel‹ indicates the flavor of the cocoa, determined by cocoa beans rather than add-itional ingredients.

With: Susanna Dulkinys, Jane Metcalfe, and Louis Rossetto

As precious as banknotes and there-fore printed with gold guilloches: dark chocolate by TCHO

Designer

The corporate design for Messe Frankfurt was a big challenge for SpiekermannPartners, because of the institution's 700-year history. The first thing to do was arrange the many different product brands into some sort of hierarchy, in order to provide the trade fair organizer with a single recognizable umbrella brand. The Messe Frankfurt image was designed to invoke sympathy, trust, and satisfaction.

Adrian Frutiger's typeface ›Univers‹ was exclusively adapted for the job by Erik Spiekermann, who renamed it ›Messe Univers‹. It plays a major role in the brand design in Latin, Greek, and Cyrillic script. Another innovation was that (nearly) all the brand names were written in lowercase.

With: Fabian Rottke and Katrin Wenke

Greeting cards with margins in 5:8 proportion in the company colors

256

»Achtung! Erik Spiekermann« is the title of Erik Spiekermann's monthly column in the British architectural magazine ›Blueprint‹. »That headline has to do with the Brits' continuous stereotyping of us Germans as heel-clicking, order-shouting men in jackboots. I have long since learnt that the best way to live with that pre-occupation is to go along with it,« Spiekermann writes on his blog.

Column from April 2009. The articles deal with thoughts on visual communication and developments in society that affect design. The publisher does not specify a topic.

ACHTUNG! ERIK SPIEKERMANN

25

Drawing is the greatest means of communication for architects and designers with or without a brief. Getting the ideas on to paper is another matter, but a foolproof strategy for designing does exist

When Le Corbusier 'designed' the Cabanon in 45 minutes, what exactly did he do? Did he scribble a complete building – plan, elevation and section – on to the back of that proverbial envelope? Or was it just a doodle that was then deciphered and translated by assistants who were familiar with the master's handwriting? We all know that a quick sketch can be both the beginning of a process or the end of it. It all depends on what you call 'designing'. Does it only happen while actually working on paper or screen, or does a problem, a brief, or a project leach itself to the inside of your head without you even knowing it's there? And then come out, fully developed as a building, a painting, a chair, a lamp, or a bookcover?

For myself, I have identified five distinct strategies to start designing. (They apply to writing as well.)

1. AVOIDING
Need the car washed, emails answered, receipts filed? When the deadline already casts a long shadow on your conscience, you suddenly feel the urgent need to tidy up all those loose ends. You can only sit down to work when everything is tidy, in your mind and on your desk. I have to go through this phase every time. By now, I recognize it and use it to actually finish all these little annoying tasks that keep piling up.

2. THINKING
Our brain is an amazing tool: unlimited capacity, works at the speed of light and is incredibly flexible. Unfortunately the problem is never lack of capacity but retrieval. We know it's in there, but cannot find it. Just sitting down (after having cleaned up the desk, of course) and putting your mind to a problem for a few minutes is an amazing experience that we hardly ever allow ourselves to enjoy. If you do not look at emails, switch off the phone, keep your door

and the books on your desk closed, you'd be surprised how quickly you start getting things sorted, in your head at least.

3. SKETCHING
After a few minutes of plain old pondering the issue at hand, it can be useful to start making marks on paper. Not necessarily proper mind maps or floor plans, but anything that will still

MELVIN GALAPON

be visible a day later. Picturing thoughts, even if you cannot draw at all, is amazingly effective, especially if you have to remember what you thought about a day later or communicate it to someone else. You can buy expensive software to help with this, but I find that the time spent mastering the learning curve of a new application would be better applied to learning to sketch simple little drawings. Everybody – especially clients – loves a designer who can actually draw. As a type designer I am loathe to admit that a picture does sometimes say more than a thousand words.

4. RESEARCHING
Knowledge is good, and looking around for signs of other intelligent solutions to a similar task may help. Gathering background facts also builds confidence and may help convince a client. Looking at too many annuals full of other peoples' work can be dangerous though: you either get totally discouraged because everybody else's stuff looks so good,

or you – inadvertently, of course – imitate something, often later, when you think you cannot recall anything you've seen.

5. COLLECTING
This is an ongoing activity. I do not know one designer, writer or architect who doesn't keep things that are 'interesting'. That doesn't always have to amount to a complete collection of Braun hi-fi equipment from 1957 until today, as in my case, but anything that you could not throw away at the time survived for a good reason: it spoke to you. If you can make your

collection bring back that original inspiration, you can trigger parts of your brain that may have encountered the same problem before, even without knowing it at the time.

All these strategies work. One after the other, if not in the order mentioned above, but more often than not concurrently. We carry a design brief around with us all the time, not just during the hours we can actually charge a client. It just needs the right moment to manifest itself. That's why Le Corbusier probably knew exactly what he wanted to do when he took out his pen. What these anecdotes fail to mention, however, is that after the first strike of genius, most of us have to spend much, much longer getting scribbles made into plans, ideas turned into prose and proposals into commissions.

WE ALL KNOW THAT A QUICK SKETCH CAN BE BOTH THE BEGINNING OF A PROCESS OR THE END OF IT. IT ALL DEPENDS ON WHAT YOU CALL 'DESIGNING'

Erik Spiekermann set up MetaDesign and FontShop, and worked in London from 1973 to 1981. A teacher, author and designer, he travels between the Spiekermann Partners offices in Berlin, and homes in London and San Francisco.

Courier New	11. Jan	19,70 €
Andale Mono	11. Jan	19,70 €
Verdana	11. Jan	19,70 €
Lucida Sans	11. Jan	19,70 €
Arial	11. Jan	19,70 €
Georgia	11. Jan	19,70 €
Calibri	11. Jan	19,70 €
Axel Regular	11. Jan	19,70 €
Axel Bold	**11. Jan**	**19,70 €**

›Axel‹ uses less space than comparable typefaces without losing legibility. Or it looks bigger with the same space.

In 2008 FontShop Germany planned to release a typeface that was space-saving and good for tables and small text sizes. Spiekermann devised a simplified version of ›Officina‹ for them called ›Axel‹, whose name caused quite a stir on the web. Spiekermann explains the name: »All my typefaces have had four-letter names since the early '90s, ›ITC Officina‹ being the exception, since it was older. Really, I wanted to call the new typeface Exel, but my colleagues at FontShop Germany were worried that a certain big company in Seattle wouldn't see the funny side. I don't think it really would have been a problem, but I didn't want to cause the company any bother just in case. So we call it ›Axel‹ instead.«

With: Ralph du Carrois and Erik van Blokland

Erik on Erik

My first contact with Erik Spiekermann was in the last year of the eighties. Just van Rossum, one year my senior, had ventured out to West-Berlin to work at MetaDesign. His description of the projects (a typeface catalog!), the clients (Berthold! Apple!) and the daily routine (type! computers!) at Meta were intriguing.

When Spiekermann visited Amsterdam for a symposium, Just introduced me to Erik. After a brief talk he invited me to come and work on a type project. Barely graduated from the Royal Academy, this vote of confidence and the promise of adventure was intoxicating. I ditched my carefully planned internship at a Dutch design agency (forms!) and took the train east.

I was not aware of the earlier instances of MetaDesign or the who's who of German typography. I walked into the Meta office at Motzstraße that summer and I saw friendly faces (Bobby! Thomas! Alex! Petra! Joan!), funny type posters on the wall, and a computer on every desk.

Those computers were a big deal. At that time there were three in the whole Royal Academy, I had bought a Mac SE, and experimented with making bitmap fonts and ran a custom version of Petr's Ikarus M. However, apart from Just, Petr, and a handful of others, computing just was not part of the design practice.

But it definitely was part of design at Erik's MetaDesign. He had probably sketched the things he wanted to do with these machines decades before they were available. All this seemed logical at the time, in retrospect it was not at all.

Many design agencies struggled with digitization for years and even when they did buy computers often they didn't know what to do with them. There are many other metrics by which to measure Erik's achievements, but I've always been impressed with his understanding of technology. Maybe not always the how – I remember a heap of gadgets and devices that almost worked, in this respect he struggled like the rest of us. But he has an uncanny sense for the why.

Having access to these resources, Spiekermann's enthusiasm and profound love of type and typography made that office a very welcoming environment for all sorts of ideas. The first random fonts were conceived and constructed at Motzstraße. Spiekermann followed the work closely and encouraged us at every step. Eventually Just and I left a reunited Berlin, Spiekermann remained a good friend and a terrific colleague. I can only guess why he so confidently hired Dutch type geeks right out of school and gave them toys and work, but I'm grateful he did.

Erik van Blokland (born 1967) runs the innovative font label LettError with Just van Rossum, and created such trailblazing typefaces as ›Beowulf‹, ›Trixie‹, ›Hands‹, and ›Federal‹. He lives and works as a typeface designer, designer, and illustrator in The Hague.

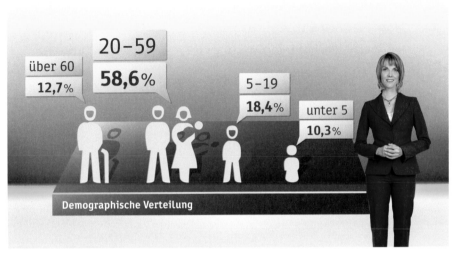

An interdisciplinary team worked for three years on the redesign of the TV news programs ›ZDF heute‹ and ›ZDF heute journal‹. Edenspiekermann worked as consultants on the marketing strategy and information design. The team working around Erik Spiekermann also created the typeface for pop-ups and icons, and the infographics concept. A new font family emphasized the originality of the design. A comprehensive pictogram set completed the typography.

»Graphic designers can now choose from over 300 partially animated characters for designing the weather forecast and using explanatory graphics,« says Fabian Rottke, who managed the project at Edenspiekermann.

With: Ralph du Carrois, Susanna Dulkinys, Fabian Rottke, and Julia Sysmäläinen

Right: Each character in the pictogram fonts has several available states with which animation can be produced quickly and easily.

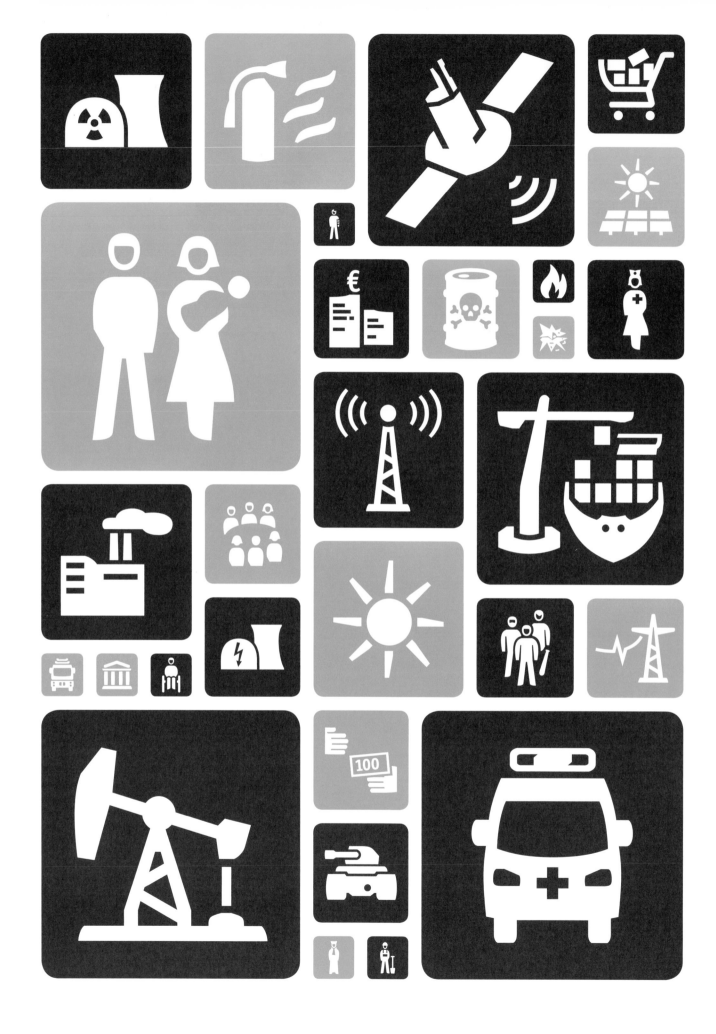

SpiekermannPartners created an entire new corporate design for the porcelain manufacturer Hering Berlin. Its website, catalog, image brochures, and all other media were adapted to the new layout.

»The challenge for us was how to combine pure information design, which makes the huge variety of the porcelain collection and its many combinations easy to manage, with a more sensuous design,« says Ralf Weißmantel, who led the project at SpiekermannPartners. The entire collection of some 980 pieces was displayed beautifully in a 700-page catalog and on the website.

The brochures and catalogs won the Silver European Design Award in 2009.

With: Eva Schekorr and Ralf Weißmantel

Cover and double page from the 700-page collection overview of Hering Berlin

22. 1. 2009
at the office with more on my list
than i can hope to do.

11. 6. 2013
1. Helvetica sucks for OS
2. Helvetica Light sucks more
3. Helvetica Light & tight übersucks.
   #ios7

9. 7. 2013
Can we all please remember:
It's Neue (German for new) Helvetica,
not Helvetica Neue. Repeat after me:
Neue Fu**ing Helvetica!.

Back in January 2009, when the social media platform was still toddling, Erik Spiekermann published his first tweet under his account @espiekermann: »at the office with more on my list than i can hope to do«. In the meantime (mid-2014) he has amassed 290,000 followers and written 15,000 tweets. A selection of Spiekermann's most retweeted tweets: »love statistics, especially when they are funny.

Relationship between the use of IE and the murder rate...«, »How to design a logo? 1. Set the name in a retail typeface 2. Cut off some corners in Illustrator 3. Cash a big check cuttingedgelogos.tumblr.com«

Spiekermann explains his tweeting: »Images get clicks, but even tweets without images get a big response, as long as I stick to what I know, which happens to be typography.«

In 2009 SpiekermannPartners merged with the Amsterdam company Eden Design & Communication; they became Edenspiekermann. The combined agency with offices in Amsterdam, Berlin, San Francisco, and Stuttgart engages in design, brand development, digital production, and service design.

According to the company profile: »We design meaningful, smart, and seductive brand experiences so that your customers become your followers.« It now has over 100 employees from 15 countries working for clients such as Red Bull Music Academy, Volkswagen, Ottobock, the Silicon Valley bank, Bosch, and the Kröller-Müller Museum.

With: Pia Betton, Hans Booms, Steven Cheek, Susanna Dulkinys, Joost Holthuis, Rik Koster, Oliver Schmidthals, Jürgen Siebert, Robert Stulle, and Edo van Dijk.

The office at 126 Friedrichstraße: big enough for SpiekermannPartners, too small for Edenspiekermann

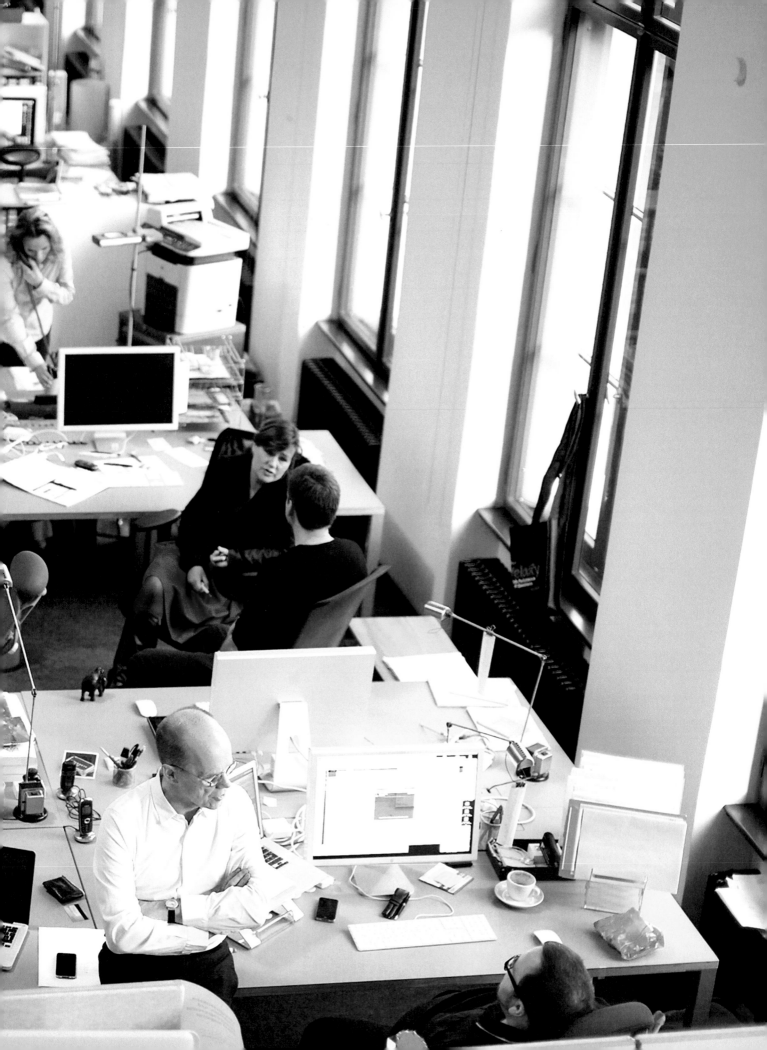

»Who is that guy walking around? Is he one of us?«

The long road from MetaDesign to Edenspiekermann, and why a coffee machine is so important.

By Julia Sysmäläinen

The world we find ourselves in is called »Espi«. Espi stands for Edenspiekermann, rather than Erik Spiekermann, as some new clients erroneously write. Erik is only in the second – though notably larger – part of the word. The shorter first bit belongs to our Dutch friends from the partner office in Amsterdam; small and beautiful. The name in itself is an interesting construct; one has to imagine it on a business card: Edenspiekermann_prof. dr. h.c. erik spiekermann.

The many letters at the beginning of the second line serve to differentiate between company and person. Or spoken, in my case: »Good morning, this is Julia Sysmäläinen, Edenspiekermann, Berlin.« How long would that take to spell out over the telephone? With my last name it takes a good two minutes, like buying a ticket for the Berlin metro using an electronic cash card – long enough to miss the train that has just arrived. With a name combination like that you get to test the humor of whoever is at the other end of the line. If they are not altogether humorless, you already have a topic for small talk. However, Espi was not always Espi; there were other names before it.

The first was UDN – United Designers Network – a nightmare for Office users. Every time you write the company name it automatically becomes a filler word, the German word for »and« being »und«. Und und und… as though thoughts and sentences could never be completed. We designers liked the name though. We liked it because it expressed what we wanted to do: be designers and work together. The clients – i.e. big fat Germans – didn't know what to make of the name. Nobody knew precisely who the designers were. What did they do? Perhaps they were a student collective? Oh! Such a lack of authority in a name is not helpful. So at some point UDN disappeared, and along with it the simple designer existence, lost to the past.

Next came the era of SpiekermannPartners. A funny, chaotic, hectic, ugly time. A time when some people desperately wanted to be partners, while the others wanted to know what was so good about the partnership in the first place. That was the time of the move: out of the old student digs, and into Berlin Mitte. A time when one was not always sure who that guy mooching around the office is. Is he one of us? A delivery man? Anyone? The time when the second Espi foundation stone was laid. We will never know whether the big fat clients liked the new name, but Spieki was bound to be right. For the first time since MetaDesign, Erik's name was

used in connection with a company, and so directly too. A lot of people were surprised: Ah, really? He's not at Meta anymore? Since when? But by then seven long Erik-less Meta years had already passed.

Espi had its home in Berlin Mitte for a long time. The building belonged to a publishing house that had taken over the former school compound sometime in the 1990s. It took them ten years to realize they didn't need half as much space. The front house was gradually rented to other companies and was, despite the proud inscription on the front of the building, barely used by the publishing company, who were now free to enjoy the relative quiet of the back house, along with its elevator.

The Espi floor was right at the top, and consisted mainly of windows. That meant brightness during snowy winters, heat in summer, and dark holes on pre-presentation nights at any time of year. Dark because the brilliant interior architects who converted that former gymnasium, and who still occasionally dropped by with visitors, had by and large decided not to bother with designing lighting. Maybe they thought the gigantic windows would somehow capture the city lights at night?

Are nightshifts unhealthy? It is hard to say how things managed to run, but without a bunch of standing lights and glowing computer screens one felt like a cat in a giant's bag.

The office had – not counting Erik – two main features: the gallery, and the coffee machine. Of course, the second is the more important, since a designer is only half a designer without latte-cappuccino-espresso. Mornings were an enthusiastic, noisy hive of grinding and frothing activity taken as group therapy; single coffees for those feeling antisocial, second waves of coffees for the especially addicted, coffees for meetings, coffees for clients. The machine was Erik's personal pride. It was referred to on the website, and at office and agency presentations. It was even often used as an argument for meeting at our office: Come to us, at least we have good coffee here… When anyone ever hung up the telephone on us because of all the dreadful construction noise in the background, then it was a clear sign that someone in the office had simply run out of coffee again.

Julia Sysmäläinen is a philologist and designer with Finnish-Russian roots. She works at Edenspiekermann and also runs her ›Carelian type foundry in the middle of Berlin‹ under the motto: »Working hard to get quality and humor together in type design.«

The first statement in the Edenspiekermann manifesto:
We work for your customers. We may have to take their side at times.

Challenge us. Complacency is the enemy of great work.

We don't give answers. Unless we can explore your question.

We are not suppliers. Partnership gets the best results.

Talk to us.
We thrive on feedback.

Trust us. You hired us because we do something you cannot.

Pay us. Our work adds to your bottom line, so invest in our future.

Göran on Erik

Most people who read this book will probably have an interest in Erik as the icon of typography that he is. I'm afraid I have to admit my interest in typography is very limited. I guess this is partly because I was brought up in a family of printers and typographers and got my fair share of it already at an early age. Partly because I'm just not that interested and therefore lack the knowledge and enthusiasm to be able to share Erik's passion.

This is where Erik is not in the least like myself. Erik can share any passion with any person he meets. He is a true »Jack of all trades«, knowledgeable in anything thing from concrete construction to the taxonomy of the Gravenstein apple.

To have Erik as a passenger on board at 40 knots or guide him in a kayak among the 24,000 islands of the Stockholm archipelago is a true delight. Does he know a lot about navigation or kayaking? No, in fact he knows very little about these things. But his still (in spite of his now considerable age) young and open mind makes him absorb everything around him and immediately turn it into knowledge, making him act and sound as if he were born on ship.

So, does this make a competent mariner? No, he is a lousy swimmer and cannot differentiate between a ketch and a yawl. But his enthusiasm and willingness to share a passion makes him not only an excellent friend and companion in any adventure but also qualifies him to be appointed a first class Swedish mariner!

Göran Lagerström (born 1945) is a branding and marketing expert and chairman of Edenspiekermann. The former IKEA manager, advertiser, and professor loves design, sailing, mountains, and Africa. He lives with his family in Stockholm.

Designer

ottobock.

Kent
C-Leg wearer.
San Francisco,
California

Quality for life

Cody McDonald, CPO.
San Francisco,
California

Great Partnerships.
Great Stories.
C-Leg®. The best care for my patients.

ottobock.

Quality for life

Aaron Holm,
bilateral C-Leg wearer.
Minneapolis,
Minnesota

Robert Tillges, CPO
Minneapolis,
Minnesota

Great Partnerships.
Great Stories.
C-Leg®. The best care for my patients.

In 2010 Edenspiekermann took over the corporate design for Ottobock Healthcare, the leading global brand of prosthetics. They created the campaign »Great Partnerships, Great Stories«. The company logo used until then was still based on Ottobock's own signature in the old German Sütterlin script, which presented an obstacle for the international market. The new image, in which Ottobock staff were also involved, is clear and modern in its design language: logo, typography, and color are all applied with this in mind.

The design team placed an emphasis on authentic photos that reflect the company's dedication, respect, and understanding of its customers.

With: Susanna Dulkinys, Katja Grubitzsch, Oliver Schmidthals, and Julia Sysmäläinen

People with prosthetics have stories to tell, like their partners in hospital and at Ottobock, who help them get back »on their feet«. That was the starting point for a campaign in which these stories are told in thought-provoking videos.

In 2011 the scientific book publisher Walter de Gruyter commissioned Edenspiekermann to design the typography for the inside of all their books. They wanted to change the complexity and confusing mix of styles they had to a unified and modern appearance. ›Meta Sans‹ and ›Meta Serif‹ are the new company typefaces; working with Carrois Type Design, they were further developed into ›DG Meta Science‹, a

typeface with over 4,000 characters in each weight, with which all scientific texts can be produced. It is rich in contrasts, creates tension, and is full of character and definition. The de Gruyter black line and the use of black as the principle company color are the chief design elements.

With: Ralph du Carrois, Eva Schekorr, and Katrin Wenke

Double page from the
De Gruyter manual, 2012

Übergreifende Fragestellung zu Methode und Darstellungsweise

—

Studien und Voruntersuchungen zur kommentierten Überlieferung und Wirkung der Abweichungen vom Text der Ausgabe und Fassung.

Herausgegeben von
Max Mustermann und Moritz Maier

Band 5/3.1

Max Mustermann

Funktion als Teil der literarischen Darstellung

—

Unterscheidung als Hilfs- und Orientierungsbegriff zur Dekodierung

2. Auflage

DE GRUYTER

1.1 Studien und Untersuchungen Kommentierung stütze

Bei meiner Kommentierung stütze ich mich weitgehend auf meine zahlreichen Vorgänger. Andererseits wird die Unterscheidung als Hilfs- und Orientierungsbegriff zur Unterscheidung, zwischen den dem gestützt durch die strikt getrennte Überlieferung. Andererseits wird die Unterscheidung als Hilfs- und Orientierungsbegriff zur Unterscheidung, zwischen den getrennte Überlieferung. Ihre der Stellen. Bei meiner Kommentierung stütze ich mich weitgehend auf meine zahlreichen Vorgänger. Andererseits wird die Unterscheidung als Hilfs- und Orientierungsbegriff zur Unterscheidung[99] zwischen dem dem gestützt durch die strikt getrennte Überlieferung. Auch umfasst die Untersuchung in der Hauptsache den Zeitraum zwischen dem Inkrafttreten und der Darstellung in seiner heute geltenden Fassung. Ihre Funktion als Teil der literarischen Darstellung und narrativen Technik enthält auch einen vollständigen textkritischen Apparat und ein Verzeichnis der Stellen.

1.2 Studien und Untersuchungen Kommentierung stütze ich mich weitgehend Kommentierung

Bei meiner Kommentierung stütze ich mich weitgehend auf meine zahlreichen Vorgänger. Andererseits wird die Unterscheidung als Hilfs- und Orientierungsbegriff zur Unterscheidung, zwischen den dem gestützt durch die strikt getrennte Überlieferung. Andererseits wird die Unterscheidung als Hilfs- und Orientierungsbegriff zur Unterscheidung, zwischen den getrennte Überlieferung. Ihre Funktion als Teil der literarischen Darstellung und narrativen Technik enthält auch einen vollständigen. Auch umfasst die Untersuchung die Hauptsache. Orientierungsbegriff zur Unterscheidung, zwischen den getrennte Überlieferung. Ihre der Stellen. Bei meiner Kommentierung stütze ich mich weitgehend auf Bei meiner Kommentierung stütze ich mich weitgehend auf meine zahlreichen Vorgänger. Andererseits wird die Unterscheidung als Hilfs- und Orientierungsbegriff zur Unterscheidung[99] zwischen dem dem gestützt durch die strikt getrennte Überlieferung. Auch umfasst die Untersuchung in der Hauptsache den Zeitraum zwischen dem Inkrafttreten und der Darstellung in seiner heute geltenden Fassung der Untersuchung. Bei meiner Kommentierung stütze ich mich weitgehend auf meine zahlreichen Vorgänger. Andererseits wird die Unterscheidung als

—

98 Vgl. von unschätzbarem Wert war die Hilfsbereitschaft der Mitarbeiter und Ehemaligen.
99 John Stewart Mill: *Funktion als Teil der literarischen Darstellung* (1768, 295–296)

Hilfs- und Orientierungsbegriff zur Unterscheidung, zwischen den dem gestützt durch die strikt getrennte Überlieferung. Meine zahlreichen Vorgänger. Andererseits wird die Unterscheidung als Hilfs- und Orientierungsbegriff zur Unterscheidung[100] zwischen den dem gestützt durch die strikt getrennte Überlieferung. Auch umfasst die Untersuchung in der Hauptsache den Zeitraum zwischen dem Inkrafttreten und der Darstellung.

1.3 Studien und Untersuchungen Kommentierung stütze ich mich weitgehend Kommentierung Untersuchung in der Hauptsache den Zeitraum

Auch beim Konzept[101] der ästhetischen Bildung von Wissen und dessen möglichst rasche und erfolgsorientierte Anwendung verspielen Einsichten und Gewinne ohne den Bezug auf die um 1900 entwickelten. Auch umfasst die Untersuchung in der Hauptsache den Zeitraum zwischen dem Inkrafttreten und der Darstellung[102] in seiner heute geltenden Fassung. Ihre Funktion als Teil der literarischen Darstellung und narrativen Technik enthält auch einen vollständigen textkritischen Apparat[103] und ein Verzeichnis der Stellen. Auch umfasst die Untersuchung in der Hauptsache den Zeitraum zwischen dem Inkrafttreten und der Darstellung in seiner heute geltenden Fassung. Ihre Funktion als Teil der literarischen Darstellung und narrativen Technik[104] enthält auch einen Vollkommentierung stütze ich mich weitgehend auf meine zahlreichen Vorgänger. Orientierungsbegriff zur Unterscheidung, zwischen den dem gestützt durch die strikt getrennte Überlieferung. Auch umfasst die Untersuchung in der Hauptsa-

—

100 Von unschätzbarem Wert war die Hilfsbereitschaft der Mitarbeiter und ehemaligen.
101 Karl Auer: *Übergreifende Fragestellung zur besseren Darstellungsweise* (1768, 295–296),
um 1900 entwickelt Argumentationen für die anlaufenden und nicht mehr einsetzbaren Fragen.
102 Daniel Petersen: *Funktion als Teil der literarischen Darstellung* (1768, 295–296),
103 Von unschätzbarem Wert war die Hilfsbereitschaft der Mitarbeiter und ehemaligen Kollegen des Lehrgebiets; abgesehen von einem knapp gehaltenen Exkurs in die Zeit des gemeinen Rechts.
104 Des gemeinen Rechts, steht die Analyse der Texte in ihrer überlieferten Form immer im Vordergrund.Auch beim Konzept der ästhetischen Bildung von Wissen und dessen möglichst rasche und erfolgsorientierte Anwendung verspielen Einsichten und Gewinne ohne den Bezug auf dieum 1900 entwickelten Argumentationen. Ihre Funktion als Teil der literarischen Darstellung und narrativen Technik enthält auch einen vollständigen textkritischen Apparat und ein Verzeichnis der Stellen. Bei meiner Kommentierung stütze ich mich weitgehend auf meine zahlreichen Vorgänger.

German Design Award

The German Design Award, conferred each year by the Federal Ministry for Economic Affairs and Energy, is the highest distinction for design in Germany. The »personality award« category honors prominent German designers for their lifetime achievement. Recent famous award winners include Wolfgang Joop, Ingo Maurer, and Richard Sapper. The 2011 personality award went to Erik Spiekermann. The award ceremony was held on February 2, 2011 in Frankfurt. The laudatory speech was given by John L. Walters, British editor of the design magazine ›Eye‹ and an old friend of Spiekermann's. This is his speech.

When I went to Berlin a couple of years ago, in preparation for ›Eye‹ 74, our Berlin special, I kept running into Erik Spiekermann. Not literally, though I did later spend a pleasant evening in the company of Erik and his wife Susanna. But I quickly realized that I couldn't avoid encountering Erik and his legacy. For a start, nearly every person I met had some connection to him: either they had collaborated with him, or worked for him, or they'd been taught or otherwise encouraged by Erik early in their career. And even people who didn't know him very well, or who had never met him, seemed to have an opinion about him. They knew him as a designer, as a typographer, as a type evangelist and as a writer – chiefly on the subject of typography, but with opinions about every other subject: politics, society, culture, art, music, and so on. Also, quite apart from all the people I met, there were traces of Erik everywhere I went, on the subway, in the signs and the many different civic and commercial public projects that bore the stamp of one of his design practices, or that used one of his typefaces.

So that's why we called the ›Eye‹ 74 piece »Six degrees of Erik Spiekermann«. We devoted a gatefold information graphic to all the connections that he had made throughout his career, spanning the years since 1979, when the company that would become Meta was founded, to the present-day activities of Edenspiekermann. Like Kevin Bacon, Erik seemed to connect anyone who was anyone in graphic design, visual communication, branding, and typography. Yet if our world were Hollywood, Erik would perhaps be more like Steven Spielberg than an actor, even an Oscar-winning one. Erik is both a generalist and a specialist.

The first time I ran into him, at an international typography conference, he asked me how I could stand to be surrounded by so many »nerds«? He knows how designers and typographers think, in the most minute detail, because that's the way he thinks, too. Yet he's managed to lift his head above the cubicle that defines the graphic design world and look dispassionately at commerce and government and charities, taking the time to understand how they think, too. I have daily reason to be grateful for Erik's advice, since his ideas of the Rundbuero, expressed in Unit Edition's book ›Studio Culture‹, helped me make some small changes in the way I organize my own office.

William Owen described Erik (in ›Eye‹ 18) as a »consummate pluralist«, while also taking on Erik's own definition of himself as a »typographic designer«, who designs »from the word up«, a phrase later used for a slim volume on Meta's work. William also noted that Erik »valued work of a kind he could never or would never want to do.« But that is not surprising. It is almost the definition of anyone with a rounded interest in culture and the world at large: you don't have to sing opera to value ›Nixon in China‹, nor do you have to paint in oils to appreciate art.

I think it is Erik's ability to work and show curiosity at both micro and macro levels (and all points between) that makes him a good writer, as well as a good designer. His writing is clear and to the point, whether in a column for ›Blueprint‹ magazine or in an email containing directions to his house. Even if he had done little else, the book he wrote with E. M Ginger, ›Stop Stealing Sheep & Find Out How Type Works‹, would be an international calling card of huge proportions, since it's one of the few genuinely informative, entertaining, and readable books about type written in the past few decades.

When I first watched the DVD of Gary Hustwit's ›Helvetica‹, whose extras section includes an extended interview with Erik, I was amused to hear him say how much he liked being an »unknown designer«. Today's ceremony seems an odd place to talk about Erik's lack of recognition. Yet he was making an important point about the role of design – graphic design, type design, and typography in particular – in civic life. As Erik explains in that documentary, neatly diverting the director from too many questions about a typeface he doesn't much care for, a nation's culture, the stuff that surrounds us, is made of good architecture and building, good food and cafés, and supposedly nerdy things like the small type in timetables for public transport, or the signs in stations, or the little details that make your iPhone work intuitively.

Erik gets a kick out of being the unknown author behind some of this stuff, even when the money is terrible, and he has to fight »the system« – the conventional way of doing something – to make things just a little bit better. Few people might notice, or remark out loud that the timetable has acquired more legible, readable type, or better navigation, but as Erik would say, »That is the point.« Many designers get a kick out of making things better, of finding a solution, whether their name's on the finished thing or not. So I think we could regard this prize as one that Erik can share, just a little bit, with all the unknown designers out there, who play their part in making our lives better, our small print more legible.

Around the time I became editor of ›Eye‹, we published an updated version of Ken Garland's ›First Things First‹, calling on designers to examine their priorities.

The manifesto included these sentences: »Unprecedented environmental, social, and cultural crises demand our attention. Many cultural interventions, social marketing campaigns, books, magazines, exhibitions, educational tools, television programs, films, charitable causes, and other information design projects urgently require our expertise and help.« Erik was one of 33 designers who put their names to ›First Things First 2000‹, and that statement sounds just as relevant today – throw mobile devices and social media into the mix and it still holds good.

I agreed to come here on the strict understanding that the Designpreis would not signify or herald any slowing down of Erik's furious pace. He still works at a furious pace. He even has a proofing press in his house, where he's cooking up plans to combine digital and analog, making plates with a laser cutter. And in addition to all the usual client work, he is publishing a series of booklets of writings that he likes, more little red books of his own work – the thoughts of Chairman Erik.

These thoughts are worth sharing. Erik is concerned about nerdy details, and he loves to construct the big picture. He's a great advocate of design's role in civilized society, all the boring, behind-the-scenes stuff, but he is also quick to spot what is new and cool, and to champion and mentor young talent – the new Edenspiekermann scholarship is a significant addition to this aspect of Erik's life and work. For all these reasons, Erik is a worthy recipient of whatever awards get thrown his way – and they won't go to his head.

John L. Walters is an editor, composer, and music producer. In the early 1980s he had two big hits in the UK with the band Landscape. Later he produced music by Kate Bush, Twelfth Night, Mike Gibbs, and others. Since 1999 Walters has edited the design magazine ›Eye‹. He also writes about music for ›The Guardian‹.

Designpreis
Deutschland
2011

PERSÖNLICHKEIT

Für seine besonderen Verdienste um eine ganzheitliche und zukunftsorientierte
Unternehmens- und Produktkultur verleihe ich

Prof. Dr. h.c. Erik Spiekermann

den Designpreis der Bundesrepublik Deutschland.

Für die hohe konzeptionelle und gestalterische Qualität zeichne ich diese Designleistu
des Preisrichterkollegiums vom 24. August 2010 mit dem Designpreis der Bundesrepul

Rainer Brüderle

Rainer Brüderle
Bundesminister für Wirtschaft und Technologie
Berlin, den 11. Februar 2011

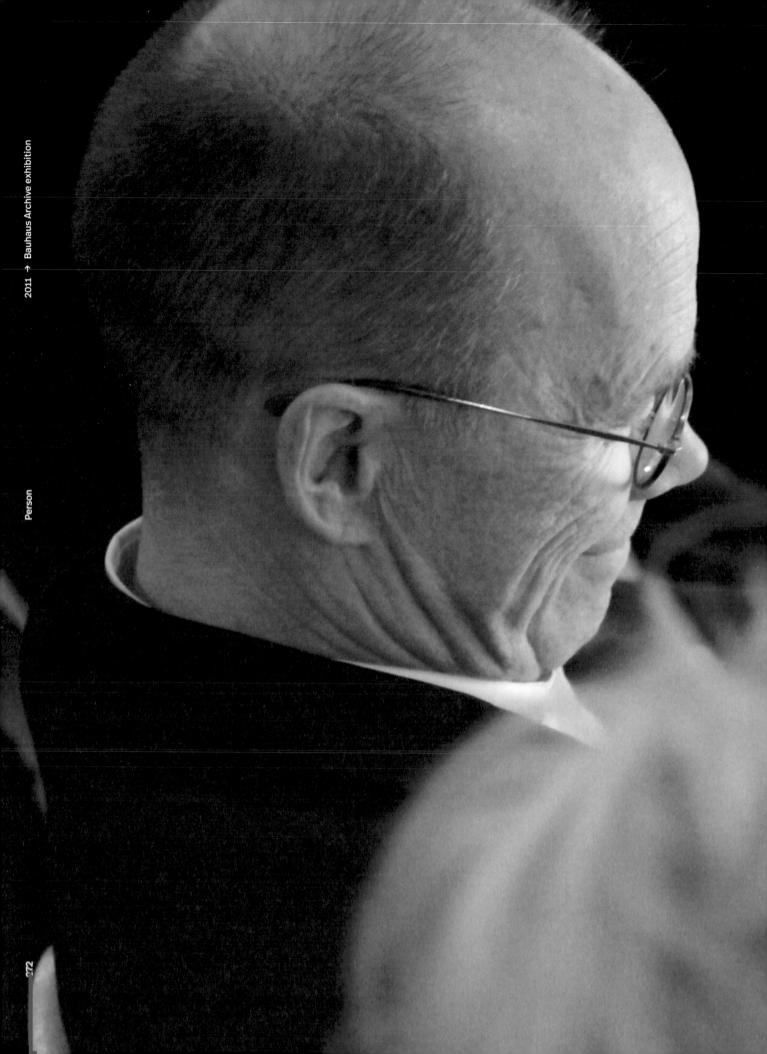

From March to June 2011 the Bauhaus Arc
hive held the exhibition ›erik spiekermann. the
face of type‹. Typefaces dating from 1979 to
the present were presented on more than 30
banners. Also on display were his corporate
design projects for ›The Economist‹, Deutsche
Bahn and Düsseldorf airport; the passenger
information system he devised for BVG (the
Berlin public transport company), and his own
publications. His global network of design
studios and graphic designers were represented in a picture that originally appeared in the
Berlin edition of ›Eye‹ magazine.

With: Susanna Dulkinys, Lars Krüger, Dr. Thomas Maier,
Ferdinand Ulrich, and Paul Weihe

Spiekermann listens to Johannes Erler
as he gives the introductory speech
for the exhibition at the Bauhaus Archiv
in Berlin.

s t u v w x y z a b c
o p q r s t u v w x y
g h i j k l m n o p q
b c d e f g h i j k l
g h i j k l m n o p q
z a b c d e f g h i j
l m n o p q r s t u v
f g h i j k l m n o p
s t u v w x y z a b c
e f g h i j k l m n o
d e f g h i j k l m n

Berliner Grotesk
FF Meta
LTC Officina Serif
FF Info
Nokia Sans
DB Serif
DB Sans Condensed
FF Meta Serif
FF Unit Slab
FF FENN Dynamic Display
FF

schriftgestalten | the face of type

23. 3.– 6. 6. 2011
bauhaus-archiv
museum für gestaltung

bauhaus-archiv

Klingelhöferstraße 14 · 10785 Berlin · www.bauhaus.de
Täglich außer Dienstag · Daily except Tuesday 10–17:00
U Nollendorfplatz · Bus M29, 100, 106 & 187 >Lützowplatz

© 2011 erik spiekermann

Spiekermann himself designed the poster
for the exhibition using letters from his
own fonts. The title was thought up by the
Bauhaus Archive curator, Sibylle Hoiman.

Explain the world to me

Berlin exhibits the work of graphic designer
Erik Spiekermann. By Melanie Mühl

Take Berlin as an example: without the typographer and communication designer Erik Spiekermann one would find it harder to get around, provided one does not know the city well to start with. One would probably stand on some train platform or other and squint at the subway or overground train map before possibly heading off in the wrong direction. The signage designed by Erik Spiekermann for the Berlin transport authority makes such errors impossible, since it is so easy to use one could leave any seven-year-old alone to travel across the city.

Or take the news magazine ›The Economist‹: Spiekermann and his team redesigned the outmoded publication in 2001. They changed the font and the table of contents, introduced information hierarchies, added color to the pages, and suddenly the whole thing had a brand new feel about it. The circulation, which was still 500,000 at the start of 2001, almost doubled to nearly a million by the end of the year.

Or Düsseldorf airport: child's play to find one's way around. Spiekermann developed the well-known typefaces ›FF Meta‹ and ›ITC Officina‹, which have since become classics. He is the co-founder of MetaDesign, one of the largest design agencies in Germany, and his current agency Edenspiekermann did the corporate design for various companies, including Volkswagen and Audi. The list goes on endlessly. Erik Spiekermann has helped simplify the world for us all. This year he is being honored for his life's work, which is why the Bauhaus Archive is dedicating an exhibition to him, which amply catalogs his achievements. There was alphabet soup at the opening; graphic designer Johannes Erler held a talk and was happy to be in Berlin, where for once he did not have to begin with a basic explanation of the word »design«. According to him, Spiekermann is driven by the fact that he simply loves to gas; he has a need to explain things and make them clearer.

Spiekermann's unostentatious design has certainly crept into the way we perceive things, without us noticing it. The art lies in its implicitness. His creativity is not dictated by aesthetic principles. Instead, organizational principles, which require competence, help keep vanity in check. Spiekermann demonstrates this in a short, modest talk in which he thanks those with whose support he has realized countless projects over the past decades, and who equally deserve the accolades. One often hears this said during thank-you speeches, but in this case it seems genuinely heartfelt.

Melanie Mühl is a journalist and author.
She works as an editor for the Arts section of the
›Frankfurter Allgemeine Zeitung‹.

At the exhibition: partition walls
made of corrugated board, and the
pages of a whole book laid out

Erik Spiekermann has long been a bicycle enthusiast. In 1985 he bought his first real racing bike; in 1995 he paid 3,500 German marks for his first custom-made bike, which was sadly stolen at some point. He currently owns 13 bicycles, including ones by Cicli Berlinetta, Waterford Precision Cycles, De Rosa, and Swiss Cresta: eight in Berlin, two in San Francisco, two in London, and one in Amsterdam.

»One can never have too many bikes, as long as there's enough room for them. All my bikes put together still cost less than a car, and they're much cheaper to use,« says Spiekermann, who has described his passion for bicycles as a source of inspiration. »Both things – my work and cycling – are practical as well as nice, get you from A to B, and are good for your well-being and everyone else's.«

Person

According to Spiekermann the formula for the optimal number of bicycles one should own is »n+1«. Here are his Berlin bikes gathered in his yard for a clean.

A day without a bike ride is a wasted day

Interview: Philipp Poll, radzeit

His design is seen in public and in the media every day by people in Berlin and elsewhere. Philipp Poll interviewed the multiple award-winning typographer Erik Spiekermann for ›radzeit‹ magazine.

You are an internationally respected designer of fonts, logos, and corporate designs, having worked for the city of Berlin, Deutsche Bahn, BVG, but also for German car manufacturers. When will the German bicycle industry receive a contemporary image design? When the »German bicycle industry« exists. It would have to lose its geeky image first. After all, cycling is everything: healthy, practical, lifestyley, contemporary, technically fascinating, and, most of all, viable for the future. Unfortunately the industry consists of a few lifestyle companies, some honest manufacturers, and a bunch of geeks. It's hard to unite them all under one brand, but it would be good for everyone.

You made the logo for the bicycle show VELOBerlin. What is the Spiekermann-bicycle connection? I cycle because it's practical, especially in Berlin; because it's fun, because it's sensible, healthy, and an aesthetic and physical pleasure.

I've heard you're a real bike nut; is that true? What fascinates you about cycling? I'm a pragmatic cyclist. In Berlin and London I usually ride with simple single-speeds, converted from old racing bikes. In winter weather I change to a solid city bike; in Amsterdam I have a Gazelle, of course; in San Francisco a racing bike (custom made) with 2×11 gears, since it gets really steep. I also have a mountain bike for country tours, and a small collection of classical racing bikes – including a De Rosa and a Wilier. After various knee operations I can no longer ride every bike over long distances, so I've had custom frames built in Berlin and San Francisco. I only ride steel bikes – I'm old-fashioned in that way. I don't usually get to do more than one longish tour on a weekend. Here in San Francisco the weather's good enough to do a little 40 kilometer or more round trip nearly every day. I think I have 12 bikes altogether, but then I do live in three cities, plus I have to go to our office in Amsterdam occasionally.

So you ride a bike everywhere: in San Francisco, London, and Amsterdam. How are they different from Berlin? Well for one thing, in London I get around faster by bike than on public transport, and a car is useless there. In San Francisco a lot of people think I'm weird because I wear normal street clothes on a racing bike. Over there cycling is still mostly treated like a sport, with a crazy amount of equipment. They still haven't realized that they don't actually need special shoes to be able to pedal. In Amsterdam you simply have to ride a bike because pedestrians are at risk. And in Berlin it's a real joy, since you get around quickly, see a lot of the city, and sleep well at night if you ride at least 20 kilometers, which is easy to do if you ride to work and to the shops. It's the perfect mix of practical, healthy, and relaxing. A day without a bike ride is a wasted day.

You are known for a clear, puristic style. Do your bikes look like your typography? That's why I only have steel bikes. The more puristic, the more I like them. My racing bike in San Francisco has no graphics whatsoever, and I only let the guys at Cicli Berlinetta put a couple of little logos on my Berlin racer. The graphics on the old bikes is pretty kitschy for my usual criteria, but their style – usually created by design amateurs – just happens to be like that, and we ought to celebrate it.

When will we see the Meta Bike, the Spiekermann bike? I'm trying to help a friend in San Francisco set up a city bike company. I help decide the colors and style of the bikes by Public Bikes. They are simple but cheerful. I would love to make a bike according to my ideas. It would probably be more of an everyday bike like my single-speeds: light, simple, colored.

The Allgemeine Deutsche Fahrrad-Club e.V. (ADFC) promotes cycling and improved road safety. It represents cyclists' political, administrative, and economic interests, and produces numerous publications on bicycles and cycling. The article »A day without a bike ride is a wasted day« appeared in March 2013 in ›radzeit‹, the ADFC magazine for Berlin/Brandenburg. www.adfc-berlin.de

Spiekermann cycling: on the Golden Gate Bridge in San Francisco, 1989; in the Grunewald in Berlin, 2013; in a conference hall during the judging of the Eurobike competition in Hanover, 2009

The name of the new typeface for Firefox OS, the mobile operating system of the Mozilla Foundation for smartphones, was contentious to begin with. ›Fira‹ was first called ›Feura‹, but when an English speaker pronounces it, it sounds too much like »Führer«. »I would never give a typeface a name like that, especially one from Berlin,« says Erik Spiekermann. Thus, it was rechristened ›Fira‹. The typeface was optimized for use on displays of various sizes, and has a broad range of weights and language versions. The combination of narrowish characters and a tall x-height make it both space-saving and easy to read.

With: Ralph du Carrois

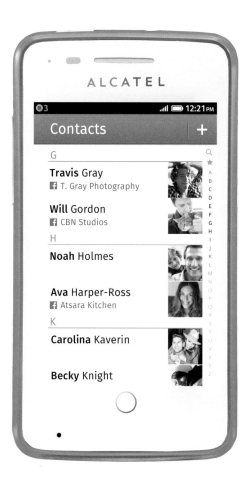

A typeface for small screens has to be clearly legible, while at the same time retaining the brand character.

In late 2013 Erik Spiekermann announced he would be stepping down as chairman at Eden-spiekermann in May 2014 (on his 67th birthday) and joining the supervisory board. He has prepared plenty to do afterwards: At the beginning of 2014 Spiekermann installed his printing press in a beautiful white room in a former girls' art school in the back courtyard of a house in Potsdamer Straße, directly opposite Eden-spiekermann. It is called Galerie P98a after its street and house number.

There are six proofing presses by FAG, Korrex, and Grafix; one Heidelberger platen press, various Boston platen presses, cutting and creasing machines, eyelet punches, a lot of wooden poster type, and even more lead type. There is also a polymer making machine, a digital Risograph printer, plus everything else one might need for printing and typesetting using old or new methods.

Soon the legendary Rixdorfer printers' workshop will be added to the collection. The Rixdorfer book and poster artists gave their whole workshop to Spiekermann on condition it be reassembled in its new home on Potsdamer Straße – a pleasure and a responsibility at the same time.

Spiekermann and partner Jan Gassel want to see how the old printing methods can be mixed with digital tools. A few wooden fonts are being worked on; starting in summer there will be workshops on hand composition and letterpress. And, in collaboration with Jena University, large poster fonts will be made using 3D printing.

To finance the venture they sell signed prints in small editions. The ›SpiekerDigest‹ with collections of interesting texts by Spiekermann and colleagues is going to be printed on the Riso, and many other books and prints will follow.

P98a is a bit »back to the future« for Spiekermann. It closes the big circle of his professional life, which began with metal type and a platen press and led him into the wide world of design and typography, ending back in Berlin at almost the exact same spot where he once learnt to compose type and print as a schoolboy. Spiekermann will keep busy, since being idle does not interest him. He will continue to dabble with all things analog and digital. And should there be a little spare time left, there are plenty of personal dreams and desires to fulfill. He talks about these on page 288.

Spiekermann in his printing and type-setting workshop. The traditional compositor's apron protects from printer's ink, machine grease, and dust from the old type cases.

Large type made of wood and Plakadur (an artificial resin that is particularly durable and produces sharp contours) has inspired Spiekermann to produce works of art using them, since they are little works of art in themselves.

12p Akzidenz-Grotesk mager

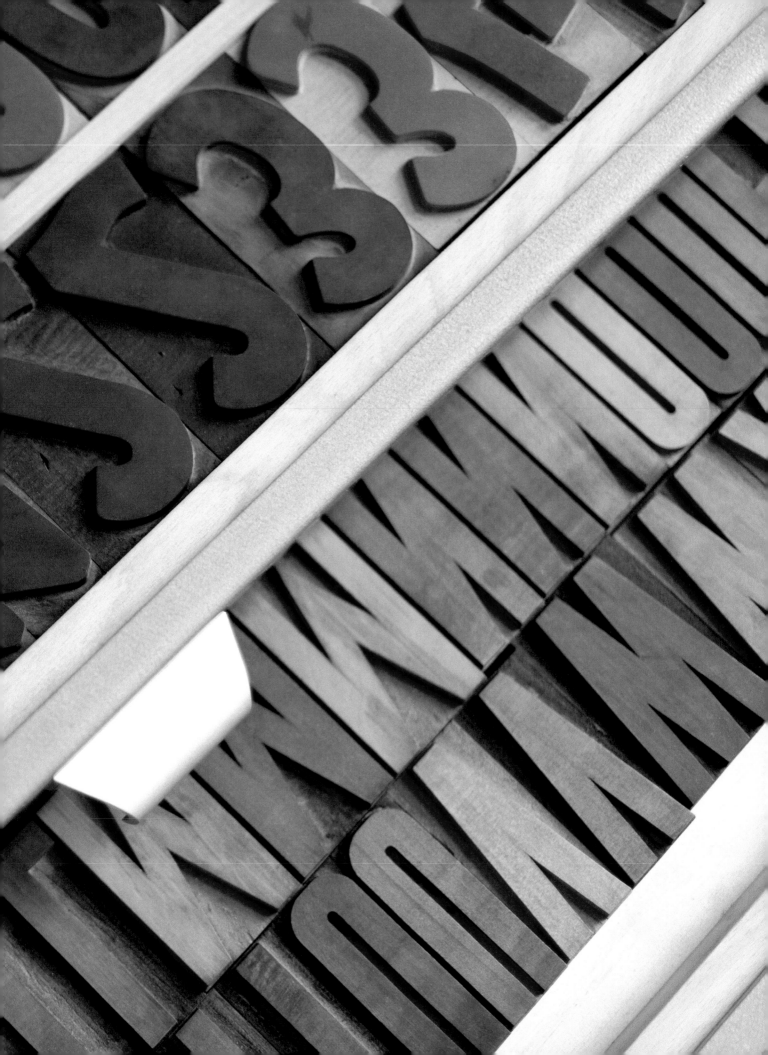

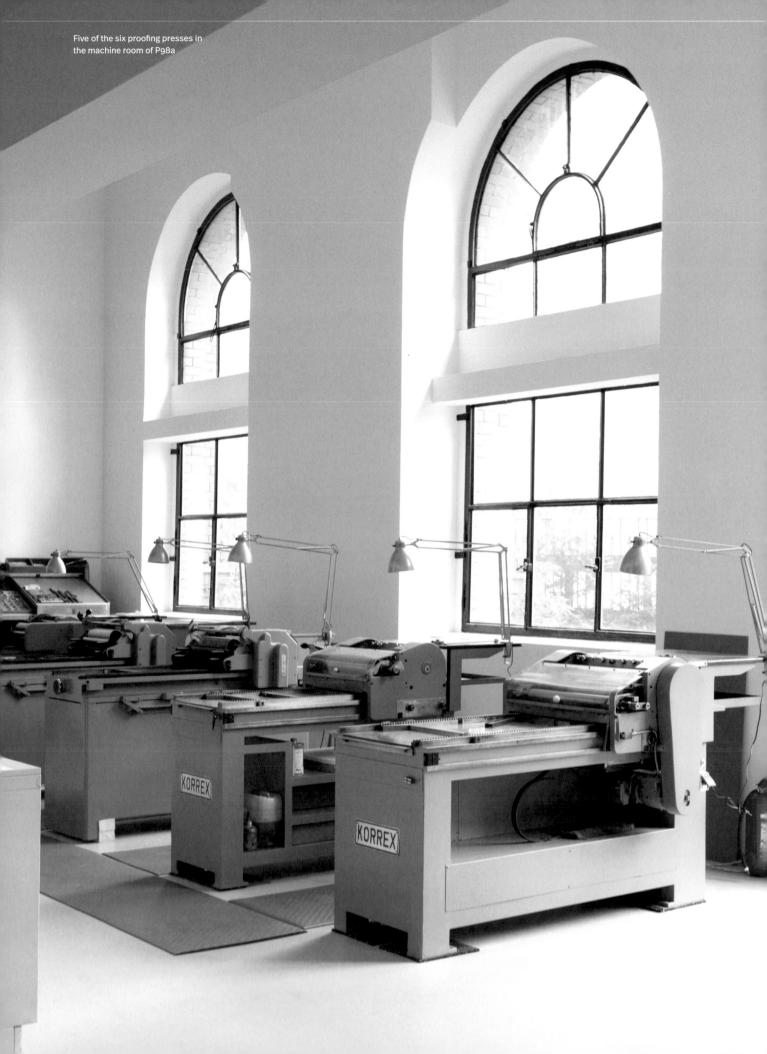

Five of the six proofing presses in
the machine room of P98a

Top: The collection of wood type from
Germany and the USA is not only
for display – the letters are also used
for printing.
Bottom: Measuring and testing is
an essential part of setting metal and
wood type.

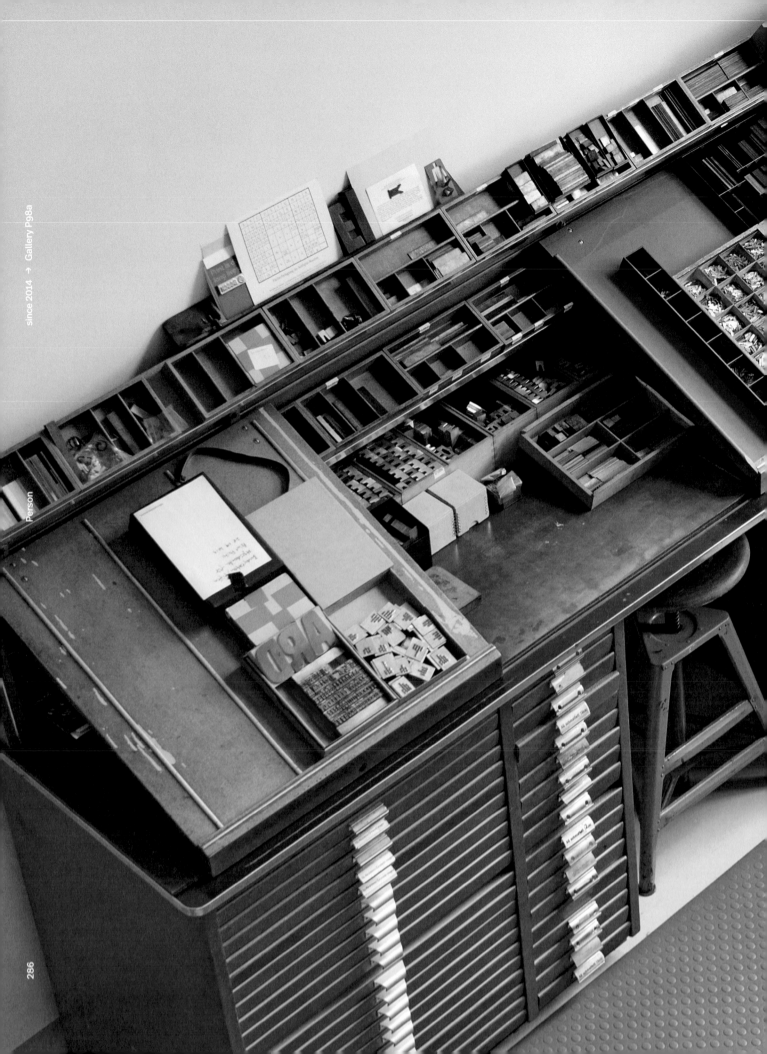

The Spiekermann gallery workshop in Potsdamer Straße, Berlin combines traditional handwork with digital technology such as Risographs and 3D printing.

And now?
»One cannot not communicate.« Spiekermann likes to quote this famous saying by Paul Watzlawick. Using the same logic, one cannot not do anything. And so, after all the jobs, typefaces, businesses, we have to ask the question: Erik, what does the future hold?

What seven typefaces would you still like to design?

1. A typeface for German highway signage
2. A typeface for German street signage
3. A typeface for pedestrian signage in Berlin
4. A classical Renaissance Antiqua (›MetaAntiqua‹)
5. An OS typeface for Apple
6. ›MetaFraktur‹
7. Large wood fonts for my proof presses

What seven jobs would you still like to do?

1. A complete book design each month
2. Signage for the German highways
3. Signage for German streets
4. Signage for US highways
5. Pedestrian signage for Berlin
6. Branding for an airline
7. Design for a big public institution, such as the EU or the internal revenue, or the UN, but with total control and without meetings or middle men

What seven
companies would
you still like
to found?

1 A design studio that
won't bend over
to please clients with
bad taste, bad manners,
weak decisions, and
too little money

2 A publishing house
that only makes
beautiful books to
give away

3 A radio station that
only plays my favorite
kind of music

4 A workshop for every-
thing (carpentry,
metal shop, electrics,
electronics, printing
etc.), where there are
competent, friendly
professionals of all
trades, and where
customers are
encouraged to join
in the work

5 A bicycle shop that
does any kind
of repair, where the
mechanics have
greasy hands, but
that also sells
the coolest clothes.
In the hipster shops
that do sell clothes,
they're usually clue-
less about mechanics

6 A café that instantly
puts anyone who enters
it in a good mood

7 A café that only
serves cheesecake
and hot cocoa

What seven technical innovations would you still like to see in your lifetime?

What seven texts, books, films, or presentations would you still like to write?

1 The endless data storage device that never gets full

2 Milk that always stays fresh without any kind of preservative

3 Chocolate that only melts once it's in your mouth

4 Music that I alone can hear, but without having to stick things in my ears

5 An electric bike with a motor small enough to fit in a trouser pocket

6 A keyboard on which I can type blind at night using all ten fingers

7 A screen that becomes a book with pages when you touch it

1 A proper novel, for once

2 The story of all of my typefaces

3 A monograph on Louis Oppenheim (LoType et al.)

4 The general presentation on visual communication that I can do anywhere in the world for lots of money

5 The second part of ›Typomania‹, a TV program I once made for the BBC

6 A travel guide of all the places I've ever been

7 An interview with anyone who has ever meant a lot to me

What seven people would you still like to meet?

What seven wonders would you still like to see?

1 My father, who died 13 years ago; we still had a lot to say to each other
2 Everyone who has meant something to me, and whom I would still like to interview
3 My great-grandchild
4 Ry Cooder
5 Paul Smith
6 A client with good taste and good manners, who isn't weak-willed, and has a sufficient budget. Someone who knows what they want, but lets us get on with it without interfering
7 The person who makes the vanilla quark by Butter Lindner

1 All seven

Erik Spiekermann's typefaces

The summary on the following pages lists
25 typefaces. They were created between 1976
and 2014. Some were drawn by Spiekermann
on his own but most were collaborations
with other type designers. The introductory
texts are by Spiekermann himself.

ARTZ

The Hamilton Wood Type & Printing Museum in Wisconsin made a wood font that Erik Spiekermann designed for his print workshop in Berlin. He donated the digital version to the museum. It is named after one of the last punchcutters there. Any earnings go to the museum.

Released: 2014
Foundry: Exclusive to Hamilton Wood Type

Styles

ARTZ REGULAR

Characters ARTZ Regular

ABCDEFGHIJKLMNOPQRSTUVWXYZ
0123456789

Sample ARTZ Regular 18/22

THE QUICK BROWN FOX JUMPED OVER THE LAZY DOGS. VICTOR JAGT ZWÖLF BOXKÄMPFER QUER ÜBER DEN GROSSEN SYLTER DEICH. PORTEZ CE VIEUX WHISKY AU JUGE BLOND QUI FUME. UM PEQUENO JABUTI XERETA VIU DEZ CEGONHAS FELIZES. MA LA VOLPE, COL SUO BALZO, HA RAGGIUNTO IL QUIETO FIDO. FILMQUIZ BRACHT KNAPPE EX-YOGI VAN DE WIJS. SPHINX OF ALL BLACK QUARTZ JUDGE MY VOW. STANLEYS EXPE-DITIONSZUG QUER DURCH AFRIKA WIRD VON JEDERMANN BEWUNDERT. QUEL FEZ SGHEMBO COPRE DAVANTI. DOCH BEP, FLINK SEXY QUA VORM, ZWIJGT. CRAZY FREDERICK BOUGHT MANY VERY EXQUISITE OPAL JEWELS. JEDER WACKERE BAYER VERTILGT BEQUEM ZWO PFUND KALBSHAXEN. BUVEZ DE CE WHISKY QUE LE PATRON JUGE FAMEUX. QUALCHE NOTIZIA PAVESE MI FA SBADIGLIARE.

Axel

Numbers and text in tables must be both space-saving and easy to read, often a contradiction. ›Axel‹ was an initiative of Jürgen Siebert's at FontShop Berlin in order to solve this contradiction. The typeface, based on ›ITC Officina‹, was condensed, improved and adapted with help from Erik van Blokland and Ralph du Carrois. The name sounds similar to a certain well-known computer program. → page 258

With: Ralph du Carrois and Erik van Blokland
Released: 2009
Foundry: FontShop

Styles

Axel Regular
Axel Bold

Characters Axel Regular

Aa Bb Cc Dd Ee Ff Gg Hh Ii Jj Kk Ll Mm
Nn Oo Pp Qq Rr Ss Tt Uu Vv Ww Xx Yy Zz
0123456789

Sample Axel Regular 9/12

The quick brown fox jumped over the lazy dogs. Victor jagt zwölf Boxkämpfer quer über den großen Sylter Deich. Portez ce vieux whisky au juge blond qui fume. El veloz murciélago hindú comía feliz cardillo y kiwi. La cigüeña tocaba el saxofón detrás del palenque de paja. Um pequeno jabuti xereta viu dez cegonhas felizes. Ma la volpe, col suo balzo, ha raggiunto il quieto Fido. Filmquiz bracht knappe ex-yogi van de wijs. Quizdeltagerne spiste jordbær med fløde, mens cirkusklovnen Walther spillede på xylofon. Høvdingens kjære squaw får litt pizza i Mexico by. Flygande bäckasiner söka hwila på mjuka tuvor. Sphinx of all black quartz judge my vow. Stanleys Expeditionszug quer durch Afrika wird von jedermann bewundert. Voyez le brick géant que j'examine près du wharf. A rápida raposa castanha salta por cima do cão lento. The quick brown fox jumped over the lazy dogs. Victor jagt zwölf Boxkämpfer quer über den großen Sylter Deich. Portez ce vieux whisky au juge blond qui fume. El veloz mur-ciélago hindú comía feliz cardillo y kiwi. La cigüeña tocaba el saxofón

Sample Axel Regular 12/16

The quick brown fox jumped over the lazy dogs. Victor jagt zwölf Boxkämpfer quer über den großen Sylter Deich. Portez ce vieux whisky au juge blond qui fume. El veloz murciélago hindú comía feliz cardillo y kiwi. La cigüeña tocaba el saxofón detrás del palenque de paja. Um pequeno jabuti xereta viu dez cegonhas felizes. Ma la volpe, col suo balzo, ha raggiunto il quieto Fido. Filmquiz bracht knappe ex-yogi van de wijs. Quizdeltagerne spiste jordbær med fløde, mens cirkusklovnen Walther spillede på xylofon. Høvdingens kjære squaw får litt pizza i Mexico by. Flygande bäckasiner söka hwila på mju-ka tuvor. Sphinx of all black quartz judge my vow. Stanleys Expeditionszug quer durch Afrika wird von

Berliner Grotesk

The new family was created from ›Berliner Grotesk Light‹ from 1913 and ›Block Semi-Bold‹ from the 1920s. ›Berliner Grotesk Light‹ and Bold were redrawn for phototypesetting and released in 1979. → page 53

Released: 1979
Foundry: H. Berthold AG

Styles

Berliner Grotesk Light

Berliner Grotesk Medium

Characters Berliner Grotesk Regular

Aa Bb Cc Dd Ee Ff Gg Hh Ii Jj Kk Ll Mm Nn Oo Pp Qq Rr Ss Tt Uu Vv Ww Xx Yy Zz 0123456789

Sample Berliner Grotesk Regular 18/22

The quick brown fox jumped over the lazy dogs. Victor jagt zwölf Boxkämpfer quer über den großen Sylter Deich. Portez ce vieux whisky au juge blond qui fume. El veloz murciélago hindú comía feliz cardillo y kiwi. La cigüeña tocaba el saxofón detrás del palenque de paja. Um pequeno jabuti xereta viu dez cegonhas felizes. Ma la

Sample Berliner Grotesk Medium 18/22

The quick brown fox jumped over the lazy dogs. Victor jagt zwölf Boxkämpfer quer über den großen Sylter Deich. Portez ce vieux whisky au juge blond qui fume. El veloz murciélago hindú comía feliz cardillo y kiwi. La cigüeña tocaba el saxofón detrás del palenque de paja. Um pequeno jabuti xereta viu dez cegonhas felizes. Ma la volpe, col suo balzo, ha raggiunto

Boehringer

Originally designed for the Boehringer Ingelheim signature, Ole Schäfer expanded this Antiqua to a family. It is based on ›Concorde Nova‹ by Günter Gerhard Lange. There is a condensed Grotesque in the tradition of Anglo-American Gothics for product names and small print.

With: Ole Schäfer
Released: 1996
Foundry: Exclusive to Boehringer Ingelheim

Styles

Boehringer Antiqua Regular

Boehringer Antiqua Regular Condensed

Boehringer Antiqua Regular Italic

Boehringer Antiqua Bold

Boehringer Sans Regular

Boehringer Sans Regular Condensed

Boehringer Sans Regular Italic

Boehringer Sans Bold

Boehringer Sans Bold Condensed

Characters Boehringer Sans Regular

Aa Bb Cc Dd Ee Ff Gg Hh Ii Jj Kk Ll Mm Nn Oo Pp Qq Rr Ss Tt Uu Vv Ww Xx Yy Zz 0123456789

Sample Boehringer Antiqua Regular 9/12

The quick brown fox jumped over the lazy dogs. Victor jagt zwölf Boxkämpfer quer über den großen Sylter Deich. Portez ce vieux whisky au juge blond qui fume. El veloz murciélago hindú comía feliz cardillo y kiwi. La cigüeña tocaba el saxofón detrás del palenque de paja. Um pequeno jabuti xereta viu dez cegonhas felizes. Ma la volpe, col suo balzo, ha raggiunto il quieto Fido. Filmquiz bracht knappe ex-yogi van de wijs. Quizdeltagerne spiste jordbær med fløde, mens cirkusklovnen Walther spillede på xylofon. Høvdingens kjære squaw får litt pizza i Mexico by. Flygande bäckasiner söka hwila på mjuka tuvor. Sphinx of all black quartz judge my vow.

Sample Boehringer Sans Regular 9/12

The quick brown fox jumped over the lazy dogs. Victor jagt zwölf Boxkämpfer quer über den großen Sylter Deich. Portez ce vieux whisky au juge blond qui fume. El veloz murciélago hindú comía feliz cardillo y kiwi. La cigüeña tocaba el saxofón detrás del palenque de paja. Um pequeno jabuti xereta viu dez cegonhas felizes. Ma la volpe, col suo balzo, ha raggiunto il quieto Fido. Filmquiz bracht knappe ex-yogi van de wijs. Quizdeltagerne spiste jordbær med fløde, mens cirkusklovnen Walther spillede på xylofon. Høvdingens kjære squaw får litt pizza i Mexico by. Flygande bäckasiner söka hwila på mjuka tuvor. Sphinx of all black quartz judge my vow. Stanleys Expeditionszug quer durch Afrika wird von jedermann bewundert. Quel

Bosch

›Akzidenz Grotesk‹ and ›Baskerville‹ were the Bosch corporate typefaces. Both families were not very extensive, and combining them required a lot of tweaking, since their x-heights and widths were incompatible. The ›sans serif‹ face was supposed to appear warm and familiar, while the Antiqua was to follow the classic shapes, but more sturdy than ›Baskerville‹. ›Scheltersche Grotesk‹ is one of the precursors of ›Akzidenz Grotesk‹ and was the inspiration for ›Bosch Sans‹, while ›Bosch Serif‹ is based on the model developed by Richard Austin in the early 19th century, called ›Scotch Roman‹ in the USA. Christian Schwartz in New York digitized the extensive font family. → page 230

With: Christian Acker, Joshua Darden, and Christian Schwartz
Released: 2004
Foundry: Exclusive to Bosch GmbH

Styles

Bosch Serif Regular
Bosch Serif Regular Italic
Bosch Serif Bold
Bosch Serif Bold Italic
Bosch Sans Light
Bosch Sans Light Italic
Bosch Sans Regular
Bosch Sans Regular Italic
Bosch Sans Medium
Bosch Sans Medium Italic
Bosch Sans Bold
Bosch Sans Bold Italic
Bosch Sans Black
Bosch Sans Black Italic
Bosch Sans Condensed Regular
Bosch Sans Condensed Regular Italic
Bosch Sans Condensed Bold
Bosch Sans Condensed Bold Italic
Bosch Office Regular
Bosch Office Italic
Bosch Office Bold
Bosch Office Bold Italic

Characters Bosch Sans Regular

Aa Bb Cc Dd Ee Ff Gg Hh Ii Jj Kk
Ll Mm Nn Oo Pp Qq Rr Ss Tt Uu
Vv Ww Xx Yy Zz 0123456789

Cisco

Ralph du Carrois and Erik Spiekermann adapted and completed the existing house face for the American network technology manufacturers, which looked like a smoothed ›Helvetica‹ but whose details were somewhat messy. The new narrow version ensures family consistency on displays and in technical texts. It is space-saving and easy to read.

With: Ralph du Carrois
Released: 2010
Foundry: Exclusive to Cisco Network Systems

Styles

Cisco Sans Thin
Cisco Sans Thin Oblique
Cisco Sans Extra Light
Cisco Sans Extra Light Oblique
Cisco Sans Regular
Cisco Sans Regular Oblique
Cisco Sans Bold
Cisco Sans Bold Oblique
Cisco Sans Heavy
Cisco Sans Heavy Oblique
Cisco Sans Condensed Thin
Cisco Sans Condensed Thin Oblique
Cisco Sans Condensed Extra Light
Cisco Sans Condensed Extra Light Oblique
Cisco Sans Condensed Regular
Cisco Sans Condensed Regular Oblique
Cisco Sans Condensed Bold
Cisco Sans Condensed Bold Oblique
Cisco Sans Condensed Heavy
Cisco Sans Condensed Heavy Oblique

Characters Cisco Sans Regular

Aa Bb Cc Dd Ee Ff Gg Hh Ii Jj Kk
Ll Mm Nn Oo Pp Qq Rr Ss Tt Uu Vv
Ww Xx Yy Zz 0123456789

Sample Cisco Regular 9/12

The quick brown fox jumped over the lazy dogs. Victor jagt zwölf Boxkämpfer quer über den großen Sylter Deich. Portez ce vieux whisky au juge blond qui fume. El veloz murciélago hindú comía feliz cardillo y kiwi. La cigüeña tocaba el saxofón detrás del palenque de paja. Um pequeno jabuti xereta viu dez cegonhas felizes. Ma la volpe, col suo balzo, ha raggiunto il quieto Fido. Filmquiz bracht knappe ex-yogi van de wijs. Quiz-deltagerne spiste jordbær med fløde, mens cirkus-

The new typeface for Deutsche Bahn had to be able to do everything the old house face ›Helvetica‹ could and much more. The typeface has to represent the brand on forms and schedules, newspapers, magazines, and advertisements. It also has to fulfill very specific functions, be available everywhere, and be thoroughly built-out, so that there can be no excuses not to use it. ›DB Type‹ is a type system where all necessary versions are derived from a common repertoire, but which also have enough of an independent character of their own. Christian Schwartz worked with Erik Spiekermann on the concept and realization. → page 221

With: Christian Schwartz
Released: 2006
Foundry: Exclusive to Deutsche Bahn

Styles

DB Serif Regular
DB Serif Regular Italic
DB Serif Bold
DB Serif Bold Italic
DB News Regular
DB News Regular Italic
DB News Bold
DB News Bold Italic
DB Head Light
DB Head Light Italic
DB Head Regular
DB Head Regular Italic
DB Head Bold
DB Head Bold Italic
DB Head Black
DB Head Black Italic
DB Sans Light
DB Sans Light
DB Sans Light Italic
DB Sans Regular
DB Sans Regular Italic
DB Sans Bold
DB Sans Bold Italic
DB Sans Black
DB Sans Black Italic
DB Sans Condensed Regular
DB Sans Condensed Italic
DB Sans Condensed Bold
DB Sans Condensed Bold Italic

DB Sans Condensed Black
DB Sans Condensed Black Italic
DB Sans Compressed Regular
DB Sans Compressed Regular Italic
DB Sans Compressed Bold
DB Sans Compressed Bold Italic
DB Sans Compressed Black
DB Sans Compressed Black Italic

Characters DB Sans Regular

Aa Bb Cc Dd Ee Ff Gg Hh Ii Jj Kk Ll Mm Nn Oo Pp Qq Rr Ss Tt Uu Vv Ww Xx Yy Zz 0123456789

Sample DB Sans Regular 9/12

The quick brown fox jumped over the lazy dogs. Victor jagt zwölf Boxkämpfer quer über den großen Sylter Deich. Portez ce vieux whisky au juge blond qui fume. El veloz murciélago hindú comía feliz cardillo y kiwi. La cigüeña tocaba el saxofón detrás del palenque de paja. Um pequeno jabuti xereta viu dez cegonhas felizes. Ma la volpe, col suo balzo, ha raggiunto il quieto Fido. Filmquiz bracht knappe ex-yogi van de wijs. Quizdeltagerne spiste jordbær med fløde, mens cirkusklovnen Walther spillede på xylofon. Høvdingens kjære squaw får litt pizza i Mexico by. Flygande bäckasiner söka hwila på mjuka tuvor. Sphinx of all black quartz

Sample DB Head Black 12/16

The quick brown fox jumped over the lazy dogs. Victor jagt zwölf Boxkäm pfer quer über den großen Sylter Deich. Portez ce vieux whisky au juge blond qui fume. El veloz murciélago hindú comía feliz cardillo y kiwi. La cigüeña tocaba el saxofón detrás del palenque de paja. Um pequeno jabuti xereta viu

Sample DB Head Black 18/22

The quick brown fox jumped over the lazy dogs. Victor jagt zwölf Boxkämpfer quer über den großen Sylter Deich. Portez ce vieux whisky au juge blond qui fume. El veloz murcié-

EcoNewtype

Gunnlaugur Briem's original text face was readapted by Aurobind Patel in the late 1980s. It was set too tight in the magazine and looked somewhat overloaded and noisy. It was freed of its own ballast and cleaned up. The bold weight was made a little stronger to create the correct contrast to the text weight. Ole Schäfer digitized the family for the magazine's redesign in late 2000. → page 208

With: Ole Schäfer
Released: 2000
Foundry: Exclusive to ›The Economist‹

Styles

EcoNewtype Regular
EcoNewtype Italic
EcoNewtype Bold
EcoNewtype Bold Italic
EcoNewtype Head

Characters EcoNewtype Regular

Aa Bb Cc Dd Ee Ff Gg Hh Ii Jj Kk Ll Mm Nn Oo Pp Qq Rr Ss Tt Uu Vv Ww Xx Yy Zz 0123456789

Sample EcoNewtype Regular 9/12

The quick brown fox jumped over the lazy dogs. Victor jagt zwölf Boxkämpfer quer über den großen Sylter Deich. Portez ce vieux whisky au juge blond qui fume. El veloz murciélago hindú comía feliz cardillo y kiwi. La cigüeña tocaba el saxofón detrás del palenque de paja. Um pequeno jabuti xereta viu dez cegonhas felizes. Ma la volpe, col suo balzo, ha raggiunto il quieto Fido. Filmquiz bracht knappe ex-yogi van de wijs. Quizdeltagerne spiste jordbær med fløde, mens cirkusklovnen Walther spillede på xylofon. Høvdingens kjære squaw får litt pizza i Mexico by. Flygande bäckasiner söka hwila på mjuka tuvor. Sphinx of all black quartz judge my vow. Stanleys Expeditionszug quer durch Afrika wird von jedermann bewundert. Voyez le brick géant que j'examine près du wharf. A rápida

Sample EcoNewtype Head Regular 18/22

The quick brown fox jumped over the lazy dogs. Victor jagt zwölf Boxkämpfer quer über den großen Sylter Deich. Portez ce vieux whisky au juge blond qui fume. El veloz murciélago hindú comía feliz cardillo y kiwi. La cigüeña tocaba el saxofón detrás del

Explo

Designer Bill Hill needed a signage typeface for the Exploratorium in San Francisco that could combine the style of the stenciled signs in the historical harbor building with a new text face. ›FF Unit‹ is the new house typeface of the Exploratorium, and Ralph du Carrois created a new stencil face from ›FF Unit Bold‹.

With: Ralph du Carrois
Released: 2000
Foundry: Exclusive to Explo

Styles

EXPLO STENCIL

Characters Explo Stencil Regular

AA BB CC DD EE FF GG HH II JJ KK LL MM NN OO PP QQ RR SS TT UU VV WW XX YY ZZ 0123456789

Sample Explo Stencil Regular 18/22

THE QUICK BROWN FOX JUMPED OVER THE LAZY DOGS. VICTOR JAGT ZWÖLF BOXKÄMPFER QUER ÜBER DEN GROSSEN SYLTER DEICH. PORTEZ CE VIEUX WHISKY AU JUGE BLOND QUI FUME. EL VELOZ MURCIÉLAGO HINDÚ COMÍA FELIZ CARDILLO Y KIWI. LA CIGÜEÑA TOCABA EL SAXOFÓN DETRÁS DEL PALENQUE DE PAJA. UM PEQUENO JABUTI XERETA VIU DEZ CEGONHAS FELIZES. MA LA VOLPE, COL SUO BALZO, HA RAGGIUNTO IL QUIETO FIDO. FILMQUIZ BRACHT KNAPPE EX-YOGI VAN DE WIJS. QUIZDELTAGERNE SPISTE JORDBÆR

Fira

The Mozilla Foundation developed the browser Firefox. ›FF Meta‹ has long been Mozilla's corporate typeface. It made sense to develop the new typeface for the mobile operating system Firefox OS (hence the name) from Meta, to emphasize the brand similarity. ›Fira‹ is wider, calmer, and optimized for small screens. Programmers like the version with equal character widths. There will be other weights and versions of ›Fira‹. → page 279

With: Ralph du Carrois
Released: 2013
Foundry: Exclusive to Mozilla Firefox OS

Styles

Fira Sans Light
Fira Sans Light Italic
Fira Sans Regular
Fira Sans Regular Italic
Fira Sans Medium
Fira Sans Medium Italic
Fira Sans Bold
Fira Sans Bold Italic
Fira Mono Regular
Fira Mono Bold

Characters Fira Regular

Aa Bb Cc Dd Ee Ff Gg Hh Ii Jj Kk Ll Mm Nn Oo Pp Qq Rr Ss Tt Uu Vv Ww Xx Yy Zz 0123456789

Sample Fira Regular 9/12

The quick brown fox jumped over the lazy dogs. Victor jagt zwölf Boxkämpfer quer über den großen Sylter Deich. Portez ce vieux whisky au juge blond qui fume. El veloz murciélago hindú comía feliz cardillo y kiwi. La cigüeña tocaba el saxofón detrás del palenque de paja. Um pequeno jabuti xereta viu dez cegonhas felizes. Ma la volpe, col suo balzo, ha raggiunto il quieto Fido. Filmquiz bracht knappe ex-yogi van de wijs. Quizdeltagerne spiste jordbær med fløde, mens cirkusklovnen Walther spillede på xylofon. Høvdingens kjære squaw får litt pizza i Mexico by. Flygande bäckasiner

Sample Fira Mono Regular 9/12

The quick brown fox jumped over the lazy dogs. Victor jagt zwölf Boxkämpfer quer über den großen Sylter Deich. Portez ce vieux whisky au juge blond qui fume. El veloz murciélago hindú comía feliz cardillo y kiwi. La cigüeña tocaba el saxofón detrás del palenque de paja. Um pequeno jabuti xereta viu dez cegonhas felizes. Ma la volpe, col suo balzo, ha raggiunto il quieto Fido. Filmquiz bracht knappe ex-yogi van de wijs. Quizdeltagerne spiste jordbær med fløde, mens

Govan

The city of Glasgow was »UK City of Architecture & Design« in 1999, and its image was based on the many possibilities afforded by Erik Spiekermann's ›Glasgow‹ type, with its alternative letters and ligatures. Ole Schäfer drew a commercial version of this exclusive typeface in 2002, published as ›FF Govan‹ (named after an area of Glasgow). → page 192

With: Ole Schäfer
Released: 2001
Foundry: FontFont

Styles

Govan Regular
Govan Condensed Regular
Govan Expanded Regular

Characters Govan Regular

Aa Bb Cc Dd Ee Ff Gg Hh Ii Jj Kk Ll Mm Nn Oo Pp Qq Rr Ss Tt Uu Vv Ww Xx Yy Zz 0123456789

Characters Govan Regular Alternate

Aa Bb Cc Dd Ee Ff Gg Hh Ii Jj Kk Ll Mm Nn Oo Pp Qq Rr Ss Tt Uu Vv Ww Xx Yy Zz 0123456789

Sample Govan Regular and Alternate 18/22

The quick brown fox jumped over the lazy dogs. Victor jagt zwölf Boxkämpfer quer über den großen Sylter Deich. Portez ce vieux whisky au juge blond qui fume. El veloz murciélago hindú comía feliz cardillo y kiwi. La cigüeña tocaba el saxofón etrás del palenque de paja. Um pequeno jabuti xereta viu dez cegonhas felizes. Ma la volpe, col suo balzo, ha raggiunto il quieto Fido. Filmquiz bracht knappe ex-yogi van de wijs. Quizdeltagerne spiste jordbær med fløde, mens cirkusklovnen

Gravis

The new Gravis logo symbolizes the connection of analog and digital. Susanna Dulkinys and Julia Sysmäläinen developed an entire alphabet and dozens of icons from the logo shape to go with Gravis Round, the basic typeface for the brand: an FF Unit with rounded end strokes. → page 246

Hybrid with: Susanna Dulkinys and Julia Sysmäläinen
Round with: Christian Schwartz
Released: 2006
Foundry: Exclusive to Gravis

Styles

Gravis Hybrid
Gravis Round

Characters Gravis Hybrid Regular

Aa Bb Cc Dd Ee Ff Gg Hh Ii Jj Kk Ll Mm
Nn Oo Pp Qq Rr Ss Tt Uu Vv Ww Xx
Yy Zz 0123456789

Characters Gravis Round

**Aa Bb Cc Dd Ee Ff Gg Hh Ii Jj Kk Ll
Mm Nn Oo Pp Qq Rr Ss Tt Uu Vv Ww
Xx Yy Zz 0123456789**

Sample Gravis Round 12/16

The quick brown fox jumped over the lazy dogs. Victor jagt zwölf Boxkämpfer quer über den großen Sylter Deich. Portez ce vieux whisky au juge blond qui fume. El veloz murciélago hindú comía feliz cardillo y kiwi. La cigüeña tocaba el saxofón detrás del palenque de paja. Um pequeno jabuti xereta viu dez cegonhas felizes. Ma la volpe, col suo balzo, ha raggiunto il quieto Fido. Filmquiz bracht knappe ex-yogi van de wijs. Quizdeltagerne spiste jordbær med fløde, mens cirkusklovnen Walther spillede på xylofon. Høvdingens kjære squaw får litt pizza i Mexico by. Flygande bäckasiner söka hwila på mjuka tuvor.

Heidelberg

In the late 1990s Linotype belonged to the Heidelberg group. Thus, the model for a sans serif face for the new brand design was a version of News Gothic published by Stempel AG for phototypesetting but never digitized. Under Spiekermann's direction Erik Faulhaber at Stempel created a family with small caps, old style figures, and all the subtle details befitting a leading printing machine manufacturer. → page 200

With: Erik Faulhaber
Released: 1999
Foundry: Exclusive to Heidelberg

Styles

Heidelberg Gothic Regular
Heidelberg Gothic Italic
Heidelberg Gothic Bold
Heidelberg Gothic Bold Italic

Characters Heidelberg Gothic Regular

Aa Bb Cc Dd Ee Ff Gg Hh Ii Jj Kk Ll
Mm Nn Oo Pp Qq Rr Ss Tt Uu Vv Ww
Xx Yy Zz 0123456789

Sample Heidelberg Gothic Regular 9/12

The quick brown fox jumped over the lazy dogs. Victor jagt zwölf Boxkämpfer quer über den großen Sylter Deich. Portez ce vieux whisky au juge blond qui fume. El veloz murciélago hindú comía feliz cardillo y kiwi. La cigüeña tocaba el saxofón detrás del palenque de paja. Um pequeno jabuti xereta viu dez cegonhas felizes. Ma la volpe, col suo balzo, ha raggiunto il quieto Fido. Filmquiz bracht knappe ex-yogi van de wijs. Quizdeltagerne spiste jordbær med fløde, mens cirkusklovnen Walther spillede på xylofon. Høvdingens kjære squaw får litt pizza i Mexico by. Flygande bäckasiner söka hwila på mjuka tuvor. Sphinx of all black quartz judge my vow. Stanleys Expeditionszug quer durch Afrika wird von jedermann bewundert. Voyez le brick géant que j'examine près du wharf. A rápida

Sample Heidelberg Gothic Regular 12/16

The quick brown fox jumped over the lazy dogs. Victor jagt zwölf Boxkämpfer quer über den großen Sylter Deich. Portez ce vieux whisky au juge blond qui fume. El veloz murciélago hindú comía feliz cardillo y kiwi. La cigüeña tocaba el saxofón detrás del palenque de paja. Um pequeno jabuti xereta viu dez cegonhas felizes. Ma la volpe, col suo balzo, ha raggiunto il quieto Fido. Filmquiz bracht knappe ex-yogi van de wijs. Quizdeltagerne spiste jordbær med fløde, mens cirkusklovnen Walther spillede på xylofon. Høvdingens kjære squaw får litt pizza i Mexico by. Flygande

Info

This typeface was first used for the signage at Düsseldorf International airport in 1997. It is space-saving but easier to read than ›Helvetica‹ et al due to its open letter shapes. The rounded end strokes help avoid halo effects on backlit signs and are easier to cut with a plotter. ›FF Info‹ is based on a typeface that Erik Spiekermann had drawn for an Italian pharmaceutical company but that was never used. Ole Schäfer expanded the family with a version for body text and added ›Info Correspondence‹. The icons and pictograms are based on ›FF Transit‹. → page 191

With: Albert Pinggera and Ole Schäfer
Released: 1996
Foundry: FontFont

Styles

Info Display Regular
Info Display Regular Italic
Info Display Book
Info Display Book Italic
Info Display Medium
Info Display Medium Italic
Info Display Semibold
Info Display Semibold Italic
Info Display Bold
Info Display Bold Italic
Info Text Regular
Info Text Regular Italic
Info Text Book
Info Text Book Italic
Info Text Medium
Info Text Medium Italic
Info Text Semi bold
Info Text Semi bold Italic
Info Text Bold
Info Text Bold Italic
Info Correspondence Regular
Info Correspondence Regular Italic
Info Correspondence Medium
Info Correspondence Medium Italic
Info Correspondence Bold
Info Correspondence Bold Italic

Characters Info Regular

Aa Bb Cc Dd Ee Ff Gg Hh Ii Jj Kk Ll Mm
Nn Oo Pp Qq Rr Ss Tt Uu Vv Ww Xx Yy Zz
0123456789

Infoscreen

Infoscreen is a company that operates electronic screens in public transport vehicles and on the streets in Austria. This typeface was developed exclusively for that use – mainly subtitles and short news. It is space-saving, somewhat idiosyncratic, and, most importantly, easy to read in the relevant circumstances. Ralph du Carrois digitized it for Erik Spiekermann.

With: Ralph du Carrois
Released: 2012
Foundry: Exclusive to City Channel Infoscreen

Styles

Infoscreen Hairline
Infoscreen Regular
Infoscreen A
Infoscreen B
Infoscreen C

Characters Infoscreen Regular

Aa Bb Cc Dd Ee Ff Gg Hh Ii Jj Kk Ll Mm Nn Oo Pp Qq Rr Ss Tt Uu Vv Ww Xx Yy Zz 0123456789

Sample Infoscreen Regular 12/16

The quick brown fox jumped over the lazy dogs. Victor jagt zwoelf Boxkaempfer quer ueber den grossen Sylter Deich. Portez ce vieux whisky au juge blond qui fume. Um pequeno jabuti xereta viu dez cegonhas felizes. Ma la volpe, col suo balzo, ha raggiunto il quieto Fido. Filmquiz bracht knappe ex-yogi van de wijs. Sphinx of all black quartz judge my vow. Stanleys Expeditionszug quer durch Afrika wird von jedermann

Sample Infoscreen Regular 18/22

The quick brown fox jumped over the lazy dogs. Victor jagt zwoelf Boxkaempfer quer ueber den grossen Sylter Deich. Portez ce vieux whisky au juge blond qui fume. Um pequeno jabuti xereta viu dez cegonhas felizes. Ma la volpe, col suo balzo, ha raggiunto il

LoType

Spiekermann's first phototypesetting typeface for H. Berthold AG appeared in 1979. The ›Lo‹ typeface was originally a hot metal typeface drawn by Louis Oppenheim between 1911 and 1914, hence its name: ›Lo‹. By looking at old type specimens, Spiekermann discovered that each type size was drawn differently, so he had to start by finding the ideal shape for all sizes. He also completed missing characters and added a new weight, ›LoType Regular‹. The proofs were corrected by Günter Gerhard Lange, Berthold's artistic director. → page 54

With: Günter Gerhard Lange
Released: 1980
Foundry: H. Berthold AG

Styles

LoType Light
LoType Regular
LoType Medium
LoType Medium Condensed
LoType Medium Italic
LoType Bold

Characters LoType Regular

Aa Bb Cc Dd Ee Ff Gg Hh Ii Jj Kk Ll Mm Nn Oo Pp Qq Rr Ss Tt Uu Vv Ww Xx Yy Zz 0123456789

Sample LoType Regular 18/22

The quick brown fox jumped over the lazy dogs. Victor jagt zwölf Boxkämpfer quer über den großen Sylter Deich. Portez ce vieux whisky au juge blond qui fume. El veloz murciélago hindú comía feliz cardillo y kiwi. La cigüeña tocaba el saxofón detrás del palenque de paja. Um pequeno jabuti xereta viu dez cegonhas felizes. Ma la volpe, col suo balzo, ha raggiunto il quieto Fido. Filmquiz bracht knappe ex-yogi van de wijs. Quizdeltagerne

Messe Univers

Representing the many product and brand hierarchies of Messe Frankfurt requires many easily distinguishable fonts which must not run too wide. ›Univers‹ was a given as the Messe corporate typeface, but some shapes were designed more openly to help differentiate them. The regular weight was made slightly narrower and extrapolated to four new weights by Erik van Blokland using his superpolator. → page 256

With: Erik van Blokland
Released: 2007
Foundry: Exclusive to Messe Frankfurt

Styles

Messe Univers Light
Messe Univers Light Italic
Messe Univers Regular
Messe Univers Regular Italic
Messe Univers Bold Italic
Messe Univers Black
Messe Univers Black Italic
Messe Univers Condensed Light
Messe Univers Condensed Light Italic
Messe Univers Condensed Regular
Messe Univers Condensed Regular Italic
Messe Univers Condensed Bold
Messe Univers Condensed Bold Italic

Characters Messe Univers Regular

Aa Bb Cc Dd Ee Ff Gg Hh Ii Jj Kk Ll Mm Nn Oo Pp Qq Rr Ss Tt Uu Vv Ww Xx Yy Zz 0123456789

Sample Messe Univers Regular 12/16

The quick brown fox jumped over the lazy dogs. Victor jagt zwölf Boxkämpfer quer über den großen Sylter Deich. Portez ce vieux whisky au juge blond qui fume. El veloz murciélago hindú comía feliz cardillo y kiwi. La cigüeña tocaba el saxofón detrás del palenque de paja. Um pequeno jabuti xereta viu dez cegonhas felizes. Ma la volpe, col suo balzo, ha raggiunto il quieto Fido. Filmquiz bracht knappe ex-yogi van de wijs. Quizdeltagerne spiste jordbær med fløde, mens cirkusklovnen Walther spillede på xylofon. Høvdingens kjære squaw får litt pizza i Mexico by. Flygande bäckasiner söka hwila på mjuka tuvor.

Meta

After Deutsche Post had rejected the original version as its house face (under the name ›PT55‹), it lay around until new software made it possible to produce type on an Apple Macintosh. Just van Rossum and Erik van Blokland converted Spiekermann's Ikarus data, completing missing characters and creating an exclusive typeface for MetaDesign, hence the name. In 1990, as ›FF Meta‹ it became one of the first FontFonts and the first of a new class of alternative humanist sans serif faces with old style figures and several other features that had previously belonged solely to Antiquas. Dubbed the »Helvetica of the '90s«, Meta remains one of the most successful new typefaces. Many people worked on expanding it, among them Lucas de Groot, Ole Schäfer, Jay Rutherford, Christian Schwartz, and Oded Ezer. New Zealander Kris Sowersby also joined the team for ›Meta Serif‹. → page 152

With: Lucas de Groot, Oded Ezer, Ole Schäfer, Christian Schwartz, Kris Sowersby, Jay Rutherford, Erik van Blokland, and Just van Rossum
Released: 1990
Foundry: FontFont

Styles

Meta Hairline
Meta Hairline Italic
Meta Thin
Meta Thin Italic
Meta Light
Meta Light Italic
Meta Normal
Meta Normal Italic
Meta Book
Meta Book Italic
Meta Medium
Meta Medium Italic
Meta Bold
Meta Bold Italic
Meta Black
Meta Black Italic
Meta Condensed Normal
Meta Condensed Normal Italic
Meta Condensed Book
Meta Condensed Book Italic
Meta Condensed Medium
Meta Condensed Medium Italic
Meta Condensed Bold
Meta Condensed Bold Italic
Meta Condensed Extra Bold
Meta Condensed Extra Bold Italic

Meta Condensed Black
Meta Condensed Black Italic
Meta Correspondence Regular
Meta Correspondence Regular Italic
Meta Correspondence Bold
Meta Correspondence Bold Italic
Meta Headline Light
Meta Headline Regular
Meta Headline Bold
Meta Headline Black
Meta Headline Condensed Light
Meta Headline Condensed Regular
Meta Headline Condensed Bold
Meta Headline Condensed Black
Meta Headline Compressed Light
Meta Headline Compressed Regular
Meta Headline Compressed Bold
Meta Headline Compressed Black
Meta Serif Light
Meta Serif Light Italic
Meta Serif Book
Meta Serif Book Italic
Meta Serif Medium
Meta Serif Medium Italic
Meta Serif Bold
Meta Serif Bold Italic
Meta Serif Extra Bold
Meta Serif Extra Bold Italic
Meta Serif Black
Meta Serif Black Italic

Characters Meta Regular

Aa Bb Cc Dd Ee Ff Gg Hh Ii Jj Kk Ll Mm Nn Oo Pp Qq Rr Ss Tt Uu Vv Ww Xx Yy Zz 0123456789

Nokia

The exclusive house face for Nokia originated as a project for which Spiekermann had made bitmap fonts in many sizes for displays. What they all had in common was the marked contrast between vertical and horizontal lines. This is the basic design principle of the typeface. Ole Schäfer produced a first outline font from Spiekermann's designs before Spiekermann himself added several variants, including the serif version. The finishing touches and production were carried out by Jelle Bosma at Monotype, who also added further weights to ›Nokia Sans‹ and expanded it into an extensive font family. → page 210

With: Jelle Bosma and Ole Schäfer
Released: 2002
Foundry: Exclusive to Nokia

Styles

Nokia Sans Light
Nokia Sans Regular
Nokia Sans Semibold
Nokia Sans Bold
Nokia Sans Condensed Regular
Nokia Sans Wide Regular
Nokia Sans Wide Italic
Nokia Sans Wide Bold
Nokia Sans Title Semibold
Nokia Sans Title Bold
Nokia Serif Regular
Nokia Serif Bold

Characters Nokia Sans Regular

Aa Bb Cc Dd Ee Ff Gg Hh Ii Jj Kk Ll Mm Nn Oo Pp Qq Rr Ss Tt Uu Vv Ww Xx Yy Zz 0123456789

Sample Nokia Sans Regular 12/16

The quick brown fox jumped over the lazy dogs. Victor jagt zwölf Boxkämpfer quer über den großen Sylter Deich. Portez ce vieux whisky au juge blond qui fume. El veloz murciélago hindú comía feliz cardillo y kiwi. La cigüeña tocaba el saxofón detrás del palenque de paja. Um pequeno jabuti xereta viu dez cegonhas felizes. Ma la volpe, col suo balzo, ha raggiunto il quieto Fido. Filmquiz bracht knappe ex-yogi van de wijs. Quizdeltagerne spiste jordbær med fløde, mens cirkusklovnen Walther spillede på xylofon. Høvdingens kjære squaw får litt pizza i Mexico by. Fly-

Officina

In 1988 Spiekermann proposed a new design with the working title ›ITC Correspondence‹ for the International Typeface Corporation as a substitute for typewriter fonts that were no longer practical on a laser printer. It was released as ›ITC Officina Sans‹ in 1989. Just van Rossum drew serifs on the ›Sans‹: ›ITC Officina Serif‹. Ole Schäfer, a student in Bielefeld at the time, proposed designs for further weights in 1995, using the occasion to expand the family to include small caps and old style figures. ›Officina Display‹ was created for the redesign of ›The Economist‹ in London in 2001, first by Ole Schäfer exclusively for ›The Economist‹, before being adapted by Christian Schwartz for publication by ITC. → page 115

With: Ole Schäfer, Christian Schwartz, and Just van Rossum
Released: 1989
Foundry: ITC

Styles

Officina Sans Book
Officina Sans Book Italic
Officina Sans Medium
Officina Sans Medium Italic
Officina Sans Bold
Officina Sans Italic Bold
Officina Sans Extra Bold
Officina Sans Extra Bold Italic
Officina Sans Black
Officina Sans Black Italic
Officina Serif Book
Officina Serif Book Italic
Officina Serif Medium
Officina Serif Medium Italic
Officina Serif Bold
Officina Serif Bold Italic
Officina Serif Extra Bold
Officina Serif Extra Bold Italic
Officina Serif Black
Officina Serif Black Italic
Officina Display Light
Officina Display Regular
Officina Display Bold
Officina Display Black

Characters Officina Regular

Aa Bb Cc Dd Ee Ff Gg Hh Ii Jj Kk Ll Mm Nn Oo Pp Qq Rr Ss Tt Uu Vv Ww Xx Yy Zz 0123456789

Real

Designed specially for this book. Spiekermann always wanted to do a version of ›Akzidenz Grotesk‹ based on a particularly light version of the medium weight that only existed as wood type for very large sizes. ›Real‹ is slightly lighter than that one but still stronger than regular text faces, most of which Spiekermann regards as being far too light. Ralph du Carrois did not miss the chance to expand ›Real‹ to a family. → page 3

With: Ralph du Carrois
Foundry: Exclusive to this book

Styles

Real Text Regular
Real Text Book
Real Text Bold
Real Text Heavy
Real Head Regular
Real Head Book
Real Head Bold
Real Head Heavy

Characters Real Text Regular

Aa Bb Cc Dd Ee Ff Gg Hh Ii Jj Kk Ll Mm Nn Oo Pp Qq Rr Ss Tt Uu Vv Ww Xx Yy Zz 0123456789

Sample Real Text Regular 9/12

The quick brown fox jumped over the lazy dogs. Victor jagt zwölf Boxkämpfer quer über den großen Sylter Deich. Portez ce vieux whisky au juge blond qui fume. El veloz murciélago hindú comía feliz cardillo y kiwi. La cigüeña to-caba el saxofón detrás del palenque de paja. Um pequeno jabuti xereta viu dez cegonhas felizes. Ma la volpe, col suo balzo, ha raggiunto il quieto Fido. Filmquiz bracht knappe ex-yogi van de wijs. Quizdeltagerne spiste jordbær med fløde, mens cirkusklovnen Walther spillede på xylofon. Høvdingens kjære squaw får litt pizza i Mexico by. Flygande bäckasiner söka hwila på mjuka tuvor. Sphinx of all black quartz judge my vow. Stanleys Expeditionszug quer durch Afrika wird von jedermann bewundert. Voyez le brick géant

Sample Real Head Regular 18/22

The quick brown fox jumped over the lazy dogs. Victor jagt zwölf Boxkämpfer quer über den großen Sylter Deich. Portez ce vieux whisky au juge blond qui fume. El veloz murciélago hindú comía feliz

TERN

Initially the project brief only asked for bitmap fonts to appear on electronic displays on European highways (Trans European Road Network). Only once those were completed did the client also ask for print fonts. The first version consisted solely of outlines around the bitmap shapes. Ralph du Carrois was brought onboard to add an italic, a condensed and a narrow version. TERN Condensed has since become the standard typeface for use on all roads in Austria. → page 234

With: Ralph du Carrois
Released: 2008
Foundry: Exclusive to the European Commission

Styles

TERN Narrow
TERN Condensed
TERN Regular
TERN Italic
TERN VMS One Four
TERN VMS Two Zero
TERN VMS Two Four
TERN VMS Three One

Characters TERN Regular

Aa Bb Cc Dd Ee Ff Gg Hh Ii Jj Kk Ll Mm Nn Oo Pp Qq Rr Ss Tt Uu Vv Ww Xx Yy Zz 0123456789

Sample TERN Regular 18/22

The quick brown fox jumped over the lazy dogs. Victor jagt zwölf Boxkämpfer quer über den großen Sylter Deich. Portez ce vieux whisky au juge blond qui fume. El veloz murciélago hindú comía feliz cardillo y kiwi. La cigüeña tocaba el saxofón detrás del palenque de paja. Um pequeno jabuti xereta viu dez cegonhas felizes. Ma la volpe, col suo balzo, ha raggiunto il quieto Fido. Filmquiz bracht knappe

Transit

After German reunification in 1989 the Berlin transport authorities needed a new signage system for the city. ›Transit‹ is a condensed version of ›Frutiger‹ with several changes such as different descenders, round dots, and varied stroke widths for back or front-lit signs, in negative and positive versions respectively. With several hundred pictograms, ›Transit‹ is a solution for signage systems everywhere. Henning Krause and Lucas de Groot worked on the typeface alongside Spiekermann at MetaDesign. → page 130

With: Lucas de Groot and Henning Krause
Released: 1992
Foundry: FontFont

Styles

Transit Print Regular

Transit Print Regular Italic

Transit Print Bold

Transit Print Bold Italic

Transit Print Black

Transit Front Negativ Regular

Transit Front Negativ Regular Italic

Transit Front Negativ Bold

Transit Front Positiv Regular

Transit Front Positiv Regular Italic

Transit Front Positiv Bold

Transit Back Negativ Regular

Transit Back Negativ Regular Italic

Transit Back Negativ Bold

Transit Back Positiv Regular

Transit Back Positiv Regular Italic

Transit Back Positiv Bold

Characters Transit Regular

Aa Bb Cc Dd Ee Ff Gg Hh Ii Jj Kk Ll Mm
Nn Oo Pp Qq Rr Ss Tt Uu Vv Ww Xx Yy
Zz 0123456789

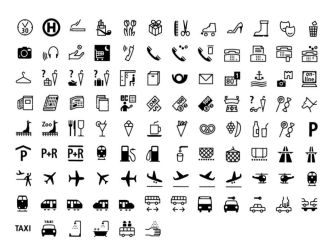

The quick brown fox jumped over the lazy dogs. Victor jagt zwölf Boxkämpfer quer über den großen Sylter Deich. Portez ce vieux whisky au juge blond qui fume. El veloz murciélago hindú comía feliz cardillo y kiwi. La cigüeña tocaba el saxofón detrás del palenque de paja. Um pequeno jabuti xereta viu dez cegonhas felizes. Ma la volpe, col suo balzo, ha raggiunto il quieto Fido. Filmquiz bracht knappe ex-yogi van de wijs. Quizdeltagerne spiste jordbær med fløde, mens cirkusklovnen Walther spillede på xylofon. Høvdingens kjære squaw får litt pizza i Mexico by. Flygande bäckasiner söka hwila på mjuka tuvor. Sphinx of all black quartz judge my vow. Stanleys Expe-

The quick brown fox jumped over the lazy dogs. Victor jagt zwölf Boxkämpfer quer über den großen Sylter Deich. Portez ce vieux whisky au juge blond qui fume. El veloz murciélago hindú comía feliz cardillo y kiwi. La cigüeña tocaba el saxofón detrás del palenque de paja. Um pequeno jabuti xereta viu dez cegonhas felizes. Ma la volpe, col suo balzo, ha raggiunto il quieto Fido. Filmquiz bracht knappe exyogi van de wijs. Quizdeltagerne spiste jordbær

The quick brown fox jumped over the lazy dogs. Victor jagt zwölf Boxkämpfer quer über den großen Sylter Deich. Portez ce vieux whisky au juge blond qui fume. El veloz murciélago hindú comía feliz cardillo y kiwi. La cigüeña tocaba el saxofón

Unit

Before Deutsche Bahn knew that they needed a new typeface, Christan Schwartz proposed a bold and straightened version of ›FF Meta‹ for a DB poster campaign. Like the postal service before them, Deutsche Bahn were not interested, so Spiekermann and Schwartz named the typeface after United Designers and used it as an exclusive house face. When they expanded the family as a FontFont, Schwartz, Spiekermann, and Sowersby decided to adapt ›Unit Slab‹ to be compatible with ›MetaSerif‹ and vice versa. ›FF Unit‹ is a bit like an older sister to ›Meta‹, a little more serious and responsible. → page 216

→ page 216

With: Christan Schwartz and Kris Sowersby
Released: 2006
Foundry: FontFont

Styles

Unit Thin
Unit Thin Italic
Unit Light
Unit Light Italic
Unit Regular
Unit Regular Italic
Unit Medium
Unit Medium Italic
Unit Bold
Unit Bold Italic
Unit Black
Unit Black Italic
Unit Ultra
Unit Ultra Italic
Unit Rounded Light
Unit Rounded Regular
Unit Rounded Medium
Unit Rounded Bold
Unit Rounded Black
Unit Rounded Ultra
Unit Slab Thin
Unit Slab Thin Italic
Unit Slab Light
Unit Slab Light Italic
Unit Slab Regular
Unit Slab Regular Italic
Unit Slab Medium
Unit Slab Medium Italic
Unit Slab Bold

Unit Slab Bold Italic
Unit Slab Black
Unit Slab Black Italic
Unit Slab Ultra
Unit Slab Ultra Italic

Characters Unit Regular

Aa Bb Cc Dd Ee Ff Gg Hh Ii Jj Kk Ll Mm Nn Oo Pp Qq Rr Ss Tt Uu Vv Ww Xx Yy Zz 0123456789

Sample Unit Regular 9/12

The quick brown fox jumped over the lazy dogs. Victor jagt zwölf Boxkämpfer quer über den großen Sylter Deich. Portez ce vieux whisky au juge blond qui fume. El veloz murciélago hindú comía feliz cardillo y kiwi. La cigüeña tocaba el saxofón detrás del palenque de paja. Um pequeno jabuti xereta viu dez cegonhas felizes. Ma la volpe, col suo balzo, ha raggiunto il quieto Fido. Filmquiz bracht knappe ex-yogi van de wijs. Quizdeltagerne spiste jordbær med fløde, mens cirkusklovnen Walther spillede på xylofon. Høvdingens kjære squaw får litt pizza i Mexico by. Flygande bäckasiner söka hwila på mjuka tuvor. Sphinx of all black quartz judge my vow. Stanleys Expeditionszug quer durch Afrika wird von jedermann bewundert. Voyez le brick géant que j'examine près du wharf. A rápida

Sample Unit Regular 12/16

The quick brown fox jumped over the lazy dogs. Victor jagt zwölf Boxkämpfer quer über den großen Sylter Deich. Portez ce vieux whisky au juge blond qui fume. El veloz murciélago hindú comía feliz cardillo y kiwi. La cigüeña tocaba el saxofón detrás del palenque de paja. Um pequeno jabuti xereta viu dez cegonhas felizes. Ma la volpe, col suo balzo, ha raggiunto il quieto Fido. Filmquiz bracht

Sample Unit Regular 18/22

The quick brown fox jumped over the lazy dogs. Victor jagt zwölf Boxkämpfer quer über den großen Sylter Deich. Portez ce vieux whisky au juge blond qui fume. El veloz murciélago hindú comía feliz cardillo y kiwi. La cigüeña tocaba el saxofón

ZDF News

The ubiquitous ›Helvetica‹ was too cold and stiff as the broadcaster's house face. ›ZDF News‹ introduces the irregularities of a typewriter font, making it lively like live TV news. Several hundred pictograms follow the style of the typeface and visualize numbers and facts. Many of these characters are animations contained within the fonts. Ralph du Carrois and Erik Spiekermann designed the typeface; Julia Sysmäläinen and Susanna Dulkinys devised the concept for the pictograms, which were in turn realized by Ralph. → page 260

With: Ralph du Carrois, Susanna Dulkinys, and Julia Sysmäläinen
Released: 2009
Foundry: Exclusive to Zweites Deutsches Fernsehen

Styles

ZDF News Screen Regular
ZDF News Screen Medium
ZDF News Screen Bold

Characters News Screen Regular

Aa Bb Cc Dd Ee Ff Gg Hh Ii Jj Kk Ll
Mm Nn Oo Pp Qq Rr Ss Tt Uu Vv Ww
Xx Yy Zz 0123456789

Sample Figures News Screen Regular 12/16

The quick brown fox jumped over the lazy dogs. Victor jagt zwölf Boxkämpfer quer über den großen Sylter Deich. Portez ce vieux whisky au juge blond qui fume. El veloz murciélago hindú comía feliz cardillo y kiwi. La cigüeña tocaba el saxofón detrás del palenque de paja. Um pequeno jabuti xereta viu dez cegonhas felizes. Ma la volpe, col suo balzo, ha raggiunto il quieto Fido. Filmquiz bracht knappe ex-yogi van de wijs. Quizdeltagerne spiste jordbær med fløde, mens cirkusklovnen Walther spillede på xylofon. Høvdingens kjære squaw får litt pizza i Mexico by. Flygande bäckasiner söka hwila på mjuka tuvor. Sphinx of all black quartz judge my vow. Stanleys Expeditionszug quer durch Afrika wird von jede

Most of the projects presented in this book were the result of a collaboration between Erik Spiekermann and various colleagues. The following overview contains brief introductions to these colleagues and describes what they are doing today, insofar as they could be researched.

Abdullah, Rayan

Abdullah (b. 1957) worked as project manager at MetaDesign Berlin from 1993 to 2001. Since 2001 he has been professor of typography at the Academy for Visual Arts Leipzig. In 2002 he founded the Markenbau agency.
www.rayan.de
→130

Acker, Christian

Acker (b. 1979) founded the design studio Adnauseum in New York City in 2002. He created typefaces including ›Mene One Mexicali‹, ›Meskyle Laid Back‹ and ›Sabe Ghetto Gothic‹ for his font label Handselecta.
www.handselecta.com
→ 231, 295

Acornley, Ben

Acornley (b. 1973) worked as a graphic designer at MetaDesign London from 2000 to 2001. Today he is a partner and creative director at the Applied design studio in London.
www.applied-espi.com
→ 207

Barney, Gerry

Barney (b. 1938) is one of the most renowned British graphic designers. In 1978 he founded the design company Sedley Place in London with three partners. Besides many global branding projects, his best-known work is the corporate design for British Rail.
www.sedley-place.com
→ 61, 87

Berkenbusch, Anna

Berkenbusch (b. 1955) was the first MetaDesign employee in 1979, and stayed there until 1982. Today she runs her own company, Anna B. Design, and is professor of communication design at Burg Giebichenstein University of Art and Design in Halle.
www.annabdesign.de
→ 61, 64, 72

Betton, Pia

Betton worked as a designer and design manager at MetaDesign from 1991 to 2002. Today she is a partner and director of consulting at Edenspiekermann in Berlin.
www.edenspiekermann.com
→ 168, 171, 172, 175, 264

Blumberg, Gail

Blumberg worked as a designer, art director, and creative director at Adobe, and today runs her design company Blumberg Communication Design in Menlo Park, California.
www.blumbergdesign.com
→ 109

Booms, Hans

Booms worked as a graphic designer at various Dutch design studios before joining Edenspiekermann Amsterdam in 1999, where he has been a partner and design director since 2009.
www.edenspiekermann.com
→ 264

Bosma, Jelle

Bosma (b. 1959) worked as a type designer for Scangraphic and Monotype before starting his own studio in The Hague, Netherlands. He developed various typefaces (including ›Cursivium‹ and ›Cambria‹), and is known for his non-Latin fonts.
→ 210, 303

Botez, Timon

Botez (b. 1973) worked as a freelance graphic and information designer at MetaDesign London. After years spent in the USA and England, he is now an artist in Oslo.
www.botezco.com
→ 207

Branczyk, Alexander

Branczyk (b. 1959) worked as a graphic designer at MetaDesign Berlin from 1988 to 1994. Afterwards he founded the design company xplicit in Frankfurt and Berlin with Thomas Nagel and Uwe Otto. He has also taught at various universities, most recently in Dortmund.
www.czyk.de
→ 102, 120, 134

Brody, Neville

Brody (b. 1957) is one of the best-known graphic designers in the world. He was art director of British magazines ›The Face‹ and ›Arena‹, and designed record covers, typefaces, and corporate designs at Neville Brody Studios before founding Research Studios in London in 1994, who now have branches in Berlin, Barcelona, and Tokyo. In 1998 he founded FontShop International with Erik and Joan Spiekermann, and initiated the FUSE conference in 1995, which later became TYPO. Brody is also the dean of the art and communication department at the Royal College of Art, London.
www.researchstudios.com
→ 122, 137, 138, 181

Christ, Gerald

Christ worked as a graphic designer and project manager at MetaDesign Berlin. Today he is professor of visual communication and typography at the design department of Anhalt University of Applied Sciences. He is also a design consultant and photo artist.
www.geraldchrist.com
→ 170

Cleary, Ed

Cleary directed the London typesetters Filmcomposition before emigrating to Toronto, where he became director of FontShop International Canada. Cleary died in 1994.
→ 43, 46, 52, 139

Coates, Stephen

Coates was art director of magazines such as ›Blueprint‹, ›Eye‹, ›Tate‹, and ›Sight & Sound‹. Today he runs his own design studio and works as an advisor and publicist.
www.stephencoates.co.uk
→ 149

Cook, Steven

Cook worked as a graphic designer and project manager for the fashion designer Marc Jacobs before becoming creative director and partner at Edenspiekermann in Berlin.
www.edenspiekermann.com
→ 264

Curtis, Gayle

Curtis is a software and online designer. He teaches visual thinking and human-computer interaction at Stanford University.
www.gaylecurtis.com
→ 169

Darden, Joshua

Darden is a typeface designer (›Birra‹, ›Corundum‹, ›Freight‹, ›Jubilat‹, ›Omnes‹, et al) who runs Darden Studio in New York City. He also teaches at various universities.
www.dardenstudio.com
→ 231, 295

De Groot, Lucas

De Groot (b. 1963) worked at MetaDesign in Berlin from 1993 to 1998, when he developed his typeface ›Thesis‹. Afterwards he started his font label LucasFonts, who specialized in designing fonts for businesses (›ARD‹, ›PLUS‹, ›Spiegel‹, ›TAZ‹). He is professor of type design at Potsdam University of Applied Sciences.
www.lucasfonts.com
→ 152, 168, 172, 175, 302, 305

Doerrié, Gerhard

Doerrié (1936–1984) was a co-founder of MetaDesign in 1979. He was a trained compositor. In 1960 he moved to Montreal where he worked as a graphic designer and professor. In the late 1970s he returned to Germany, and died a few years later.
→ 59

Du Carrois, Ralph
Du Carrois (b. 1975) designs typefaces at his Studio Carrois Type Design for various clients e.g. Edenspiekermann and Erik Spiekermann (e.g. ›Fira‹, ›ZDF News‹, ›Cisco Sans‹ and ›Meta Science‹).
www.carrois.com
→ 235, 258, 260, 279, 293, 295, 297, 298, 300, 304

Dulkinys, Susanna
Dulkinys is a founding partner at Edenspiekermann, SpiekermannPartners, and United Designers Network.
www.edenspiekermann.com
→ 196, 220, 246, 247, 252, 255, 260, 264, 268, 273, 299, 307

Esterson, Simon
As art director of ›Blueprint‹, ›Domus‹ and ›The Guardian‹, Esterson became one of the most prolific British editorial designers. In 2008 he took over the design magazine ›Eye‹ with John L. Walters, and has been its art director ever since. He also runs the design company Esterson Associates in London.
www.estersonassociates.co.uk
→ 149

Etter, Michael
Etter (1949–2007) studied advertising sales before founding the Berlin advertising agency »Etter and partners – the last agency before the Wall«, after which he founded the publishing company »Inkognito – the society for great big surprises« in 1990, where he sold postcards, posters, and other satirical products such as the »Angie citrus press«.
www.inkognito.de
→ 134

Ezer, Oded
Ezer was a musician and poet before engaging in graphic design on the threshold of art and typography. He has lived in Jerusalem, London, and the Negev desert, and currently resides in Tel Aviv.
www.odedezer.com
→ 152, 302

Faulhaber, Erik
Faulhaber (b. 1966) is a graphic and type designer (for example, ›Xenois‹, ›Aeonis‹, ›Generis‹). He wrote a book about the ›Frutiger‹ typeface, and teaches at various universities.
www.effont.com
→ 299

Fendley, Tim
Fendley is a graphic designer who was a founding partner of MetaDesign London. Today he runs the design studio Applied, which specializes in urban information systems.
www.applied-espi.com
→ 178, 195

Fischer, Christa
Fischer is an interior architect who has worked with her company for MetaDesign since the 1990s, and subsequently also for United Designers Network, Edenspiekermann, and Erik Spiekermann.
www.fischerinnen.de
→ 177

Fischer, Florian
Fischer (b. 1940) co-founded MetaDesign in 1979. He studied interior architecture plus product and graphic design before starting the design agency Fischer & Scholz, and today works as a consultant and publicist in Berlin.
www.der-naechste-schritt.ff-wey.com
→ 41, 59, 61, 64, 72, 86

Frech, Charly
Frech worked as a graphic designer before becoming a board member at MetaDesign from 1991 to 2002. Today he is a partner at Fuenfwerken Design and consultant for various design initiatives. He is also a professor in Würzburg and Potsdam.
www.carlfrech.de
→ 130, 172

Ginger, E. M.
Ginger is a typographic advisor and publicist. With her company 42-Line she produces digital editions of valuable typographic print works.
www.42-line.com
→ 162

Greisner, Inken
Greisner worked as a graphic designer at MetaDesign from 1987 to 1988 before starting her own company Typoly.
www.typoly.de
→ 102, 112

Grubitzsch, Katja
Grubitzsch worked as graphic designer at ›Wired‹ magazine in San Francisico and subsequently at MetaDesign Berlin. Today she is creative director and member of the management team at Edenspiekermann.
www.edenspiekermann.com
→ 268

Hartwig, Brigitte
Hartwig worked as a graphic designer at MetaDesign Berlin from 1990 to 2000. In 2001 she started the design company Embassy in Berlin. Since 2004 she has taught design at the Anhalt University of Applied Sciences in Dessau.
www.embassyexperts.com
→ 130, 189

Heil, Dieter
Heil coordinated the German projects for the London design agency Wolff Olins before co-founding MetaDesign in 1979. His current activity is not known.
→ 59, 61, 86

Henze, Karsten
Henze (b. 1965) worked as design manager at MetaDesign from 1996 to 2000. Since 2001 he has been responsible for the appearance and creative aspect of Deutsche Bahn. He is chairman of the board of IDZ, International Design Zentrum Berlin.
www.idz.de
→ 130

Hill, Bill
Hill is a graphic designer. He founded MetaDesign San Francisco in 1992 with Terry Irwin, and remained its chairman until 2010. Today he runs his own studio, Bill Hill Design, and is a consultant to the branding company Rebrand in San Francisco.
www.rebrand.com
→ 109, 158, 169

Holthuis, Joost
Holthuis worked as design director from 1999 at Eden Design. Today he is creative director and partner at Edenspiekermann in Amsterdam.
www.edenspiekermann.com
→ 264

Holzwarth, Hans Werner
Holzwarth is a trained photographer skilled at graphic design. He was one of the early employees at MetaDesign in Berlin. Today he works with publishing companies and galleries on books about contemporary artists.
www.holzwarth.de
→ 90, 101, 102, 106, 107, 112

Hooper Woolsey, Kristina
Hooper Woolsey is a scientist who works on exploring the potential of multimedia for education and further education. As the »mother of multimedia« she worked for Atari and Apple, and taught at numerous universities.
www.beispiel.de
→ 169

Irwin, Terry
Irwin is a graphic designer. She founded MetaDesign San Francisco with Bill Hill before dedicating herself to teaching at various schools. Since 2009 she has run the Carnegie Mellon School of Design in Pittsburgh.
www.design.cmu.edu
→ 158, 169

Kahlfeldt, Paul
Kahlfeldt (b. 1956) is an architect who runs Kahlfeldt Architekten in Berlin with his wife. He is also professor at the Technical University of Dortmund, and is on the board of Deutscher Werkbund and Internationale Bauakademie Berlin.
www.kahlfeldt-architekten.de
→ 177

Kahlfeldt, Petra

Kahlfeldt (b. 1960) is an architect who runs Kahlfeldt Architekten in Berlin with her husband. She is also a professor at Beuth University of Applied Sciences in Berlin, and works on various councils and advisory boards.
www.kahlfeldt-architekten.de
→ 177

Kim, Scott

Scott studied computer science and graphic design at Stanford University. He works with visual puzzles such as anagrams.
www.scottkim.com
→ 169

Klein, Manfred

Klein (b. 1932) started as a compositor before learning typography and type design under G.G. Lange. He developed many often experimental typefaces and fonts, including ›Birds‹, ›FF Johannes G‹ and ›FF Schoensperger‹.
→ 156

Köble, Rainer

As an independent economist Köble was responsible for the project management of Meta-Haus at MetaDesign. He runs Köble Consult and is chairman of the board at FontShop AG.
www.koeble-consult.de
→ 177

Kolaschnik, Axel

Kolaschnik was design and communications manager at MetaDesign before becoming a freelance communication advisor. He is professor for corporate identity at the design faculty of Mannheim University, and is active as a counselor in numerous communication initiatives.
www.axel-kolaschnik.de
→ 170

Koster, Rik

Koster is a graphic designer. He was design director and partner at Eden Design from 1999; since 2009 he has been creative director and partner at Edenspiekermann in Amsterdam.
www.edenspiekermann.com
→ 264

Krause, Henning

Krause worked as a graphic designer at MetaDesign in Berlin from 1990 to 1993. He subsequently founded Büro Formgebung and manages Monotype Font Production. Krause was president of BDG Berufsverband der Deutschen Kommunikationsdesigner for several years, and is currently president of Deutscher Designertag.
www.formgebung.com
→ 130, 305

Kreitmeyer, Jens

Kreitmeyer worked as a graphic designer at MetaDesign in Berlin from 1984 to 1989, and at MetaDesign West in San Francisco from 1992 to 1995. Today he is freelance in Berlin, concentrating on web and interface design.
www.visualengineering.de
→ 90, 106, 107, 112

Krüger, Hans C.

As salesman and manager, Krüger was a co-founder of MetaDesign plus in 1990. He left Meta in 2002 and went to Oakland, California where he is CEO of the digital design studio Futuredraft.
www.futuredraft.com
→ 144

Krüger, Lars

Krüger wrote his master's thesis on the BVG project by MetaDesign, making him an important contributor to the Spiekermann exhibition at the Bauhaus Archive in Berlin.
www.ghostarmy.de
→ 273

Lange, Günter Gerhard

Lange (1921–2008) is one of the most internationally important typographers and promoters of quality type of the 20th century; he greatly influenced type design post-1945. He was the long-term director of H. Berthold AG, and was awarded numerous medals, prizes, and honorary memberships throughout the world.
→ 54, 301

Lohmann, Andreas

Lohmann started the company Biofarben in Berlin in 1983. The business grew from a small ecological paint shop to an international business for environmentally friendly paints and building materials. Since 2007 Biofarben also has a base in London.
www.biofarben.de
→ 213

Mader, Petra

Mader worked during the 1990s as management assistant at MetaDesign in Berlin. Today she works as concept developer, editor, and author in Jena.
www.petramader.de
→ 112

Martini, Anke

Martini is a graphic designer who worked at MetaDesign in Berlin from 1990 to 2013. Today she is a partner at the design company Friends in Design in Berlin.
www.friendsindesign.com
→ 129, 130, 171, 172

Maier, Dr. Thomas

Maier wrote his doctoral thesis on the history of typesetting, supervised by Erik. He returned the favor by helping with the Spiekermann exhibition at the Bauhaus Archive in Berlin.
→ 273

Mayer, Uli

Mayer (b. 1958) is a graphic designer and set designer who founded MetaDesign plus with Erik Spiekermann and Hans C. Krüger as a successor to Spiekermann's first incarnation of MetaDesign. She still runs the company today. Mayer also lectures at various schools and institutes.
www.metadesign.com
→ 144, 175, 189

Metcalfe, Jane

Metcalfe (b. 1961) founded Wired Ventures, who publish ›Wired‹ magazine, with her husband Louis Rossetto. The couple sold the business in 1998. Today they dedicate themselves to various projects related to technology, media, and real estate with their investment company Força da Imaginação. Metcalfe also engages in cultural and social projects.
→ 255

Middendorp, Jan

Middendorp writes about and teaches typography and graphic design. He is the author of numerous books and advises companies such as FontShop, LucasFonts, Linotype, and MyFonts. He lives in Berlin and teaches at the Berlin Weissensee School of Art.
www.dorpdal.com
→ 242

Nagel, Thomas

Nagel (b. 1962) worked as a graphic designer and project manager at MetaDesign in Berlin and San Francisco between 1988 and 1994. In 1994 he founded the design studio xplicit in Frankfurt and Berlin with Alex Branczyk and Uwe Otto.
www.xplicit.de
→ 102, 129, 168

Pinggera, Albert

Pinggera is a type and graphic designer. After a few years abroad, including a stint at MetaDesign in Berlin, he returned to his native Italy in 1997 and founded design.buero in San Leonardo in Passiria. He also teaches type design at the University of Urbino.
www.design.buero.it
→ 191, 300

Poynor, Rick

Poyner is a design journalist and founder of the British design magazine ›Eye‹, where he was chief editor between 1990 and 1997. He is the author of numerous art and design books; he was a visiting professor at various universities and has curated exhibitions on design. He also writes regularly for various magazines. He was coordinator of the ›First Things First‹ manifesto in 1999.
→ 149

Pratley, Mike
Pratley is a graphic and type designer. He spent many years at Sedley Place Design.
→ 87

Richmond, Robin
Richmond is a graphic designer and co-founder of MetaDesign London, where he worked from 1995 to 2001. Today he works as a design consultant, lecturer, and organizer of design conferences.
→ 178, 195

Robeck, Sylvia
Robeck is a product designer who worked as a designer and project manager at MetaDesign in Berlin. Today she is a freelance designer and author in Berlin.
→ 177

Rossetto, Louis
Rossetto (b. 1949) founded the company Wired Ventures, who publish ›Wired‹ magazine, with his wife Jane Metcalfe. They sold the business in 1998. Today they dedicate their time to various projects related to technology, media, and real estate with their investment company Força da Imaginação. Rossetto was also CEO of the chocolate company TCHO.
www.tcho.com
→ 255

Rottke, Fabian
Rottke started as a graphic designer at Meta-Design. Later he worked at SpiekermannPartners before becoming creative director and member of the management team at Edenspiekermann. Since 2013 he has run the design company wenkerottke in Berlin with Katrin Wenke.
www.wenkerottke.com
→ 214, 220, 221, 228, 233, 252, 256, 260

Rutherford, Jay
Rutherford (b. 1950) worked as a graphic designer and typographer at MetaDesign in Berlin. Today he is professor for visual communication at the Bauhaus University in Weimar.
www.jayrutherford.net
→ 152, 302

Schäfer, Ole
Schäfer (b. 1970) is a type designer. Between 1995 and 1999 he worked at MetaDesign in Berlin, working on typefaces such as ›FF Meta‹ and ›FF Info‹, in addition to numerous corporate projects. In 1999 he founded the font label Primetype. His best-known typeface is ›FF Fago‹.
www.primetype.com
→ 115, 192, 207, 208, 209, 210, 294, 297, 298, 300, 302, 303

Schekorr, Eva
Schekorr is design director at Edenspiekermann in Berlin.
www.edenspiekermann.com
→ 228, 233, 241, 262, 269

Schmidt, Bruno
Schmidt was a teacher and later marketing director at the textbook publisher Cornelsen. In 1992 he became project manager at MetaDesign in Berlin. Since 2000 he has been a partner at MetaDesign in Zurich.
www.metadesign.com
→ 130, 189

Schmidthals, Oliver
Schmidthals (b. 1963) was key account manager at MetaDesign between 1994 and 2002. After stints elsewhere he became managing partner and director of consulting at Edenspiekermann in Berlin in 2009.
www.edenspiekermann.com
→ 189, 200, 214, 220, 252, 264, 268

Schoepflin, Tina
Schoepflin worked at various design agencies including MetaDesign. Today she is a freelance creative director in New York.
www.linkedin.com/in/tinaschoepflin
→ 246

Scholz, Peter
Scholz worked as a designer and advisor at Sedley Place Design and other design and advertising agencies. In 1990 he founded Fischer & Scholz with Florian Fischer. Today he runs Team Peter M. Scholz, who specialize in strategic communication.
www.t-ps.de
→ 86

Schuler, Marianne
Schuler was an assistant at MetaDesign in Berlin between 1991 and 2001. In 2001 she followed Spiekermann to United Designers Network, and is now office manager at Edenspiekermann.
www.edenspiekermann.com
→ 220, 252, 264

Schwartz, Christian
Schwartz (b. 1977) is a type designer who first worked at MetaDesign on various Spiekermann typefaces (including ›FF Meta Serif‹, ›FF Unit‹, ›DB Type‹). In 2001 he founded the font label Commercial Type with Paul Barnes, publishing typefaces such as ›Guardian‹, ›Lyon‹, ›Stag‹ and ›Publico‹.
www.commercialtype.com
→ 214, 216, 221, 223, 231, 295, 296, 299, 302, 303, 306

Schwemmer-Scheddin, Yvonne
Schwemmer-Scheddin writes about design and typography. She writes books and has written for magazines, holds presentations, and works at various institutes. She is on the board of the ATypI and Typografische Gesellschaft in Munich.
→ 156

Siebert, Jürgen
Siebert is chairman of FontShop and a member of its TypeBoard. He studied physics and founded the publishing magazine ›PAGE‹ in 1986, for which he still writes. In 1991 he joined FontShop in Berlin and initiated projects such as FUSE, FontBook, and the TYPO conference, of which he is program director. He is also the founder of the FontBlog, where he writes regularly about design and the type scene.
www.fontblog.de
→ 137, 139, 181, 182, 185

Sowersby, Kris
Sowersby is a graphic and type designer. In 2005 he founded the font label Klim Type Foundry in Wellington, New Zealand. In addition to ›FF Meta Serif‹, he created typefaces such as ›National‹, ›Metric‹ and ›Domaine‹, and helped develop logotypes for the ›Sunday Times Magazine‹ or Condé Nast, amongst others.
www.klim.co.nz
→ 214, 216, 302, 306

Spiekermann, Joan
Spiekermann founded FontShop in 1989 with her then husband Erik, and later founded FontShop International with Erik and Neville Brody. She is still a partner at FontShop and is on its supervisory board. She lives in England.
www.fontshop.de
→ 72, 122, 137, 138

Sprent, Mary
Sprent is a TV producer and director. Between 1985 and 2007 she worked for the BBC in London. Subsequently she worked for the private production company Glasshead, also in London.
→ 119

Steinbeck, Carolyn
Steinbeck studied dressmaking before going on to graphic design. She worked from 1996 to 1999 at MetaDesign in Berlin, after which she founded Carolyn Steinbeck Gestaltung, which she still runs today.
www.carolynsteinbeck.de
→ 200

Steinen-Broo, Frido
Steinen-Broo worked as a senior designer at MetaDesign in Berlin between 1993 and 1996. In 1997 he founded the design studio eStudioCalamar in Figueres, Spain, which he still owns and runs. In 2012 he became a partner at Friends in Design in Berlin.
www.friendsindesign.com
→ 175

Stulle, Hansjörg

Stulle (b. 1938) is a trained compositor and typographer. In 1964 he founded the layout typesetters Stulle and published writings on typography. He taught at the Academy of Art in Stuttgart and became a professor in 1985. He is a member of the communications agency Visuell in Stuttgart.
www.visuell.de
→ 68

Stulle, Robert

Stulle worked as a graphic designer at Meta-Design in Berlin from 1995 to 1997. After working at various other places he became a creative director and partner at Edenspiekermann.
www.edenspiekermann.com
→ 252, 264

Sylvester, Allan

Sylvester is a co-founder of the architects ullmayersylvester in London. He teaches at Brookes University in Oxford.
www.ullmayersylvester.com
→ 213

Sysmäläinen, Julia

Sysmäläinen is a philologist and designer. She works at Edenspiekermann and runs her »Carelian type foundry in the middle of Berlin«.
www.juliasys.com
→ 220, 246, 260, 268, 299, 307

Thi Troung, Mai-Linh

Thi Troung is senior project manager at FontShop International and database manager and co-publisher of FontBook.
www.fontshop.de
→ 139

Ullmayer, Silvia

Ullmayer is a co-founder of the architects ullmayersylvester in London. She also works as an examiner at Cambridge University.
www.ullmayersylvester.com
→ 213

Ulrich, Ferdinand

Ulrich (b. 1987) is a graphic designer. He runs a design studio in Berlin and works as an artistic assistant at Burg Giebichenstein University of Art and Design in Halle.
www.ferdinandulrich.com
→ 273

Van Blokland, Erik

Van Blokland (b. 1967) is a type designer, typographer, and software developer. He worked at MetaDesign in Berlin before founding the innovative font label LettError with Just van Rossum, developing trailblazing typefaces such as ›Beowulf‹, ›Trixie‹, ›Hands‹ and ›Federal‹. He lives and works as a typeface designer, designer, and illustrator in The Hague.
www.letterror.com
→ 115, 152, 216, 258, 293, 301, 302

Van Blokland, Petr

Van Blokland (b. 1956) is a graphic designer, typographer and type designer. Since 1980 he has been a designer and partner at Buro Petr van Blokland + Claudia Mens in Delft, Netherlands, who deal with typography and the design of interior spaces and environments. He teaches at various Dutch universities.
www.petr.com
→ 139

Van Dijk, Edo

Van Dijk is a graphic designer who is a co-founder and creative director of Edenspiekermann in Amsterdam, prior to which he was a partner at Eden Design and co-founder of the branding agency Designyard, a partner agency of Edenspiekermann's.
www.edenspiekermann.com
→ 264

Van Rossum, Just

Van Rossum (b. 1966) is a type designer, typographer and software developer. He worked at MetaDesign in Berlin (›ITC Officina‹ et al) before founding the font label LettError with Erik van Blokland in 1989, for which he developed such well-known typefaces as Randomfont ›FF Beowulf‹, the handwriting font ›FF Justlefthand‹, the typewriter font ›FF Trixie‹ and many more.
www.letterror.com
→ 115, 152, 302, 303

Walter, Eva

Walter worked as a graphic designer at MetaDesign in Berlin and San Francisco before founding her studio designing.it in San Francisco.
www.designing.it
→ 170

Weihe, Paul

Weihe worked as IT and project manager and designer at United Designers Network and Edenspiekermann. He helped organize the Spiekermann exhibition at the Bauhaus Archive in Berlin.
www.paulweihe.de
→ 273

Weishappel, Theres

Weishappel was a graphic designer and partner at MetaDesign in Berlin between 1985 and 1988 before founding Büro für Gestaltung in 1988, and Typoly in 1999, of which she is still a partner. She is a visiting professor at the University of the Arts Bremen and has lectured at various other universities.
www.typoly.de
→ 90, 102, 106, 107, 112

Weißmantel, Ralf

Weißmantel worked as a graphic designer, type designer, and art director at various agencies including MetaDesign, United Designers Network, and Edenspiekermann. Today he is professor of corporate design and information design at Aachen University of Applied Sciences, and works in Berlin.
www.ralfweissmantel.de
→ 214, 220, 221, 233, 241, 252, 262

Weitz, Petra

Weitz worked as an assistant at Sedley Place in Berlin before joining FontShop. Today she is managing director of FontShop International.
www.fontshop.de
→ 137

Welt, Harald

Welt worked for several years as a graphic designer at MetaDesign in Berlin. In 1995 he founded the design agency Welt Design in Frankfurt.
www.weltdesign.de
→ 170

Wenke, Katrin

Wenke worked as account director and member of the management team at Edenspiekermann in Berlin between 2004 and 2013. In 2013 she founded the branding and communication agency wenkerottke with Fabian Rottke.
www.wenkerottke.com
→ 256, 269

Wollein, Priska

Wollein is a graphic designer who worked at MetaDesign in Berlin between 1991 and 1995. After various stints in France and Germany she became a partner at the media agency M8 in Berlin in 2011.
www.macht.de
→ 129

Zwerner, Jeff

Zwerner was one of the first employees at MetaDesign San Francisco. Later he became a partner at Factor Design. Today Zwerner is vice president of branded products at the software company Evernote, where he is responsible for the company image and design of analog lifestyle products.
www.evernote.com
→ 169

Johannes Erler
The author and publisher
Johannes Erler conceived and realized
this book. He had the idea for it when he
picked up the lovely book about Tibor
Kalman by Michael Bierut. Erler liked
the personal manner of the monograph
and decided to do a similar book about
Erik Spiekermann. On July 4, 2009 he
asked Spiekermann in an email whether
he could imagine doing it. Five years
later the book was finally complete.

Johannes Erler (b. 1965 in Hamburg)
is one of the leading figures of the
German design and creative scene. He
founded Factor Design, recipient of numerous awards, with Olaf Stein in 1993.
He left Factor Design in 2010 and founded ErlerSkibbeTönsmann with Henning
Skibbe and Christian Tönsmann. In
2012 Erler became art director of the
German weekly magazine ›Stern‹, and
was responsible for the magazine and
brand's award-winning relaunch. Erler
lives with his family in Hamburg.
www.erlerskibbetoensmann.com

Inga Albers
The designer
In April 2013 Erler asked the graphic
designer Inga Albers whether she would
like to spend a couple of weeks working
on the design of this book. It turned
into a full year's intensive work, and
Albers became the crux of the entire
production. She gave the book its form
and designed it from the first to the
last page. She was the central point
of contact for everything and provided
information that Erler would not have
had access to.

Inga Albers (b. 1987 in Reckling-
hausen) studied communication design
at the Düsseldorf University of Applied
Sciences, the Royal Danish Academy of
Arts in Copenhagen, and the design
department of the Hamburg University
of Applied Sciences. She lives and
works in Hamburg.
www.ingaalbers.de

Ferdinand Ulrich
The archivist
To make a book about a designer, the
main thing one needs is the body of
work itself. In Erik Spiekermann's case
this was not easy, since much of it was
scattered about or had disappeared
altogether. That changed when Spiekermann appointed the graphic designer
and typographer Ferdinand Ulrich as
his assistant. Ulrich's superb detective
work forms the backbone of this book.

Ferdinand Ulrich (b. 1987 in
Schönebeck/Elbe) studied visual communication at the Berlin University of
the Arts and Carnegie Mellon University
in Pittsburgh. He runs a design studio
in Berlin and travels between there and
Halle, where he is an artistic assistant
at Burg Giebichenstein University of Art
and Design.
www.ferdinandulrich.com

Walter Schießwohl
The photographer
At some point it became clear that the
book would only be half as good if the
beautiful formats, sizes, and patina of
many works were mere photocopies.
Real photos were needed – a lot of
them, quickly. The photographer Walter
Schießwohl lost no time in coming up
with the goods when Erler asked him.

Walter Schießwohl (b. 1967)
started as a painter before becoming
a photographer. He feels at home with
landscape, still life, and architecture
photography. He grew up in southern
Germany, and has spent over 20 years
with his family in Hamburg.
www.schießwohl.com

Anne Beyer
The project describer
Anyone can write long texts, but to
describe a complex topic in a few lines
is a real craft. Anne Beyer wrote most of
the texts about projects, checking them
with Erik Spiekermann – and she did it
very quickly.

Anne Beyer (b. 1980 in Rostock)
studied German and musicology. She
works with her »copy company« in
Berlin for businesses, organizations, and
publishing companies.
www.maßtexterei.de

Isabelle Erler
The family researcher
Quite a bit was already known about
Erik Spiekermann, but few people knew
where he was from and how he became
what he is. Through long talks with him
and his sister, Isabelle Erler created a
sensitive portrait of someone who had
to learn independence from an early age.

Isabelle Erler (b. 1967 in Düsseldorf)
studied German and art history (MA),
and works as an editor and author. She
develops and writes texts, books, and
other publications for businesses, institutions, and publishing companies as
Punkt und Pünktchen – Das Textbüro.
www.punktpuenktchen.de

Urs Willmann
The interviewer
Typography is something for nerds.
After all, who can tell the difference
between a ›Helvetica‹ and an ›Arial‹?
And does it really matter? The journalist
Urs Willmann, who knows little about
typefaces, let Spiekermann explain to
him exactly why type is more than just a
bunch of letters.

Urs Willmann (b. 1964 in Winterthur)
works as editor on the science and
education section of the German weekly
newspaper ›Die Zeit‹. He lives with his
family in Hamburg.

Dylan Spiekermann
The translator
Dylan Spiekermann was the perfect
candidate for all translations from German into English, particularly personal
stories. The reason is simple: Dylan is
Spiekermann's son.

Dylan Spiekermann (b. 1968 in Ber-
lin) is a musician and translator (›Adrian
Frutiger – Typefaces: The Complete
Works, amongst others‹). He lives in
London.

Sonja Knecht
Die Übersetzerin
When more and more English texts
appeared that needed translating
into German there was a snag: Dylan
Spiekermann was ideal for German to
English but not vice versa. Fortunately,
Sonja Knecht came to the rescue. Fast,
uncomplicated and always friendly.

Sonja Knecht (born in Jakarta) is
a communications consultant, copy
writer, translator, and director text at
Edenspiekermann in Berlin.
www.txet.de

I need to thank the people who helped
me with their work, time, and so many
good ideas without ever complaining.
Okay, here goes...

Many thanks to:

Inga Albers for her amazing sense of
calm, friendliness, and perseverance
throughout the realization of this book.
Inga, your name is also on this book in
great big letters!

Ferdinand Ulrich, who did all the real
grassroots work in Erik's dusty forsaken
archives.

Walter Schießwohl, who I hardly
knew but who helped me as only a
friend would.

Robert Klanten and Pauleena Chbib
at Gestalten, who pestered me until the
book was finally ready.

Henning Skibbe for his typographic
eye, Jonas Buntenbruch for the first
design ideas, and Prof. Heike Grebin,
who found me Inga.

Jürgen Siebert and Alex Branczyk,
who not only wrote nice contributions
but also supplied me with a lot of
material.

Hu-Ping Chen, Susanna Dulkinys,
Marc Eckardt, Steven A. Heller, Bill
Hill, Hans Werner Holzwarth, Gerhard
Kassner, Tobias Benjamin Köhler, Nils
Holger Moormann, Stefan Müller,
Yvonne Schwemmer-Scheddin, Stefan
Schilling, Zubin Shroff, Rowan Thomas,
Ferdinand Ulrich, Jons-Michael Voss,
Paul Weihe, and Max Zerrahn, who all
contributed photos to this book.

Paul Davis, Jens Kreitmeyer, Lars
Krüger, Mark Leet, Alexander Roth, Erik
van Blokland, and Maartje van Caspel,
who made other images available.

Anne Beyer, who managed to
supply the project texts so quickly and
efficiently, and the writers Melanie Mühl,
Yves Peters, Philipp Poll, Petra Schmidt,
Julia Sysmäläinen and John L. Walters,
whose texts I was allowed to print here.

Michael Bierut, Mirko Borsche, Nev-
ille Brody, Christoph Busse, Susanna
Dulkinys, Bill Hill, Jürgen Korzer, Andrej
Kupetz, Göran Lagerström, Christoph
Niemann, the late Wally Olins, Robin
Richmond, Stefan Sagmeister, Bruno
Schmidt, Christian Schwartz, Joan
Spiekermann, and Erik van Blokland for
their wonderful guest contributions.

Julia Bähre, Tanja Metzner, Anna
Prochnow for countless scans, and
Jan Gerds and Stefan Reimers from
Alphabeta Druckservice for the image
processing.

Angelika Arndt for her fond memories of a young Erik.

Isabelle, who wrote a fine text and
also got me back on track whenever I
hit a snag.

Emil and Fritz, because I spent way
too much time in front of the computer
over the last two years.

And, of course, I have to thank Erik
himself. You really are a remarkable
person!

A

Abdullah, Rayan → 130, 308
Achtung! Blueprint column → 257
Acker, Christian → 154, 231, 295, 308
Acornley, Ben → 207, 308
Adviser at Filmcomposition → 52
Aldus PageMaker templates → 107
Alliance '90/ The Greens CD → 134
Apple → 104
Arndt, Angelika → 12, 13, 21, 41
ARTZ → 293
Audi corporate design → 172
Axel → 258, 293

B

Bank für Gemeinwirtschaft CD → 41, 61
Barney, Gerry → 61, 87, 308
Baseline → 100
Bauhaus Archive → 272, 274
Bauwelt redesign → 228
BDG → 84, 96
Berkenbusch, Anna → 59, 61, 64, 72, 308
Berlin corporate design → 168
Berliner Grotesk → 53, 294
Berliner Verkehrsbetriebe (BVG) design
concept → 112
Berliner Verkehrsbetriebe (BVG) signage and
corporate design → 130, 133
Berthold Berliner Grotesk → 53, 294
Berthold Block Italic → 56
Berthold corporate design → 102
Berthold exclusive brochures → 64
Berthold LoType → 54, 64, 301
Betton, Pia → 168, 171, 172, 175, 264, 308
Bicycles → 276, 278
Bielefeld University of Applied Sciences → 57
Bierut, Michael → 4, 227, 251
Block Italic → 56
Blueprint column → 257
Blumberg, Gail → 109, 159, 308
Boehringer → 294
Booms, Hans → 264, 308
Borsche, Mirko → 153
Bosch corporate design → 214
Bosch → 230, 295
Bosma, Jelle → 210, 303, 308
Botez, Timon → 207, 308
Branczyk, Alexander → 102, 120, 134, 135, 308
Brody, Neville → 122, 126, 127, 137, 138, 181,
186, 251, 308
Bund Deutscher Grafikdesigner (BDG) CD → 96
Bund Deutscher Grafikdesigner (BDG) → 84, 96
Busse, Christoph → 37
BVG → 112, 130, 133

C

Christ, Gerald → 170, 308
Cisco → 295
Cleary, Ed → 43, 46, 52, 139, 308
Co-founder of Eye magazine → 149
Co-founder of Forum Typografie → 82
Coates, Stephen → 149, 308
Committee member of BDG → 84
Cook, Steven → 264, 308
Curtis, Gayle → 169, 308

D

Darden, Joshua → 231, 295, 308
Darkroom → 62
DB → 222, 224, 296
De Groot, Lucas → 135, 152, 168, 172, 175, 302,
305, 308
De Gruyter book typography → 269
Design Within Reach (DWR) house numbers →
238, 240
Deutsche Bahn corporate design → 221
Deutsche Bahn → 222, 224, 296
Deutsche Post corporate design → 86
Doerrié, Gerhard → 59, 308
Du Carrois, Ralph → 3, 235, 258, 260, 279, 293,
295, 297, 298, 300, 304, 307, 309
Dulkinys, Susanna → 166, 167, 196, 220, 246,
247, 252, 255, 260, 264, 268, 273, 299, 307, 309
Düsseldorf airport signage and CD → 188

E

EcoNewtype → 208, 297
Edenspiekermann → 264, 266
EDEN → 124
Erik Spiekermann graphics and hand press →
20, 29, 31, 32
Erler, Isabelle → 11
Erler, Johannes → 4, 184, 202, 273, 275
Esterson, Simon → 149, 309
Etter, Michael → 134, 135, 309
European DEsigners Network (EDEN) → 124
Exhibition Bauhaus Archive → 272, 274
Explo → 297
Eye magazine → 149
Ezer, Oded → 152, 302, 309

F

Fall of the Berlin Wall → 126
Faulhaber, Erik → 299, 309
Fendley, Tim → 178, 195, 309
FF Govan → 192, 298
FF Info → 189, 191, 300
FF Meta → 86, 106, 152, 154, 171, 216, 238,
298, 302
FF Transit → 130, 133, 300, 305
FF Unit → 216, 218, 228, 246, 297, 299, 306
Fidia → 42, 189, 191
Filmcomposition → 21, 43, 52, 53
Fira → 279, 298
First London Period → 38
First Things First 2000 manifesto → 201
Fischer & Spiekermann → 21, 41
Fischer, Christa → 177, 309
Fischer, Florian → 22, 41, 59, 61, 64, 72, 86, 112,
185, 309
Fleischmann, Gerd → 57
FontBook → 139, 140, 142
FontFont → 138
FontShop corporate design → 120
FontShop International (FSI) → 136
FontShop → 51, 120, 122
Form column → 226
Forms & Schedules infobox → 109
Forum Typografie → 82
Founding Type Directors Club (TDC) London →
43, 187

G

Frech, Charly → 130, 172, 309
FUSE conference → 180

G

Gallery P98a → 280, 282, 284, 286
German Design Award → 270
German Design Council board member → 198
German Design Council → 198
Ginger, E. M. → 162, 309
Glasgow corporate design → 194
Glasgow → 192, 298
Govan → 192, 298
Gravis corporate design → 246
Gravis → 246, 299
Greisner, Inken → 102, 111, 112, 135, 309
Großplakate Deutschland → 28
Grubitzsch, Katja → 268, 309
Grützmacher → 35

H

Hartwig, Brigitte → 77, 130, 133, 189, 309
Heidelberger Druckmaschinen CD → 200
Heidelberg → 299
Heil, Dieter → 22, 59, 61, 86, 309
Helvetica, Neue/ type specimens → 80
Helvetica documentary → 250
Henze, Karsten → 130, 309
Hering corporate design → 262
Hermann Miller corporate design → 106
Heute Journal corporate design → 260
Hill, Bill → 109, 158, 159, 169, 297, 309
Holthuis, Joost → 264, 309
Holzwarth, Hans Werner → 90, 94, 101, 102,
106, 107, 110, 309
Hooper Woolsey, Kristina → 169, 309
House in Berlin → 247, 249
House in London → 212
House in San Francisco → 196
House numbers → 238, 240
HWT ARTZ → 293

I

Ikarus/ Peter Karow → 42
Im Reich der Schilder documentary → 236
Infoscreen → 300
Info → 189, 191, 300
Installing a darkroom → 62
Irwin, Terry → 158, 159, 169, 309
ITC Officina → 67, 114, 115, 116, 293, 303
ITC Review Board → 114

K

Kahlfeldt, Paul → 177, 309
Kahlfeldt, Petra → 177, 310
Karow, Peter → 42
Kim, Scott → 169, 310
Klein, Manfred → 156, 310
Kolaschnik, Axel → 170, 310
Korzer, Jürgen → 173
Koster, Rik → 264, 310
Krause, Henning → 130, 305, 310
Kreitmeyer, Jens → 82, 90, 94, 106, 107, 111,
112, 159, 204, 310
Krüger, Hans C. → 125, 144, 310

Krüger, Lars → 273, 310
Kunstamt Kreuzberg programs → 81
Kupetz, Andrej → 6, 199
Köble, Rainer → 177, 310

L

Lagerström, Göran → 267
Lange, Günter Gerhard → 3, 54, 77, 181, 184, 294, 301, 310
Last train from Berlin → 74
Leaving MetaDesign → 202, 204, 206
Lecturing at Bielefeld University of Applied Sciences → 57
Le monde diplomatique redesign → 232
Letraset Baseline → 100
Lohmann, Andreas → 213, 310
London College of Printing → 21, 38, 127, 179
London → 38, 46, 48, 50, 212
LoType → 54, 64, 301

M

Mader, Petra → 111, 112, 310
Made with FontFont → 242, 244
Maier, Dr. Thomas → 273, 310
Martini, Anke → 129, 130, 171, 172, 310
Mayer, Uli → 144, 175, 189, 310
Messe Frankfurt corporate design → 256
Messe Univers → 256, 301
MetaCafé → 65, 72
MetaDesign (Mark I) → 58, 60
MetaDesign (Mark II) → 94
MetaDesign London → 178, 195, 207
MetaDesign plus (Mark IV) → 144, 146
MetaDesign West → 109, 158, 160
Meta Gesellschaft für Design (Mark III) → 110
MetaHaus → 176
Meta → 86, 106, 152, 154, 171, 216, 238, 298, 302
Metcalfe, Jane → 255, 310
Middendorp, Jan → 242, 310
Moving back to Berlin → 65
Moving the hot metal press to London → 44

N

Nagel, Thomas → 102, 129, 135, 165, 168, 310
Neue Helvetica type specimens → 80
Niemann, Christoph → 318
Nokia → 210, 303

O

Objects & Posters → 20, 34
Officina → 67, 114, 115, 116, 293, 303
Olins, Wally → 46, 47
Olympic postage stamps → 150
Oppenheim, Louis → 54, 301
Os mundi LP → 36
Ottobock corporate design → 268

P

P98a → 280, 282, 285, 286
PAGE column TYPOthek → 128
Personality Posters → 19, 20, 28, 34
Peters, Yves → 154

Pinggera, Albert → 191, 300, 310
Poynor, Rick → 149, 251, 310
Pratley, Mike → 87, 311
Professorship at University of the Arts Bremen → 148
PT55 (MetaPost) → 87, 88, 152
PTT-Post Olympic postage stamps → 150

R

Real → 3, 304
Rhyme and Reason → 76, 78
Richmond, Robin → 159, 178, 179, 195, 311
Ro 80 → 98
Robeck, Sylvia → 177, 311
Rossetto, Louis → 255, 311
Rotbuch-Verlag cover → 74
Rottke, Fabian → 214, 220, 221, 228, 233, 252, 256, 260, 311
Rutherford, Jay → 152, 302, 311

S

Sagmeister, Stefan → 184, 185, 187, 251
Scangraphic type specimen book → 92
Schekorr, Eva → 228, 233, 241, 262, 269, 311
Schmidt, Bruno → 130, 145, 189, 311
Schmidthals, Oliver → 189, 200, 214, 220, 252, 264, 268 , 311
Schoepflin, Tina → 246, 311
Scholz, Peter → 86, 311
Schuler, Marianne → 220, 252, 264, 311
Schuppenhauer, Hucki → 20, 34
Schwartz, Christian → 115, 152, 154, 216, 217, 223, 231, 246, 295, 296, 299, 302, 303, 306, 311
Schwemmer-Scheddin, Yvonne → 156, 311
Schäfer, Ole → 115, 152, 191, 192, 209, 210, 294, 297, 298, 300, 302, 303, 311
Second London period → 46, 48, 50
Siebert, Jürgen → 123, 137, 139, 181, 182, 184, 185, 186, 293, 311
Sowersby, Kris → 152, 154, 216, 302, 306, 311
Spiekermann, Dylan → 20, 29, 38, 39, 50, 51, 65, 185, 213
Spiekermann, Joan → 19, 20, 31, 50, 51, 72, 122, 123, 137, 138, 311
Spiekermann, Michael → 12, 20, 34
Spiekermann Condensed Form column → 226
SpiekermannPartners → 252
Sprent, Mary → 119, 311
Springer corporate design → 174
Stadtinfo information system → 90
Steinbeck, Carolyn → 200, 311
Steinen-Broo, Frido → 175, 312
Stop Stealing Sheep → 162, 164
Studentenfutter → 68, 70
Stulle, Hansjörg → 68, 312
Stulle, Robert → 252, 264, 312
Susanna → 166
Sylvester, Allan → 213, 312
Sysmäläinen, Julia → 220, 246, 260, 266, 268, 299, 307, 312

T

TCHO Packaging → 254
TDC International Conference → 108
TERN → 234, 304

Teutonic Typewriter → 67
The Economist redesign → 207
Thi Troung, Mai-Linh → 139, 185, 312
Trans European Road Network (TERN) → 234, 304
Transit → 130, 133, 300, 305
Twitter → 263
Type and Typographers → 156
Type Directors Club → 43, 187
Typesetters Grützmacher → 35
TYPO conference → 182, 184, 186
Typographic Circle → 43, 187
Typomania film → 118
TYPOthek → 128

U

Ullmayer, Silvia → 213, 312
Ulrich, Ferdinand → 273, 312
United Designers Network → 216, 220
Unit → 216, 218, 228, 246, 297, 299, 306
University of the Arts Bremen → 148

V

Van Blokland, Erik → 115, 137, 152, 154, 155, 184, 216, 258, 259, 293, 301, 302, 312
Van Blokland, Petr → 42, 139, 312
Van Dijk, Edo → 264, 312
Van Rossum, Just → 115, 152, 184, 259, 302, 303, 312
Verkehrsbetriebe Potsdam CD → 129
VizAbility infobox → 169
Volkswagen (VW) corporate design → 170
VW corporate design → 170

W

Walter, Eva → 170, 312
Walters, John L. → 270, 309
WDR corporate design → 171
Weihe, Paul → 273, 312
Weishappel, Theres → 90, 94, 102, 106, 107, 111, 112, 135, 139, 312
Weitz, Petra → 137, 186, 312
Weißmantel, Ralf → 214, 220, 221, 233, 241, 252, 262, 312
Welt, Harald → 170, 312
Wenke, Katrin → 256, 269, 312
Westdeutscher Rundfunk (WDR) CD → 171
Wiescher, Gert → 17, 34
Wolff Olins → 22, 41, 46, 47, 59, 61, 170, 179
Wollein, Priska → 129, 312

Z

ZDF → 260, 307
ZDF heute journal corporate design → 260
Zwerner, Jeff → 159, 165, 169, 312

Header
Photo: Steven A. Heller, 1988
Scan: Alphabeta

4
Photos: Johannes Erler
Scan: J. Bähre, T. Metzner, A. Prochnow

10, 11
Photos: Erik Spiekermann archive
Scans: Tanja Metzner, Anna Prochnow

12
Photos: Angelika Arndt archive
Scan: J. Bähre, T. Metzner, A. Prochnow

13 – 15
Photos: Angelika Arndt archive
Scans: Alphabeta

17, 18
Photos: Erik Spiekermann archive
Scans: Tanja Metzner, Anna Prochnow

20
Top left: Angelika Arndt archive
Other photos: Erik Spiekermann archive
Scans: Tanja Metzner, Anna Prochnow

23
Photo: Tilman Schwarz
Scan: J. Bähre, T. Metzner, A. Prochnow

28
Artwork: Erik Spiekermann archive
Photo: Walter Schießwohl

29, 30
Artwork: Erik Spiekermann archive
Scans: Tanja Metzner, Anna Prochnow

31
Artwork: Erik Spiekermann archive
Photo: Walter Schießwohl

32
Artwork: Erik Spiekermann archive
Scan: J. Bähre, T. Metzner, A. Prochnow

34
Artwork: Erik Spiekermann archive
Scan: Alphabeta

35, 36
Artwork: Erik Spiekermann archive
Photos: Walter Schießwohl

38, 39
Slides: Erik Spiekermann archive
Scans: Tanja Metzner, Anna Prochnow

40
Photo: Tilman Schwarz
Scan: J. Bähre, T. Metzner, A. Prochnow

41
Artwork: Erik Spiekermann archive
Photo: Walter Schießwohl

42
Slide: Tilman Schwarz
Scan: J. Bähre, T. Metzner, A. Prochnow

43
Poster: James Alexander, Jade Design

44
Slide: Erik Spiekermann archive
Scan: J. Bähre, T. Metzner, A. Prochnow

46
Artwork: Erik Spiekermann archive
Photo: Walter Schießwohl

48 – 50
Artwork: Erik Spiekermann archive
Scans: Tanja Metzner, Anna Prochnow

51
Photo excerpt from ›Rhyme & Reason‹,
p. 140, Mainz 1994

52, 53
Artwork: Erik Spiekermann archive
Scans: Alphabeta

54 – 56
Artwork: Erik Spiekermann archive
Scans: Tanja Metzner, Anna Prochnow

57
Artwork: Erik Spiekermann archive
Photo: Walter Schießwohl

58
Photo: Hu-Ping Chen
Scan: J. Bähre, T. Metzner, A. Prochnow

60
Artwork: Erik Spiekermann archive
Photo: Walter Schießwohl

61
Artwork: Erik Spiekermann archive
Scan: Alphabeta

62
Artwork from Berthold Phototype
GmbH, fk 3 repromat; Scan: Alphabeta

64
Artwork: Erik Spiekermann archive
Photo: Walter Schießwohl

65
Photo: Tilmann Schwarz

66, 67
Artwork: Erik Spiekermann archive
Scans: Tanja Metzner, Anna Prochnow

68
Photo: Walter Schießwohl
Drawing: Erik Spiekermann
Scan: J. Bähre, T. Metzner, A. Prochnow

69 – 71
Artwork: Erik Spiekermann archive
Photos: Walter Schießwohl

72, 73
Artwork: Erik Spiekermann archive
Scans: Tanja Metzner, Anna Prochnow

74, 75
Drawings: Erik Spiekermann
Scans: Tanja Metzner, Anna Prochnow
Book photos: Walter Schießwohl

76 – 81
Artwork: Erik Spiekermann archive
Photos: Walter Schießwohl

82
Advertisement top left from ›Deutscher
Drucker‹, No. 34, 1983
Bottom: Erik Spiekermann archive,
Scans: Tanja Metzner, Anna Prochnow

83
Illustrations for the 8th Forum Typografie:
Hans Eberhard Ernst in ›Sonderdruck des
Druckmagazins Offsetpraxis‹, Fellbach and
MetaDesign, Berlin
Scan: J. Bähre, T. Metzner, A. Prochnow

84
Artwork from ›Form‹ issue 115, 1986, p. 91
Scan: J. Bähre, T. Metzner, A. Prochnow

86, 87
Artwork: Erik Spiekermann archive
Scans: Tanja Metzner, Anna Prochnow

88
Drawing: Erik Spiekermann
Scan: J. Bähre, T. Metzner, A. Prochnow

90, 91
Artwork: Erik Spiekermann archive
Scans: Tanja Metzner, Anna Prochnow

92, 93
Artwork: Erik Spiekermann archive
Photos: Walter Schießwohl

94, 95
Artwork: Erik Spiekermann archive
Scans: Tanja Metzner, Anna Prochnow

96 – 99
Artwork: Erik Spiekermann archive
Scans: Tanja Metzner, Anna Prochnow
Photo: Walter Schießwohl

100
Artwork: Erik Spiekermann archive
Photo: Walter Schießwohl

102
Artwork: Alexander Brancyzk archive
Photos: Walter Schießwohl

103
Artwork: Erik Spiekermann archive
Scan: J. Bähre, T. Metzner, A. Prochnow

104
Photo: Hans Werner Holzwarth
Scan: J. Bähre, T. Metzner, A. Prochnow

106, 107
Artwork: Erik Spiekermann archive
Photos: Walter Schießwohl

108
Photo: Yvonne Schwemmer-Scheddin
Scan: J. Bähre, T. Metzner, A. Prochnow

109
Artwork: Erik Spiekermann archive
Photo: Walter Schießwohl

110
Artwork from »Blueprint« magazine,
MetaDesign reprint, April 1988
Photo: Tilman Schwarz
Scan: J. Bähre, T. Metzner, A. Prochnow

112
Artwork: Erik Spiekermann archive
Scan: Alphabeta

114
Artwork: Erik Spiekermann archive
Scan: J. Bähre, T. Metzner, A. Prochnow

115
Photo: Hans Werner Holzwarth
Scan: J. Bähre, T. Metzner, A. Prochnow

116
Drawing: Erik Spiekermann
Scan: J. Bähre, T. Metzner, A. Prochnow

118
Screenshots from ›Typomania‹, BBC, 1988.

120
Artwork: Alexander Branczyk archive
Scan: J. Bähre, T. Metzner, A. Prochnow
Photos: Walter Schießwohl

121
Artwork: FontShop archive
Photos: Walter Schießwohl

122
Artwork from ›PAGE‹ No. 3, May/ June
1989, Hamburg
Photo: Walter Schießwohl

123
Photo: Gerhard Kassner

124, 126
Artwork: Erik Spiekermann archive
Scans: Tanja Metzner, Anna Prochnow

127
Photo: Marc Eckardt

128
Artwork from ›PAGE‹ No.3, May/
June 1989, Hamburg. Photo: Walter
Schießwohl

129
Artwork: Erik Spiekermann archive
Photos: Walter Schießwohl

130
Photos: Erik Spiekermann
Scans: Tanja Metzner, Anna Prochnow

131
Photo: Stefan Schilling

132
Photo: Ferdinand Ulrich

133
Scans: Lars Krüger

134
Artwork: Alexander Branczyk archive
Photo: Walter Schießwohl

136
Artwork: Erik Spiekermann archive
Scan: J. Bähre, T. Metzner, A. Prochnow

138 – 140
Artwork: Erik Spiekermann archive
Photos: Walter Schießwohl

142, 143
Artwork: Jürgen Siebert, FontShop
Photos: Walter Schießwohl

144
Artwork: Erik Spiekermann archive
Photos: Walter Schießwohl

146
Photo: Erik Spiekermann archive
Scan: J. Bähre, T. Metzner, A. Prochnow

148
Contract: Erik Spiekermann archive
Book: Victor Malsy, ›El Lissitzky‹,
Verlag Hermann Schmidt, 1990.
Photos: Walter Schießwohl

149
Artwork from ›Eye‹ No.1 Vol. 1, London 1990
Photo: Walter Schießwohl

150
Artwork: Erik Spiekermann archive
Scan: J. Bähre, T. Metzner, A. Prochnow

152
Artwork: FontFont, ›Focus No. 4, Meta‹
Design: Wim Westerveld
Photo: Walter Schießwohl

155
Drawings: Erik Spiekermann
Poster: Erik van Blokland

156, 157
Artwork: ›Type & Typographers‹,
V + K Publishing. 1991.
Photo: Walter Schießwohl

158
Photo: Erik Spiekermann archive
Scan: J. Bähre, T. Metzner, A. Prochnow

162 – 164
Book: ›Stop Stealing Sheep‹, Adobe
Press, Mountain View, California, 1993
Photos: Walter Schießwohl

166, 168
Artwork: Erik Spiekermann archive
Scans: Tanja Metzner, Anna Prochnow

169
Artwork: Erik Spiekermann archive
Photo: Walter Schießwohl

170
Artwork: Erik Spiekermann archive
Scan: J. Bähre, T. Metzner, A. Prochnow

171
Artwork: Anke Martini private archive
Photo: Walter Schießwohl

172
Top photo: Erik Spiekermann archive
Bottom photo: Jons-Michael Voss

174
Artwork: Erik Spiekermann archive
Photo: Walter Schießwohl

175
Artwork: Erik Spiekermann archive
Reconstruction: Inga Albers

176
Artwork from excerpt from the catalog
for the exhibition ›Transformatoren |
Transformationen‹ at Aedes East Forum
Photo: Stefan Müller
Scan: J. Bähre, T. Metzner, A. Prochnow

178
Artwork: Erik Spiekermann archive
Scan: J. Bähre, T. Metzner, A. Prochnow

180, 181
Photos: Gerhard Kassner

182
From ›Form‹ online archive
Poster design: MetaDesign Berlin

183 – 186
Photos: Gerhard Kassner
Photos TYPO SF 2013: Jürgen Siebert

188 – 190
Photos: Stefan Schilling

191
Graphics: Alexander Roth,
FontShop International

195
Artwork: Erik Spiekermann archive
Scan: J. Bähre, T. Metzner, A. Prochnow

196, 197
Photos: Zubin Shroff

198
Photo: Nils Holger Moormann, 2008
Scan: J. Bähre, T. Metzner, A. Prochnow

200
Artwork: Erik Spiekermann archive

201
Poster: insert in ›Adbusters‹, Vancouver
Design: Chris Dixon
Photo: Walter Schießwohl

204
Photo montage: Jens Kreitmeyer

207
Artwork: ›The Economist‹, London
No. 8221, May 12 – 18, 2001
No. 8273, May 18 – 24, 2002
No. 8470, March 25 – 31, 2006
No. 8725, March 19 – 25, 2011
Photos: Walter Schießwohl

208
Artwork from ›The Economist‹
March 19 – 25 2011, London
Scan: Alphabeta

210
Artwork top: MANGO Design
Management, August 2001
Bottom: Erik Spiekermann archive
Scans: Alphabeta

211
Drawing: Erik Spiekermann
Scan: Alphabeta

212, 213
Photos: Ullmayer Sylvester, 2008

214
Artwork: Erik Spiekermann archive
Scan: Alphabeta
215
Logo: Robert Bosch GmbH

18
Graphics: Alexander Roth,
FontShop International
220
Photos: Christa Fischer
221
Artwork: Erik Spiekermann archive

222
Artwork: Erik Spiekermann archive
Scan: J. Bähre, T. Metzner, A. Prochnow

224
Artwork: Erik Spiekermann archive

225
Artwork from »Ihr Reiseplan,
EC9 Hamburg–Chur«, 2013
Scan: J. Bähre, T. Metzner, A. Prochnow

226
Artwork from ›Form‹, No. 195,
March/ April 2004, Neu-Isenburg
Photo: Walter Schießwohl

228, 229
Artwork: ›Bauwelt‹, 38.06,
October 6, 2006, Berlin
Photos: Walter Schießwohl

232, 233
Artwork: ›Le Monde diplomatique‹, Ger-
man edition, May 2005, taz Verlags- und
Vertriebs- GmbH, Berlin
Photos: Walter Schießwohl

234
Photo: Tobias Benjamin Köhler

236, 237
Screenshots from ›Leitsysteme für
Menschen – Im Reich der Schilder‹,
Arte 2005

238
Photo: Ferdinand Ulrich

240
Photos: Paul Weihe

241
Artwork: Michael Erlhoff and Tim Mar-
shall, ›Wörterbuch Design, Begriffliche
Perspektiven des Design‹, Berlin 2008.
Deutscher Designer Club e.V., ›Gute
Gestaltung 08.‹, Frankfurt 2008.
Photo: Walter Schießwohl

242 – 245
Book: Jan Middendorp, Erik Spiekermann, ›Made with FontFont‹, Amsterdam
2006. Photos: Walter Schießwohl

246
Photo: Erik Spiekermann

247 – 249
Photos: Max Zerrahn

250, 251
Screenshots from ›Helvetica‹,
a documentary film by Gary Hustwit,
New York 2007

252
Artwork: Erik Spiekermann archive
Photo: Maartje van Caspel
Scan: J. Bähre, T. Metzner, A. Prochnow

254
Photo: Mark Leet

256
Artwork: Erik Spiekermann archive
257
Artwork from ›Blueprint‹ magazine, April
2009, London 2009
Photo: Walter Schießwohl

259
Photo: Marc Eckardt

260
Artwork: Edenspiekermann

262
Artwork: ›Hering Berlin‹, Berlin 2008
Photos: Walter Schießwohl

264
Photo: Edenspiekermann

266
Drawings: Paul Davis

268
Artwork: Edenspiekermann

269
Artwork: Edenspiekermann,
presentation September 29, 2011
Photos: Walter Schießwohl

271
Photo: Erik Spiekermann

272, 274
Photos: Jens Winter

274
Poster: Erik Spiekermann

276
Photo: Erik Spiekermann

278
Top photo: Bill Hill
Scan: J. Bähre, T. Metzner, A. Prochnow
Middle photo: Susanna Dulkinys
Bottom photo: Roman Thomas

279
Artwork: Mozilla Press Center
Montage: Alphabeta

280 – 287
Photos: Max Zerrahn

288 – 291
Drawings: Erik Spiekermann
Scans: Alphabeta

292
Photo: Tilman Schwarz
Scan: Alphabeta

313
Photo bottom: Xenia Kern

319
Illustration: Christoph Niemann

Header back
Photo: Max Zerrahn

Christoph on Erik

Christoph Niemann (born 1970 in Waiblingen) is an illustrator, graphic designer, and author of various books. His work has appeared on the covers of the ›New Yorker‹, ›Atlantic Monthly‹, the ›New York Times Magazine‹, ›ZEIT magazine‹, and ›Süddeutsche Zeitung Magazine‹. Niemann lived in New York from 1997 to 2008 before moving to Berlin with his wife and three sons.

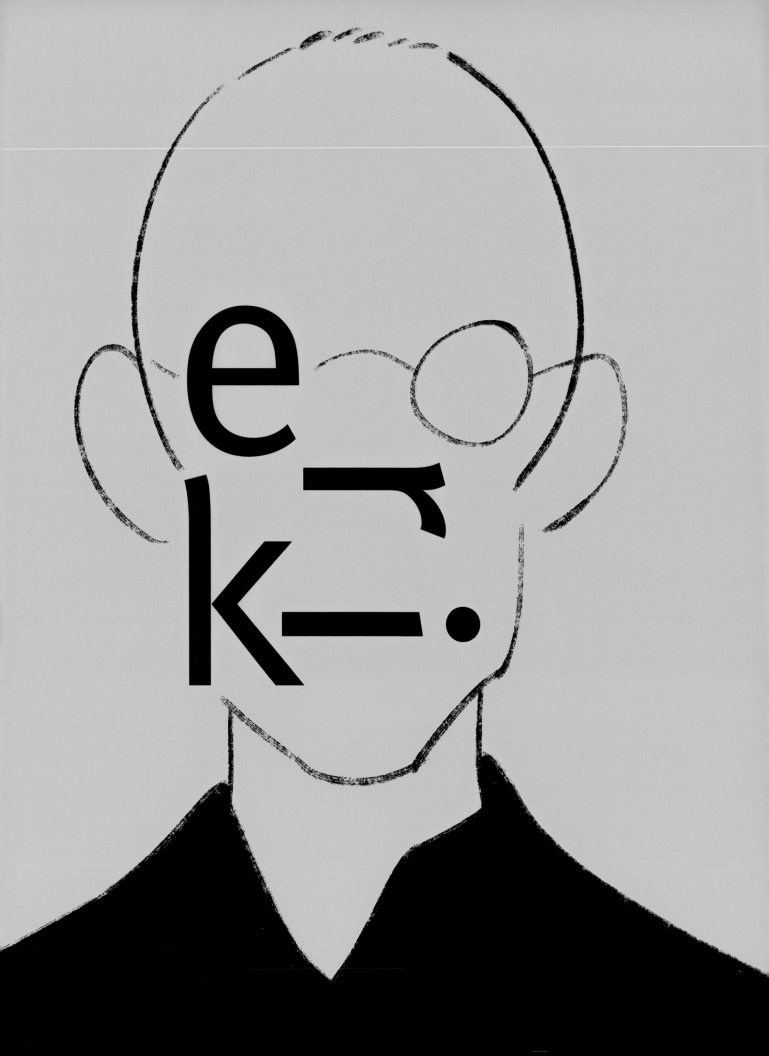

Colophon

Hello I am Erik
Erik Spiekermann: Typographer, Designer, Entrepreneur

Edited by Johannes Erler

Texts: Anne Beyer, Michael Bierut, Mirko Borsche, Neville Brody,
Christoph Busse, Susanna Dulkinys, Isabelle Erler, Johannes Erler,
Bill Hill, Jürgen Korzer, Andrej Kupetz, Göran Lagerström, Melanie Mühl,
Wally Olins, Yves Peters, Philipp Poll, Robin Richmond, Stefan Sagmeister,
Bruno Schmidt, Petra Schmidt, Christian Schwartz, Erik Spiekermann,
Joan Spiekermann, Julia Sysmäläinen, Erik van Blokland, John L. Walters,
and Urs Willmann

Design: Inga Albers
Typeface: ›Real‹ by Erik Spiekermann and Ralph du Carrois

Translation from German by Dylan Spiekermann
Proofreading by Bettina Klein

Printed by Nino Druck GmbH, Neustadt/Weinstraße
Made in Germany

Published by Gestalten, Berlin 2014
ISBN 978-3-89955-519-6

For more information, please visit www.gestalten.com.

Bibliographic information published by the Deutsche Nationalbibliothek.
The Deutsche Nationalbibliothek lists this publication in the Deutsche National-
bibliografie; detailed bibliographic data are available online at http://dnb.d-nb.de.

This book was printed on paper certified according to the standard of FSC®.

Gestalten is a climate-neutral company. We collaborate with the non-profit carbon
offset provider myclimate (www.myclimate.org) to neutralize the company's carbon
footprint produced through our worldwide business activities by investing in projects that reduce CO_2 emissions (www.gestalten.com/myclimate).

Free Download

To download the regular weight of the ›Real‹ typeface by Erik Spiekermann for free, please go to fontshop.com. Add the ›Real Regular‹ font to your shopping cart.

During the checkout process, you will be asked for your personal promo code. Enter the following code in the promo field:

uldg8i

Checkout, and enjoy using your Erik Spiekermann font!

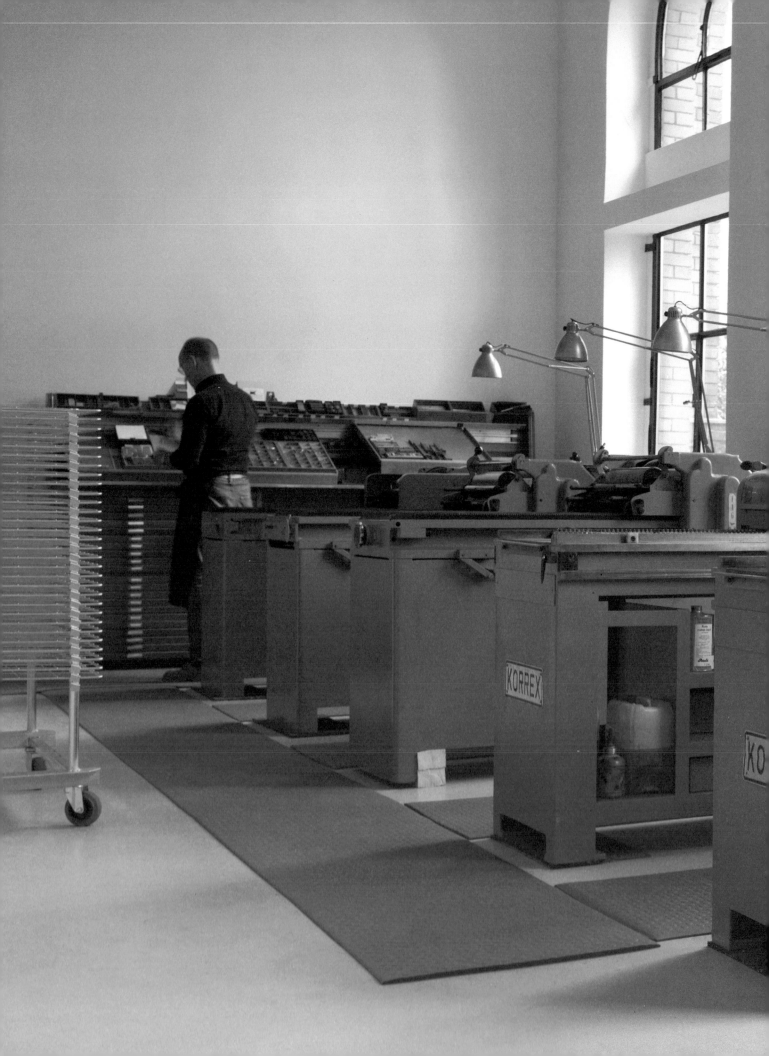

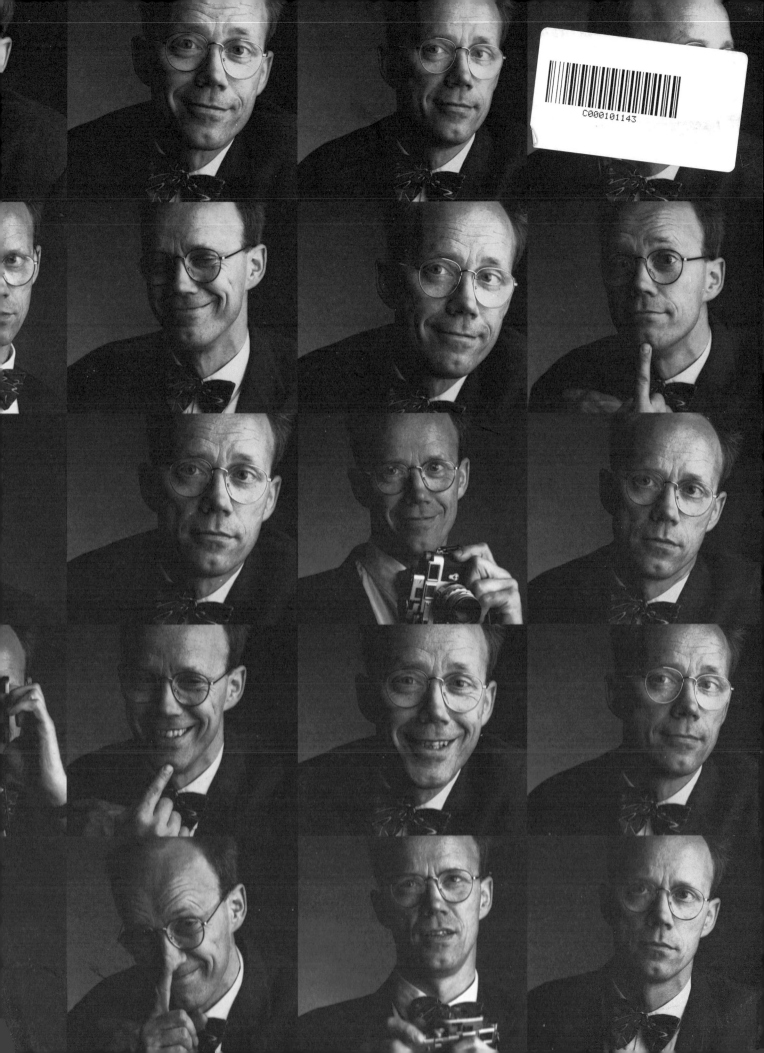